Where Asia Smiles

Contemporary Ethnography

Kirin Narayan and Paul Stoller, Series Editors

Where Asia Smiles

An Ethnography of Philippine Tourism

Sally Ann Ness

PENN

University of Pennsylvania Press

Philadelphia

10   9   8   7   6   5   4   3   2   1

Published by
University of Pennsylvania Press
Philadelphia, Pennsylvania 19104-4011

Library of Congress Cataloging-in-Publication Data

Ness, Sally Ann
    Where Asia smiles : an ethnography of Philippine tourism /
Sally Ann Ness
        p. cm. (Contemporary ethnography)
    ISBN 0-8122-3685-8 (cloth : alk. paper) ; ISBN 0-8122-1826-4
(pbk. : alk. paper)
    Includes bibliographical references and index.
    1. Ethnology—Philippines. 2. Culture and tourism—Philippines.
3. Tourism—Economic aspects—Philippines. 4. Philippines—Social life
and customs. 1. Title. II. Series
GN671.P5 N47   2002
305.8′009599—dc21   2002028503

This work is dedicated to the fond memory of my good friend, José Locsin, and to his fellow residents of Davao, past, present, and future.

Contents

Illustrations

Preface

My history with tourism began long before I set foot in Davao City, and the perspective developed in this study has far deeper roots than those related to my research in the Philippines. Some account of this prior history seems necessary, and I include the following autobiographical sketch toward that end.

My history with tourism began in 1969, when I was nine and my family moved from Oakland, California to a small town in rural Idaho. It was a community of roughly two thousand residents, 5,000 feet up in the central Idaho Mountains. The village, as the settlement was semi-officially designated, was nestled at the northern end of an alpine valley on the edge of a large, deep glacial lake. The exceptional natural beauty of the location, in the midst of highland ranching country, perched on the edge of Idaho's vast wilderness and primitive areas, was well known throughout the state by this time. Summer cabins dating back to the 1920s and '30s dotted the more picturesque coves and bays on the lake's western side. Summer camp properties for a number of religious and civic organizations were long established around the lake's eastern shore, serviced by a single lane dirt road. The few seasonal inhabitants of these recreational properties kept their activities largely to themselves. Although the town had an in-state reputation as an attractive mountain destination, it was only minimally developed for tourism at the time of my family's arrival.

During my adolescence I lived through the transformation of this community from a forest service station and logging town, whose surrounding mountains served as a source of lumber and whose lake as a storage pond, to a full-blown resort destination, whose mountains were reimagined as ski developments and whose lake became an aquasports facility. The transformation involved my family and myself as it did nearly every other member of the community. We all became incorporated into the town's emerging *tourate*—its population of tourism service providers and "locals." It was a process that changed all our lives permanently. It echoes, faintly but clearly, throughout the pages that follow.

My earliest encounters with tourists visiting my hometown in growing numbers occurred at the smaller of our two local ski hills. This was a tiny facility by contemporary downhill ski resort standards, a one-lift T-bar, three-and-a-half-run hill. Just a mile outside the northern city limit, it had been in operation since the early decades of the twentieth century. Almost everyone in the community patronized the hill, children as well as parents, rich to working class. The local nordic and alpine ski teams—from the children's "Mighty Mites" to the senior high school leagues and beyond—trained on the hill. It was not the only hill close by, but the little ski hill was so close to town that it was impossible to separate it from the town's identity. To belong to one was to belong to the other.

It was obvious when the "Turkeys" started to arrive. We called them turkeys because we knew that turkeys were the stupidest animals. The visitors were loud and raucous in their movements like the gawky birds. They came on weekends and holidays in small groups and acted as though they owned the hill. They skied in high-tech, state-of-the-art equipment, which at the time included buckle boots, step-in bindings, and skis made of fiberglass, not wood. They sported matching parkas and warm-up overalls of brightly colored synthetic fabrics ("Turkey suits," we called them). These contrasted sharply with the hodge-podge, usually second-hand, jury-rigged outfits and equipment we wore and used. The Turkeys' technique on the slopes was rough and risky. They were no match for the best of our local racers—we were unimpressed by their fast and loose recreational style. In our eyes, the Turkeys simply had no sense of the etiquette that had developed for the little hill. They were too busy playing at being racers to realize that their conduct was offensive, not to mention dangerous.

The animosity toward "flatlander" tourists, as my mother preferred to call the growing numbers of visitors that were driving up from the more densely populated southern lowland areas of the state, was shared by adults as well as children. Some local residents started wearing T-shirts with the phrase, "Turkeys go home," printed on them. When the tourists did leave, at the end of a holiday or weekend, we breathed sighs of relief, glad to have our world back to ourselves, with only those who belonged in it present.

This early experience with tourism left its mark. I developed a local identity that formed in opposition to the growing tourist crowds. It was not a neutral identity, but one in relation to which the tourist was seen in a negative light. That identity has remained. Throughout my fieldwork, I have found myself struggling with an ingrained tendency to fall back into or align with such a "local" anti-tourist identity, as it had originated in these adolescent encounters.

As I grew older and began to work in the summers to pay for college at the University of Idaho, I became more directly involved with the tourism industry, working as a sales clerk at a gift shop on the busiest corner of the village main street. We sold Idaho jasper jewelry, set in silver and gold, sculpted wooden boxes and bowls made by Idaho artists, and a variety of international goods from Africa, Europe, the Middle East, and China. I worked for slightly over minimum wage with a 5 percent commission and earned enough in the summers to make ends meet during the rest of the year. I grew adept at selling the shop's luxury goods to Turkeys—our main clientele. I learned how to tell a real spender from a window shopper and the many ways to cultivate a big sale. I grew sensitive to the rhythm of commercial activity generated by the holidays, grew to understand how the merchants in the town depended on a big Fourth of July to get them through to Labor Day, on Labor Day to get them through to Christmas, and on Christmas to get them through to the February Winter Carnival, the profits of which had to last them all the way to Memorial Day. With this experience, I learned what it could mean to be complicit in the tourism industry's operations. "Complicit" was not a concept I employed at the time; I was only aware that my understanding of tourism changed as a result of the job, as I benefited from tourism's presence while still resenting the influx of strangers the industry brought with it. A mixed attitude began to develop, part accepting, part resistant, grudgingly grateful, wistfully disappointed, that was to have an enduring presence in my consciousness as well.

Other members of my family also went into tourism-related work. My older sister worked summers at the state park on the southeastern edge of town, assigning permits to campers and working on park maintenance and upkeep. My younger sister went to work for the lakeside lodge, starting out as a desk clerk. This employment track, which continued through high school, eventually led her to a major in hotel management at Michigan State University and a career in resort development. Today she manages a Trendwest Resorts, Inc. sales office for vacation ownership, with resort developments all over the world. The experiences of these siblings also contributed to my understanding of the tourism industry.

My father, a retired lawyer, became caught up with tourism during these years as well, although in a more political way. Not long after his arrival in Idaho, he accepted a volunteer appointment to chair a newly formed municipal planning and zoning commission, charged with creating a comprehensive plan for the village and its surrounding "impact area." The commission was set up in response to general alarm in the community raised by the construction of the first condominium development in the town center, a project that had failed to make good on promises to town leaders concerning its landscaping. The commission's plan was adopted in 1979.[1]

The volunteer service my father performed gave me an indirect but extensive education in the politics of tourism development in a small scale, rural, democratic social context. During his years on the commission, there were often contentious, heated sessions involving the agents of the tourism development boom as well as their more extreme opponents. "P-and-Z," as my family came to call the commission, was a major flash point in the tourism development process. It was the town's main line of authoritative civic defense standing in the path of the developers. I was a teenager during this time, or coming home sporadically from college. As a result, I never witnessed first-hand the conflicts and debates over the years that resulted in the construction of a selected array of upper middle and elite class resort establishments. I do remember many mornings, however, when my mother would wearily report that Dad had once again arrived home long after midnight from another overcrowded meeting of P-and-Z. I would hear the summary version of the latest initiative and its response over breakfast.

By the 1990s the town did develop into a regional resort destination. It currently hosts tens of thousands of visitors every year, winter and summer. It now has a much expanded Winter Carnival and additional summer festivals as well, all part of its tourism promotion program. The gentrifying changes to the lakeshore, village center, and outlying ranch lands have been dramatic. However, tourism has by no means completely altered the locality. My mother still resides in the same house where we always lived, across from the high school where we all graduated, surrounded by the same neighborhood houses and even some of the same neighbors. Her grandchildren have spent a good part of every summer of their lives with her there. I often wonder if we would still have access to, or any desire to visit, that now long-time family home, had it not been for P-and-Z and the relatively moderate pattern of development it served to bring about.

Through all my early experiences with tourism in this small scale community, I gained an appreciation for the tremendous power of the tourism industry as well as for the appeal it can have for communities like this one, vulnerable communities experiencing the loss of other forms of livelihood and industry. I also developed the understanding that tourism was not necessarily an omnipotent force. Individual and collective action could and did change the course of tourism development in this rural community, even when very large scale interests were involved. These impressions of the industry have remained with me. They served in part as the personal background against which I conducted my research in Davao City, Philippines.

I assumed one other role in the tourism industry, after leaving Idaho to start graduate school at the University of Washington in 1981. This time I became a part-time tour guide, leading groups of around thirty tourists on hour-long, tongue-in-cheek, historical walking tours in Seattle's Pioneer Square underground district. Again, this employment sensitized me to the ebb and flow of tourist bodies that did continually arrive and depart from this location. In the August high season, our tour company could handle as many as five hundred tourists a day. The customers came from all over the United States and countries around the world.

This work experience placed me on the front lines of a mass tourism enterprise in a cosmopolitan, high volume destination. In contrast to the experiences of rural Idaho, the tourists drawn to this context were not in a position to threaten some vulnerable, highly local way of life. On the contrary, tourists formed only one segment of a vast network of incoming and outgoing visitors to the city. Tourism itself occupied a relatively humble position in the city's complex and dynamic structures of commerce and industry. I sensed no absentminded proprietariness from the tourists in this setting as I had done on the little ski hill. Tourists taking the walking tour conveyed no sense that they had taken over and claimed as their own the landscape in which their touristic experience was situated. Quite the contrary—the tourists I guided for the Seattle tour company tended to see themselves as relatively vulnerable characters vis-à-vis the city's more knowledgeable residents. In this touristic setting, it was the tourists who were in need of assistance in coming to feel at home in an unfamiliar urban landscape.

Another contrast to the village tourate experience emerged in relation to the professional status I assumed in the role of tour guide while working for the underground tour company. I discovered in the Seattle context that, as a *guide*, I, as much as the sights seen, became one of the attractions of the amusement service. This was particularly true of the tour company for which I worked. The underground tour had in part built a distinctive touristic reputation on the cultivation of an irreverent, nonconformist, even politically incorrect style of interaction. The narratives each guide developed for his or her own personal tour script typically included several taunting points along these lines, the main one being to inform the tourist clientele that there was nothing of real merit to be seen on this particular tour. Tourists, the scripts asserted, had paid good money mainly for the opportunity to see a series of "dirty basements" that ordinary people with a modicum of common sense would have avoided altogether. In developing such counternarratives to more standard tourism discourses, the underground tour guide scripts played openly with a kind of "Turkey" identity for tourists of their own design. In this setting, however, the playfully offensive strategy served only to increase the tour's unconventional popular appeal. Tourists usually seemed to find the scripts refreshing and amusing, enjoying the opportunity to laugh at their own predicament of trying to find ways to fill their vacation hours at a destination that didn't always serve their every need every minute.

In this role as a tour guide, I became more than a local worker, as I had been in my previous college job. Here I was interjected into a highly competitive touristic system, whose diverse market and complex social organization allowed for various forms of status play to develop between tourists and their service providers. The tour guides, in this business, were much more than native yokels who knew the ways into and out of the Pioneer Square district underground. Guides were also introduced and expected to perform as seasoned, heckle-drawing storytellers, experts in the crafts of objectification and narration. The crowds I worked assumed I was a professional entertainer, working more and less improvisationally, giving as good as I got in the presence of the tourist gaze and voice. As part of this theatrical "yuppie" tourate, I experienced and learned to wield the magic of touristic fantasy "space," transforming busy storefront doorsteps with a few carefully voiced phrases into miniature scenic viewpoints and proscenium arches, conjuring up hilarious episodes out of the city's past amid the unrestored (genuinely filthy) rubble of its neglected, abandoned basements. A guide's rhetorical spin could turn the most ordinary and even repulsive working-world setting into a captivating scene in the story of a grand old city. Even the occasional live rat or cockroach could be used to add excitement and authenticity to the experience of venturing into Seattle's wild west history, populated by philanthropic prostitutes, dastardly mayors, savvy Native Americans, and a host of colorful folkloric personalities.

Through this job, however, I also learned the dehumanizing effects of touristic mass production, as I delivered my narrative goods four times a day, five or six days a week during peak season to crowd after crowd after crowd. The repetitions drained my voice, which was lost completely by every day's end. They also dulled my interpretive faculties to such an extent that I lost the capacity to sense the humor of my own tall tales, after a few days of retelling them continuously. As my experience increased, a bizarre semantic rift opened between myself and the groups I led. I learned to memorize the phrasing patterns of a story's delivery and ignore its content, like a puppet of my own ventriloquism, uttering punch lines as if they were a kind of singing, not talking, in order to produce consistently humorous effects and timing. In the end, the performances became ironically mechanized and I found myself engaged in a masquerade, playing the part of an unaffected spontaneous commentator—the character type that I found worked best to relax and engage the tourists.

Most of the guides, like myself, were part-time employees, pursuing careers elsewhere as educators or performing artists. When we went home after work, the tourist landscape was left behind us. We all lived far outside the historic district, in residential areas of the city that had not been developed for tourism. There were clear geographical boundaries around the tourism industry for us in this regard. Our work force moved into and out of its touristic world with little or no ambiguity. This situation again differed dramatically from the village tourism development experience. It gave me the understanding that tourism could be kept quite literally within bounds and limited to one aspect and one space of working life.

I kept the guide job until I finished my doctorate, giving tours while teaching cultural and linguistic anthropology courses on the side until 1987. I left the position five years before my work on tourism in Davao City began. The guide experience overall was important in teaching me how different urban tourism could be from the rural situation with which I'd grown up and how varied tourist clientele could be as well. The nonconformist tour company also provided an example of the flexibility that was potentially available within the tourism industry for developing unpredictable but highly lucrative service niches. Unlike other industries where certain environmental or cultural givens were essential for a sustainable business to develop, in the case of tourism the underground tours served as living proof that enterprises could be created virtually out of thin air, or even out of seemingly undesirable circumstances. The importance of touristic *narrative* and its performance in generating a touristic market was brought home to me with special force and significance by this work experience as well. I came to understand tourism as an essentially performative, imaginative phenomenon, an orientation that is preserved throughout the account that follows.

In addition to the tourate roles just recounted, I have had, of course, numerous experiences of being a tourist or, in the postmodern mode, of "playing tourist."[2] I have purchased airport art, had myself photographed on monument steps, surrendered travel responsibilities (fretfully) to hired guides and guidebooks, peered with uninitiated awe into sacred temples, and amused myself for countless hours in the museums and public gardens of foreign lands and places. I have even, at my own request and with no research agenda or notebook involved, spent whole 100-degree-plus days with friends, waiting in line after hour-long line, like sheep if not like turkeys, to ride the roller coasters of Magic Mountain during August—high tourist season. My understanding of the industry develops from these experiences as well.

My intention throughout this study has been to record the insights of those dealing with tourism as I have done, in their home territories. I have attempted to observe closely and "thickly" the cultural consequences of tourism's way of operating at one particular location that qualifies as a "developing" or "underdeveloped" place. It is my hope that such perspectives and observations may suggest lessons that can be constructively applied to future developments in analogous locations. It is also my intention to document the fact that tourism itself is a far more complex, uniquely human phenomenon than has heretofore been recognized in the ethnographic literature.

In my father's spirit, and for what remains of that offended child on the little ski hill, I will never be a tourism enthusiast. However, as a person whose education and whose family's well being has been in no small part supported by the industry, I will never see tourism as evil personified. Neither will I ever see the industry and its practices as something wholly foreign, regardless of how unfamiliar the circumstances or the places may be in which I may encounter them. Tourism has been part of my geo-cultural reality for far too long. As something more than a "halfie"[3] engulfed within the pressures of its operations, I, too, find myself obliged to understand how to live with tourism and find a home within its presence in as sane and decent a way as possible. It is this shared predicament that motivates the ethnographic account that follows.

A Note About Pseudonyms

With the exceptions listed below, pseudonyms have been used for all individuals and establishments mentioned in the text by nickname, first name, or full name. Whenever possible, anonymity for those directly represented in the study has been preserved. However, in the case of officials whose statements were a matter of public record—regional tourism director Catalina Santos Dakudao, DATA presidents Margarita Moran-Floirendo and Mary Ann Maceda Montemayor, and former tourism secretary Narzalina Lim—no pseudonyms have been used. Also, when historical or documentary records had already been well established for a site, no pseudonyms were used for either the site or its owners or governing officials. This was the case for the Samal Island Tourism Estate, Pearl Farm Beach Resort, Davao Insular Intercontinental Inn, Apo View Hotel, and GAP Farming.

Part I
Orientation

Chapter 1
Tourism and Culture

Tourism has become an un-ignorable subject in cultural anthropology, an industry of utmost importance to the developing world. One of the largest employers worldwide, it currently involves an enormous percentage of the developing world's populations and commands an enormous and rapidly growing percentage of the world's capital.[1] Moreover, in an age where socio-cultural identity is conceptualized more and more in terms of movement, tourism has mobilized humankind in the largest geographical movements ever known for reasons other than war.[2] Theoretically, tourism is an industry that literally cannot be thought about without a recognition of the distinguishing features of contemporary cultural reality—globalization, diasporic multiculturalism, advanced capitalism, transnationalism, postcoloniality, and the profound uncertainties of postmodern forms of self-consciousness, to mention only a few.

This book concerns the relation of tourism and culture, taking as its ethnographic focus one Southeast Asian urban site located in the Philippines, Davao City, on the southern island of Mindanao. The study's approach is interpretive, seeking to integrate a small though varied sample of perspectives on tourism development from Davao City's million-plus residents with an account of what I observed and participated in during a series of visits to the city that began in 1992 and ended in 1996. This was a period of boom in the Southeast Asian, or in geopolitical terms, the "ASEAN" economy.[3] It was a time when tourism was growing faster in the Asian and Pacific Islands than anywhere else in the world.[4] Davao City was a prime target of transnational tourism development during these years, before the 1997 fires in Indonesia, the Asian financial crisis, and the end of the Ramos administration brought about an abrupt—though temporary—end to the development boom. In this regard, Davao City's transformations in the mid-1990s represent a fairly classic example of rapid, advanced capitalist tourism development in its earliest stages, the industry's presence being largely the consequence of an extraordinarily optimistic moment in the city's as well as the nation's and the region's intertwined economic histories.

My intention in developing the ethnography was to use tourism as a lens through which to understand the cultural aspects of transnationally moti-vated "development"—or, as the local context might have termed it, the "ASEAN-ization" of everyday life—the reorientation of local practice around the development activities of the ASEAN member states. I sought to observe and understand how the most newly arriving operations of trans-national capitalism became lived experience, what the day-to-day impact of them meant "on the ground." The focus on tourism, I assumed, would fore-ground this globalizing cultural transformation.[5] As time went on, however, and various instances of such transformation occurred, I came to realize that tourism, while it was to be sure a manifestation of the global and transnational forces of "development," was also peculiar in certain respects. Its semiotics in particular were relatively complicated, and its cultural dimensions were more difficult to delimit and define than those of its competitor industries, both heavy (mining, oil, logging) and light (fashion, furniture, food, flowers). The longer I observed the industry in action in Davao City, the more my interests shifted or reversed. I moved from seeking to understand advanced capitalist development through tourism to trying to understand tourism itself, both through the forces of transnational and global capitalism that were feeding it and through the specific individuals who were bringing it to "real" life, into the realm of the ordinary and into everyday practice. This interest, the understanding of tourism and its cul-tural consequences, remains the central theme of this book.

To understand the reality of all that was going on in the name of tour-ism and ASEAN in Davao City and the connections to "things cultural" it entailed, I devote this first chapter to a discussion of tourism itself as a subject of cultural study. The global tourism industry currently works on a scale that makes it virtually impossible to form any generalizations, let alone universal theories, about its character, particularly its cultural conse-quences. As recent scholarship on the industry has shown, it is nearly impos-sible for anthropology's classical paradigms of culture[6] to handle tourism, since it tends to involve global or "supercultural," as well as multicultural, pseudocultural, and transcultural processes.[7] Moreover, it is also problem-atic to attempt to apply the classical methods of ethnographic research to the whole of what tourism can entail, culturally speaking, since the major-ity of its participants are not the kind of subjects who can be understood through the "depth" strategies of long term participant/observation at a given, generally peripheral geographical site.[8] The global industry cannot adequately be characterized in terms of its belonging to some larger national or cultural whole. Neither is the ethnographer's cultural position easily understood in relation to tourism and its personae, let alone its actual personnel. The ethnographic study of tourism requires some redefinition of the ethnographer's own persona as well as those of the subjects of research. It is to this project that I devote this opening chapter, examining first the problematic relationship between tourism and anthropology, and then presenting a few conceptual strategies for understanding tourism, both as a geocultural matrix and as a deformation of the cultural institution of home.

Tourism and Anthropology

Tourism's long-standing relationship to anthropology reveals a conflict inherent in touristic and anthropological identities and practices. The conflict stems from the common cultural legacy shared by tourism and anthropology. Both are journey-centered pursuits, the one excursionary and indulgent, the other expeditious and disciplined, coming of age in nineteenth-century northwestern European social life. Tourism was, as it still is, conceived as a form of mass leisure; anthropological science, as an elite form of professional work.[9] Each belonged to a separate hemisphere of modern, industrializing, "Western" life. The two hemispheres of practices—the two sides of life defined for the middle and upper classes by their engagement in or freedom from some form of *industry*, or industriousness defined most broadly—together formed the most basic parts of a complex cultural whole, a grounded worldview, balancing exertion and recuperation, work and play, time off and office hours.[10] These two hemispheres defined an ideal structure of social reality in this cultural-historical moment.[11] And, as with any such systemic cultural construct, confusing or merging the two hemispheres could produce chaos, dysfunction, internal conflict, and a loss of the sense of reality.

Studying tourism, even in the twenty-first century, must still entail some recognition of this antiquated though influential conflict. Even in contemporary contexts, in post-industrial, postmodern, even in some views postcultural times, tourism remains a troubling, even painful subject for cultural anthropology and cultural anthropologists. While objective evidence may insist that tourism is a historic form of cultural contact, no more no less, the subject is still widely believed to degrade and confound the enterprise of cultural anthropology, or, at best, to distract the discipline from its main mission.[12]

An incident that occurred during the later phases of my research in Davao City illustrates how this conflict manifests in a contemporary cultural context: In 1996 the host of a beach resort where I had been residing for several weeks and I were engaged in conversation after dinner one evening. It was the time of day when I tended to settle down someplace on the resort's grounds, on a wooden bench or at a nipa-shaded table, where I could relax alone. I hoped to attract a word or two of conversation with the resort owners in the cooling air, now that their day was finished, or just to sit and enjoy the sunset views of pumpboat traffic still streaming silently by offshore. On this evening, talk turned to my work interviewing persons displaced by a large scale tourism development project. Eventually we began discussing the budget for the research. Upon hearing the amount I was being charged for assistance by one of the local NGO directors, my host became incensed. As soon as the figure was out of my mouth, his eyes grew wide with disbelief, his face livid. He bellowed a question back at me by way of response, a question that came spontaneously, without a moment's deliberation. "What does he think you are?" he fumed, "A *tourist*!?" He repeated the word, "tourist," several times in the moments following, shaking his head in vehement disapproval. "Tourist" seemed to be exactly the right word for indicating the worst possible way in which I might have been identified and treated.

Hearing his reaction, I felt a sense of loss for the wasted resources and some shame for having negotiated the research partnership ineptly. However, there was also a rush of relief upon hearing that, at least in this resort owner's mind, I was something quite other than a tourist. I had yet to let go of the desire (also a common tourist's desire) to become a part of the "real" world of Davao, where life went on without the presence of tourists. Although I soon remembered that being identified as a tourist was not necessarily a bad thing given my research interests, and that it might even have been considered an achievement in some respects, at the time the tourist identity was not a neutral, let alone a desired role where I was concerned, but one by definition opposed to that of the ethnographer.

Whenever I assumed or was granted a modern ethnographer's or social scientist's identity in the process of conducting research on the tourism industry in Southeast Asia, I found myself in a context where "the tourist" was regarded as a character antithetical to my own, yet potentially belonging to my own cultural identity. This circumstance occurred, if not constantly, then quite regularly. Regardless of my theoretical stance on the issues, in practice I found myself time and again living out scenarios of modernity, still the local cultural dominant in Davao City at this time, and the conflict between tourism and culture they entailed. The conflict pitted me against and within the very subject of my research. It undermined whatever objectivity I attempted to construct and compromised my ability to establish a good faith rapport in its presence.

This troubled relationship between the figures and fields of the anthropologist and those of the tourist has already been well analyzed and documented.[13] To summarize the observations made by the subject's leading scholars: in just the ways cultures and natives are understood to be real or authentic, tourist destinations and their inhabitants are known to be fantastic and artificial; in just the ways culture is understood to be profound, enduring, time-honored, meaningful, and original, touristic practices are known to be superficial, temporary, devalued, and for sale, meaningless, and dependent on alien contingencies. In just the ways culture is believed to be complex, and difficult to apprehend—requiring years of graduate study, local involvement, and language acquisition—touristic systems are believed to be hyper-accessible, reductively simplified, and user-friendly, available to "anyone." Finally, in just the way that culture is believed to be a "whole," an autonomous, independent, even sovereign way of life, tourism is understood to be a "part," a neo-imperialistic form of commerce operating within larger cultural contexts. It is an industry devoted to the production and consumption of "hyperspaces,"[14] places that have lost their integrity and become contaminated through global contact. Tourists likewise possess not whole, but contingent cultural identities, transient characters (some of them even modeled on the anthropologist), embodied only on a part-time basis, partial personae that function amid a host of other modern or postmodern identities.

No other industry has done as much to frustrate or undermine the work of cultural anthropology, classically conceived, as the leisure industry of tourism. Few other personae are as much a threat to the ideal figure of the cultural anthropologist, classical or contemporary in conception, as that of the tourist—that shallow, short term, self-serving and self-centered, sightseeing, pleasure-seeking, ever-photographing, orientalizing stranger, who is stereotypically a deserving object of ridicule, annoyance, or contempt from any native's point of view, and who, *like the ethnographer*, does not really belong in the place. As Jamaica Kincaid, taking the position of the native vis-à-vis the tourist, succinctly writes, "The thing you have always suspected about yourself the minute you become a tourist is true: A tourist is an ugly human being" (1988: 14). The tourist defines the nemesis of the character that the standard ethnographer typically has sought to embody.

This conflict between tourism, culture, and the ethnographer remains a problem for contemporary ethnographers of tourism, regardless how cosmopolitan or nuanced their own outlook on cultural phenomena, globalization, and their own cultural position in a given research context may be. The basic partitionings of the hemispheres of work and leisure remain a feature of contemporary life in the present global order for the middle classes of the world, even as we move into the twenty-first century. The working ethnographer, in practice, is still pitted against the tourist and tourism. The problem has not gone away. Quite the contrary, it appears to be growing even more intense as tourism becomes more ubiquitous.

One is tempted to think the conflict can be solved by simply abandoning the role of the ethnographer and fashioning some more feasible contemporary, globalized, postmodern equivalent. This is easier said than done. Moreover, in doing it, a humanistic, interpretive understanding of the industry and those it involves—an understanding generally under-represented in the anthropology of tourism,[15] would probably be lost in the process. In this regard, I chose to live with the problem rather than attempt to transcend or escape it—to remain "resolutely late modern" in Paul Rabinow's terms.[16] I chose to keep working the way interpretive ethnographers of my generation have typically worked, staying with situations until the stereotypes associated with being a stranger gradually lost their power, participating in, observing, and describing life's cultural minutiae, noting how and where they manifested, who embodied them, and in what particular condition they appeared to be—globalized, nationalized, or localized; integral or fragmented; enduring or temporary; unqualified or represented, postmodern, modern, colonial or neocolonial; imploded, decentered or marginalized; appropriated, contaminated, or even authentic. This is not to say that I conformed completely to the standard model. I was compelled to incorporate a greater amount of travel back and forth to work in Riverside, California than the classic models of fieldwork would have sanctioned. My time in residence, although it was preceded by a much earlier period of residence at a related Philippine location,[17] was limited and intermittent and totaled only around nine months altogether.[18] As I was in a cosmopolitan location and dealing to a considerable extent with cosmopolitan people, I was also often compelled to depart from the standard methods of ethnographic research, conducting formal interviews and surveys instead of relying on intensive informal rapport-building as a means of study.[19] Since there was no common native language in Davao, and no person who was fluent in all of Davao's local languages, I did not master one, let alone all, of the verbal means of expression employed in the city, but struggled with several, including Philippine-style English. Finally, since there was no common localized culture or community—no homogeneous "local people" among whom I could "be"—I invented a few social circuits for myself through a variety of relationships, a patchwork of friendships and acquaintances, nothing like a comprehensive network.

The above notwithstanding, however, it was still the case that, to the extent a middle-class Californian—and a thirty-something Euro-American woman—could assume the practices and dispositions of the standard interpretive ethnographer in a cosmopolitan location, I did. I led an uncontroversial life focused solely on my research agenda, immersed in a niche-finding odyssey vis-à-vis the city's society. I studied intensively its most widely spoken language, and listened to the narratives, formal and informal, only partially comprehensible, that came my way. In sum, I preserved the practice of *dwelling* in Davao (versus *seeking* its culture, as a tourist might), of becoming a displaced homebody, as James Clifford (1997: 22) has described it. It was in this relatively planted mode that I was able to watch Davao's globalized world go by at an accelerating pace. Who exactly it was that I was dwelling among became an ethnographic question as a result, not a given, as did the question of what constituted "community" and "locality."

This somewhat outmoded methodological choice appeared to be the only way to keep asking questions about tourism's human/cultural effects in Davao City, questions that couldn't be framed or phrased, or even posed at all without a considerable amount of Davao-specific understanding. Davao was, after all, a locality that had an enduring existence. In a modest, impure way, it was a source of culture, even while its inhabitants were growing more and more heterogeneous and deterritorialized with every passing instant.

While the conflict between tourism and culture fractured, even maddened some aspects of the ethnographer's character I assumed during my research process, it left other aspects relatively undisturbed. It did not alter, for example, the ethnographic spirit, the realistic, particularistic spirit, in which the research was undertaken. Neither did it affect the ethnographic commitment to conceiving and pursuing a humane, even "humanizing" research agenda. It did not alter my belief that there was nothing new under the sun where the general character of humankind was concerned. Moreover, while the conflict exposed the ethnographer's identity as a contingent one, that is to say not universally operative, and as a compromised one, in terms of neutrality and membership in the places I frequented, it nonetheless left many relationships more or less alone and unaffected. The influence of the tourism industry and the state of transnationalization and globalization more generally were still far from absolute or omnipresent in the city at this time.

I would not say that I grew grateful for the conflict's presence. At the same time, it came to serve as a more or less constant reminder of the changing times in which I lived and worked, times in which the choice to adopt the role of the ethnographer was itself not as effective as it once might have been believed to be. The conflict, ironically, became something of a reality check in a study that led me further and further into forms of touristic production designed, among other things, to mystify, obscure, and confuse.

Tourism: The Geocultural Matrix

Even without an ethnographer's conflicts, the task of grasping fully what kind of "industry," or human phenomenon more generally speaking, tourism actually is, is far from easy. Tourism is both more and less than an industry, more and less than a cultural phenomenon, more and less than a form of leisure. Its character is as quintessentially human as the faculty of language, yet it is a relatively late arrival to the human condition. All the same, it is currently a global presence, a development phenomenon with innumerable discursive practices and micro-techniques of intervention, articulation, and production.[20]

The general understanding of tourism from which this case study develops does not preserve, but rather shifts markedly away from classical cultural anthropological standpoints and characterizations—away from the now much critiqued "culture"-centered or "centered culture" or "peoples and cultures" perspectives.[21] I have adopted a "geocultural" orientation that aligns with the geographically fluid, movement-based analyses or mappings of cultural identity and cultural practice developed by Arjun Appadurai, James Clifford, James Ferguson, Akhil Gupta, Michael Kearney, and George Marcus, among numerous others.[22] Tourism is conceived from this perspective, not as a newly added industrial part of some discrete "complex whole" of a cultural entity, but, rather as a globalized service industry—part and parcel of what Gayatri Spivak (1999: 3) has termed the "financialization of the globe." Its best analogy would be that of a complex, unruly, all-too-human, living *matrix*—in the numerical as well as the geological sense of the term.[23] Unlike an empire, with a center and periphery, or a force, with a linear trajectory and impact, a matrix is a leaderless, multidimensional array of flows and bodies, changing in areas of density as it constantly replicates its distinctive features—its commercial and corporate discourses and practices, its networks of agents and clientele, its capital, material resources, and predominantly servile employment "opportunities." The matrix does not seek purposefully to destroy, but rather to capitalize, which results in continuous reorganizations of all its constituent elements. It is an ever-growing integrative composite, neither essentially external nor internal to its sites of growth, although its power structures tend to reconstruct and conserve older patterns and hierarchies.[24] The matrix can exert and is responsive to pressures that result in deformations of previously existing social and natural formations, new fabrics and structures. Its deformations create spaces of growth and repression, collaboration and resistance. These acquire histories of inhabitation and exploitation involving both local and nonlocal agents. Perhaps the only basic fact that can be assumed about the matrix is the constant temporal pressure it is under to proliferate its spaces and its operations, and to do so ever more quickly at a profit.[25]

Put somewhat more specifically, the tourism matrix is dedicated to the production, replication, and maintenance of hyper-consumable landscapes—displaced, liminoid, constructed spaces grafted onto developable locations worldwide by the more established interests of advanced capitalism, big and small. It is a matrix that deforms cultural identities and practices, among other more material things, in its landscaping operations. It negotiates ("mediates," as Erve Chambers has characterized it[26]) generates, and imposes a variety of *-cultural* contexts—multi-, post-, pseudo-, cross-, inter-, national-, meta-, super-, trans-, and so on—in relation to an ever enlarging, ever more generic, defamiliarized market of consumers and their service providers. It is not, of course, an industry without competitors, all of which together form a global industrial field whose movements continuously transform and reconfigure in planetary magnitudes the cultural terrains encountered, from their foundations on up.

As with others in the discipline of cultural anthropology working on such contemporary phenomena, I have found it necessary to shift away from the classical paradigms of cultural anthropology because they are rooted in a certain kind of naturalism as far as cultural givens or "the world" are concerned. The world from which (always already pre-modern) cultures classically were understood to have emerged and existed was a world of "fields"—pre-industrial, pastoral, or even "wild" places—where the forces of nature governed life.[27] The dilemma here is that no one can observe or participate in the global tourism industry's matrix and maintain such a paradigm without severe difficulties. The industry, as an outgrowth of modernity, is primarily concerned with the blatantly unnatural construction and production of scenic destinations.[28] While the themes of its landscaping— or cityscaping or seascaping—may vary greatly, from ethnically or culturally coded destinations foregrounding historical, aesthetic, or religious attractions, to recreational sport oriented sites, to environmentally oriented eco-sites, to entirely fantastic theme parks, the designated landscaping of tourism denaturalizes the world, creating colossal stages, or realms of narration and representation.[29] Life is governed on these landscapes, not by the laws of nature but by the semiotics of market forces.[30]

Taking into account its staged, unnatural character as well as its matrix-based relations of production, I have chosen not to approach tourism from a "tourist-centered" perspective, as many of the leading anthropologists and sociologists on the topic have done.[31] Be they "action seekers," "off-beats," "charters," "drifters," or "high class" types,[32] I have chosen not to give primary agency or emphasis to the sign-reading, reinventing consumers of the tourism industry and the consequences of their polyvocal, individualized touristic play. Rather, I am concerned with the entire spectrum of persons, on and off touristic stages, who become engaged in the cultivation of touristic landscapes, in the matrix's processes of (re)territorialization—all of them also sign-production processes.[33] Integral to them is an ever more nuanced, ever-expanding array of travel narratives that *all* those who become involved in the industry, tourists among them, internalize and make cultural as well as historical as they reappropriate, "glocalize,"[34] and reinterpret them, before handing them along to new generations of consumers and producers.

The activities of tourists form only one, albeit key aspect of the touristic landscape development process. In the Southeast Asian context, where tourism has become a top priority for ASEAN member governments, and where coping with large scale, "top down," transnationally funded development projects has become a way of life for many communities, tourism does not by any means begin, let alone end, with the arrival of tourists.[35] The cultivation of the touristic landscape, and of the human population or *tourate*[36] that will inhabit it, narrate it, appropriate it, and become associated with it as its non-tourists or "real" people—if not its representative "natives"—can begin long before individual tourists actually, if ever, arrive. As Dean MacCannell (1976) and more recently John Urry (1990) have noted with respect to the cultivation of "the" tourist gaze—in actuality there are infinitely many—such gazing cannot be left to chance or developed instantaneously on site. It involves lifelong processes of learning how, when, and where to "gaze." So, too, the cultivation and maintenance of a touristic landscape and its tourate requires the development of sensibilities and interpretive faculties related to embodying the object of that gaze, of attracting and holding it, of becoming readable in its presence. It is not a process, of course, without a politics and social life, let alone a culture, of its own.[37]

Touristic Utopics

Although the hyperspaces produced by tourism vary greatly in design, one general feature of their character, which I have found to be critical in understanding their narratives, performances, and their cultural consequences, is that they are, as Andrew Causey (1997) has observed, "utopic."[38] Too perfect to actually exist in their truest forms, utopic spaces are by definition "nowhere" places, realms that in their ultimate, absolutely ideal manifestations can have their being only in imaginary spaces, in realms of possibility. In reality they cannot be located in the "real" or natural world. Their approximation, however, can, and from some theoretical perspectives *must* be attempted in order for their ever-deferred perfection to itself become a proven, articulated fact. Utopic spaces, both physical and imaginary, transcend and transform to various extents the ideological and material constructs of the ordinary, the everyday, the natural, and the functional. The worlds in which they can be conceived and finally, totally, and completely fulfilled, are extraordinary, supernatural, meta-functional places, upgraded, reformed, refined, and emended worlds of dreams, hopes, desires, plans, and fantasies.

As Causey notes, utopic spaces are by their nature narrative, dynamic, emergent, and, most important, playful, in the broadest and most profound sense of the term. They are open to explorations of possible ways of enhanced being, ways that tend to run counter to or invert some aspect or aspects of whatever dominant ideology or ideologies they attempt to perfect.[39] Their actual or imagined foundations in this respect must take the form of a neutral "gap," a spatial void, ideologically as well as physically. Their places must evidence nothing but the utopia as envisioned, their grounds blank in order for their representations to serve as convincing realizations.[40] Only such a gap—between ordinary existence and untamed possibility—can allow for the mental and physical play of narratives, the dialogues with ideology, to occur realistically enough to produce utopic experience in actual practice. The first step in realizing a utopic space, pseudo or genuine is the neutralization, the voiding, of a given place, the production of a neutral gap. The politics of such a move in "real life" circumstances, of course, tend to be devastating.[41]

One main concern of this study is this very foundational deformation—

the material and symbolic implosion of tourism's neutral gaps/utopic land-scapes onto the homes, homelands, and natural citizens of a cosmopolitan developing location. In Davao City such gaps tended to vary greatly, in size as well as in character and consequence. At one end of the spectrum, for example, the gap created by one private resort was understood as a pre-existing natural given, and this "original" voided character of the destina-tion became a distinguishing and highly productive feature, foregrounded even in the name of the establishment: GAP Farming. At the other end of the spectrum, however, in the largest of the large scale developments, the Samal Island Tourism Estate, the gap was understood as a traumatizing, even monstrous phenomenon, consuming entire communities in its land-scaping operations. No general character for the neutral gaps of the matrix in Davao City was evident. Its understanding was a matter of contingencies that varied from enterprise to enterprise.

In the case of touristic landscaping, where the gap produced has mate-rial as well as imagined aspects and the play is typically only a degenerate form of what Clifford Geertz might have termed deep utopic play, "work" generally becomes the dominant ideological counter concept in opposi-tion to which pseudo-utopic, physical landscapes unfold and develop their narratives and practices. Tourists enter utopic worlds where, regardless of other variations, they are not supposed to work in the industrial or post-industrial sense. In some cases, in some of the more exoticized, primitively coded touristic landscapes, they explore worlds where they believe no one works in such a sense. They play in touristic landscapes with the possibility of worklessness, perhaps even with freedom from materialism or capital-ism.[42] Inside the matrix, in the stories they tell themselves in their utopic hyperspaces of choice, they can reject aspects of their own existence they find problematic, suspend conventional necessities of manner and thought, and invent new ideal social roles, perhaps egalitarian, perhaps magisterial, roles that run counter to those of their ordinary lives.

The play that occurs in a utopic neutral gap—a play that involves not only tourists but tourates as well—creates a plurality of individual interpre-tations and internalizations. It is not a plurality without hegemony, since the matrix encourages, supports, even rewards the reinvention of some nar-ratives over others. However, it is a plurality that nonetheless allows for qualified agency, resistance, and even transformation to occur, and which produces contradictions and inconsistencies the resolution of which, as Causey observes, is no one's responsibility. There is no primary commit-ment to truth or falsehood in the narratives of a utopic landscape, only to perfection. Likewise, there is a different understanding of transgression as enacted through play, an understanding inapplicable to the world "outside" the neutral gap. These orienting assumptions form the basis of a utopic worldview in the neutral gaps of tourism. They can have permanent, life-altering consequences anyplace, however, whether within the matrix or beyond it. In Davao City the utopic worldview, or rather a range of such worldviews, were still largely in the process of forming, but, as the chapters ahead will illustrate, the formations were steadily gaining currency, and generating conflicting understandings of what might count as a cultural standard for conduct and practice in so doing.

Touristic Hysteria

One general effect of touristic landscapes, which is a consequence of their playful denaturalization of the world, is something I have come to call, for lack of a better term, touristic hysteria. By this I don't mean the kind of excessive affect display most generally associated with the term "hysterical"—although such experience does tend to be cultivated in the more "hyper" hyperspaces of the tourism matrix, such as in roller coaster theme parks, for example. I have a more clinical definition in mind in relation to the entire spectrum of touristic productions generated by the matrix—the fact that tourist landscapes are designed to impair to varying extents the capacity of their consumers to distinguish between fantasy and reality. They blur the boundary between the pseudo- and the genuine, between what might once have been referred to as the natural and the constructed, and also between what Gregory Bateson characterized as the sacramental and the metaphoric.[43] They impair the ability to distinguish between what is understood as an "own" or an "other" experience or location. The loss of the capacity to distinguish the real from the unreal, taken to a pathological, uncontrollable extreme, defines the general condition of hysteria.[44] The landscapes produced by tourism, insofar as they are effective in playing with the "real" world, are hysterical landscapes in this clinical sense of the term. They are designed, of course, to keep their impairments confined to playful limits—temporary, reversible, controllable, limits—but their basic operations move in the direction of generating hysteria nonetheless.

Put in the capitalistic terms of claims to ownership, touristic landscapes, regardless of their details, are designed to realize two contradictory falsehoods that are asserted to be coming true simultaneously. These (un-)truths are (1) "This World (of Pleasure) Belongs to You (Consumer)" and (2) "This World is not the World to which You (Normally) Belong." The selling power of the landscape derives in part from the perceived right to enact these dreams of trespass on it, exercising a bought-and-paid-for "right" to move in and through the landscape with impunity, paying no other dues of membership in the process. The (always imperfect) realization of such a promised "trespass" produces one general form of quasi-hysteria in the neutral gaps of tourism and becomes a general feature of their worldview as well.[45]

With regard to these tendencies to fuse and confuse fantasy with reality, touristic landscapes can be understood as the embodied materializations of the advertising industries that design and market them. John Urry (1990:13) has argued this point, recognizing tourism as the paradigm case of imaginative pleasure seeking that contemporary consumerism inspires. It acts out scenarios literally constructed in consumers' imaginations through advertising media. Touristic landscapes employ the same array of duplicitous performative tropes that are used in the advertising industry—masquerade, ventriloquism, and magic, among others—to sell their various venues and stagings.[46] These tropes in the context of touristic practice become embodied and are performed at venues that are often mystified and constructed for the most effective presentation/illusion possible.

Understanding the cultural specificities of tourism must entail an understanding of which hysterical tropes are being played with in relation to what sort of utopic site or stage and how they are being "choreographed"—made corporeal and animate—as well as narrated. These elements bring definition to the landscape of a particular touristic destination. Their histories of construction, usage, value, ownership, and maintenance constitute the cultural significance of a hyperspace in the tourism matrix.[47]

In Davao City a wide array of performative tropes were in the process of being cultivated during the East ASEAN growth years. The majority of enterprises were invested in developing masquerades of one form or another—the romantic native paradise looming particularly large among them. However, ventriloquism was also playing a key role, as the tourate personnel occupying positions on the front lines of the industry were preparing themselves to act as the mouthpieces of global enterprises, learning to give voice to the discourse and embody the "song and dance" of internationally standardized service provider role models. The trope of magic was also occasionally called into play, particularly in the more fanciful and imaginative destinations.

To add even more complexity to this ethnographic project, however, is the circumstance that the landscapes of tourism, and the varying forms of hysteria they produce, must also be distinguished from one another in terms of the degree of control the matrix itself exercises over them and those entering them. At one extreme, for example, is the case of the theme park, hermetically sealed off from the "real" world outside its concrete walls, more or less completely controlled by its developers. The theme park is only an extreme case in landscape development, however. In the majority of tourist destinations—and certainly in most of those under development in Davao City—control over the landscape and its population is not so absolute. The boundary between touristic and nontouristic contexts in the majority of destinations, is not so clear cut. Heavily touristed destinations, whether the would-be theme parks of Atlantic City or Waikiki Beach or more complex world class destinations such as Paris or Bangkok, tend to produce more ambiguous kinds of quasi-hysteria, keeping perpetually open the question of their status as real places or fantasy lands. Aspiring destinations, such as Davao City was, can produce Wonderland effects of contradiction and confusion while engaged in the cultivation process of attempting to transform their localities into globally consumable landscapes. I came to understand Davao's contemporary cultural predicament primarily in this way, as a place where the tourism matrix was continually appearing and disappearing, materializing and evaporating, slipping into and out of various occasions and locations, getting itself going into a full tilt operation, only to suffer a sudden breakdown and collapse. Sometimes these disturbing transformations occurred from moment to moment, sometimes they spanned much longer periods of interaction. The overall effect was one of uncertainty and heightened potential—a sense that times were changing and about to change dramatically.

In the more ambiguous, industrially heterogeneous sites, tourism becomes an aspect of everyday life, a potential and contingent presence, regularly available, typically transcendable, occasionally unavoidable, and perpetually invokable. It is as such an aspect of everyday life that the cultural consequences of tourism became the most far reaching in the contexts I was participating in and observing in Davao City. I studied tourism, its landscapes, narratives, and performances, mainly as such an aspect of a more complicated contemporary cultural reality.[48] It integrated itself into the city's increasing involvement with a broad array of regional commerce and trade initiatives developing throughout the East ASEAN area. It grafted itself onto a wide array of longstanding local identities—turning business travelers and long-lost relatives into tourist "arrivals" and domestic helpers into "room staff." College folkdance groups became "cultural entertainers." Tourism also inserted itself into several of the city's most well-established facets. It fit neatly into the city's identity as a place where newcomers were a familiar, welcomed presence and where narratives fashioned by visitors were already considered to be of special consequence to the maintenance of a family's good name. It added itself smoothly to the city's reputation as an outpost where industrialists were repeatedly pioneering new enterprises. Last but not least, tourism joined itself into a host of practices reinforcing the city's self-proclaimed status as a place where hospitality was already understood as a cultural institution, if not a source of livelihood. In all these respects, tourism operated as an aspect of an elaborate, multifaceted cultural reality.

To summarize the conceptualization I have developed thus far, the tourist industry creates utopic landscapes, worlds within the worlds of advanced capitalism, where illusions of reality become embodied, material reality. It produces spaces where tourists and tourates play and work with the narratives of work and leisure, both real and imaginary. Even while some of the contexts in which it is situated, and the tourists and tourates it cultivates, are not themselves entirely or even predominantly utopic in character, the tendency of the industry is to force movement in this quintessentially postmodern direction. The contemporary cultural consequence of tourism, in this general respect, is one of contestation, in which various pre-existing forms of cultural practice and identity contest to varying extents the quasi-hysterical practices and identities produced within the play of touristic landscapes. It is this contestation—as it manifested in Davao City—that I have attempted to document.

Tourism and Home

There is one final conceptual strategy—an oppositional strategy in this case—that I have found to be essential in understanding tourism in general terms. This is the opposition between being in tourism and being at home. As Urry (1990: 2) has noted, home and work form two particularly salient contrasting realms (I will call them "lifescapes") in relation to touristic practices and identities. While the opposition of tourism to work looms somewhat larger in both scholarly and common sense perceptions of the industry,[49] I will argue that the opposition of home to tourism is of equal, if not greater importance. The concept of home sheds light on why and how it is that tourism moves people, in every sense of the term, how it fundamentally alters the sense of place for all who engage in its operations, tourists and tourates alike.

An excerpt from the popular U.S. periodical *Filipinas* illustrates an aspect of the opposition I am referring to in this regard. Gemma Nemenzo, an affluent Filipina and a longtime U.S. resident, recounted her "Balikbayan" ("return country") visit to the Philippines with her teenage Philippine-American daughter Maia. The visit, described in summary terms, included stops in Manila and Cebu (to visit family), a tour of the University of the Philippines Dilliman campus, shopping, spending time at the beach ("where my hectic life in America became a memory"), and repeated episodes of gorging on Filipino food. The itinerary, supplemented with idyllic descriptions of the sites visited, read as though duplicated from a Philippines Department of Tourism promotional brochure. To close the narrative, however, the author writes:

At the end of our all-too-brief visit . . . I wanted to hold on to the taste of the country for as long as I could. Maia, however, asked for a big American breakfast when we landed in San Francisco. She was just visiting the Philippines. I went home. (Nemenzo 1999: 29)

One cannot be at home and be a tourist—or so it would seem for the Balikbayan traveler. Her identity, contrasted to her daughter's "visiting" status, is asserted at the end of her account to have remained unambiguously inside a home-and-family Philippine lifescape. Destinations of tourism are typically understood inside the industry in this manner, as un-homely places *for tourists*. This sense of place is assumed to go a long way toward creating a tourist identity. Tourism, if it is nothing else, is the kind of travel, the kind of geocultural movement, that specifically leaves the place of the traveler's home behind. As Valene Smith defines the tourist, the role is embodied by a person "who voluntarily visits a place *away from home* for the purpose of experiencing a change" (1989: 1, my emphasis).[50] The minute tourists begin to believe they have "come home," their identity as tourists falls into question, or, as with the Balikbayan, becomes plausibly deniable.

Being a tourist thus appears to require a foray into the world where one is not at home, a foray that, as with the enacting of any form of travel, necessitates a change in status as it achieves a change of place.[51] The cultural logic of tourism is founded on a certain understanding of the dynamic relationship between home and status in this regard. Distance from home is correlated to elevation in status. The landscapes of tourism produce unhomely status-increasing spaces for their consumers. Home can be understood, from within the narratives of the industry, as that other essential space which, together with the spaces of tourism, define a complex, modern "omni-scape," or livable world, a whole world of upwardly spiraling status inflation, yet balanced in terms of stability and mobility. The relation of home to tourism, as the industry would have it, is a relation of place to movement, or root to route, in Clifford's terms (1997: 3),[52] of humble dwelling to lordly journey, of birth (read female) to life (read male),[53] of a safe, familiar center to a free and foreign field.[54] The matrix, in other words, needs "homes," or the belief in them, to proliferate itself.

Yet another profoundly disturbing form of touristic quasi-hysteria that is generally produced by the matrix occurs in relation to the understanding of home. The reality play touristic landscapes encourage is one that plays, not only with worklessness, but first and foremost with home. The impairment of the ability to judge what is home and what is not is a key objective of touristic systems, the production of home's distinctive features a goal to which their service operations aspire.[55] The landscapes of tourism, in this regard, produce contradictory and equally ungrounded sets of messages that simultaneously assert two profoundly meaningful propositions: (1) "You Have Left Home" and (2) "You Are Now Home."[56] In the case of transnational diasporic individuals—such as the Balikbayan—such messages undergo additional layers of semantic reversal, when home becomes a destination, and the tourist persona becomes an ever-present aspect of personal identity, deniable, yet ever open to question.[57]

Home, or *domus*, unlike tourism, is not a cultural construct that arose with modernity. Even in the strict sense of the English language "home," there is a history of cultural practice more than ten centuries long connected with the term. The concept and the practices it and others analogous to it around the world have referenced over the millennia cannot be understood as originating or existing in a simple opposition to tourism or to modernity more generally, even though in the contemporary context of globalization tourism's matrix is coming to define more and more what homes around the world can be and mean.[58] The relation of home to tourism, nonetheless, is in some respects a relation of antiquity to modernity and postmodernity.[59] Home is something of a cultural survival in contemporary globalized life, persisting, adapting, transfiguring, yet enduring and still, in some aspects, continuing as an ancient, perhaps *the* ancient cultural institution.

Although home is generally conceived in terms of "where-ness," as a fixed space in the world—a little corner of it, perhaps—it is also one of those believed-in, practiced phenomena that are defined by more than their material elements or physical existence.[60] This is why, in the unusual case—and more and more frequently in the nomadic cases most representative of contemporary life—"home" can be defined in terms of practice or actions alone, regardless of location.[61] Home is personally bonded space/time, a "called" space/time, the place/action one calls home. As such, the sense of home, even the reality of home, can live in memory and dreams, in nonlinear, atemporal thoughts and feelings as well as in the performance of life's most ordinary, most intimate personal habits. As Gaston Bachelard noted, "all really inhabited space bears the essence of the notion of home" (1958:5). The travels of tourism, in this regard, are not just initially but continuously enmeshed in the practices of leaving and coming, establishing and dismantling, longing for and finding home. As long as the practices of home-making continue—resting, cleaning, and feeding, among others—somehow, somewhere, the seeds of home's presence are constantly replanted.

Michael Jackson's work on home (1995) takes such a place-less understanding of home one step further, dislocating it even from the habitual practices of home-making. Jackson achieved his desired understanding of home, or rather it encompassed him, in what he recounts as an unanticipated moment of *consonance* in the Tanami Desert of Central Australia. As he writes,

At that moment . . . I think I knew what it means to be at home in the world. It is to experience a complete consonance between one's own body and the body of the earth. Between self and other. It little matters whether the other is a landscape, a loved one, a house, or an action. Things flow. There seems to be no resistance between oneself and the world. The *relationship* is all. (1995:110–11)

Home, in Jackson's extraordinary experience, is a matter of harmonious accord between bodies. The consonance of home can occur in a single moment, as an isolated, instantaneous manifestation.[62]

Jackson's identification of a harmonious relationship between bodies as a definitive indicator of the real presence of home is particularly apt for understanding the non-linear reappearances, manifestations, and experiences of home that occur in the presence of the contemporary landscapes of tourism. Such consonances, radically displaced yet authentic realizations of home, and their resulting sense of "flow," of comfort and comfortableness, their consequential ease of interaction, are a distinct and well understood possibility at tourist destinations for all who populate them. Under ordinary circumstances, of course, such a consonance as Jackson recounts between the bodies he identifies requires years, even generations of practice to produce. Nonetheless, the possibility that tourists and tourates may likewise achieve something like this extraordinary consonance in the landscapes of tourism and narratives of its realization abound in tourist discourses. The industry's semiotics at every stage—from pre- through post-consumption phases—are designed to have its tourists and their tourates feel, and in feeling *be* "at home in the world."

And, yet, as the cliché reminds, "There's no place like home." True home, as in that place where the sign truly hangs reading, "Home, sweet home." Home, where one's roots have been planted, as well as one's ancestors, where there is not the smallest doubt coming from any quarter that one belongs, because one is born belonging there, or because one was born to belong there, or, perhaps, because those to whom one's life belongs are there, permanently, enduringly there. There may be no future there, no jobs there, no upwardly mobile reason on earth to be living there, yet, as Carol Stack's work on African Americans returning to the American South has so poignantly shown, the power of such locations—and they are indeed address-touting locations—can be second to none in shaping a life experience.[63]

One is understood at such familial and ancestral home places as well as one understands oneself, for better and for worse. As Nigel Rapport and Andrew Dawson (1998:9) define home, "Home . . . is where one best knows oneself—where 'best' means 'most', even if not always 'happiest.'" Familial and ancestral homes are proving grounds of such knowledge. One's identity becomes established there, sometimes suffocatingly, unenduringly so. Familial and ancestral homes are not places of contingent, detachable identities. They are "high context" identity spaces, to borrow Edward Hall's once popular concept, places where clichés become inadequate, recognizably superficial and impotent, and where more intimate, individual, nuanced representations become necessary. At a familial or ancestral home, the cost of being who one is can exceed the benefit—a striking contrast to the tourist's world, where such a possibility is written out of the landscape.

Familial and ancestral homes, more than anything else, are the places in the world that are more than the self, yet given to it for its sustenance and shelter, however short of the mark they actually may fall. Jackson quotes Robert Frost in this regard, who once wrote, "Home is the place where when you go there they have to take you in."[64] One tends to be treated well at such a home, or at least better than elsewhere.

Such familial and ancestral homes still do exist, although for fewer and fewer in the contemporary developing world. Their cultivation is not a growing trend in the twenty-first century. Some even now may find such homes not only unrealistic but unimaginable. Fewer and fewer individuals either know or have access to such a "where" in which they have so belonged. Such homes cannot be built, materially or symbolically, in a day or a moment. They cannot be displaced and remain what they are. They are old growth, slow growth entities, impossible to manufacture in rapid development. Whether they are familial or ancestral, such homes tend to inspire a deep sense of gratitude. They are the places people have died for. As Thomas Friedman (1999:27) has observed, few things are more enraging, more devastating in the current events of globalization, than the stripping away or foreign conquest of such homes, in imagination or in reality.

The extremes I have just described—the ever present home of home-making practice, transient, incomplete, and ever-multiplying; the poetic home of momentary consonance; the soil-rich familial/ancestral home of a locationally continuous life history—form some of the outer reaches of what might be understood as the lifescapes of home. Between them, the practices and places of actuality tend to form other more or less abiding, displaced, loving, understanding, and temporary homes—the homes with which the tourism industry concerns itself, both inside and outside its matrix.

What the global tourism matrix produces and projects onto home places and homelands around the world are various landscapes of ludic pseudo-homelessness/homefullness—commitment-free, supposedly playful variations on what many have argued to be the basic condition of contemporary life.[65] From the consumer's point of view, tourism's productions are self-imposed and temporary. For the rest of those involved with the industry, however, the homelessness/homefullness produced in the cultivation of a touristic landscape can be quite real, if not absolutely real, causing the displacement or dispossession of a community in whole or in part, in imagination or in reality, onto stages, however subtly constructed, of commercial activity. The tourism industry's operations, in this regard, produce an arena in which a struggle to define home, and the cultivation of all that home supports (cultural identity and practice not least among them) take place.[66] In Davao City this struggle was still in its initial phases with regard to all the destinations observed and documented. It was evident, everywhere, however. Sometimes it emerged as a tragic losing battle along David and Goliath lines; sometimes it became a duel between more equal contestants on relatively level playing fields; sometimes it was conceived as a series of victorious revolutions in which the transformations were understood as progressive and in the best interests of all involved. In every case, however, the meaning of home was in one way or another explicitly at stake.

Conclusion

The tourism industry has long been recognized as having both darker and brighter potentials. It has been cast, with compelling evidence to support the claim, as yet another degrading, dehumanizing, land-robbing, commoditizing, oppressive intervention of the global onto the local, a neo-imperialistic industry founded solely on the production of Big Lies. It has also been cast, with persuasive reason, as the greenest and most humane of the world's relatively hideous array of lucrative and invasive global industries—the last, best, most enabling hope of sustainable development for creating win-win opportunities within the establishments of advanced capitalism as it promotes cultural revitalization, peace, and understanding worldwide.[67]

As the evidence from Davao City presented in the chapters that follow illustrates, it is impossible, if one is willing to pay close attention to the whole of what tourism can entail, to take a consistent side on this controversy. In my observation and experience, tourism, in Davao City as well as elsewhere,[68] for both its consumers and its producers, is unpredictable in its outcomes. The question whether tourism is a nightmare or a godsend or some combination of the two in a given location is not one that currently can be foreseen with any certainty. It depends on an array of circumstances too vast and complex to model in general terms. My orientation in this regard is basically aligned with what Robert Wood (1997: 3) has identified as a "postnormative" trend in tourism studies, which avoids making global judgments on tourism's positive or negative character. I also make a strong distinction between the industry in general and its specific manifestations in given locations. I defer normative claims about the industry *as a whole*, but I have adopted normative perspectives on the industry's operations with regard to the specific cases I have studied and lived through. It is for the purpose of developing this case-specific normative capability, in fact, that I would argue ethnographic studies of the tourism matrix are particularly appropriate and meaningful at this historical juncture, while the matrix's powers are still limited, its outcomes uncertain, and its influence incomplete. Through ethnography, and particularly interpretive ethnography, designed as it is to enlarge the record of perspectives given on the topic at issue, it becomes possible to take a valid normative stand for or against the industry's operations and influence its development.

Regardless of the questions of goodness or evil, however, tourism must be recognized as a subject that brings unique, even vital insight to the study of contemporary cultural phenomena. It is an industry that, in selling extraordinary movements, illuminates by contrast the ordinary landscapes of the practices of everyday globalization, particularly those of home and work. In this regard, the discipline of anthropology can learn much from studying tourism as a cultural subject, despite the conflicts entailed. This ethnography attempts to make a contribution to that effort, preserving what remains viable from standard ethnographic method when possible, and adjusting to the given circumstances of the contemporary research context when otherwise necessary.

Chapter 2
Davao Arrival

Tourists and those who work within the tourism matrix pay particular attention to arrivals. From the tourist's perspective, arrival is a defining experience, containing the lasting impact of "first" impressions and the trauma of extraordinary uncertainty related to the loss of all familiar placement and its accompanying sense of existential control.[1] From the industry's point of view, arrival is the single most important act of consumption, prerequisite for all subsequent acts. A tourist is generally classified as an "arrival" in the discourse of the industry. A single person becomes a series of arrivals on a tour as he or she moves to new destinations in the matrix. The act disfigures the individual, in rhetoric if not in fact. The thing done displaces the being.

The tourism industry worldwide counted around 600 million "arrivals" in 1996. They generated U.S. $423 billion in receipts. Roughly one sixth of those arrivals occurred in the Asian-Pacific region.

The Philippine tourism industry counted around two million international arrivals during the same year. While this represented a relatively tiny sliver of the region's entire market, the two million mark was nonetheless a figure up by 10 percent from that of 1995. It evidenced a rate of growth in the Philippines industry twice that of the average growth rate for tourism in the Asia-Pacific region and more than three times that of the world industry as a whole. However, it represented roughly only one fifth the number of arrivals occurring in the domestic tourism sector for the same year.

These statistics translated into one general fact: by 1996 the business of servicing arrivals had become a vital one, one of the top three industries in the nation in terms of earnings in foreign exchange. The Philippines government projected that the global industry would continue to grow inside its borders by 10 percent every year through the turn of the century.[2]

On March 12, 1996, I arrived in Davao for the seventh time. The first arrival had been on June 16, 1992. The most recent had been only a few weeks before, on January 23, 1996. Each of these arrivals in Davao was a story unto itself, a story of attaining a safe haven within a particularly unruly, unfinished sector of the tourism matrix. Each arrival was something of an adventure, although the quality of adventurousness diminished with

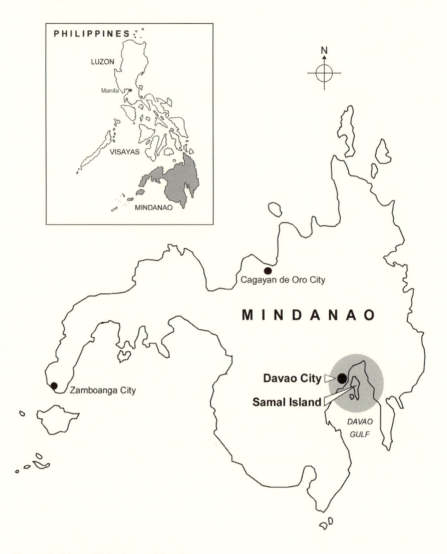

Figure 1. Map of Mindanao Island.

every passing experience. This was in part because of my own increasing familiarity with the landscape. Even as Davao's touristic markers grew more and more prominent, my ability to read them as a tourist gradually became weaker. But the diminishing sense of disorientation was also in part due to progress in the matrix's ongoing construction through the years, which worked in its own way to make the city globally accessible—a process that was still far from complete when my research ended.

I found myself over the years using my own arrivals as a way to gauge the development of the tourism matrix and document its utopic effects. I allowed the matrix to do its work on me, to the extent it could, and reflected on its character through the experiences each arrival generated. I was not attempting to study a tourist persona itself, so much as I was investigating the interventions of the tourism matrix into the locality as they could be perceived or evidenced via the act of arrival. Toward that end, I always arrived by plane as any foreign tourist would; I always arrived alone, as only an international or "foreigner" tourist would; I always found my way into the city by a taxi, as a professional non-elite person would; and I always went directly to the same hotel, as a returning business person would, foreign or domestic. In this way, I practiced arriving over the years, noting the changes to the pattern that occurred.

Each arrival entailed bearing witness to new developments in the city's landscape. In 1993 Victoria Plaza, a huge two-story air-conditioned indoor shopping mall, appeared, as did multi-story air-conditioned dealerships for Honda, Nissan, Toyota, Yamaha, and Mazda and a new block-long office building housing the regional Philippine Tourism Authority and Department of Tourism offices. In 1995 a new highway overpass, the first in Davao (a city of over one million residents), appeared in place of a clogged intersection on the airport-downtown route. In 1996 an Internet Cafe and MailBoxes, Etc. arrived downtown, making affordable and dependable international communication services widely available to sub-elite private sectors for the first time. Because of these changes and countless others, being a repeat arrival in Davao thus brought with it an expectation of change, as was the case with other repeat arrival destinations in the region.

No one participating in the arrivals I enacted ever took me for a tourist, despite my being counted as such by immigration. Even when I spoke English instead of the most commonly used dialect, Cebuano, I was generally taken to be a person of some non-tourist sort, most often a missionary.[3] These identifications were also indicators to me of the largely incomplete condition of the tourism matrix still under construction in Davao.

All the same, I proceeded to build a concept of how an international tourist arrival was being constructed in Davao through my practice. To be sure, I was somewhat ahead of the global schedule. I encountered no cultural tourists taking seriously the industry's invitation to visit what it was then already billing as the Philippines's most richly diverse cultural destination: exotic Mindanao. No arrival hordes were currently seeking the much-advertised land of the Tasaday, Bagobo, Maranao, and myriad other cultural groups. No crowds had yet assembled to witness the picture perfect *vinta* sailboats that so often served as the central image for travel posters of the region, or to consume the precious gold and silk threaded *malongs*, the solid silver, snake-bladed *kris* daggers, or the brass gongs and ornately carved mahogany drums and frames of the *kulintang* orchestras that were then being promoted by the tourism industry as still being traded in local markets at something like local values. The construction of arrival was occurring well ahead of the bodies who would eventually enact it.

With each passing arrival, Davao's landscape became more and more congruent with the particular utopic design developed for it. With each arrival, the narratives, choreographies, and venues of tourism appeared less incredible, ludicrous, and contradictory in relation to the built environment and the services developed for its maintenance. To illustrate something of this evolving condition of the matrix as it existed by the end of my research process, I recount the final episode of my own arrival practice, and some of the memories it both evoked and instilled.

Descent

On March 12, 1996, as I landed in Davao for the seventh time the jet's ventilation system spewed white steam into the cabin through the vents beneath the overhead storage bins. This went on for a few moments after touchdown and halted after the flight attendants had opened the main hatch for disembarking. As the air-conditioning system was abruptly shut off, the plane interior quickly transformed from its cool airborne self into a stuffy hothouse. Passengers made haste down the center aisle in efforts to escape the suffocating inner cabin. I did the same and collected myself on the top of the stairway outside the hatch with a slight sense of relief at having emerged successfully.

It was a small and now familiar struggle to keep balanced on the wobbly mobile stairway used to assist passengers in disembarking. I was carrying all the various instruments of documentation that accompanied me on these journeys—the camcorder, tape recorder, camera, and, since 1995, laptop. Turning myself part way around toward the plane's body as I emerged from its open hatch, I descended earthward somewhat backwardly for safety's sake. My consciousness centered on the several pieces of luggage hanging off my shoulders, which seemed to take on lives of their own in relation to the wobbles of the mobile staircase, swinging back and forth—a traveler's waltz with portable technology made all the more challenging by the long hours of sitting while in flight. After a few moments, however, I found myself, without mishap, at the bottom step of the stairway. One foot had already set itself on the black tarmac of the Davao International Airport. The other I now set beside it, with just the faintest sense of triumph. "Made it," the thought came to me, happily. There had been no fall from grace in this first movement of arrival. No other passenger had been jostled or delayed. So far, so good.

The hot wind whipped at the lightweight plaid cotton blazer I wore. The mid-afternoon sunlight caused a sharp heat to rise off the hair on the crown of my skull and also from the plastic frames of my sunglasses. The climate that had been controlled inside the jet seemed a distant memory before even a second or two on the ground had passed. The rate of change was tremendous, the sense of the weather as a ferocious force all encompassing.

A short episode of disorientation occurred. Was it 1995? I asked myself. No certain response was forthcoming. Wasn't it already 1996? or was it 1992? Was it 1993? The steps in descent had so fully absorbed my attention. There had been no clear temporal cues throughout the process. It had always been like this disembarking: the heat, the wind, the charged air, the sense that the light had itself somehow grown dense, the wobbly stairway, the loss of the seat on the plane and all to which it was connected. A brief struggle to regain temporal certainty ensued. Fatigue was a problem. Shifting the weight of the computer bag around, adjusting the resting position of the new sunglasses, tracing a fingertip around the shape of the frames, these actions brought a return to actuality and its specific facts. Not more than a second had passed before the time frame was back in place.

Each time I descended a stairway to disembark from an aircraft in Davao, the drama of the surrounding landscape as I'd scanned it from the window nearest my airplane seat had just had a natural impact, virtually identical in kind. The terrain of Mindanao from the air is an unforgettable landscape. Images of Bali, Bora Bora, Hawaii, and other island destinations on the Pacific Rim have nothing on Mindanao. There is a comparable quality of paradise: the absence of air pollution; the brilliant blues and greens of the

Figure 2. Davao International Airport arrival.

waters lit by the tropical sun—the Celebes Sea to the west and south, the Philippines Sea to the north and east, and the Gulf of Davao to the south; the dense blackness of the mountains rising steeply from the lush green of the lowlands, peaks steep, smooth, and dark, their giant cones alive in some massive, sleek way, slightly sinister, hauntingly elegant, terrifying, imposing, awe-inspiring. The mountains of Mindanao, dominated by the 10,000-foot volcano Mount Apo, possess a majesty worthy of global attention. The clouds that nearly always surround them appear symphonic in shape and movement, cumulonimbus plumes shooting up into the atmosphere in fountains of exuberant cottony material. Their celestial formations lend a distinctive beauty to the location, generated in perfect harmony, as they are, with the existent conditions of the natural environment.

Davao was inspiring from above, from afar in 1996. The experience of this beauty was enhanced markedly when one looked down on the clouds from a vantage point that included all the comforts a commercial airline service could provide. It was a moving scene, a scenic wonder, providing no disappointment for even the most discriminating arrival's gaze. My own repetitions of arrival had served only to reaffirm the wisdom of the Philippine government's logic in this regard, in selecting Davao as a site for large-scale tourism development.

Having walked down the steps off the plane, now crossing to the terminal building, I noted in 1996, as was a habit now, how the terminal building itself, with its distinctly shaped roof, reminiscent of the peaked roofs of the Minangkabao and Toraja of Indonesia, or even those of the palatial temples of Bangkok, was the most impressive human-made sight in the immediate landscape. Davao's terminal building was different from those I'd seen elsewhere in the Philippines, where such an architectural style was never apparent in monumental institutional structures. From the moment a person at all well-traveled in the Philippines stepped off the plane in Davao, it was clear that Luzon and the Visayas had been left behind. The non-Christian nations of ASEAN loomed larger here as well as nearer. There was no mistaking the fact that this was a very different end of the archipelago from that over which Manila had for centuries cast its shadow. The new terminal's design asserted a very different cultural and historical identity in no uncertain terms to all who might arrive by air.

The Lower Level

After reorienting myself on the tarmac, I made my way toward the terminal. The entry into the terminal building, a space that in 1992 had seemed mysterious and unmarked, now appeared transparent in its meanings. The indoor arrival area contained no surprises. It was, as always, framed by the well-worn wooden partitions that separated this section of the terminal's large, high ceilinged, open-air upper level from the waiting areas for departure. I passed under the enormous chandeliers made of seashell disks, passed over the off-white linoleum floor, passed by the hand-painted billboards advertising the orchid gardens and beach resorts of the vicinity, and on by the now unoccupied dark wooden desks and counters used by various officials for international arrivals. I glanced beyond the head-high partitions to the rows of anchored yellow plastic chairs that sat facing the runway on the other side, and to the small gift shop/snack bar open for business along the far end wall of the upper level. Same as ever.

The terminal's open air upper level hall was spacious and tranquil, virtually empty with only a few PAL staff milling about. It had always been this way in my experience—I remember my pleasure of this at first encounter, appreciating the gracious and serene welcome that the dark wooden terminal building had staged, the wisdom embodied in the distinctive architectural design, the lack of noise, the appropriateness of the materials, the magnificent sense of shelter underneath the huge mahogany colored wooden beams, and the comfort of the freely moving air, wafting in and out over the uncrowded balconies that lined both long sides of the structure. The airport itself was expanding, with a new addition under construction and much more in the planning stages to accommodate a rapidly growing international flight schedule, but this arrival area had preserved its generous, informal character over the years in which I had come to know it. The effect of this initial venue—understated, unchanging, and charmingly far from the cutting edge in its touristic signage—was an enduring one.

The baggage claim area on the lower level, however, was a different world entirely. It was not a large room, and it was generally crowded with uniformed porters. Once inside the terminal building, a passenger could reach the lower level in only one way, down a narrow, winding set of steps. This downward spiraling passage staged a transition from the global to the local. On the upper level, one was either "cleared" for take-off or still in transit. One was still a part of the wider world of airline travel. Starting down the steps to the lower level to claim bags, however, one entered a new stage of practices, mediated by different signs, governed by different forces, originating from different circumstances. On the upper level one was still connected to the world of one's point of departure. On the lower level of the terminal building the standards of the global matrix were no longer in control.

The airport didn't always work as it did on this particular arrival. When I had flown in from Manado, the 40-seat Boraq Airline propjets had carried only a couple of dozen passengers. In those cases we claimed our bags Greyhound style outside on the tarmac as the crew took them out of the plane, with no other middlemen involved. I'd had no dealings with porters and left the terminal carrying my bags myself, clearing customs and immigration in minutes, bypassing the lower level operations altogether. Because these flights were small, there were fewer taxi drivers waiting around outside the terminal. The international Indonesia-Philippines arrival experience was a much smaller scale operation than the Manila-Davao flights, and was handled in a more personal way. The contrast was in line with the current travel statistics for the nation, which recorded domestic travel arrivals occurring on a much larger scale than international arrivals.

When I had arrived at this point in the journey for only the fourth time, back in July 1995, I had interpreted the advance of the porters toward the arrivals descending the steps as something like an onslaught. Caught off guard, I went along with the stream of life and complied with the first request for my claim tickets, giving them to a person with the name of "Rudy" and "#59" boldly printed on his blue T-shirt. Rudy pointed to his number repeatedly after I had given him the tickets, emphasizing wordlessly the means by which I should identify him later, as well as the primitive limits available to us for any further communication as far as he was concerned. His speechlessness and its signed alternatives created the initial voiding of a neutral gap between us and around us. I recognized them as the initial moves of constructing a utopic space where his first language, he rightly assumed, would not be uttered. The touristic stage had reached only this crude phase of construction on the lower level, even in July 1995.

Despite the efforts he made to make himself distinguishable to me, Rudy soon passed off my business to "Jozen" (#48) when some more pressing business came along, and it was Jozen who wheeled my bags outside the terminal where a van driver grabbed one away from him, heading off toward a minivan. At no point was I brought into the choreographing of this tourist-transporting process.

Today, in March 1996, I arrived amid a large incoming mainstream Manila crowd. I decided this time to surrender to the local style of claiming and relinquished my two baggage checks to one of the porters. Too many repetitions had occurred for a stranger's panic to ensue, even though the "onslaught" was staged in a manner similar to those of previous visits. It was I who selected a porter on this particular day. I made a choice and signaled it by making eye contact with one of the porters toward the edge of the crowd, keeping my face dead pan and making no movement in gesture save for a slight lift of the eyebrows. The one I signaled understood the sign without hesitation, as it was a common one for such purposes. He took my claim tickets and did his job, handing over my baggage to a taxi driver who led me to his vehicle—a weatherworn minivan of Japanese manufacture. There was no denial of linguistic competence; language simply didn't enter into the process.

The driver wanted 100 pesos (then U.S. $4.00) for the thirty-minute trip into the heart of town. Anticipating my protest, he hurriedly went on to say he had no meter to calculate the exact fare, assuming I knew, as indeed I did, that working meters had for a year or so been standard technology for this service. Grateful for the apparent (nontouristic) candor in the driver's opening line, I countered his price immediately with an offer of 80 pesos.

I was relieved that he had started at 100 pesos instead of 200 or even 500, which had happened before. This would have meant we would have stood in the searing heat outside the van much longer while we fixed the price and that I would have been worried the whole way in about whether this was going to be the time I would end up robbed, kidnaped, or worse. It was always a worry with an unknown driver.

The driver immediately consented to my counter-offer of 80 pesos. Immediately. No refusal, no additional-counter offer, no frown of irritation or exhalation of frustrated disgust, no laughing shaking of the head, no repetition of the original price, in short, no protest of the various forms I had come to recognize as reactions to counter offers that were too low. Neither was there a gleeful nod, aborted song-line, deflected half-whistle, or overly quick acceptance. There were no questions during the ride about my situation in Davao City or offers of additional service in the days to come, as I had come to expect with counter-offers that had been too high. There was just neutral acceptance, and we went on to the next phase of our business. At this moment in my journey, the symbolic dimension of the tourism matrix vanished into thin air.

A stir of satisfaction had spread across my consciousness as I registered how quickly the price settling interaction had been accomplished. We had established a price in a verbal exchange of just two moves. It seemed a little work of art in and of itself, getting the price fixed in just two utterances. Previous epic-length interactions had taught me that. There was no magic involved, however. Neither was it luck. Behind the exchange on both sides had been an extensive daily practice of fare negotiation, hundreds, maybe thousands of trials and errors over the years. How exactly had I been able to let him know, without words, that I knew he knew I knew what I was doing, I didn't even know myself. It wasn't something I could ever have put into words. Somehow, however, I had shown it—staged it—in a manner that was persuasive. Somehow, I had demonstrated that I knew he ought to realize I was offering him 15 pesos more than the metered fare would have come out to be in 1996. I had made it evident that I knew a 15-peso tip was more, significantly more, than he could expect from his average airport customer, even a wealthy customer, although it was less than what he'd have made from a novice foreign arrival. And somehow I had made it clear I knew that there was a world of difference evident between an 80- and a 100-peso fare, even though the actual monetary difference amounted to less than one U.S. dollar in 1996—as I was certain we both knew. Novice foreigners, as we also both knew, calculated in increments of 100 pesos. This was the only difference I had really wanted understood, for the sake of my peace of mind on the ride into town. I hadn't spelled any of this out, yet it all seemed to have been communicated. We evidently shared the opinion that 80 pesos was a reasonable fare, an acceptable deal, given the going prices.

Not that these prices were somehow inherently reasonable. But they were what they were, and that was "life" in Davao, in 1996, and we both knew it. On this occasion, when it had come time to take a ride outside the airport's lower level, where local forms of play still tended to rule over the global, I had chosen to exit the tourism matrix. It was not a conscious choice but an impulse. I felt compelled to drop out of the matrix and make it evident that I was operating on home ground. And so on we went, now in the absence of the matrix.

Reentry

The final phase of arrival was a short journey into the city's center. The roads of Davao no longer impressed me as they once had—as relatively wide and well paved compared to those of Cebu and Manila. The driver was silent on this occasion, which was typical in 1996. Since air-con taxis had become standard, drivers more often than not chose to play radio music so loudly that conversation was impossible. We turned onto the National Highway heading southwest along the waterfront of Davao Gulf for the first quarter of the journey. We passed the Nestle plant and headed away from the loading facilities of the international and domestic Sasa Seaport that loomed not far off. The oil storage facilities of Caltex, Mobil, and a few other large companies were the first landmarks on the way into town. This stretch of highway was particularly significant for most locally oriented forms of touristic life in Davao, because it was where people turned off down to the waterfront to catch the outrigger ferries that ran between the city and the beach resorts of the northwest coast of Samal Island, a few hundred meters off the Mindanao shore in the interior of the Davao Gulf. These half dozen or so establishments could be reached only by ferry, and they catered mainly to weekend tourist groups heading over to the beaches to eat their midday meal, swim, celebrate some festive occasion like a birthday or the arrival of a visiting relative, or otherwise enjoy a day of leisure.

The billboard for the most popular of these establishments, Fantasy Isle Park, stood out prominently on the highway at the turnoff for its ferry landing. It had been pointed out to me on my first arrival in 1992 by my driver then, who recommended it as a destination when I gave him to understand I was interested in tourism. However, the actual landmark for the day tourists coming this way from Davao's city center stood on the opposite side of the road. This was the family residence of the owners of "Fantasy." The residence was impossible to miss along the highway, as it was one of only a handful of pre-World War II residences left standing in the city. Its handsome wooden facade, painted a somewhat muted shade of green when seen against the tropical background, and its formal front yard, gated with ornate antique wrought iron, contrasted starkly with the other dwellings along the roadside, all of them relatively nondescript and of much more recent construction. Although the residence was not large enough to be called a mansion, the force of the house's architectural historicity alone created an extraordinary presence on the roadside. I never met an individual in Davao who didn't know the place and something of its family history.

We next passed the enormous white archway of the Minflo orchid exhibition grounds. The booming orchid industry had used the orchid blossom as a new symbol of local and transnational commercial identity in Davao during the early 1990s. Orchids were linked to tourism in a number of essential respects. I was always reminded in passing by Minflo's sign of the city's recently developed annual Kadayawan festival and the various explosions of orchids that event produced every August. The 1995 festival had been organized, in fact, by the owner of Minflo.

We came soon to the inland fork in the road, where most drivers would turn away from the shore and proceed onward on J. P. Laurel Avenue for the main portion of the journey. This turnoff had been made recognizable by another key touristic venue, although key to an entirely different form of touristic expression: the Insular Century Hotel. Originally the Davao Insular Inter-Continental Inn, the only international hotel firm operating in Davao, the resort loomed large in Davao's touristic landscaping. "Insular," as it was known locally, was for many years Davao's grandest hotel by a considerable margin. Rooms started at around 1500 pesos (then U.S. $75) a night—more than ten times the going rate for a room downtown.

Various events had brought me to Insular over the years—celebrations, conventions, meetings, festivals, and special visitors of various kinds. Every time I passed its glamorously carved wooden sign, planted majestically in stone at its entrance on the National Highway in a manner resembling the minor monuments used to mark the boundaries of national forests of the U.S., I felt the lure of its multinational power source. Insular's entrance was strikingly unlike any other on the route into the city center. It was reminiscent of a plantation driveway, a long single lane of smoothly paved road, lined with palms and manicured lawns, welcoming foreigners into its reception area. Jeepneys didn't venture inside and, given the length of the walk from the highway to the hotel steps, taxis and private cars were the only means by which a person could comfortably arrive at the hotel. The scale of the grounds served to weed out lower income visitors.

Insular had been a presence in Davao since the 1950s, managed always by European expatriates. During my years in the city it had dramatically changed its facade as well as its ownership, management, staff, and business practices. Ownership had shifted in 1996 from the Intercontinental to the Century chain, signaling a new touristic era in Davao—one marked by growth, new investment, and increasing conformity to global service standards, aesthetics, and economies. The staff, particularly the more key positions, changed from lifetime to temporary slots, breaking ties in the process with local patrons who had long established relationships with the older work force. The hotel's more public areas were upgraded, redesigned in more technologically sophisticated, environmentally sensitive open air architectural forms. The lobby was supplied with museum-quality installation areas for the display of locally associated artifacts, asserting that Mindanao did in fact possess world class material culture. In some respects Insular's specific transformations appeared microcosmic, evidence of the more general changes taking place in the city with respect to tourism and the changing forces behind it.

Leaving the hotel and waterfront behind, the taxi proceeded through the district of Lanang, an area already relatively rich in touristic landscaping. We passed the distinctly peaked dark roof of the large Damosa building, headquarters of the House of Travel, a leading player in the local private sector tourism development game. Also along this stretch of J. P. Laurel Avenue, on the opposite side, stood the older of the city's two golf courses, the Lanang Country Club and Golf Course. It was owned by a family connected prominently with tourism in the 1990s, the Dakudao family. The regional director of the Department of Tourism, in fact, was Catalina "Kiling" Santos Dakudao.

As I passed the golf course, I thought of Carmen Dakudao Locsin, a *tita* or "aunt" (by marriage) of the director, and the younger daughter of the family's original immigrant to Davao, Dr. Santiago Dakudao. Carmen Dakudao had managed the clubhouse and supervised the gardens, overseeing the orchids planted along the fairways that had put the golf course on tourist maps several decades ago during the earlier Marcos tourism era. I remembered her on the golf course when we had played a round together in 1992. She was close to seventy years old at the time, wearing violet golf shorts, pink shirt, and violet blazer—every inch the lady golfer. She drove her ball down the fairways like thunder in dead straight shots, complaining nonetheless that she had lost her "snap" with age.

We came next to the new overpass heading up to the affluent Buhangin district and the Stanfilco (Dole Philippines, Inc.) offices. It was a turnoff I had taken countless times in the past, most often to escape the research on the tourism matrix. The Marcos-era Ladislawa subdivision was located there, a gated community where all the streets were quiet and well paved and the homes large, modern, heavily landscaped, and surrounded by high, sturdy brick or concrete walls. Ladislawa was off limits to tourists. My first acquaintance in Davao, Grace, lived there. Grace was the daughter of a Chinese-Philippine businessman and a Visayan schoolteacher from the northwestern side of Mindanao, among the youngest of thirteen children and the mother of three children herself. She was married to a son of the owner of the city's main downtown hotel—a relationship that had bestowed on her a position inside the local tourism sector, at an inner margin of the city's elite.

When I first arrived in Davao, Grace had been starting a small local business in jewelry and metallic artwork. In four years time, the business had grown into a transnational enterprise, shipping products to the United States and Europe as well as to various destinations in the ASEAN region. Grace's company was one of many small businesses in Davao that were enjoying the booming transnational economic climate brought on by the ASEAN trade agreements. In 1996 she was exploring possibilities for expanding her home-based production into a larger warehouse. She was working on the idea that her future manufacturing space and showroom could also be developed for tourism, built as a theater so that tourists could observe the various stages of jewelry production. Grace's commercial sense included the recognition that tourism would become part of her future one way or another. She was designing her own built environment to take best advantage of the integration of the matrix's operations with her own, including a viewing area and a cafe to accommodate tourists.

After the turnoff, the first signs of the downtown tourist landscape began to appear. The new facade of the Villa Margarita appeared, followed by the Durian Hotel and, on the opposite side of the road, the recently closed Casino Filipino, whose upper stories still showed the signs of a devastating fire. It was another monument to the end of the Marcos-dominated touristic era. Next, the new office of APTTI (Asian and Pacific Tourism Training Institute) appeared. I wondered whether the new occupants knew yet of its building's reputation for being haunted. Then the fortress-sized cream-colored walls of Victoria Plaza and the gigantic Ronald McDonald Clown figure just beyond it came into view. Seeing them, I knew I was more than halfway home. The densest areas in the older parts of the city were now to come, areas largely untouched as yet by the tourism matrix.

I have no recollection which route brought us to Thomas Claudio Street (now Elpidio Quirino Avenue), the final street of my reentry. We passed by a weatherbeaten, elaborately shuttered wooden edifice, the Palma Gil Elementary School—a rare artifact of the American colonial era. Then we drove through several blocks of dingy storefronts, their street level interiors wide open for business. Halfway to where one could now see Claudio Street dead-ending, at the Davao River, a calachuchi tree in full white bloom stood out on the left. Its organic form appeared in high contrast to the water-stained concrete, neon signs, asphalt, and rusty galvanized iron surfaces that otherwise constituted the scene. We continued on past it and rounded one of the oldest corners in the city, onto Magallanes Street (renamed A. Pichon). Magallanes, one of the original three streets of the city, dated to the tiny Spanish pueblo built in 1848, although no trace of that history remained.

The taxi pulled into the driveway of Marjorie's Inn, braking and lurching as always while negotiating the two-inch cement lip that separated the driveway from the street pavement. The lip never failed to jar me a bit more strongly than I anticipated. No matter how many times I pulled into this parking area, the design in concrete forced an abruptly unmediated transition. Traversing it had become a rite, symbolic not only of the quality of my own arrival in the city, but also of the more general character of the relationship between public and private sectors as it tended to manifest itself in the city's less globalized spaces. If there was ever any doubt as to when exactly it was that I finally arrived in Davao on a visit, the lip resolved it with a shock and a jostle. Surviving the lip, I was there.

I emerged from the taxi, glad to be done traveling. Marjorie's Inn had been my place of residence in Davao throughout my years of coming and going, and it had changed relatively little in that time. Here, I knew, I would live both inside and outside the tourism matrix, and the changes in aspect would come in rapid and unpredictable fluctuations.

Familiar faces smiled at me from the small front desk beyond the inn's open doorway. I moved forward to respond to the welcome. A few minutes later my head hit a pillow in "my" room, #303. My final arrival was at last complete.

Chapter 3
Davao Understandings of Tourism

What awaited me on all my arrivals in Davao was a host of diverse touristic narratives, as well as the agents, audiences, histories, and other social contexts of their performance. The array was too numerous to collect or inhabit in some representative manner. Of the many occasions I did attend where narratives of tourism were produced, two stand out. These were two of the most prestigious narrative events in which I took part. Taken as a pair, they give some sense of the range of opinion that was present among the most powerful segment of Davao society regarding the local significance of the tourism industry during these years. The first event explicitly focused on tourism, the second virtually ignored it. Together they indicate the differences and similarities in perspective voiced in two highly contrasting types of narrative contexts in the city: those of public life, where the tourism matrix was already well established, and those of affluent private life, where it was not.

Davao Tourism Association Induction

In late July 1995, a valedictory address was given at a special anniversary meeting of the Davao Tourism Association, a civic organization commonly referred to in Davao as DATA. The service organization was created in 1974 during the early years of martial law, when Imelda Marcos had been a driving force behind the proliferation of the tourism matrix throughout the Philippines.[1] In 1992, however, after a decade of intense local conflict and political strife in the Mindanao region, less than thirty members remained active in DATA. Nonetheless, by 1995 DATA had gained the support of nearly one hundred establishments: roughly thirty hotel- and resort-type enterprises, thirteen travel agencies, all four of the city's largest orchid farms, both its golf courses, all four of its local airline offices,[2] thirteen restaurants, five car and bus transport companies, five handicraft and gift shops, several department stores, a college, a career center, a theater collective, a city newspaper, and the local offices of Coca Cola, San Miguel Beer, Anflocor,[3] and Nestle Philippines. Multinational names were not lacking from its membership—Avis, Grayline, Sanyo, Intercontinental, and Nissan were present in addition to Coca Cola and Nestle. However, the large majority of establishments were not themselves global entities, and only around a dozen—most of them fast food or retail merchandise chains—were even nationwide in terms of their commercial reach. The bulk of DATA's membership was local, and the growth of the membership reflected the growth of interest in tourism that had occurred over these years largely at the local level.

With the majority of businesses involved in tourism now represented among its ranks, DATA was Davao city's premier private sector tourism organization. The association put most of its service energy, however, into enhancing government-initiated projects and activities. It maintained close links to the regional Philippine Tourism Association (PTA) and Department of Tourism (DOT) offices and officials. It sent officers and members to accompany DOT officials to trade fairs, conventions, and travel marts where Davao was to be represented. It also coordinated tourism development seminars, festivals, and other events held in Davao itself with which the DOT and PTA were involved, if not in charge. DATA could to some extent be called the government's private sector mouthpiece, so close was the alignment of the organization with the local branches of the Philippine tourism bureaucracy. However, given the array of Davao-based families and businesses involved, and the extent of their influence and input into the organization, such a characterization was far from adequate. DATA expressed the collective consciousness of the city's most actively involved tourism entrepreneurs, a consciousness that entailed personal, familial, and professional perspectives, as well as those originating in the government.

On the evening of the 1995 anniversary meeting, when the main agenda was the induction of a new slate of officers as well as fourteen newly joining businesses, DATA's more mundane service work had been set aside temporarily for the purpose of celebrating its own membership. The collected assembly on this occasion was looking its most glamorous. Ten committees staffed by twenty-six members had been hard at work attending to every detail of the event—from invitations to banquet menus to member-produced song and dance "intermission numbers" to award presentations—in order to ensure a most memorable and elegant event. Every feature of the swearing in, gavel transferring, and plaque bestowing sequences had been planned according to the letter of the bylaws so as to proceed without the slightest disturbance or misstep. Music, spotlights, and slides had been prepared and coordinated with sets of remarks for the emcee that would make the awards presentation segment move along in an entertaining and theatrical manner. The crowd, around 150 members and guests, were coifed, perfumed, bejeweled, and dressed "to the nines," as the local press might have reported it the following day. The level of *palabas*[4]—or joie de vivre Filipino-style—was at a cultural apogee. All this signaled unambiguously that DATA was at this moment an organization of central importance to Davao's contemporary social life, one of those networks where the current cutting edge of social action was actively ongoing.

I was invited to attend the DATA induction as a guest of the owners of Marjorie's Inn. As we arrived on the scene—the large Apo View hotel—shortly after sunset, the crowd was just beginning to swell to its fullest. The organization's cumulative fashionable and festive effect was nothing short of dazzling. In addition to the occasional black chiffon cocktail dress, every variation on Filipiniana themes seemed richly represented. Butterfly sleeves of every pastel color flitted about on the ladies' shoulders. Meshes and mazes of *jusi* and (even more coveted) *piña* fibers, looking like veils of mist and stars, formed the "substance" of numerous shirts and dresses. Hawaiian floral print evening dresses added a certain loud accent to the party as well. But the predominant fashion statement, oddly enough in this overwhelmingly Roman Catholic assembly, was Islamic in design—*moro*, as local discourse still tended to designate it. "Moro," from the Philippine Catholic perspective, referred to the once-dreaded seafaring enemies of the lowland Christian agriculturists of the previous century. Moros had raided Spanish-governed settlements with terrifying success on a regular basis throughout the Visayas and Mindanao—in what was now considered a bygone premodern age.[5] Moro costuming entailed straight, *sarong*-styled skirts, brocade evening jackets, sashes, and *malong*-sized[6] heavy scarves, all of which were being worn on this evening by the majority of its leading ladies and a handful of its more daring gentlemen. These fashions, I gathered, were worn with the intention of representing the traditional precolonial clothing styles of the region.

No one, I noted, had come in an authentic costume. The fabrics and dress patterns were postmodern, neoethnic pastiches. They were made with contemporary silks, chiffons, and satins that had been embroidered, appliqued, and often sequined using the latest technology in metallic fiber weaving. Some combined Christian with Islamic designs. The lucky lady who later turned out to be the evening's raffle grand prize winner, for example, wore a sequined green evening gown with butterfly sleeves that was decorated with a brass and beaded moro-style medallion, fastened at the waist. Regardless of the contemporary materials, combinations, and cuts, however, many of the fabrics did use woven designs that resembled, in some cases with museum-quality accuracy, the distinctive abstract imagery identified with the Islamic minority groups indigenous to the Southern Philippines: the Maranao, Magindanao, and Tausug, to mention only a few. Intricate gold and silver patterns, stitched into emerald green, garnet red, jet black, sunflower yellow, and myriad other bold backgrounds, presented rows upon rows of swirling, scrolling, zigzagging, scalloped, droplet, rosette, diamond, and crescent shaped shining forms. These cumulatively set the crowd aglitter in ways not entirely disconnected from those of the region's ancestral ruling

classes, who had for centuries used similar artwork in their climactic cere-
monial events. It was definitely a night for Southern Philippine symbolism
to shine, sparkle, and bask in the limelight.

Whether this appropriation of indigenous imagery was intended to create
linkages to some national Philippine "Past," as it had already been reified
in the artifacts of its southern minority cultures in museum's throughout
the world, or whether it was meant to identify with some transnational
future involving countries such as Indonesia, Malaysia, and Brunei—whose
national costumes were virtually identical in design—was unclear. I pon-
dered these possibilities silently as I took a seat among the crowd. Both associations, I imagined, would be desirable. I grew more curious to hear how
the evening's rhetoric would play out in this regard.

The Apo View Hotel's newly remodeled grand ballroom was a fitting site
for such a spectacular local gathering. This hotel was a landmark local institution, particularly where tourism was concerned. It had been built in 1947,
in the wake of independence and the mass exodus of the Japanese from the
area. It was a family-owned and managed establishment, by a family who
had ancestral ties to the Central Luzon region of Pampanga among other
Philippine locations, but who had been Davao-based for several generations. The Apo View had a history that reflected the city's own major events.
It had been a high profile target of civil unrest in the 1980s and had been
severely damaged and closed temporarily in 1988 in one of the more spectacular and brutal of a series of hotel fires that had been set throughout the
archipelago during this time. People tended to remember this about the
place when it came up in conversation. Currently, however, the hotel was
expanding rapidly, adding an entirely new wing to its premises, symbolizing
in this development the city's booming economic climate. While Apo View's
city center location was largely without manicured grounds and entirely
without shoreline, its rooms were handsome and its other facilities were
roughly equal in quality and price to those of the five-star Insular Inn.
Social events of great prominence were held in both locations. The choice
of Apo View on this occasion, I assumed, was most likely due to the recent
opening of the grand ballroom, which according to local *chismis*[7] had been
deemed superior in ambiance to anything comparable at Insular.

The ballroom was indeed grand. It accommodated 1,200 persons at maximum capacity. Its gleaming stone floors were inlaid with coral or marble of
a kind I couldn't easily identify. Round tables set for twelve had been placed
across the floor, and a dais with room for seven was set up at the front of the
hall. A buffet was at a back corner was serving a Pacific Rim smorgasbord:
lechon (roast pig), meatloaf, callos stew, fried shrimps, green beans, sashimi,
macaroni salad, rice, fruit and several desserts. There was every item that
I had come to expect at banquets of this deluxe class.

The ballroom's high white walls were almost entirely mirrored, creating
an even more cavernous and magical effect. However, the outstanding

feature of the ballroom was its enormous chandeliers. These were made from horns of water buffalo ("carabao," as they were known locally) in a seeming tribute to the history of local agriculture that, until the arrival of modernity not so long before the Apo View's construction, had been dependent on the labor of the carabao. The chandeliers had been designed to match the elaborate sculptures of the hotel's main open-air lobby, which presented ornate clusters of the same type of horns, assembled there with copper- and silver-gilded branches and leaves to form gigantic, one might even say imperial, bouquets of a type seen nowhere else in the Philippines. Grace had designed them—I knew her work well enough to know this at a glance. The sculptures in the lobby area were further enhanced by huge bunches of white orchids placed on the handsome hardwood check-in counter and around the main lobby. These were placed with such frequency as to create a splendid, even glorious effect. One of the hotel family members was in the orchid business. In the ballroom, however, the relatively unadorned chandeliers of carabao horns brought a more rugged, rustic element to the otherwise wedding-cake aesthetics of the hall. The ballroom was a space of mixed messages, of reflection, allusion, and East-West intersection, framed on a magnificent scale.

When I'd first entered the Apo View in 1992 (it was the first night I spent in Davao) I'd been impressed to find a Balinese painting hanging in the main lobby hall, a huge piece, the only reference I'd seen to Bali during my travels throughout the tourism destinations of the Philippines. It had signaled to me that a critically different orientation to tourism was in the making here as it was nowhere else in the nation. I interpreted a regional ASEAN-centered orientation that I'd expected to see more widely understood at other Philippine resort areas but had not. Apo View's imagery had been an influential factor in my decision to work in Davao, although, as it happened, I learned later that the painting was merely a rather idiosyncratic acquisition of one of the hotel's family members and did not carry the broader meaning I'd interpreted. Nonetheless, only three years later, at the 1995 DATA anniversary meeting, the program's speakers were about to announce in unambiguous, euphoric terms the actual manifestation of just such an orientation as I'd originally come seeking, as they celebrated the public success of ASEAN and the local awakening it was bringing to Davao and its apparently blossoming tourate.

The valedictory address by the outgoing DATA president was the most substantive speech of the evening and as such best represented the historical narrative of tourism development I had hoped to witness in attending the occasion. It was the first of several speeches that together formed the core of the evening's four-hour program, a program that was, except for the occasional spontaneous Tagalog remark, conducted entirely in English. Despite its relatively rich content, the valedictory address was given the humblest position of all the evening's keynotes. It preceded the speeches by the evening's most honored guests and served as a precursor to the acceptance speech of DATA's incoming president, the former Miss Universe, Margarita "Margie" Moran-Floirendo, wife of the eldest son of Davao's economic super tiger, Antonio "Tony Boy" Floirendo. The address was not to be buttressed by the array of impressive statistics that Kiling Dakudao, in her role as DOT regional director, would soon afterward utter. Kiling, dressed this evening in a ravishing gown and shoulder sash of deep maroon chiffon, embroidered moro-style with sparkling green and golden threadwork, her hair French braided up the back of her head and swept into a twist anchored by a gorgeous golden fan-like comb, would soon comment from the dais that tourism was up 400 percent in Davao this year. She would then project that the tourism estate about to begin construction on nearby Samal Island was going to make 1,150 new jobs for local workers. Neither was the outgoing DATA president's valedictory address to be enhanced by the spirited comments of Eduardo Juaquin, Philippines undersecretary of Tourism and general manager of the Philippine Tourism Authority. The undersecretary had flown down from Manila for the occasion and was adorned this evening by a lei of pink orchids. He would soon wax poetic about the particularly advantageous situation Davao now enjoyed for tourism development as a "gateway city," likening the healthy government (led by "the loveliest Regional Director of Tourism in the Philippines") and the even healthier private sector (emphasizing here the Floirendo family's Pearl Farm Beach Resort, which the undersecretary hailed as largely responsible for putting Davao on the international tourist map) to the twin fires needed for the roasting of a good *bibingka* ricecake.

Regardless of its modestly positioned situation, the valedictory address summarized the main events of the organization from 1992 through 1995 and documented in some detail the changes in scope, focus, and activity DATA had undergone during a period when the global tourism matrix, long dormant since the final phases and aftershocks of the Marcos regime, had begun to stir somewhat grudgingly back into life again.

DATA's outgoing president was Mary Ann "Baby" Maceda Montemayor. She was a member of the prominent Manila-based Maceda family, a relative of the famous Philippine career politician Senator Maceda. However, she was also the wife of Leon Garcia Montemayor, Jr., the eldest son in one of Davao City's most powerful families. The president's in-laws included a local congressman and the wife of a provincial governor. Her mother-in-law, a member of the powerful Davao-based Garcia family, was popularly revered as something like a queen figure in the city's elite social circles. Baby Maceda Montemayor, like everyone of her social class, also had family living in Los Angeles—a fact she mentioned to me in an interview I did with her a few days after the induction, the only occasion where I interacted with her personally. DATA's outgoing leader, whose term had coincided with the beginning of a new era of tourism in Davao, was a person whose transnational, national, and local ties were powerful, notorious, and profound.

Baby Maceda Montemayor was small in stature by Filipina standards. However, her posture, as she assumed the podium, was so exceptionally well aligned, exhibiting such a lithe, almost athletic vertical emphasis, that she appeared statuesque regardless of her height. On this evening, her simply cut short hair was unadorned. She wore a green evening gown, similar to Kiling Dakudao's in its moro-inspired design, but simpler. Her skirt was solid green with only one thick band of golden threaded weaving about a foot wide toward the bottom. Her shoulder sash was also golden, and she wore a large gold medallion hanging from a long golden chain around her neck. She bore this small treasury easily, without officiousness, utterly without the self-important air of the celebrity that indeed she was.

Despite her unpretentiousness, the president's final presidential performance was anything but unofficial. She spoke in formal, sober, yet melodically rich and gracious tones throughout the fifteen-minute speech. Her diction was maturely phrased into a style of speaking that evidenced a sort of practiced clarity only seasoned stage actors typically possess. It must have taken her five minutes to list every party to whom she bade welcome at the outset of her remarks—a welcome that was truly presidential in its regard. People had started to chat among themselves by the time she finished her immaculately enunciated array of names and groups. Regardless of the audience's lapse, Baby's earnestness remained at an extraordinary level of intensity, such that I judged it at the outset to be seemingly unsustainable. Yet somehow she managed to maintain and even at times to increase the affect as she reviewed the highlights of her term. Only in the final moments did her composure fleetingly break down. She broke into tears at the end of her speech, overcome by the whole experience. It was only seconds, however, before she regained her composure and proceeded to the awards portion of the program. Statesmanlike polish soon covered any residual grief she may have been experiencing.

"Allow me," said the president, "to take you down memory lane and highlight some of our major accomplishments of the past three years." This request followed several minutes of jubilant introductory effusiveness, during which "a perfect team" of officers and members were acknowledged as having "functioned magnificently" for "the greater good of the DATA community." The president described herself as "on top of the world!" and "profusely thankful" to all those who had assisted her during her term of office. "Now I realize," she stated in the closing moments of the introduction, "that society, indeed, is a series of interdependencies. To be in a community is to be in partnership." The invocation of partnership at this point in the evening produced a moment of rhetorical brilliance worthy of the diamond-studded event. The concept was an ethical cornerstone of progressive discourse among Davao's development network, conservative and liberal factions alike. It was the word that linked what was happening in the city to the best of what was supposed to be happening in the name of advanced capitalism worldwide. The incorporation of "partnership" in this manner, at the outset of the program's most serious moments, served effectively to connect DATA's membership to the heart of world class rhetoric on sustainable development. The president could not have chosen a more cogent means of elevating the evening's ceremonies to the stature of an international event.

"Friends," she began again, "when I assumed the presidency three years ago, it was like taking possession of an attractive shell bereft of life." The melodramatic metaphor hung in the air, evidently increasing in poignancy for the now silent crowd. "There were a handful of us, however," she continued, "who still believed in the dream." After another series of compliments touching on the vision, strength, and faith of her officers, the president proceeded with her recollection. "Even then," she reminisced, "we saw DATA as merely a sleeping giant whose time had come." Her metaphor, this time evoking fairy tale, adeptly reinvented the history of the 1980s—a time when kidnappings, assassinations, bombings, and torture were occurring on a close to routine basis in Davao, and when members of the president's own family had relocated to the United States. The metaphor recast this period as a serene and passive waiting period for the tourism sector. The turbulence of this still recent past, largely the result of the ending of the Marcos regime and its accompanying political chaos,[8] was written out of the tourism development landscape in the narrative and replaced by the peaceful figure of a slumbering mega-industry.

The accomplishments the president proceeded to enumerate, clustered according to each of the three years of her term, began modestly enough. She started with the organization's having been awarded "best booth" at a travel convention held in Manila. Even this humble success, however, she recalled, carried a lasting significance, as it marked the precise moment when the slogan, "Visit Davao . . . we have it all!" was launched and the campaign to bill Davao, "as the destination of the 90s" began. "The 90s," a new decade fortuitously providing historical reinforcement for a new narrative, loomed large in Davao's touristic discourse. "The 90s" created a conceptual disjuncture between the turmoil of "the past" and the commercial opportunity of "the present." "The 90s" was an essential figure in the creation of Davao's utopic neutral gap. Without its temporal boundaries, no perfection-oriented constructions, symbolic or material, were conceivable. With them, the locality was safely positioned on the fairer side of a chronological chasm. DATA's emergence as a leading civic organization was a transformation dependent on and constitutive of "the 90s."

Next on the list of achievements came events from 1993 and 1994, years when DATA first developed its "promotional materials"—its come-on stickers, festivity banners, discount cards, and directory brochures that documented the "all" of Davao. This identified, reified, and mass produced what were to remain the key touristic symbols of its landscape throughout "the 90s." The foul-smelling, crocodile-skinned durian fruit, the enormous, monkey-eating Philippine eagle, the rare and colorful *waling-waling* orchid blossom, and of course venerable, towering Mount Apo had all at this time been identified as the dominant set of icons destined to attract and cultivate the tourist gaze.

1993 and 1994 were also the years when the phrases "East Asean," "East Asean Growth Area," and "BIMP-EAGA"[9] first became household expressions for DATA's membership, as the organization initiated its campaign to stage Davao City as "the" convention destination for the southern Philippines, and for the transnational "growth triangle" the ASEAN-inspired geoeconomic terms defined. DATA's main achievement for this period, the president recalled, had been participating in the first East ASEAN Business Convention and Exhibits, an event she characterized as "history-making." The ASEAN-ization of DATA's practice of everyday working life could be traced to these early/middle years of the 1990s, when the initial transnational linkages were given the official stamp of government approval and launched with convention events.

As the president's narrative continued, it became apparent that the final year of her term, through 1994 and 1995, had been the period when DATA's success had become manifest on a new and larger order of magnitude, erupting from provincial into national and international registers of recognition. In late 1994 the association had received the DOT's national Kalakbay[10] award for Tourism Council of the Year. That same year it represented the tourism associations of the region in a transnational negotiation on tourism with the Brunei Association of Travel Agents, resulting in the joint signing of a memorandum "witnessed by no less than President Fidel V. Ramos." In 1995 DATA's transnational outreach had extended to include Malaysia as well, when the association sent representatives to Kuching, Malaysia to attend the first East ASEAN Tourism Forum.

The most impressive achievement of all, which the president saved for the final segment of her account, was the association's receipt of a seven-million-peso GATT grant from the Philippine government,[11] a grant that would allow DATA to begin "Manpower Skills Training" for the tourism sector in Davao City. With this funding, DATA was poised to become the main agent in Davao City for standardizing tourism service according to international guidelines. DATA in effect had been handed the task by the Philippine government of translating the global tourism industry's service operations into local terms. The funding ensured that it would be up to DATA in the months ahead to galvanize and instruct a work force who could go about the business of, first constructing and setting the stage of the locality's tourist landscapes, and then embodying and choreographing the characters that would bring their narratives to life. The GATT grant and the expansive future it represented formed the crown jewel in DATA's array of accomplishments, as the president's remarks summarized them.

The president finished her recollections with the question, "Now, ladies and gentlemen, if that is not proof enough that DATA has, indeed, gained a foothold in the world of tourism and is going 'great guns,' . . . what is?" No one in the audience felt the need to respond. Therefore, with this question and its unanimous implicit affirmation successfully placed uppermost in everyone's mind, she prepared to bow down. After a pledge to remain in active service to the "refreshing and remarkable personality" about to take the helm, Baby brought her speech to a close. She called to the membership to sustain their commitment to "strive for excellence," and finished with a short segment from the poetry of the European author Etienne de Grellet ("I shall pass through this world but once . . .") and final round of thanks.

The president's final question, a rhetorical question par excellence, captured the public mood and common sense of DATA's membership regarding the general understanding of tourism's presence in Davao as aptly as any utterance I ever heard during the course of my research. No one could, and, in fact no one in my observation ever did, publicly deny that Davao was speedily on its way to becoming a mass tourism destination for the ASEAN masses. While the arrivals themselves were just beginning to materialize, the cultivation of the utopic landscape that would be in place to greet them was well underway, with DATA taking a leading role in its creation. If there was one idea made strikingly clear at DATA's 1995 induction, it was this: that, from official points of view, tourism in Davao was understood to be a hotbed of activity, an industry that had replaced the civil unrest of "the 80s" with its own brand of "great guns." As the outgoing president's narrative amply demonstrated, tourism by 1995 had been accepted as *the* key developing service industry that had drawn the attention and engagement of some of the most powerful and prestigious characters in Davao's community, as well as in the nation and in neighboring ASEAN countries.

A Pioneer Family Dinner Party

Near the end of my visits to Davao City, in late February1996, in an entirely different context from the DATA meeting, an informal, off-the-record, entirely private occasion took place that produced another, quite different, narrative of tourism development. It was, like the DATA induction, conducted in English, and not simply for my benefit. However, I did play a more central role in this event, being one of five guests invited on the spur of the moment to attend a midday family dinner. It was not a "party" but simply a meal, an ordinary family get-together.

Despite the informality, this was not an occasion I took lightly. The invitation came from the current senior head of one of Davao's oldest Luzon immigrant families, a family with extraordinary continuity of both local residence and leadership in Davao City. This family had grown along with and adapted to the city's changing characters and fortunes, creating and recreating highly successful niches for itself over the course of several generations. It would be no overstatement to say that when transnationalism, in the guise of nationalism, began in Davao City, it began with some of the ancestors of this particular family. I felt fortunate to have been invited to attend this particular gathering. Although I had known of the family by reputation and from local historical sources, until now I had never felt I had a compelling reason to initiate any relations with them, and with no such means of legitimately establishing rapport I had made no attempt to connect with them during my visits.

The narratives produced throughout the gathering's five hours of conversation were for the most part freewheeling, Davao-focused improvisations. They were nostalgic tales of the good old days, spun out with spirited exuberance by a group of individuals uniquely positioned to give them authoritative voice. The perspectives articulated were rich in life experience, displaying a profound attachment to the hometown that Davao City was to these individuals, as well as to the metropolis it was now becoming.

Tourism reared its now not so glamorous head only once during this party, at my own initiative, toward its end. After only a few moment's engagement, the topic was changed, and the subject was not revisited. Given the interests that were represented around the family table and the stake in Davao City held by various members present, the absence of tourism talk was a telling indicator of the degree to which the DATA induction's rhetoric might have been somewhat overly enthusiastic regarding the "real life" operation of the industry. Yet the mini-narratives the mention of tourism elicited, although hardly more than a sentence or two in length, in the context of all the others also given were in fact revealing of a related understanding of the industry vis-à-vis those put forward at the DATA reception. As seen from inside this family residence, the "great guns" of the tourism matrix appeared to be of a somewhat smaller caliber than their public image pronounced. Moreover, they were not yet seen to be "going" nearly as greatly. The limits of the matrix's influence and its selective intelligence in designing Davao's utopic landscape were more clearly evident at this gathering, removed as it was from any touristic stage, imaginary or actual. Even here, however, there were moments when I observed the matrix's presence apparent and operative, and the comments left no doubt that tourism was a topic of serious concern to local interests, particularly to those who cared deeply about what kind of a hometown Davao City was and would or should continue to be.

The impetus for the party was a conversation at a semi-private social occasion, a food festival put on by the alumni organization of a local private college. I'd been invited to this celebration by one of the college's alumni members, who was like myself a longtime student and enthusiast of

Philippine dance.[12] The college was a long established institution in Davao City, where many prominent Davao families had sent their children, sometimes several generations of children, over the years, as had been the case with my friend. The festival was held at a restaurant popular among this well to do local subset. Upon arrival, we immediately encountered familiar faces from among the old time immigrant family circuit, some of whom I had collaborated with during my visits collecting information on Davao City's social history. Shortly thereafter, amid tables filled with platters of Buffalo chicken wings, pizza, tacos, lasagna, fried chicken, *lumpia*, spaghetti, rice noodles, cookies, pastries, and cassava cake, I was introduced by one of these acquaintances to the owner, who went by the nickname, Donding. Despite the youthful nickname, he was in his sixties at that time. It was Donding who at the festival's end extended the dinner invitation to myself, my companion, and another friend of my companion's, a lawyer, Celia, who practiced law in the Philippines but who lived also with her husband in California.

I was introduced to Donding by my friend, who described me as an anthropologist writing a book on Davao's history and culture. This introduction produced a cordial though quickly waning series of questions from him. It was by no means this aspect of my identity that produced the invitation to his house for dinner. Even though I knew from my own research that one of Donding's children had recently been appointed to a position in the city's tourism office, my interest in tourism stirred no particular interest in Donding. He already knew far more than I did about the key players in Davao's tourism development network and what actions they were taking with what consequences. He had no need of me for any insight into the topic, nor was he in any official position that required him to make comments about it for the record. Tourism was not to be our common ground.

Donding spent his initial time with me sketching the history of his family's residence in Davao, which went back to the middle of the 1800s. This was during "the time of abaca" as I'd come to think of it (somewhat inaccurately), following the local rhetorical style of defining chronological phases. The time of abaca—a crop known most everywhere else as Manila hemp— was the earliest and longest period of Davao's colonial agricultural development, comprised of a relatively unproductive Spanish phase followed by a large scale American phase, which together lasted nearly a century, ending with World War II.[13] Its first phase was a time when *encommiendas*, estates hundreds of hectares in size, had been set up under Spanish rule. Anyone in Davao with ancestors who had lived through this Spanish phase was assured a special status as part of the original social fabric of the immigrant settlement.[14] "Abaca" meant historicity among these "pioneer" families. It was a profoundly nostalgic concept. It was also completely absent from the contemporary tourism discourse, located outside the matrix.[15]

In Donding's case, he could trace his family line through his paternal grandmother's side back five generations, to two of the original four *cabezas de barangay*, when barangays were first established in 1853.[16] This Spanish cultural heritage still loomed large in Donding's consciousness. His parents, he remarked, were Spanish speakers, although he himself was not primarily so. Born into the later period of American rule, the Commonwealth period, he had learned to speak English as a child, along with the local Davaoeño language, which he said was now virtually extinct.[17]

It soon became clear in this introductory exchange that Donding's perspective on local Davao history was extraordinary in its scope, depth, and detail. He was of a generation that personally had crossed a kind of broad temporal divide, constituted by several decades of the twentieth century, during which the Philippines had become separated from its colonial past and had been reoriented toward its multinational future. Donding was one of a handful of individuals who possessed first-hand knowledge of what Davao City had been on both sides of this temporal divide, what it had been as a colonial port city of some 20,000 people, around the time of his birth, and what it was becoming as an ASEAN gateway of over a million. His own grandparents had lived in Davao at the turn of the twentieth century, in a city center residence so large he remembered playing badminton as a child inside its walls. When his father's father had set up his rural *hacienda*, shortly after arriving from Luzon at the turn of the century, the entire district of Davao (officially the Fourth District of Mindanao—a region that stretched around the Davao Gulf and halfway up the northeastern portion of the island) had had a population of some 30,000 souls, only 4,000 of them Christian immigrants coming from the Visayas and Luzon.[18] The majority of the district's population had belonged to various indigenous groups: Bagobo, Mandaya, Ata, Manobo, Mansaka, Samalnon, Guiangan, Bilaan, Calagan, Tagbara, Tagbili, and Tagacaolo, to mention some of the most numerous.[19] Davao itself was a small pueblo town of around 1,500 residents.[20] The grandfather had been active in local government during the early part of the American regime, at the time when the transition from military rule had ended in 1906 and civilian rule begun.[21]

Donding, however, was himself much more than a chronicler of the family's prestigious distant past. He had also lived through the transformations of World War II in Davao, and the "time of the bananas" that followed it, the violent Marcos years and, now "the 90s." Perhaps in response to my anthropologist identity, he dwelled somewhat in his conversation on the days of his youth, times when the "tribal peoples" would be seen on all the city streets, unlike today. He'd had many friends among the older members, he recalled. Nonetheless, his perspective was by no means entirely nostalgic. Donding was a major player in Davao's present moment, when the city's Christian immigrant population was currently mushrooming toward one-and-a-quarter million residents and its tribal populations—although a key focus in the touristic landscaping efforts—had shrunk to virtually invisible, legendary minorities.[22]

Donding was as well a meta-local figure who sat on the board of directors of one of the Philippines' largest corporate institutions. His world class transnational stature was evidenced most convincingly for me by the fact that he was, as he let drop, being treated for high blood pressure these days at Stanford's medical clinic. If there was anyone who might put the "whole" of Davao into some kind of graspable perspective, I believed it was a person like Donding, a person with experience, with history, and with—as was very quickly evident—an exceptionally sharp memory.

The invitation to dinner came when we were speaking of music. It was at the end of the festival, when my friend and I were sitting at a table with the lawyer, Celia. Donding had come back around to us to say hello to Celia, a woman his daughter's age, of whom he was visibly quite fond. On his re-appearance, we discontinued our discussion of the earthquake damage that was still depressing the real estate market in Northridge, California and turned to cheerier subjects. Someone made a favorable comment on the background music, a medley of early twentieth-century jazz band melodies, which caused Celia to remark that Donding had a music collection in his home that was like a library. Various orchestrations in it of "As Time Goes By," she reported, alone required half an hour just to sample. Donding mentioned an extensive set of recordings of the star he characterized as the all time favorite of Filipinos, Frank Sinatra. We fell to naming the tunes of Broadway musicals and progressed backward to American folk songs from the nineteenth and early twentieth century. The titles that sprang to various minds were all represented in Donding's library, defining an Americana musical territory spreading from Stephen Foster to Robert Goulet. Apparently moved by the extent of our knowledge and level of interest, Donding invited all of us to come and enjoy his music library and join his family for dinner. We accepted, and the date was set for the day after the following.

I arrived at Donding's house around noon, accompanied only by the husband of my friend—she had been unable to join us, as it turned out, having had guests of her own arrive. We drove in the husband's car to the residence, which was located in one of the city's older Marcos-era, affluent subdivisions. A maid let us in, and we went into the *sala* living room and started listening to music immediately. Celia was already there, along with a middle-aged couple who had lived in Davao many years previously and were now visiting from Manila.

The house itself, although built of high quality materials, was not extraordinarily luxurious, let alone decadent. The main entrance led into a wide hall with a kitchen to the right, a linoleum-floored dining area in front of it, and the sala, sunken a few steps beneath beyond that, its floor a wood parquetry forming simple small triangular patterns. A large lanai ran the width of the house off the sala's far side. To the left of the main entrance was a long stuccoed hallway, largely unadorned save for one or two small niches in which religious images had been placed and a few portraits. The hallway was raised a step or two up, and several rooms, I assumed bedrooms, opened onto it.

While the home's split level modern design, as well as its size and decor appeared comfortably suburban, generally speaking, several features stood out as indicators that this residence was extraordinary. In the dining area, one of the more beautiful large wooden dining tables of the many ornately carved varieties I'd seen in the city had been squeezed into place, with matching chairs and side piece. The rattan furniture sets in the sala and lanai were at the top end of locally available lines. The lanai, with its sleek black concrete/gravel paneled floor, its carved dark wooden railings, and fine wire mesh screening, approached a certain grandness on its own. Two furniture pieces it contained—an antique mother-of-pearl inlaid bench of Islamic style and a coffee table with coral tiled top and intricately carved dark green painted wooden legs—were of international souvenir quality (the latter, Donding informed us, he'd bought at the Export Processing Zone on Mactan Island where it had been designed and manufactured for export to Italy). A floor-to-ceiling glass-enclosed bookcase rested against one of the lanai's end walls, with several Time-Life books, a set of Reader's Digest condensed books, and a full set of *Encyclopaedia Britannica* volumes and accompanying dictionaries on its shelves. Most impressive, however, was the literal centerpiece of the home's common rooms: the music library, which took up one side of the sunken sala area, and which included an upright piano piled high with well worn music books, a CD player, stereo system, and drawers upon drawers of meticulously labeled and categorized cassettes and CDs.

We stayed in the sala before dinner, sitting on white plastic patio chairs grouped around the music collection, listening to requests and speaking little until it was time for dinner. The musical choices made were American folksongs—"My Old Kentucky Home," "I'm Coming though my Head is Bending Low," and "Gentle Annie" among numerous others. I asked at one point to hear my favorite Cebuano ballad, the classic, "Matud Nila," of which I'd never been able to locate a recording. A search of the collection revealed it was not among the holdings. I switched to "Bayan Ko," the Tagalog anthem of the anti-Marcos movement, which was quickly produced. Donding also played a tape of a child prodigy pianist, a blind boy from a poor family in Cebu whom he had been attempting to launch in a performing career. On the tape, the child was singing "I Left My Heart in San Francisco" in a blues improvisational style.

It struck me, as the musical entertainment proceeded, that the city's tourism campaign had given virtually no emphasis to popular music in its development of Davao's destination imagery, even though, as Donding's home concretely demonstrated, this untapped resource tended to occupy a cultural space of central significance in local life. The symbolism chosen for the campaign had been predominantly visual in nature, focusing on costuming, architecture, and certain products of horticulture. In the industry's imagery and discourse these were situated always against the imagined backdrop of Mount Apo or at the edges of a deserted tropical beach. Music had largely escaped the notice of tourism developers. The references to musical images and the enactment of musical performances in tourist contexts focused on indigenous instruments and their precolonial, premodern practices, not the more popular transnational music Donding's collection represented (albeit with its own specific generational emphases) and which his protégée performed with exceptional skill. This "real" music of Davao City's mainstream population, the music of everyday life, reappropriated from the global industry and played incessantly in every public and non-working private space I had ever frequented in the city, still inhabited a cultural space untapped by the tourism matrix.[23] Apparently, its transcultural character did not fit neatly enough into the landscape currently under construction.

The meal was a deluxe, superbly prepared version of a standard local menu, served family style: buko juice and water to drink, beef soup, grilled fish, roasted pork, *pinakbet*,[24] rice, an array of sauces and dried fish, and, for dessert, pineapple slices and two kinds of cake. We were joined by members of Donding's family, a group of all ages who made the large table full and busy. The newly appointed city tourism official was present during the meal, a young woman concerned entirely at this moment with attending to the eating habits of her son, who looked to be about five. I could see she was preoccupied and did not to attempt to engage her in any tourism related discussion. The daughter's professional identity produced no special commentary during the meal on the part of any family members. Her new position inside the tourism matrix and its relation to my own had no influence on the conversation. I took this as another sign of the incompleteness of the matrix's construction in the city, and the degree to which a well-placed member of its tourate could evacuate the matrix to attend to other dimensions of her identity, if, as in this case, she chose to do so.

Not wanting to appear altogether uninterested in the daughter's career, however, I caught her attention as she was about to leave the house immediately following dinner and asked her if she would be interested in doing an interview with me at some point. She responded by saying, in earnest tones, that she would have some materials prepared to send to me, taking down my address. I suggested setting a date for an interview, well aware that it would be difficult to reestablish direct contact after this fortuitous meeting. But she demurred, saying she would call me, adding that she would want to use the interview time to introduce me to the DOT director, Catalina Santos Dakudao. I made careful note of this response, as it confirmed what I had gathered from numerous previous experiences and observations: there was no great difference between the city's and DOT's tourism agenda. The city government, like DATA, tended to take its cues from the national agency.

Conversation during dinner and afterward, carried on by Donding and his wife, his friends from Manila, Celia, and myself, ranged over several topics: politics, education, the economy, and the favorite subject of the day— Davao local history. Concerning politics, discussion focused at the national level. Fidel Ramos's recently proposed antiterrorism bills and the likelihood of his attempting to maintain the presidency beyond his legal term were addressed, being the hottest news item of the day. Opinion—which history proved to be correct—inclined against the possibility. Concerning economics, discussion ranged from global to local issues. Donding spoke about his own experience with multinational business investors, reporting that the Philippines, although it was viewed by some investors as problematic as an ASEAN location because of the relatively democratic government and the labor unions it allowed, was nonetheless currently attracting investors from Malaysia who were interested in the country because the lack of a strong dictator indicated less upheaval for the long term. Surprised by this information, I asked what limits the state of the existing infrastructure in the region—the widespread lack of basic public works and services—was having on multinational investment. Both Celia and Donding responded to this question, acknowledging the seriousness of the obstacles to investment posed by these conditions and commenting in tones of somewhat resigned frustration on the difficulty presented by the Philippine bureaucracy in making progress with public works. The dim view taken on government procedures, however, did not result in a hopeless forecast for multinational investment. Donding's remarks indicated that the international pressures driving investment in the Philippines were in general greater than the internal roadblocks presented by its infrastructural shortcomings.

On the party's favored topic, Davao history, the limits of history with respect to Davao's immigrant settlement record were traced out for my benefit. Celia and Donding remarked that most early nineteenth-century commerce and social life on Mindanao had been in the towns of Caraga to the east, and Surigao to the north.[25] Davao had not been a center for much of anything until after 1848, and really not until the 1910s.[26] The Bangoy family—the family generally regarded as the original landholding aristocrats in the region—was probably Visayan, coming originally from the island of Bohol, Donding speculated. No women of established families from the northern islands would have been willing to come to Davao in the early days. The men coming in must have married native women and then changed their names for the record.

Toward the end of dinner, Donding produced a damaged photograph from around 1907 of the family house that had been built in the town's center in 1906. It was a large square structure, wooden, one story, with a high Chinese style roof. The shutters were made with shells. The veranda had a wooden railing, as did the roof. It was no different from the houses of that period I had seen from anywhere else in the Visayas and Mindanao.

There were again no signs of grandeur. The house was raised off the ground about four feet, and Donding commented that pigs had been kept underneath it until a canal was built around it and lilies grown. He remembered catching fish out of the canal in later years. There was no yard or garden in the picture, only some fenced areas for animals. The place looked like a working farm.

Several times during the afternoon the group stressed how small a town Davao had been until the 1960s—the time when the population first exploded from "town" to "city" magnitude. Donding remarked about the loss of the bats, birds, and other creatures once common in the natural environment that had come with growth and the Marcos regime (the second "time of logging"[27]). Celia commented that in the old days locals knew each other's faces and strangers would stand out. Donding and Celia both remarked that the small contingent of pioneer immigrant families had been "landed" and enjoyed a wealthy life—Donding cited in this regard the example of his own grandmother, who once gave forty hectares of land back to the government simply because she was tired of paying the taxes on it. He then attributed what he characterized as a relative lack of political prominence of the Davao provinces and the city at the national level to this historical situation and the complacency it had tended to produce.

Everyone in the group agreed that Davao remained a "family-oriented" city in many respects, even now that its population had increased to over a million people. Donding, by way of illustration, related that he had expected 600 guests at a reunion he recently hosted, so strong were his extended family ties at present. Even more than 600 had in fact shown up, he reported. He offered several additional examples of the family's contemporary scope and vitality, sharing stories of meeting in distant cities individuals who could identify themselves as members of his family tree.

This family-oriented side of the locality, a large part of what made Davao "home" to the party here gathered, was like music a feature of local life virtually unrepresented in tourist discourses. No images of old time residences, plantation fields, or famous figures—Dakudao's, Bangoy's, Garcia's, or any others—appeared among the flowers and fruits in the industry's designs, either lodged beneath the slopes of Mount Apo or rising behind the shores of the Davao Gulf. While the pre-1960 immigrant network of local families and their agricultural enterprises were still understood to be a real force in the city's social and cultural life, they had yet to be written into the landscapes of tourism in any significant way. Once again, the limits of the tourism matrix became visible in the party's conversation.

Donding, taking a final tack in the discussion of local history, made a few remarks about the Japanese era of Davao City's early twentieth-century history. The time of abaca, as it happened, in its later American phase was also a time of Japanese presence in Davao City and its environs. Japanese laborers recruited during the early years of American rule had lived and worked in Davao in large numbers—the largest numbers anywhere in South-east Asia.[28] Their influence and industry had been such that Davao had been popularly referred to as "Davao Kuo" or "little Japan" prior to World War II. The Japanese had built their own settlement within the city's boundaries and come to occupy a variety of key commercial and professional niches in the city's society, working in close association with the Philippine immigrant community and indigenous local groups.[29] According to Donding, the Japanese were adept, progressive caretakers of the abaca fields and effective managers of the plantation labor force. In his view, the success and later the failure of abaca in Davao had been due in large part to the presence and then the absence of the Japanese developers.[30]

Donding also commented that, while he had felt hatred at times because of the atrocities committed during World War II by Japanese soldiers in the Philippines—and specifically in Davao—he also had been moved toward equally strong positive feelings toward the Japanese as a result of some of his own family's experiences working and living with the Japanese throughout the American period. He cited the case of one Japanese man whom he had known to come every year to his own grandmother's grave to pay his respects. During the war the grandmother had taken this man in after the Americans had returned. She had saved his life, nursing him back to health from a malaria attack. When the grandmother had died, Donding had seen the man return to her side and shed tears of grief at her death. The man's actions had impressed Donding, complicating his understanding of the meaning of the Japanese presence in Davao, which could not be reduced easily to only positive or negative stereotypes.

Celia added that she had recently accompanied another Japanese visitor around the city, following a map the man had brought with him from Japan, which indicated the location of Japanese burial grounds in Davao City. Neither she nor any local residents she knew had known about these sites. The map had been made by a Japanese organization whose members were Japanese workers who had come to Davao shortly after the turn of the century. The workers had subsequently returned to Japan when all Japanese were expelled from the Philippines at the end of World War II.

The Japanese presence in Davao was a subject I found particularly intriguing. Davao was the only location in the Philippines that had had such a historical connection to Japan, an extraordinarily productive, respectful, and enabling connection, adeptly managed on both Philippine and Japanese sides. The Japanese colony that had been in the city was a feature of true distinction in the Philippine context. It had given World War II a remarkably different meaning at this location from virtually anywhere else in Southeast Asia. I'd heard many a heroic counternarrative detailing acts of extraordinary humaneness, performed both by and for various Japanese residents of Davao vis-à-vis their Philippine immigrant counterparts. Like those described by Donding, these were acts of personal and local loyalty undertaken at the risk of a traitor's execution, in the face of some of the most extreme national enmities the war generated anywhere in the world.

The discussion focusing on the Japanese brought home to me once again the specificities of Davao's fledgling tourism industry and the selective nature of its utopic landscaping. This was not the first time I had heard of burial maps of Davao that had been printed in Japan, maps made for the purpose of assisting Japanese visitors in their ancestral pilgrimages—maps that had never been duplicated locally. The tourism landscape was not being designed to encourage the already established trickle of Japanese visitors to Davao or to exploit the distinctive Japanese-Philippine pre-World War II connection. At the same time, this history was one of the few sources of genuine transnational attraction Davao had going for it, one of the few ways Davao already existed as a destination in the minds of one small but economically strong segment of a Pacific Rim population.

Why this feature of the locality's historical identity had not been seized on for touristic exploitation, bound as it was to tap into a more general global market in World War II historical tourism, remained a mystery to me throughout my research visits. Yet it was certainly the case that no references to the Japanese colony of days gone by were foregrounded in the dominant symbols of the industry's discourse and promotional literature. The absence seemed to indicate that the World War II-inspired hatred of which Donding had spoken might still be something of a factor at all levels of the Philippine imaginary, precluding the association of Davao, even in the age of ASEAN, with Japan identifications or with its role in U.S.-Japanese conflicts.[31] On the other hand, the Japanese tourism might simply have been too transnational—that is to say not Filipino *enough*—to catch on as a strategy for a nationally sponsored campaign to embrace.

The picture of Davao that emerged from this afternoon's conversation was, nostalgia aside, a complex, richly detailed one. It showed that tourism had not become a ubiquitous presence in the local imagination of reality but was still confined to a relatively narrow array of largely public domains. Its landscape currently was cultivating only a few of the available sources for attraction, objectification, and symbolic dominance.

The tourism matrix became present and influential at Donding's gathering only once during the conversation, in a lively debate that occurred at the dinner table over another noteworthy topic in the daily news: the visit to Davao of the prime minister of Papua New Guinea. The minister's arrival had been given much attention in the local media. It signaled once again how Davao was gaining recognition as a city of regional importance. Donding's wife opened the discussion, holding forth at some length about the welcome dancing that had been performed a few days previously for the visit. I knew from other sources involved in organizing this visit that the reception and welcome activities had been staged according to the standard format used for a VIP class of official visitor. It was a program identical in form to touristic welcome performances of an elite variety that had been in practice since the Marcos era, when Imelda Marcos had brought together under her own supervision tourism development and the performing arts.[32] Cultural dancing was a focal element of the VIP greeting process, ideally performed at the initial moment of transition from transit to arrival, on the airport tarmac.[33]

Donding's wife, having witnessed the arrival event, expressed the opinion that the decision made by the choreographers to present dances representing only Islamic ethnic groups, whose *moro* style of costumes and movements were among the more technically impressive of the standard array of Philippine folkdances, was a mistake. While she did not elaborate on why she considered this to be so, I interpreted her comment as recognizing the fact that the Islamic dance stylizations employed for the occasion actually were not representative of the dancing of ethnic groups indigenous to the Davao City area specifically. Rather, they were identified with groups living in other parts of Mindanao and the Sulu Archipelago to the southwest of Mindanao. Mulling this over, however, Donding's wife also recalled the reaction of a Malaysian dignitary to a Bagobo ethnic dance presentation in Davao (Bagobos being in fact indigenous to the locality). The dignitary had been shocked by the bare midriffs and "strong" style of dancing.[34] He had turned to her during the performance and asked if this was really "your dance?" She concluded from this experience that welcome presentations for foreign dignitaries might well emphasize the Spanish-derived *jota* or Maria Clara dances, which were also true to the Davaoeño identity in her opinion, but whose more demure costumes and European-styled court dance movements ensured a respectful response from visitors. Donding, however, repeatedly stressed that the Bagobos, who were indigenous to the city area, had the most admirable costumes. There was animated discussion on this. Others at the table were equally supportive of costumes attributed to different indigenous groups. Donding, however, held firm, citing the beading and the bell work of the Bagobos as the most beautifully ornate among all the costume traditions in the area.

While specific referents differed, only Donding's wife challenged the assumption that the construction of Davao's international cultural identity, particularly in ASEAN-oriented contexts, was dependent upon the symbolism of local non-Christian ethnic minority groups—as they had already been reconstructed along folkloristic lines and adapted to touristic purposes. Otherwise, there seemed to be no question at the table, a table filled by members of an authentic "pioneer" family, that such representations of minority groups should aptly serve as the Davao-defining objects of such a transnational gaze. The logic here followed that of the tourism development campaign, basing its discriminations on premodern, precolonial, indigenous understandings of beauty and the assumption of their exotic appeal. The disassociation of "Davao" from the family's own ethnic heritage and cultural practices was accepted without question by the gathering's majority. I could see in this regard—and, perhaps, only in this specific ASEAN-oriented regard—that the tourism matrix already had gained the upper hand in the imagination of Davao's identity. The group was actively participating in the proliferation of the matrix's imagery and appropriating it as their own in so doing, even though it was recognized as having the capacity to generate unwanted associations, as the group's lone dissenting voice had illustrated.

I raised the subject of tourism itself toward the end of the afternoon's discussion, after waiting through most of the party to see if it would come up otherwise through interests other than my own. It did not, and particularly not when the conversation had turned its most serious—after lunch and the end of the musical entertainment, after Donding's wife and family as well as my friend's husband had left to return to their daily routines, and when there was nothing left for the rest of us but to settle into the more comfortable chairs of the lanai and exchange views on topics of relatively serious concern. I raised the topic in this phase of the get-together at the last opportunity, just before the *merienda*[35] of French toast, sweet *suman* sticky rice, and Tang were served and the more light-hearted, pre-departure phase of conversation began.

I started with the comment that tourism seemed to me at present to be more a dream than a reality in Davao, voicing this somewhat provocative assertion in my best straight-arrow manner—what had become the rhetorical style of choice throughout this phase of the discussion. Everyone immediately agreed with me. The 400 percent increase in tourism arrivals noted at the DATA induction had not created a marked impression on anyone present, evidently. The frame of reference all assumed in response was regional. Davao, it was asserted unanimously, did not currently compete with Bali or other international tourist spots. Davao was not an actual destination yet, the gathering agreed; Davao was not yet on the global tourist's map.

The mention of Bali did not come as a surprise. Bali was currently the ASEAN tourism destination on everyone's mind—everyone who was anyone with respect to the industry's local development, in any case. I'd heard the slogan, "Davao, the Bali of the Philippines," enthusiastically used throughout the upper echelons of the tourism development network. Back in 1992, the geographical location of Indonesia was not a fact I could count on being known when I was in conversation with the average person in Davao. Back then, someone I considered to be a well educated person in the tourism network had once asked me if Indonesia wasn't an island located somewhere in the Pacific. However, in 1996, Bali had become, not only a household word, but a name generally identified with the pinnacle of touristic success. Mass tourism in the flesh may not yet have reached Davao in 1996, but the idea of tourism, Bali-style, certainly had. As far as this gathering was concerned, however, Davao was not yet in the same league with Bali and its likelihood of ever being so was not actually asserted by anyone during the conversation.

The appraisal of the tourism industry's contemporary importance for Davao, however, was not by any means bankrupt as far as the group was concerned. Celia noted that, even while tourism was not yet an actual industry, it was already having real consequences. Her main evidence was the rise in property values that had taken place recently throughout the city and its environs. No one was giving away forty hectares of land these days. Land values were increasing at exponential rates. Tourism, Celia concluded, might not be changing the way people were living, but it certainly was affecting the way people were thinking. This comment concluded the discussion of tourism for the remainder of the afternoon.

The party came to an end shortly after the *merienda*. Celia gave me a ride home, and we spoke mainly about a civil case of fraud against a cement company in Las Vegas that her husband was working on in Los Angeles. She also let me know of a new airlink into Davao from LAX she'd just started to use, flying through Kuala Lumpur on Malaysian Airlines, bypassing completely the Manila domestic airport. I was grateful for the tip, made an indefinite date with her to go out ballroom dancing some evening soon, and said good evening.

Conclusion

The two narratives—one performed center stage on the tourism matrix's most prestigious social platform, the other unfolding casually inside a private residence—illustrated two divergent perspectives on the tourism industry in Davao City during the mid-1990s, when an agenda for progressive, ASEAN-oriented regional multinational development was being implemented with noteworthy success. The perspectives differed markedly with respect to the estimation of the industry's operations in the present moment. The public view emphasized an actual increase in activity—which, indeed, there had been. The private view recognized more of a potential state of affairs, and with good reasons. Both perspectives agreed that real changes in the city had been taking place in the recent past in response to tourism's arrival, be it an imagined or an actual arrival. Both acknowledged that, at least for Davao's professional and more well established classes, people were thinking differently about tourism these days, along the lines of accepting it as a prominent feature of everyday life. Both registered the increasing market values of local territory. In the public view, however, there were no limits made apparent to the extent of the industry's reach into everyday life. In the private narrative, in contrast, the selected array of practices and symbols that had become the focal elements in the utopic landscape cultivation process were still emerging—and only beginning to emerge—as a relatively limited and even marginal subset of what local life was all about, at least from an affluent vantage point.

Looking toward the future, the public narrative presented a utopian view, emphasizing increasing employment, revenues, and a more prestigious international identity. In the private narratives, however, the achievement of such positive outcomes was envisioned with less certainty. The difficulties stemming from the lack of provincial and local infrastructure and the political machinery to produce it loomed larger. The decades of highly centralized government—the bulk of the Philippine post-colonial period—were understood to have taken a heavy toll on the maintenance, let alone the progressive development of provincial facilities and institutions. It was a toll that had been particularly heavy in Mindanao, I was aware, since resistance to Manila-based regimes had been especially fierce on this island, as it had been throughout the southern islands in general. In my own observation, the Marcos regime and its consequences had left the southern region of the Philippines in a condition of limbo, as far as the foundational services and structures of collective life were concerned, perpetually deferring institutional and technological advancement. Now, with a strategic flash, the era of globalization had come upon the locality, catching it largely by surprise. Now, the real estate was precious, the interest of Big Money was present, the attention of the ASEAN leadership was caught. Now, the key question voiced from the private perspective was: could the modus vivendi that had created the current conditions be modified in time and in performance to respond effectively to the contemporary window of opportunity?

Such had been the general question on people's minds over the course of my research period, the question motivating the general drift of tourism narratives that I encountered in Davao City during my arrivals in the mid-1990s. While the two narratives I have chosen to recount presented understandings that were obviously partial, they were not in my experience misrepresentative of others I heard on the same subject. They also indicated, as did all the others, something so basic about Davao City's past that it generally went without saying in this discourse: that mass tourism had no history of practice such as the present moment was intending to instigate. As far as Davao's "human resources" were concerned, mass tourism was for all intents and purposes starting from scratch. Whatever globalized tourate DATA or any other agents might be attempting to cultivate, they were going to be cultivating it more or less out of thin air.

It was also my observation that, given its complex of distinctive features—deeply embedded ethnic diversity, civic youth, four decades of immigrant-driven population explosion and increasing mass poverty, a history of national marginality and global invisibility, an agricultural base falling gradually into decline, and the rather sudden arrival of a contemporary wind-fall of transnational investment—the enterprise of producing an ASEAN-friendly utopic hyperspace in Davao had been destined to move in a variety of directions vigorously and simultaneously. To be sure, in the foreground of nearly all of them was the work of cultivating a tourate, since the prospect of recruiting an "expat" labor force was unthinkable, except for a few key elite professional and highly technical positions. There definitely had been considerable pressure in this regard to act as quickly, effectively, and massively as possible, so as to succeed in capitalizing on the opportunities the "time of tourism"—however fleeting it might turn out to be—was presenting. However, in addition to the tourate's development, other forms of landscape cultivation, both material and symbolic, had been steadily underway as well. Some were focusing explicitly on the introduction of global markets into Davao's "90s" local scene. Others, however, were oriented toward bringing local residents into the tourism matrix and developing the tourism market on more specifically local terms.

The chapters that follow describe in detail four kinds of developments resulting from such enterprising movements. Two of them, a luxury resort built in 1992 and a tourism estate launched in 1991, illustrate the direct consequences of nonlocal forces moving into the locality and enlisting local interests. These destinations illustrate specific reiterations of the global tourism matrix, being basically nonlocal in conceptualization, production, design, and consumption. The cultivation of their respective tourates took on relatively traumatic characters, to varying extents, and their patterns of development generated more extreme disjunctures with preexisting cultural practices. The other two, an array of economy hotels and a collection of beach resorts, exemplify the development of touristic spaces in which local control, initiative, patronage, and even genius, were more prevalent, even while the effort to produce a hyperspace essentially touristic in character remained predominant, and the urge to "go global," as well as the utilization of non-local resources, was not lacking in any instance.

Nothing in Davao, of course, ever could be wholly local. Davao City was and remained a city of immigrants, a locality that even in the oldest of its not-so-olden, pre-twentieth-century olden days always had been identified more with ethnic diversity than with cultural homogeneity. Davao, as I had come to know it, was a place of many languages, of countless arrivals and departures—a home more generally understood in terms of routes than of roots. In its more locally oriented destinations, however—which were all outgrowths of commercial enterprises that existed since well before "the 90s"—the boundaries between tourate and more established cultural identities and roles were less absolute, the continuities with time-honored practices more prevalent, and the integration of tourism into the unimaginably complex web of Davao's cultural life more finely gradated.

Taken as a collective, the four types of developments give some sense of the changing conditions that were occurring in the wake of the first major intrusion of tourism development moving through Davao City and the cultural deformations it was producing in this extraordinarily optimistic boom period of the city's history. Taken individually, the sites document the varied manifestations of the tourism landscaping enterprise. Most important, however, in my own accounting of these enterprises, the case studies attempt to give some sense of the many spectra of individual understandings that tourism was generating at each location.

Part II
Global Enterprises

Chapter 4
The Excessive Destination:
Pearl Farm Beach Resort

Pearl Farm Beach Resort, or Pearl Farm as it was commonly referred to in Davao City, was not difficult to read as a touristic landscape. It was the epitome of a "glocal" destination—a destination that generated its tourist magic through the play of local and global characters constantly masquerading in the place of one another. A five star meal posed as a "local specialty," constructions exceeding international standards of architectural design passed as "native-style dwellings," and grounds surpassing a Disneyland level of cleanliness were proclaimed indigenous "natural" settings. Pearl Farm capitalized on movements within the tourism matrix that brought the worldliest of worldly consumers into direct contact with the most colorful productions of "local color," and in so doing reinforced and accentuated the respective geocultural characters and the status gaps between them. Pearl Farm was understood unambiguously to be a high end, small scale destination, a destination designed for discriminating "long hole" (transcontinental) tourists interested in practicing a romantic (private, personal, even semispiritual) gaze.[1] Its 83 "keys," or accommodation spaces, realized paradise, for a maximum of around 350 arrivals a night. Its clientele were exclusively First World tourists, drawn to the best that Mindanao, and *only* Mindanao, could offer, both naturally and culturally.

The "only" in this last proposition bears an essential character that cannot be underestimated in comprehending Pearl Farm's touristic utopics. The resort's top-of-the-pile international luxury rating rested somewhat precariously on its being able to make good on the claim to embody all that was distinctive about the locality. Through this perfected concretization of the local, Pearl Farm was able to assert an identity that was global, being the only place *in the world* like itself. The resort's "Mindanao-ness" was the primary characteristic that justified separating it from other destinations of a more ordinary class, the characteristic that moved it—albeit only marginally—into the "world class" category of such "glocal" destinations.

My experiences with Pearl Farm, which was located across the water from Davao City on the southwestern shore of Samal Island, brought home to me one very basic fact about the tourism industry. To survive as a destination in the tourism matrix, particularly in the elite or luxury class, a landscape must be constructed of extraordinarily durable signs, signs that are *fixed*, in the way the signs of language used to make a text and the foundations used to support a building are fixed. Only through such stable components could a given landscape become a place foreordained for a specific purpose, a place set apart for a particular use that was understood prior to its actual appearance in the world, or in a given arrival's world. A luxury destination, in other words, had to be able to maintain a reputation that preceded it. It had to cultivate a clientele, not there at any given present moment, who would look forward to visiting it and who would be certain that they would not be disappointed when they did. Such reputations are not like trophies that can be won or lost in an instant. For a place to have a reputation of this kind, it had to have a habit of affecting people in a very specific way, and that required fixed-ness.

Pearl Farm in "the 90s" was such a destination par excellence, an excessively fixed utopic space. Its exceptional fixed-ness in addition to its glocalizing tendencies contributed significantly to the ways the heterogeneous array of persons in its tourate who animated and narrated its landscape were understanding the resort. I will, in the chapter that follows, give a sense of that diverse tourate array—and of how varied the resort's cultural

Figure 3. Pearl Farm Beach Resort.

consequences could be—by recounting conversations with three members of Pearl Farm's tourate, each of whom was positioned differently within and without its landscape. In this chapter, however, I first set the scene for those conversations, giving a brief account of the landscape itself, its development, design, and reputation.

The Landscape

My first observation of Pearl Farm—or rather what was to become Pearl Farm—occurred from a distance, from a vantage point located some twelve kilometers north of the resort's actual location on Samal Island's southwestern coast. It happened gradually, as I was spending a few days on the island in 1992, watching shipping traffic traveling up and down the Davao Gulf, heading into or out of the port areas of Davao City. Most of the traffic was unremarkable, small boats hustling back and forth between Davao City and the island, headed for the beach resorts scattered along the island's northwestern coast, or the principal municipal port of Babak, located just to the north. Occasionally, however, a container ship or some other type of cargo tanker would pass through the channel, riveting the attention of all who happened to be gazing out across the water at that moment, unable to resist watching such a colossal hulk displacing water at a rate many times that of the relatively tiny vessels that it seemed to scatter out of its way like so many specks of lint across the water's surface. For a few silent and inactive days, I sat by the shore and watched the traffic pass to and fro, waiting for an opportunity for some kind of active engagement in the local scene to present itself.

It wasn't long, as I developed a sense of the traffic's regular characteristics, before I began to recognize an unusual type of commerce on the water, a series of fairly large outrigger cargo boats, that were passing by somewhat regularly—more than once a day. They were well constructed boats not noticeably different in design from other locally built outrigger cargo bancas. They were hugging the shoreline, something few other boats their size did, and sometimes they had to be guided with bamboo poles as they moved slowly and deeply through the water. They were laden to maximum capacity with sacks and sacks of cement, piles of gravel, and stacks of bamboo poles. These boats stood out from the rest of the traffic, so different was their charted course over the water, and so heavily laden were their decks with unusual materials. The diverse forms of cargo were carefully arranged on board each vessel so as to use every available bit of space.

These boats, the resort staff informed me, were bound for Pearl Farm. Everyone already knew Pearl Farm, since the site had had a history of activity that stretched back to the days when it actually had been a working pearl farm in the 1960s and '70s—in the heydays of the Marcos era. However, the family business that had developed the pearl farm had closed it in 1980,

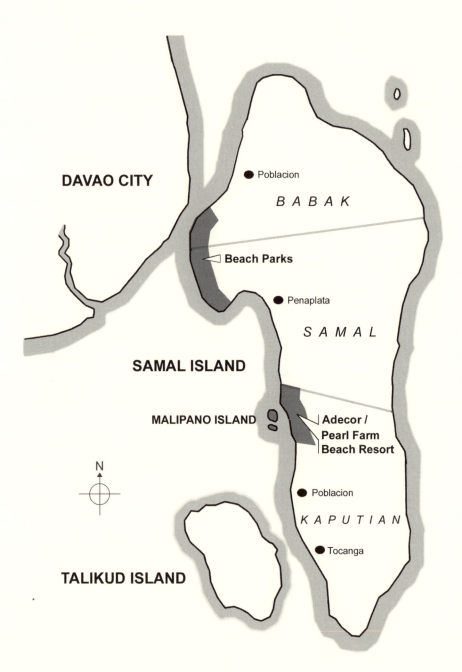

Figure 4. Map of Samal and Talikud Islands.

and the property had been sold more than once since then. The current resort was not a restoration of the old pearl farm. It was an altogether different sort of destination, a beach resort featuring aquasports as its main diversion. The newly redesigned resort was now open for business, I was told, even while it was still under construction. I made plans to charter a boat to visit it the next morning when the waters would be calm and the currents slack, curious to see what was being made out of such copious quantities of cement, gravel, and bamboo.

As I was to hear years later, long after the fact, in conversations with one of the resort's general managers, nothing constructed at Pearl Farm was brought in in a pre-fabricated condition. This was mentioned as a point of contrast to other larger scale transnational resort developments being undertaken elsewhere in the Philippines. Every physical aspect of the resort had been crafted at the site itself—a time-consuming, labor-intensive strategy that, from the management's perspective, was believed to have been particularly beneficial since it had produced that valuable margin of originality and distinctiveness in the resort's appearance that made good its claim to world class glocal status. However, at the moment when I was witnessing the resort's cargo flotilla in action, this thought did not occur, even though the future truth of it was graphically evidenced. At the time, I only remarked upon the boatfulls of gravel and wood and the small mountains of cement sacks passing by over the water—in vessels that looked to my eye as though they would have held thirty or even forty persons had they been put to the more standard uses I had newly grown accustomed to watching.

So it was that I became a witness to Pearl Farm Beach Resort's construction, and the materials which were to become the infrastructure of Pearl Farm made a lasting impression on my memory. There were so many bancas needed for their transport, so many bodies employed in poling, lifting, balancing, toting. . . . The accidental role I played in witnessing this transport process precluded my ever achieving anything like a standard tourist's gaze on Pearl Farm's landscape or giving a description of it in those terms. While the many varieties of tropical flora and marine fauna cultivated at the resort undoubtedly loomed much larger to most arrivals, to my eyes the inorganic ingredients of cement and gravel, as well as the "natural" material of harvested bamboo, were the elements that always appeared foregrounded, claiming attention. I never lost a fascination to see what had become of them.[2]

I would not venture to guess the actual cost or number of tons of concrete required to put the new Pearl Farm together and constitute its fixedness. The number, whatever it was, exceeded by an obvious margin what had been used over the years in building all the public roads of Pearl Farm's home municipality of Kaputian, the southernmost of the three municipalities on Samal Island. Kaputian, "the place of the white rock," as the name was most often translated, possessed only around 400 meters of concrete road in 1992—a single short stretch running through its población, or village center. The municipality's land area totaled more than 11,000 hectares, its population roughly 24,000 people. Even by 1996, long after Pearl Farm's construction had been successfully achieved, Kaputian's 63 kilometers of public roads were mainly "earthfill" in type—a wash of coral, mud, sand, and gravel.[3] The local road that ran to Pearl Farm, veering off the island's main circumferential route, was of this standard dirt-coral type. It was passable only to jeeps, motorcycles, and foot traffic, a difficult road even for these, so steep and rough was its grade, even when it was dry, which was, roughly speaking, a little more than half the time. "Real" visitors to Pearl Farm—its tourist clientele—always arrived by water, by way of resort-owned boats. The inland road served tourate traffic only.

The more I got to know Kaputian (which by 1996 was fairly well), the more extraordinary and excessive the boatfuls of cement and gravel destined for Pearl Farm and its 83 keys seemed in my memory. The fixedness of Pearl Farm's structure, the number of concrete-made or concrete-reinforced foundations that constituted its built environment, stood out starkly from their equivalents in both the public and the private spheres of the resort's immediate environs. This differential pattern of material resource allocation was reproduced with most other basic goods and services at Pearl Farm as well: electricity, metal piping, and gasoline, to mention a few. It was in large part this contrast that kept my memories from 1992 alive over the years.

The contrast between Pearl Farm and the rest of Kaputian was particularly striking with regard to the settlement of Adecor, whose 385 households were situated on the coast directly north of Pearl Farm and with which Pearl Farm shared a boundary. The name Adecor was a contraction of Aguinaldo Development Corporation. The settlement, which had grown out of a tiny fishing village in the 1960s, was named for the family who had developed the original pearl farm. Adecor was the *barangay*[4] from which the new Pearl Farm drew around half its total labor force of approximately 160 persons. Only a few steps away in actual distance, Adecor, with its predominantly wooden houses built on rickety pilings, most of them roofed with a patchwork of corrugated iron and wood, presented an utterly different kind of landscape from the resort. It was a landscape that appeared to be on the verge of coming unglued—a relatively fragile, vulnerable, imperfect, and unstable environment compared to the impeccably crafted, Eden-esque creation that was Pearl Farm.

In the years following my initial visit to Samal Island, during which I returned to Pearl Farm several times, concrete continued to dominate my perceptions of the resort. Even its most fluid, seemingly spontaneous, and ever-changing features—its rushing waterfall that turned into a bubbling rivulet and gurgled noisily around the resort's main walkways, its mesmerizing rimless central swimming pool, which from most angles was impossible to distinguish from the sea itself, and which gave its bathers the impression that they were one with the carefully rejuvenated marine environment off-shore—even these most liquid and mobile resort enhancements appeared to me as little more than the effects of an elaborate system of embankments, aqueducts, basins, drains, catchments, channels, and other types of foundational structures, all of them made of concrete. The seeming impermanence of Pearl Farm's breathtaking aqueous landscaping was in fact an illusion set in concrete, carefully designed to reiterate itself eternally. The refreshing play of light, color, sound, and cool wetness generated "naturally" by the artificial stone-like infrastructure was entirely fixed, predetermined, and guaranteed for the future.

However, it was not Pearl Farm's waterways but its pathways that, in my experience, most meaningfully represented the contribution concrete made to the resort's most general utopic impact. In the act of conducting oneself along the resort's walkways and staircases, all made durable in one way or another by means of concrete, the fixedness of the landscape became most powerfully evident in an embodied sense. Some of the pathways were almost like jewelry in appearance, with rock or coral mosaically inlaid, carefully, so that the fragments of indigenous material looked naturally placed but also positioned so as to create a smooth, highly walkable surface. Other paths were made of wooden planks, always winding softly along curving routes, supported over water by wooden piles sunk into invisible concrete foundations. The walkways were laid out like necklaces throughout the resort's eleven hectares of grounds, connecting different parts of the resort to one another. They linked the six two-story beach-front Samal Suites at the resort's northern end (U.S. $160 a night in 1992, up to $250 a night by 1996), to the main pool, the Maranao dining pavilion, and the Parola Bar at the resort's center. The paths then wound their way down to the nineteen uniform Samal Houses—identical single unit cottages perched on pilings above the water's edge—and then to the aquasports center and the Mandaya Village duplexes at the resort's southern end. Moving steeply inland, the pathways widened, allowing for the use of resort motor vehicles, and arrived at the resort's two Hilltop Longhouses, or "Balays,"[5] as the resort's brochures labeled them. These were fifteen hotel-type rooms set in close proximity to the resort's tennis courts and gameroom areas. In this more secluded area, billiards, table tennis, karaoke, and a variety of other relatively un-"eco"-oriented amusements were available on request.

The fixed walkways allowed a certain form of movement—utopic movement—unimaginable elsewhere on Kaputian's shores, or anywhere else on Samal Island's rugged coastline for that matter. They afforded an ease of locomotion that felt genuinely magical in its speed, regularity, and freedom, particularly when compared to the array of other possible forms of movement available to those on foot around the island's jaggedly reefed edges. My research forays into the barangay communities along Samal Island's southwestern coastline had intensified this contrast. Nowhere else on the island's shores could one cover ground the way one could at Pearl Farm. One could skip, or even run, easily, for several hundred steps, if one desired, over the resort's walkways, without having to struggle with an unstable or uneven surface of any sort. The strength and sturdiness of the material of the paths made it possible to pay very little attention to the process of moving about the resort, and to allow one's gaze to wander freely over the surrounding scenery, taking in far more than one's pathway alone.

The concrete trails of Pearl Farm choreographed various forms of relatively absentminded yet nonetheless graceful movement—extremely privileged forms of movement—that were the antithesis of those performed when, for example, one was wading ashore at any other location on the island wearing rubber slip-ons, or tennis shoes, or barefoot. Disembarking from a wobbling banca onto a slippery coral reef at low tide, or plodding across a hot dry sand or gravel beach, or picking one's way along the edge of a coral bluff overgrown with the branches of *balete* trees required altogether different forms of locomotion from those employed habitually at Pearl Farm. The difference between walking the length of Pearl Farm and walking the length of barangay Adecor could not have been more pointed in this regard. Adecor's haphazardly placed array of stilt houses, no two of them alike, ran for about a kilometer along the shore north of the resort.

Figure 5. Pearl Farm cottages.

The barangay had no public works whatsoever connecting these dwellings. Its main informal walkway, "paralleling" the shoreline in a very crooked and meandering manner, was a footpath so narrow that it allowed for only single file passage in most places. Walking through Adecor required a much more nimble practice than at Pearl Farm. It required agility, alertness, strong leg muscles, and a flexible spine. Even in its smoothest places, the footpath required constant watching out for the small but ubiquitous tricky unevennesses of its rocky coral protrusions, on which it was very easy to turn an ankle, stub a toe, or lose one's footing and fall. In its roughest places the path was not, literally speaking, walkable. It required one to duck under branches or laundry lines and clamber over a variety of boulders, tree roots, and other obstacles that made for very slow going and a constant change of movement strategy. Getting from one end of Adecor to the other was manageable, but it was no "walk in the park," as was the case with Pearl Farm.

Since a large percentage of the households at Adecor had a family member working at the resort, the difference in infrastructure was habitually encountered and registered as a bodily experience by a good portion of Pearl Farm's tourate. No one ever mentioned the difference in conversations with me. It went without saying that the concrete aspects of Pearl Farm defined a different lifeworld for its inhabitants from that of the rest of the island's population, a difference that few tourists were likely to notice or experience.

Figure 6. Adecor home.

Pearl Farm's reputation, while it grew throughout the tourism matrix as rapidly as its landscaping had been developed, was born already mature in one important respect. Its destination image was, throughout certain Philippine and international networks, more like an outgrowth of a distinctive sort, rather than an entirely new creation. Its reputation was understood in these circles as a new dimension of a reputation already well established by its owners: the Floirendo family. To know Pearl Farm well was to understand it as the "home away from home" of this extraordinary family, a family already popularly understood as glocal in a number of powerful respects.

Sometimes humorously referred to as the "Chiquitas" of the Philippines, the Floirendo's main corporate enterprise, Tagum Agricultural Development Company, or Tadeco, included in its holdings one of the Philippines's largest banana plantations, several thousand hectares in area. It employed some 12,000 laborers, many of them inmates of the Davao Penal Colony. Local sources were quick to point out this latter fact when searching for evidence of the Floirendo family's extraordinary success in cultivating profitable relations with all levels of the Philippine government.[6] The family was headed by Antonio Floirendo, who was approaching eighty at the time of my last arrival to Davao in 1996. Not a native of Davao, and sometimes typed by "pioneer" elites as "nouveau riche," or more generously as a self-made man of the post-war era, Antonio Floirendo had been active in business in the city since shortly after Philippine independence. Ford Motor Company had given him the franchise for the region of Mindanao at the end of World War II. He expanded into abaca cultivation until the crops failed in the 1960s, and then turned to bananas and stock farming. The "time of the bananas" in Davao was to a considerable extent the time of the Floirendos.

Of the many ultra-powerful names commonly linked in local discourse to the Floirendo family, the most venerable mentioned was that of Philippine President Elipidio Quirino.[7] It was mentioned specifically in connection with Antonio Floirendo himself. Far more widely cited, however, was the Floirendo family's close relationship with Ferdinand and Imelda Marcos. Floirendo's wife Nenita Rosario was in 1996 still identified locally as having been one of Imelda's favorite escorts, the once-renowned "blue ladies." Floirendo, for his part, had contributed greatly to Marcos's 1965 and 1969 presidential campaigns. He had been the chairman of Marcos's Kilusang Bagong Lipunan (New Society Movement) party in Eastern Mindanao, which was responsible for the 1986 defeat of Corazon Aquino in that area. The Marcoses had in turn been important allies for the Floirendo enterprises in Mindanao.[8] However, it was Floirendo's role as a middleman for the Marcoses' notorious dealings in the international sugar industry in the late 1970s and early 1980s that had established him globally as well as locally as an insider to the Marcoses' inner circle, for better and for worse.[9]

Pearl Farm in 1993, to the practically minded, locally informed observer's eye, looked very much like a straightforward effort to diversify the Floirendo family's holdings, since the banana market had become less lucrative in recent years. It was certainly the case that Pearl Farm represented a new business direction for the Floirendos, albeit a relatively small scale one in comparison to their colossal agribusinesses. Until this time, the family had no other tourism enterprises and had never made a bid for any market share of the tourism industry. The family's lack of experience was in fact noted by one of the more seasoned managers, who (when interviewed in 1992) had consulted extensively for the family in the initial stages of the resort's construction. That individual was quick to recognize, however, that the Floirendos' wealth more than made up for what they lacked in expertise as far as the development of the resort was concerned, and that, of the two, expendable capital definitely had been more important in creating their touristic success.

Despite the resort's significance as a diversification of the shifting of financial resources, however, Pearl Farm was also understood and noted locally as being one of the Floirendo family's own private getaway destinations. This was an interpretation that two Floirendo family members articulated themselves to me directly during interviews I conducted with them in 1995. The oldest daughter of Antonio Floirendo, Linda Floirendo Lagdameo, who was overseeing the management of the resort at the time I interviewed her, emphasized in her account of the resort's origins how her father had identified the resort initially as a personal residence. According to Ms. Lagdameo, construction on the property had begun simply as a plan for a private family beach residence. These initial efforts, however, outgrew their original purpose, and early on were transformed into a business venture. Nonetheless, in addition to the guest rooms of Pearl Farm, "villa" residences had also been constructed for Antonio Floirendo and each of his six children and their families, on the resort's tiny island of Malipano, which sat a few hundred feet off Samal Island's main shore. In the daughter's view, Pearl Farm was not conceived as just another source of revenue for the family, but as something of a personal venture as well.

The extent to which the personal motivations and interests of the Floirendos influenced the design and construction of the resort was evident in a number of respects. Roberto Mañosa of Fransisco Mañosa & Associates, the architect of the Marcos's Coconut Palace in Manila, had been called in to design the resort. Another of Floirendo's daughters, with a graduate degree in art history, had personally investigated the Bagobo, Samal, and Mandaya architectural styles that were incorporated into the resort architecture and had consulted at length with Mañosa on the resort construction. Margarita Moran-Floirendo, DATA's future president, and wife to Antonio Floirendo's oldest son, gave a similar quantity and quality of attention to the construction process, overseeing such minute details of the resort's construction as what kinds of nails were to be used in the buildings, what type of rattan wrapping would be used for the light fixtures, and what type of paper would be made especially for the Maranao dining pavilion's menus. The time and money invested in recolonizing the coral reefs and the care taken mounting and displaying museum quality textiles, pottery, and other artifacts that adorned the resort's premises also evidenced the "personal touch" the Floirendos had consciously inscribed in Pearl Farm. It was largely this touch that pushed the resort into world class ratings. The family's personal interest had complicated the resort's identity by bestowing on it something of an authentic "home place" status, which made a critical difference in the character and reputation of the destination. It intensified for its glocal arrivals the seductive duality of Pearl Farm's classic tourist fantasy narrative, promising the presence of home while at the same time delivering an exotic, foreign locale.

Regardless of family connections, however, Pearl Farm remained a tourist destination in its own right. It achieved over its first few years of operation in the mid-90s a reputation that transcended the Floriendo family's alone. Each year brought new achievements. In 1993 and again in 1994, Pearl Farm won the national Kalakbay Award from the Office of the President and the Department of Tourism for "Resort of the Year." In 1995 Pearl Farm made the cover of *Travel and Leisure* magazine, one of three resorts featured in an article proclaiming the Philippines as "Asia's New Horizon." Full page photos illustrated the resort's accommodations, captioned as "masterworks of island architecture," and the text described in vivid detail the "lush" seaside landscaping ("perfect for a dramatic meeting of Captain Hook and the Lost Chicos," 1995: 146). The magazine's correspondent even went so far as to denounce the five star Shangri-La Hotel on Mactan Island, off the cost of Cebu City, designating it as "conventional" after staying at Pearl Farm.

In 1996, when *Gourmet* magazine announced its "Local Color" photo contest, asking readers to send in "a travel image that captures your unique view of any destination in the world," the grand prize for the best entry was an eight-day "Philippine Odyssey" vacation that included two nights at Pearl Farm Beach Resort. On the eve of the Asian financial crises in 1997, and at the end of the boom era of "the 90s," Pearl Farm's success was such that it was one of only two resorts listed for the Philippines in Open World's Small Luxury Hotel world wide web site. Within a few years of its creation, Pearl Farm had established itself as *the* premier high end resort destination for Mindanao, its guests having included Corazon Aquino, prime ministers from Malaysia and Papua New Guinea, an American ambassador, and a host of lesser dignitaries and celebrities.

Pearl Farm's reputation, carefully and self-consciously crafted to impress, lure, attract, and inspire the "long-hole," long distance resort arrival—the "discriminating traveler," in the words of Margarita Moran-Floirendo—

achieved its glocality through excessive concentrations of desirable imagery. It intensified and fixed desire powerfully enough to motivate relatively costly forms of travel—international, transcontinental travel. Had its drawing power been any less potent, it could never have succeeded as a destination. The consequences of this drawing power played themselves out, however, not only on its tourists, but on the resort's tourate as well.

Chapter 5
Pearl Farm Beach Resort: Tourate Perspectives

After my initial visit to Pearl Farm in 1992, several years went by before I returned to the resort. The perspectives summarized below were documented during those return visits, which occurred in 1995 and 1996, in conjunction with a series of survey/oral history interview projects that were undertaken with approximately thirty members of Pearl Farm's tourate. The interview process combined survey and oral history methodologies, collecting life history information in a manner roughly paralleling census surveying, and, then, using oral history interviewing strategies, pursuing a schedule of open-ended questions regarding the interviewee's experiences working at, or living by, Pearl Farm. The research did not produce quantifiable "findings" but, rather, an array of relatively detailed opinions and narratives. The interviews varied in length from around half an hour to an hour and a half, and in a few cases led to additional informal discussions in the following days.[1]

On each interview visit, I identified myself as a "researcher" writing a book on tourism in Davao. I never rented a room or spent a night on Pearl Farm Beach Resort's premises, and I had no interaction with tourists while there. I had in this regard no tourist identity of any sort at the resort. Neither was I ever taken for a tourist by any of the individuals I met over the course of the research. My focus and perspective on Pearl Farm developed specifically from local/tourate, not global/tourist, points of view.

Although my direct interaction with Pearl Farm's tourate was sporadic and transient, the intermediaries who introduced me to the individuals interviewed for the project included some of the people I knew best in Davao City. The rapport the interviews established was initial and temporary, but also layered (sometimes thickly) with meaning. Below, I give extensive accounts of three interviews, done with individuals positioned very differently within and without the resort's landscape—one a manager, one a cultural entertainer, one an Adecor neighbor with family members working in the resort's rank and file. The differences in occupation, age, sex, residence, and other details of personal history contributed to very different perspectives on the resort, and because of this, each account provides a considerable amount of background information on the individual interviewees. Together the accounts give some sense of the complex identity the resort was establishing for itself as a local social and cultural institution, as well as the range of consequences it was producing for its individual tourate members. In particular, the interviews illuminate the kinds of transitions that individuals involved with the resort were undergoing at this period in time, transitions from preexisting, pre-tourate social and cultural roles to roles designed specifically for integration into the tourism matrix. These hybrid identities resulting from sustained contact with Pearl Farm—partly internal, partly external to the matrix's deformations—were in no case occurring as abrupt or complete character transformations. Rather, they were entailing relatively gradual, partial shifts of practices and values. These shifts were sometimes in harmony with, sometimes quite at odds with Pearl Farm's glocal reputation as a utopic destination.

Father Chico

In February 1996 I interviewed Pearl Farm's personnel officer, the individual responsible for keeping affairs relating to the resort staff in order. His was a low level management position, situated far behind, and literally beneath the scenes tourists typically encountered. Pearl Farm presented its personnel officer, not with a landscape to animate so much as with a basement office to occupy and a work force to monitor. The position rested on Pearl Farm's fourth rung of management, below several resident managers, a general manager, and the Floirendo family members.

As the position of personnel officer was not considered to be a "frontliner" (as employees who dealt directly with resort guests were typically called), the individual who filled this slot in 1996, like those who had preceded him, was not in the habit of submitting himself to any cultural or "native" masquerading. He performed no embodiments, narrations, or other theatrical or choreographic activities designed to further realize the resort's utopic schemes. He was a relatively "real" member of the resort's tourate, although he was also one constantly dealing with the consequences of such tourate/tourist interaction.

Despite the glamorless managerial ranking, the position carried some important duties. These included seeing to it that all employees had valid health certificates and acting as the management's somewhat sympathetic ear of first resort for "employee relations" issues, as he put it. The personnel officer was in a limited sense a go-between for staff and management, and so had a relatively detailed understanding of the resort's interpersonal dynamics. He was optimally positioned within the tourate to receive insights from a wide variety of individuals and to gain an understanding of the particular stresses and strains that different kinds of frontliner jobs tended to produce.

At our first meeting the personnel officer was introduced to me as "Father Chico." The name did not strike me as an unlikely combination of terms at the time. The use of an honorific and a nickname together had come to seem quite ordinary by 1996. "Chico" was a common nickname. "Father" was actually something of a slight misnomer, as Father Chico was not currently a priest. He had been a priest for seventeen years, however, and the title apparently had had time to affix itself permanently to his person in the minds of those who knew his history. That he was still addressed as Father, I guessed, was a recognition of his having earned the title in the first place and having devoted so many years of service to the priesthood.[2]

Father Chico had "left the convent," as he put it, in 1993 to return to secular life. He now had a wife and family of his own. He was a native of the province of Davao City, from a rural settlement in the area of the town of Toril, several kilometers down the coast from the city center. Since 1994 Father Chico had lived with his family on Samal Island, and he saw himself as a resident with a strong interest in the island's "grass roots" element. Many of his years in the priesthood, in addition to those of his youth, had been spent in rural communities. Samal Island's generally rural conditions were by no means unfamiliar to him in this regard. He was currently residing on property he owned in the barangay of Anonang, in an upland barrio close to Adecor and Pearl Farm. By 1996, he considered Samal Island his home.

Father Chico was an unusual employee of Pearl Farm with respect not only to his professional background but also to his living situation. He was not commuting from the main island, as were the other managerial personnel. However, he was also not a resident of the coastal barangay of Adecor, as were all the other Samal Island-based employees. While he was not a lifetime local, he nevertheless lived in an inland rural area—the sort of area where one was least likely to find newcomers on the island.[3]

Coastal and inland settlements differed markedly on Samal Island, as Father Chico pointed out when discussing Anonang in relation to Adecor and Pearl Farm. They were connected in many ways and people regularly trafficked back and forth between them, but their differences were significant. Along the coast, households tended to be clustered closely together hovering over the water's edge. Boats were a primary means of transportation. Fishing, although a dying industry, was generally an important occupation. The inland barangays, in contrast, were mountainous (although the highest peak was only 162 meters) and almost completely given over to the cultivation of food crops—bananas and coconuts mainly, but corn, coffee, cacao, rice, and a variety of root crops and vegetables as well. In the island's interior, households were more sparsely located and farming was the primary concern. Motorcycles—called "Skylabs" locally in recognition of the dangers their design and speed posed—were the most common form of transport over the island's steep and hazardous clay roads. They were a fairly recent innovation, having been imported well within the last ten years. Horse, bicycle, and foot traffic were also common in the interior, along with the occasional rough terrain vehicle (generally owned by "titled" persons) or commercial jeepney. In short, the daily experience of living in the island's rugged uplands was markedly different in many respects from that of the coast, particularly with regard to the degree to which off-island interests were present and influential.

Father Chico's perspectives on Pearl Farm and its significance for Samal Island as a whole carried the insight of his inland experience as well as the breadth and depth of his vocational training and years of residence in rural communities located on the main island of Mindanao. He described himself as a "grass roots" person with good reason, as he had committed himself for the whole of his adult life to looking after the best interests of small scale rural communities. When he contrasted that category with the "business" type he observed Pearl Farm generally attracting for managerial employment—the type interested in generating profits and looking after their own financial interests first and foremost—his understanding of that contrast was extensive.

The circumstances under which I first met Father Chico bear mention, as they affected significantly the views he presented in conversation, which were in some respects extraordinarily candid. The meeting took place on a day when I had hired a small banca and a pilot to make the boat trip to Adecor with two associates. The work we had intended to do in the barangay, however, turned out to be impossible on that day. With no other work in sight, my colleagues and I turned to Pearl Farm.

"Walk-ins," such as we were at that moment, did not exist as a standard category of tourist arrival at the resort, and this circumstance precluded the strategy of my assuming a tourist identity in order to gain us entry. Instead, we sought admittance at the resort's northern gate, an employee entrance, asking a security guard if it might be possible to make a courtesy call on the management. Once we were granted permission and allowed inside the grounds, one of my research associates remembered that Father Chico had joined Pearl Farm's management. He inquired about his presence from a staff member. Finding out that Father Chico was indeed on the premises and available, we went immediately to his office.

So it happened that I met Father Chico, not through the Floirendos or their management, but through one of my fellow researchers, which was an extraordinary circumstance. The Floirendos had a well deserved reputation for guarding their interests carefully and monitoring closely those who had access to information about their enterprises. Nonetheless, on this occasion, there was no chance that Father Chico perceived me as an agent of his employers. Although I was presented as a "very good friend" of the general manager,[4] my identity was connected most prominently to that of my fellow researchers.

In this regard Father Chico recognized me as a person closely connected to the nongovernmental organization with which my partners were otherwise identified, an organization that was generally highly respected around Samal Island for its projects developing low cost housing, improved water supply systems, and a variety of cooperative livelihood projects. He and one of my associates had known each other from years before, although they were not well acquainted. Father Chico's regard for me and our discussions of Pearl Farm, both during his interview and then more informally over the several days I spent interviewing people at the resort and at Adecor, were filtered through this regard. Even on the occasions when the particular researcher he had known previously was not present, the connection remained an influential factor in his commentary.

With respect to his own tourate identity, Father Chico commented that he did not see himself as a good match for Pearl Farm's enterprises, even though he described the management as having been eager to hire him when he decided to accept the position at the resort in 1994. He recalled:

> The former Personnel Officer had been gone for five months, and there was a backlog of work. They really had to find somebody. When they found out that I was a priest—imagine, seventeen years—they really wanted me, but they had to persuade me to come because I had no interest in working here—it's not my kind of place.[5]

Entering a private sector establishment was a decision Father Chico had made based on pressing financial considerations. After leaving the priesthood he had first gone to work in human resources management for a couple of local government offices and had hoped to continue in that capacity permanently through the Kaputian mayor's office on Samal Island. This kind of work would have allowed him to maintain many of his lifetime commitments to enhancing the social welfare of rural families in the nearby area that he had made when he entered the priesthood. However, circumstances had not come through such as would have allowed him to continue in government service. When he was faced with no other options, the offer from Pearl Farm had materialized, and to avoid unemployment he had taken it. He had hoped that it would be only a temporary position and that he would be able to move back into social work soon. After two years, however, no such position had been forthcoming. In this regard, Father Chico was only a reluctant participant in the tourism matrix and was in many ways a most unlikely person to find working within it.

The majority of the tourate considered positions at Pearl Farm to be rare opportunities to obtain world class commercial employment experience, and so the jobs were much sought after and highly prized. Particularly among the younger frontline staff members, who had commercial career tracks clearly in mind, a job at Pearl Farm was thought to be a dream come true. It paid better money than anywhere else in Davao city—or anywhere else for that matter. Several members of the staff had actually turned down employment opportunities abroad, preferring the working conditions at Pearl Farm. The resort had even drawn employees away from the five-star Insular Inn, offering higher pay and benefits such as a "custom living allowance" to compensate for travel to Samal Island from the main island. Father Chico also remarked that the reason virtually all the Pearl Farm local staff came from Adecor was that, if there was ever a vacancy, the Adecor families were so quick to fill it with one of their own members that the position would already have been filled by the time word of the opening might reach other barangays. In this regard, Pearl Farm's tourate had little in common with work forces managed by other Floirendo enterprises, particularly the inmates of the Davao Penal Colony employed by Tadeco. This section of the tourate, perhaps because of its global exposure and the integral role its individual frontliners played in establishing Pearl Farm's reputation, enjoyed a relatively high standard of employment.

Father Chico had been recruited to Pearl Farm by one of the resort's resident managers, who had been his neighbor in his home town, and also by the housekeeping supervisor, who had formerly been a "chapel leader" under his direction. In this regard, the people working for Pearl Farm were not simply coworkers to Father Chico, nor was he simply such to them. His nontouristic identity had not been erased by the resort's utopic neutral gap. Pearl Farm, in fact, had been a surprising source of continuity in Father Chico's working life, offering him a niche that preserved his former identity, deforming it just enough for it to work within the commercial tourist landscape. He used his counseling skills frequently in his interactions with the employees, who came to him for guidance and support when they encountered difficulties with the resort's code of behavior—a code Father Chico described as stricter than that of his own seminary training.

Rules for employee behavior at Pearl Farm were elaborately codified and rigidly enforced—fixed to an extraordinary extent. Breaking any of the "house rules" was grounds for suspension, and tardiness of even a minute in reporting for work was recorded and punished. While Father Chico chose not to elaborate with specific examples even when questioned specifically, he did note that a significant aspect of his job was acting as the sounding board for employees reacting to the resort's code of conduct.

Rather than dwell on the disciplinary dimension of the resort, Father Chico spoke at length about a number of other ways Pearl Farm had been a source of change for its tourate. The opportunities presented by the resort for transforming the livelihood of the barangay of Adecor were quite significant in his view. Adecor, he noted, was an old "sitio" or settlement, with families who had resided there for several generations, and who controlled the land and the migration of newcomers almost completely. Looking at the positive side of change, Father Chico noted that Adecor's families had been able to benefit in many material ways from Pearl Farm's renovation. "Compared to Anonang, this is a well-off barangay," he commented. "TV, karaoke, washing machines—the families have everything." Tourism had made electricity available to the village, which in Father Chico's view would never have come to the barangay but for Pearl Farm—or "through the Floirendos," as he put it.

The boundary between Pearl Farm's landscaping and that of Adecor was not as absolute as it might at first glance have seemed. While the village did not resemble Pearl Farm in most visible details, some aspects of Pearl Farm's landscape had disseminated into Adecor's environment. The resort's presence had changed most of Adecor's homes significantly, albeit from the inside out. Father Chico estimated that 70 percent of the families in Adecor had a relative working at Pearl Farm and benefiting in this way from the resort's presence.

The diffusion of the tourism matrix had occurred, not only with regard to utilities and material goods, but also, Father Chico noted, with regard to social practices, particularly economic ones. "They have money now," he commented, referring to Adecor's residents. He continued: "They can make loans now because they have a guarantor—their employment. With the husbands being employed, they [the families] can engage in lending."

Pearl Farm had become a source of long-term financial stability for Adecor, allowing the community a measure of security not enjoyed by other barangays in the municipality. Basic financial needs were not only met but safeguarded against times of misfortune or unexpected difficulty. Resort policy even allowed for salary advances in cases of urgent need. These economic consequences of Pearl Farm changed the relationship of Adecor's families with those of other neighboring barangays. The wages Adecor members were earning, and the overall stability of their community's financial situation enabled them to become small scale lenders to residents from other settlements, moving into additional economic roles and practices in so doing.

Pearl Farm had succeeded in creating a slow but steady economic "rising tide" that was indeed "raising the boats" of Adecor families along with those of Pearl Farm. The presence of the tourism matrix was strengthening the barangay's existing economic base and enlarging it in terms of relatively traditional money lending practices. This effect did not necessarily serve to create a stronger resemblance of any kind between Adecor and Pearl Farm, as the financial practices of the tourate did not replicate those carried out inside Pearl Farm's boundaries. The moneylending going on in and through Adecor was not, in other words, deformed by the presence of the resort. Pearl Farm was fueling it but not otherwise altering it.

While Pearl Farm had "spread the wealth" to Adecor in these various ways and provided a basic level of material well being, Father Chico also commented that in his view some limits of the resort's influence on its tourate were also apparent. These had to do with what he characterized as largely

unsuccessful efforts at the alteration of beliefs and practices related to livelihood in Adecor, which had not yet been transformed by either the resort's
presence or the experiences and opportunities it had provided. Father
Chico noted, for example, the repeatedly unsuccessful efforts on the part of
the management to organize Adecor residents into "micro-enterprises" and
described residents as "a little bit passive" in this regard:

> So many times Mr. Robles [the resort's general manager] has encouraged them
> to do something. He wanted to give projects to the people in the barangay . . . it was
> one way of helping them. But they were not able to take them on. The people just
> do not absorb these kinds of ideas. It is really a disappointing situation since there
> is a real opportunity now for them to get involved in starting businesses of their own.

The resort was employing mainly the male heads of Adecor households
in 1996, leaving other members of the family typically without regular jobs.
Aware of this situation, and with the intention of creating mutually beneficial "partners in development," several programs targeting employee family
members had been organized at Pearl Farm's initiative for Adecor residents.
However, these had met with no success, even when staff from the Department of Trade and Industry had been brought in to offer training seminars
in order to give the residents some additional assistance in getting new work
programs started. The opportunity to further capitalize on the presence
of tourists was not one that Adecor's unemployed sector evidently found
attractive. The tourism matrix was failing more or less completely to proliferate itself in this respect in Father Chico's observation.

Instead of complying with the resort's interest in developing the barangay into a neighborhood of tourism business partners, Father Chico commented that the unemployed barangay members tended to relate to Pearl
Farm in a manner consistent with the patron-client models of interaction
established in Pearl Farm's older incarnations. These dynamics involved
relatively dependent roles being assumed by the workers vis-à-vis their
employers—what one of my research associates called "tasking for mercy"
and what Father Chico typed a "mercenary" style of interaction. "It's not a
very pleasant concept," he remarked: "It involves sort of begging for something, like asking for charity or a dole-out. Every time there is an event in
the barangay, they come to us to borrow things—tables, chairs. And they
always ask for donations for their prizes."

Instead of aspiring to managerial kinds of positions that would enable
self-sufficiency and increase autonomy, barangay members, in Father Chico's
view, tended to remain inactive and ask for charitable contributions of one
form or another from the resort, borrowing furniture or asking for money
on an ad hoc basis whenever a need was perceived to support various collective functions occurring in the barangay. Adecor was not envisioned as
a place that was on its way to becoming more and more a part of Pearl
Farm's world. Rather, it appeared to be a community struggling to hold

onto its past, maintaining essential differences from the resort's overall outlook and relying on Pearl Farm for support when it could on its own terms,
following an established patron-client model.

In general, Father Chico noted, the barangay had resisted Pearl Farm's
initiatives whenever the changes attempted by the resort required cultural
changes of one kind or another—changes in which the established practices of everyday life or changes in the conceptualization of the local environment were at stake. The greatest attempted change along these lines
had come about when Pearl Farm's management had wanted to displace
Adecor's community in its entirety to a nearby inland location in an effort
to expand the utopic marine environment to the north of its own property.
Father Chico summarized the resort management's position on this in
straightforward terms. He reported:

> Because the resort is located right beside Adecor, the credibility of Pearl Farm—
> a world class beach resort—was affected by Adecor. That's the reason why there
> was a plan made to relocate the people, because their houses were believed to be
> an "eye sore" to the guests. Of course, the people didn't like to hear those words,
> that they were an "eye sore." When you approach the resort, however, you can eas-
> ily distinguish the two settlements. Pearl Farm Beach Resort looks so nice with uni-
> form cottages, and, then, you see this other section with scattered houses. So that
> was why.

Faced with the loss of their homes and a coastal way of life, the community had successfully fought the relocation initiative, rejecting the logic
presented by Pearl Farm's management that a park along their waterfront
would improve the overall quality of the shoreline and be good for business
for everyone. From the tourate's perspective, residence along the shore not
only afforded a relatively comfortable and familiar location, but also was
essential for livelihood reasons unrelated to Pearl Farm. It allowed residents a place to keep the fishing boats they owned constantly within their
supervision, and it also guaranteed a mobility throughout and beyond the
barangay that was considered fundamental for the community's survival.
Although negotiations over the possibility of relocating residents were not
completely shut down in 1996, the issue was largely a dead one as far as
the community leadership was concerned, in Father Chico's understanding.
Adecor's victory evidenced not only some limits to the tourate's willingness
to participate in Pearl Farm's commercial development, but also the limits
of the tourism matrix's growth and power.

On less extreme measures, and even when benefits to Adecor's residents
were significant, the same resistance to cultural changes tended to occur
among the resort's tourate, in Father Chico's observation. He recalled, for
example, that when the marine reserve first had been established and fishing had been prohibited inside its waters, residents had reacted negatively
and complained. Father Chico remembered:

That was a classic example of the residents' dissenting attitude. They were very agitated by the project. Of course, they did not like the sanctuary at first . . . they had been able to get a lot of fish in the middle of it. . . . When we made the plans to turn [the area] into a sanctuary, they reacted against it. Now, however, they have learned they can get Matambaka [fish] here instead of having to go out to the middle of the sea because of the sanctuary. . . . Their initial way of thinking was that the fish would stay within the sanctuary where they would be safe.

Eventually Adecor's residents had complied with the new restrictions, accepting that the new legal designation of the local waters was an unavoidable reality. With time, they also had come to recognize that the overall quality of fishing outside the reserve had improved with the reserve present as a breeding ground, and the change had been to their advantage. However, the process had been a gradual one that entailed, as one of my research associates had put it, "warming up to it issues."

Similarly, Father Chico recalled, when the Pearl Farm management initiated a "clean and green" program for Adecor, attempting to organize a committee whose job it would be to improve the looks of the barangay's housing, resistance to changing the everyday practices of household maintenance also had resulted. "Our general manager encouraged me in 1995 to organize all the workers residing in Barangay Adecor to promote a 'clean and green' barangay," Father Chico recounted. He elaborated:

We decided to create a real organization and elect a set of officers with the ultimate purpose of promoting "Green and Clean." But we were not able to push this through. We got caught up at the resort with so many visitors, and there were never any officers elected. Until now, we are still only intending to organize something.

The barangay had not been forthcoming with officers to staff the committee and there had been little participation in the campaign by individual residents. Some residents had even taken issue with the resort management's rhetoric in launching the campaign in the first place, since it had again involved the claim that Adecor was "an eyesore" sitting next to Pearl Farm's immaculate paradise. More than one Adecor resident pointed out that tourists were not infrequently venturing outside Pearl Farm to visit Adecor, arguing that this would hardly have been the case if Adecor were really such a repulsive destination.

Once again the limits of the tourism matrix's influence were apparent. No interest in replicating the spotless uniformities of Pearl Farm's design were visible throughout Adecor. The tourate did not accept the resort's destination image as being in fact, or even in fantasy, representative of the homes of the locality's actual residents. Father Chico's account indicated that Adecor's community had not "bought into" Pearl Farm's seductive narrative of local living, and had rejected the utopic assertion that the resort had constructed anything that might be understood as representative of a Samal Island coastal home.

Father Chico's overall perspective on Pearl Farm and its cultural consequences was ultimately somewhat mixed. His hopes for Pearl Farm as a progressive force of modernization and small scale economic growth for the residents of Adecor were not vanquished, but they had been dimmed by his observations of the community's conservative responses to the opportunities offered thus far. On the whole, in Father Chico's perspective, Adecor's tourate seemed uninterested in changing either its established vision of itself or its standard ways of operating in relation to Pearl Farm's partnership-for-development agenda. Instead, the Adecor community tended to relate to the Pearl Farm enterprise as much as possible as it had to the older pearl farm, where many of its residents had also been employed previously. The community expected regular employment and long established forms of patronage from the resort and did not want to alter community life substantially so as to develop alongside of it touristically. On the other hand, the Floirendos—a family that did not identify with the older forms of hacienda-style ownership that had prevailed on the island from agricultural development—consistently rejected the patron type of managerial role, attempting to supplant it with what it viewed to be more progressive, enabling forms of community relations. Such was the character of the contestation that, in Father Chico's observation, was seen to be occurring in the name of tourism at Pearl Farm in the mid-1990s.

Heidi Toledo

Strangely diminished from my point of view was Father Chico's emphasis on tourist-related issues vis-à-vis Pearl Farm's tourate. He made few comments about interactions between tourists and Adecor's tourate, either on or off Pearl Farm's premises, despite the fact that a significant percentage of his working life was devoted to dealing with the consequences of such relations as they created stress for the resort's frontliners. "The interaction with foreigners is really affecting them," he did assert at one point in his interview. "These people [Pearl Farm's employees] are coming from the barrios—80 percent of them from the village. They must change or it will impede the industry."

Father Chico went on to mention briefly the resort's frontliners' frequent struggles with *hiya*, or "shyness" in the presence of tourists, and he reported that the resort management recently had tried to address this condition by requiring that frontliners attend seminars with an expert in international tourist relations brought in from Manila for the purpose. The individual held a PhD in social psychology and business administration from the Asian Institute of Management. While this experience had been somewhat informative, communication between the leader and the staff had itself been difficult given the difference in backgrounds between participants. Father Chico recalled: "Dr. Claude [the expert] had traveled around the world. For 24 years he lived in the United States before coming here. And these people here are only high school graduates. They hardly speak English. It was very hard for them."

The gap between the local tourate and the global tourist orientations, and the amount of learning necessary to bridge it, had become glaringly visible to Father Chico during this brief interaction. It was one area where the "glocal" character the resort aspired to produce had not yet been achieved. For the most part, however, the tourists themselves did not occupy much space in his discourse. He spoke of Pearl Farm's meaning as a cultural force mainly in terms of its management-labor and community organizing relations and initiatives.

Maria Henrietta Goméz Toledo, or Heidi as she was introduced to me in November 1995, had a very different perspective in this regard. Heidi was codirector of the Peña Dance Company, which had been producing cultural dance shows for Pearl Farm on a semiregular basis since shortly after the resort had opened for business. Although she was not a full time employee of the resort, Heidi was a regularly engaged "service provider," designing and presenting entertainment for Pearl Farm that enhanced its cultural and recreational aspects. Heidi was a frontliner in the most dramatic sense of the term, as her work involved elaborate and theatrical forms of masquerade and exoticized cultural embodiment. It was Heidi, along with her partner and fellow company members, who crafted and then enacted before tourists' eyes a "native" fantasy of Pearl Farm, bringing its carefully unmarked stages to life. Her dance work provided the utopic landscape with something intended to suffice as living proof that the illusions of paradise on which the resort was fixated were a human as well as a material reality.[6]

Given the isolated location of the resort and the complete absence of anything its global guests might recognize as "nightlife" in the barangay of Adecor, entertainment in the evenings at Pearl Farm was characterized by the resort management as an important, even crucial feature of the resort's activity profile. Individual rooms and cottages intentionally were not equipped with televisions or videodecks, leaving guests with virtually no choice to entertain themselves in the evenings beyond participation in what the resort itself offered. As gaming and other diversionary facilities were limited, live entertainment had played a prominent role in the resort's entertainment menu during its early years. Peña under Heidi's and her husband Adam "Dani" Toledo's direction was one occasional source of such entertainment in 1996. It was a source that relied on "Culture" with a capital C to achieve a particularly prestigious utopic effect.

The choreographic content of the productions Heidi and her husband designed for Pearl Farm represented neither a new nor an original avenue of creative activity for them, but, rather, a reconstruction of a body of work they had staged in a variety of civic and social contexts previously. What the tourists at Pearl Farm were seeing in their evening dance events, in the name of "Mindanao Culture," was actually a replication in Pearl Farm's glocal landscape of an established genre of theatricalized "Philippine"-identified folk dance. The style of national folk dance Heidi and Peña presented had a long tradition—a transnational as well as a national and local tradition of presentation. It was modeled closely on the choreographies of one internationally renowned Philippine folk dance company, the Bayanihan Dance Company.[7] The genre's presentational history emphasized non-tourist as opposed to tourist-related types of performance venues. Pearl Farm was serving as a new platform for the reiteration of a national-cultural choreographic discourse that was being reappropriated and embodied by this small scale community dance troupe, now actively carving a niche for itself inside a particularly luxurious corner of the tourism matrix.

In their work for Pearl Farm, the Toledos had not been asked to reproduce their entire "Filipiniana" repertory—as the choreography was called. The Filipiniana repertory was itself only one genre of the company's entire choreographic repertoire, which included "modern," "boogie," and "swing" dance numbers as well "folk" "cultural," and "tribal" genres. Heidi in fact identified herself essentially as a "modern" dancer. The resort, however, had expressed an interest at the outset only in specific selections of Peña work, what Heidi characterized as the "tribal" choreographies, using the standard categorization the Bayanihan Company had developed for these numbers. "The wife of the mayor in Peñaplata told us, 'You should try Pearl Farm because they are looking for tribal folk dances,'" she recalled in her interview. "That's why we tried out there."[8] The selected reconstructions consisted of a dozen different five- to ten- minute routines, which presented costumed group unison renditions of basic Bayanihan-derived dance steps, each presentation associated with one of the best-known ethnolinguistic communities of Mindanao—the Bagobo, Manobo, Mandaya, Maranao, and Maguindanao ethnolinguistic groups.[9]

The neutral gap materialized by Pearl Farm had not erased, but, as with Father Chico, edited Heidi's professional identity, deforming it just enough to transform her choreographic reconstructions into commercially viable entertainment. "It was because of Pearl Farm that I really became able to do choreography," she recalled.[10] Her comments indicated that the experience was not altering but, rather, reinforcing and improving upon her previously acquired skills and understanding. The choreographies the Toledos had generated outside the tourist venue had been transplanted into it keeping the bulk of their formal details intact.

Throughout my conversations with Heidi, which took place over several weeks while I was engaged in an interview project with the Peña company, it became evident that, in her understanding, what the Peña Company was doing at Pearl Farm was essentially an edited version of "the same dancing" they did elsewhere in their performing lives. However, she was coming to assess its meaning differently because of her experiences with Pearl

Farm's tourists. The touristification of the choreography, in her perspective, was occurring via the new interpretations its transplantation was generating, not by the deformation of its embodiment or design.

Heidi, like Dani and virtually all her company members, was linked to
Samal Island through family ties. Her father was from Peñaplata, the island's
oldest and second largest municipal center.[11] He had grown up there, the
son of migrants from Cebu and Pampanga. He had been a salesman and
later on had transferred to taxi driving in Davao City, where Heidi was
born and raised. Dani's father was also an immigrant to Peñaplata, where
he had taken up farming and served for a time as a barangay councilor.
The company often held its regular Saturday rehearsals in Peñaplata at relatives' houses. It was convenient for the company members, many of whom
lived on Samal Island as well, although none of them in Adecor.

The Peña company itself numbered fourteen persons in 1995. All but
Heidi had grown up either in Samal municipality or in its more industrious
neighboring municipality of Babak, on the island's northern end. Company
members ranged in age from seventeen to twenty-eight, with the average age
around twenty-one. This was four years older than the median age of the
island itself. Four company members were married; two were gay.[12] About
half the company members were in college pursuing various degrees such
as nursing, accounting, architecture, math, engineering—none of them in
the arts. All but one had some college education, which put the company in
the top 5 percent of the island's population in terms of educational attainment.[13] Those who were not in college were employed full time in a variety
of occupations, from carpentering to midwifery.

In sum, the members of the Peña company, Heidi included, while they
might have been considered marginal characters in a global network, from
the standpoint of Samal Island's overall social profile were nonetheless
upper middle class, urbanized "yuppies." They viewed their work with the
Peña company as an enjoyable part time job that brought them extra
income[14] and considerable social recognition among their friends and
neighbors on Samal Island, and occasionally from other college students in
Davao City as well. If not for their engagement at Pearl Farm, it was unlikely
that these individuals ever would have encountered a guest there. Their
exposure to foreigners was limited mainly to a small number of missionaries working in Davao City. The experience they gained at Pearl Farm was
in this respect the stuff of their upwardly mobile dreams and aspirations, a
rare opportunity and one they recognized as such. They could not have
been more different from Father Chico in their outlook in this regard. They
were anything but "grassroots" in orientation.

Heidi in particular felt that she possessed the kind of entrepreneurial
spirit Father Chico found so lacking in himself and in his neighbors at
Adecor. An energetic woman in her mid-twenties, the mother of a five-year-
old, she had two years of college courses in commerce and marketing

behind her. Although she was most centrally involved in the production of artistic creations at Pearl Farm, she was in her own mind a practical person first and foremost. She was self-consciously "financial," as she put it, in her approach to dealing with the resort. She was in fact an exemplary micro-enterpriser along the lines the Pearl Farm management had envisioned in its outreach efforts to local Adecor residents. She developed choreography for Pearl Farm as an auxiliary business—a "sideline" as such business activities were called in Davao. Her main work was cashiering at a Shell gasoline station in Davao City. She and Dani and their son currently resided in a modern townhouse development complex in Davao City.

Heidi and Dani's share of one performance at Pearl Farm was 1,000 pesos, close to what they would earn together working one week full time at their regular jobs. This represented a significant supplement for their household income in 1995 and 1996.[15] Heidi noted that the family had recently been able to purchase a television set with savings accumulated from the work at Pearl Farm. The choreographic sideline ranked high among Heidi's various pursuits for this reason. She hoped that the dance company might become even more successful in its activities, eventually enlarging its performance schedule so that it might become their sole occupation. The sideline status, she emphasized, was currently a necessity not a choice. "Of course, we have to divide our time now," she commented. "But if we could focus only on dancing, we would only dance. However, we need additional income now. Making a living is difficult. Since our show is not permanent at the moment, so we have to find other jobs."[16]

Dani and Heidi had started their choreographic work in 1991 when they were first married. Their first program had been presented in connection with the Peñaplata mayor's office, for a fiesta on Samal island. In 1992 and 1993 the group won the municipality's fiesta dance contests in "modern," "boogie," and "tribal" dance categories. In 1994 they received a standing ovation for a performance during another municipal fiesta. The Peña company in the mid-1990s was building a reputation in Samal as a local dance company that could succeed at venues unrelated to Pearl Farm. This local reputation was significantly enhanced by the association with the resort, however: the company had already been featured on a local television program that had done a show on Pearl Farm and had been engaged for another commercial television spot as well. The touristification of the company was facilitating more opportunities both inside and outside the tourism matrix.

The experience of being hired by Pearl Farm had been an extraordinary one for Heidi. In 1992 the company auditioned directly for Margarita Moran-Floirendo, who was at that time the Floirendo family's primary overseer of the resort. They were told to come back in one week, and minor changes were suggested for their costumes and performance. Heidi described these as "corrections," indicating that they were taken as changes designed to enhance the authenticity of the productions as opposed to deforming them in some tourist-oriented respect. After their second audition the company was engaged to perform regularly. This success prompted several days of intense rehearsal for the group. Heidi recalled that Dani became ill from all the overtime work. "If it only might have been possible to back out, we really would have," she recalled. However, the group decided to push themselves to go on with their performance, even rehearsing late into the night, because, as she put it, "It was an opportunity that would have been a real pity to let go of—Pearl Farm is truly first class."[17]

Pearl Farm's fixedness proved to be a good match for Heidi's folk dance discipline, which itself involved an exacting and steadfast set of rules for mastery and an extraordinary semiotic stability in its own right. The theatrical choreographies of the Bayanihan Dance Company were legendary for their precision and meticulous craftsmanship. Despite the fact that their performances, as well as their innumerable replications throughout the archipelago, were ephemeral and transitory, the codes of bodily conduct that had been designed to reproduce them had been elaborated down to the finest detail for every posture, gesture, step, and expression. These were generally carefully adhered to, even though they were transmitted entirely through oral and visual traditions of instruction. Heidi's case was no exception. "In my observation," she stated, and "I have had experience with many choreographers, I have never worked with one who was lenient. They were really strict."[18] When Heidi assumed the role of artistic director, she had demanded that her dancers pay extremely close attention to the smallest details of the steps she was teaching, and that they practice until they were able to reproduce them perfectly. Her "strictness" as a choreographer had ensured that their learning of the dance material was comprehensive, detailed, and deeply ingrained. "At least my being strong has helped them," she commented, "That's why they now are also able to teach other people themselves."[19]

The fixedness of Pearl Farm's tourist landscape, in this regard, was imposing nothing essentially new on the dancers in the Peña company, but rather reinforcing and intensifying an existing and already demanding code of conduct they had voluntarily adopted when they had begun their folk dance training. The tourism matrix had not erased the preexisting traditions of practice. Rather, their continued presence inside the matrix was now serving new touristic ends.

Heidi's perspective on Pearl Farm developed under highly specific and in some senses ideal conditions. The company was typically ferried into the resort by Pearl Farm's transportation in the evenings, scheduled to perform for the assembled guests shortly after arrival, given a meal in the Maranao Pavilion kitchen after the performance, and then transported back home to Davao City. Through this working arrangement, Heidi saw one small slice of resort life and had only very limited contact with the resort staff and management. Unlike the residents of Adecor, she did not experience Pearl

Farm as a constant presence in what she considered to be her home community. Moreover, she was not obliged to live by the resort's house rules on a day to day basis. She was something of a visitor herself, and a specialist at that, who spent relatively little time behind the scenes of the resort's utopic venues and interacted mainly with its higher levels of management. The company's choreographies all but completely mediated Heidi's experience of the resort and its clientele. Because of this performance-oriented exposure to Pearl Farm's landscape, Heidi's perspective on the resort was close to touristic in its appreciation of the utopic experience, even while it was also that of a tourate employee.

Not surprisingly, Heidi reported overwhelmingly positive experiences at Pearl Farm, for both the company generally and herself personally. The manager with whom the Peña company had had the most contact, a French expatriate referred to as "Sir Francis," had been a key figure in her regard. Sir Francis ran the food and beverage services and was in charge of the restaurant where the group would most often perform. His encouragement had been particularly important at the outset, Heidi commented, when many company members had been intimidated or "shy" at first sight of the resort's landscape, as well as its foreigners. Sir Francis, in effect, had been the first agent of the company's glocalization at Pearl Farm. On occasion, he had contributed ideas of his own to the staging of the Peña company's choreographies. Through him the tourism matrix had been effective in creating the deformations that it in fact had produced on the folk dance performances themselves. "He really added a lot," Heidi recalled, remembering these collaborations.[20]

The company had welcomed Sir Francis's suggestions, particularly when they had been directed toward the staging of special programs put on for large collective parties—"incentive vacations," as they were typically referred to in the discourse of the tourism matrix. Such events were sponsored by large multinational corporations. Several cases involved inserting the basic steps and movements of folk dance forms into some kind of fantasy narrative concerning "native" life and custom. These were then enacted in one or another of Pearl Farm's most well manicured "natural" spaces.

As an example of the most extensive modification to her standard practice that the Pearl Farm engagement had entailed, Heidi recounted a program entitled, "Sultan Nights" that the company had staged for a large group function on the beach-front of Malipano Island at Pearl Farm. An entire evening of choreography had been designed for this event, all of it using steps and movements of the "Muslim" style as exemplified by Bayanihan Company repertory. The dancers had performed the choreography on the sand, surrounded by elaborate decorations symbolic of the communities represented by the dancing—employing as props some of Pearl Farm's artifacts. To further intensify the effect, the company, with the resort's assistance, had been able to stage a spectacular entrance; their soloist "princess" dancer arrived on the beach ferried by a small outrigger banca, literally dancing her way from the sea to the candlelit shore.

Heidi had been quite affected by this particular theatrical experience at Pearl Farm. "We were like real Muslims," she remarked in her interview.[21] The authentic props and the beachfront setting had worked to produce a belief that the performance approached a genuine replication of a traditional cultural practice. Pearl Farm's environment and additional material resources had enabled Heidi to suspend her disbelief more or less completely in this regard, and personify a "Muslim" cultural icon. In her own mind the icon had in fact become more real, not more artificial, through its actualization in the tourist landscape. In this regard, Pearl Farm as a venue had actually reinforced and heightened Heidi's belief in the veracity of the representations developed by the Bayanihan-derived folk dance choreographies, to the point of creating the impression that her performance experience had replicated the actual cultural reality of the indigenous groups the representations had attempted to depict theatrically. A cultural hysteria was in this way resulting from her choreographic work in the landscape, as the line between theater and everyday life became obscured, as well as the difference between historical fact and touristic fiction.

With respect to the tourists of Pearl Farm themselves, Heidi reported positive experiences as well.[22] Among its most positive effects, she commented, Pearl Farm had given the company exposure to foreigners who were generally appreciative and approving of the company's work, even on the occasions when they turned in a slightly imperfect performance. In this regard, the company members had experienced the process of glocalization at Pearl Farm as a heightening of self-esteem and self-confidence in relation to their dancing. Pearl Farm was changing their own estimation of their dance work, increasing its cultural value and artistic merit in general, both inside the resort and outside it as well.

As to the specifics of this glocalizing process, the identity the Peña company assumed in their performances at Pearl Farm was one of "cultural ambassadors," modeled again on Bayanihan roles. While the periods of interaction were brief, they were very personal in nature, as well as being generally respectful in kind. Audiences, Heidi and others reported, tended to watch attentively and clap politely but warmly at the end of each number. In addition to the standard presentational choreography, performances at Pearl Farm typically entailed short participatory segments at their conclusions, moments when selected guests were brought out of the audience to be taught portions of dances presented. When this occurred, the Peña company members would inevitably come into close physical contact with tourists and be required to instruct them in very personal terms about how to execute steps and gestures, as well as lead them tactilely through the dancing.

Whenever Peña dancers escorted guests onto the dance area during the participatory segments, a global/local role reversal occurred, one that epitomized the character of the glocalization process taking place in this segment of Pearl Farm's tourate. The dancers, identifying themselves as "natives" (hence, in the tourist landscape, inferior) suddenly found themselves placed in the position of relatively masterful culture bearers, possessors of desired (if exoticized) techniques of bodily conduct. In these transient though collectively witnessed episodes, the dancers were able to impart something of their Bayanihan-style theatrical dance expertise to resort guests, who, while they were certainly members of a First World leisure class, nonetheless often exhibited inadequacies vis-à-vis the movements being performed and their attempts to learn them. These were sometimes laughable in the extreme. Heidi recalled one tourist, for example, who when learning the dancing suddenly had the urge to urinate and communicated this to her, which she found exceedingly funny. Even in less extreme cases, however, the Peña company members, through their dancing, became virtually the only local residents of Samal Island allowed to meet the Pearl Farm tourists on something like a "level playing field" globally speaking, where they in fact had superior skills in relation to the activity at hand. Other opportunities for interactions at the resort were highly limited and conducted in a rigidly hierarchical manner, with tourists clearly stationed in dominant and superior roles. It was, perhaps, only in these fleeting moments of the folk dance presentation that the status tables were turned and the human beings involved confronted each other in an arena where local knowledge gave those seldom accustomed to it an international, cross-cultural advantage.

In this regard, Heidi and her fellow company members, developed a unique tourate perspective on the tourist clientele of Pearl Farm, one marked by gratitude, humor, and guarded optimism about sustaining partnerships of a more extensive kind with other globally-oriented First World foreigners in the future. Heidi even reported that some of the company members had hopes of taking the Peña company on an international tour some day, following in the footsteps of the fabled Bayanihan Dance Company. The global tourism matrix was providing the Peña company with a context in which company members could claim and begin to develop their membership in an imagined community of global professionals, a community that many of their other life experiences had already prepared them to aspire to join. As Heidi summarized the attitude, "When we were accepted, we were all "standing tall." [We thought:] "Hey, we are accepted, maybe we can even go abroad."[23]

The single negative aspect of working with tourists at the resort in Heidi's perspective, and it was one that was confirmed by other company members as well, was interacting with tourists who were not foreigners. Domestic tourists tended to be a very different population from the international arrivals. In Heidi's words:

We have had sad experiences with Filipino [audiences]. . . . They hardly clap at all. . . . It's really bad. The Filipinos only look for mistakes. They should be the first to clap because it's Filipinos [they are watching perform]. However, they are the ones who don't clap. They will even smirk.[24]

The cultural dancing at Pearl Farm was apparently having a different effect on the touristic endeavors of its non-international guests. The dancing brought out negative attitudes toward the company, who were seen to be claiming, following the resort's utopic logic, to be representing the homeland to perfection. Domestic tourist responses to the Peña company performances indicated the failure of culturally marked entertainment to support the resort's narrative of world class quality for this particular category of domestic tourists.

Other Peña company members in discussions of their experiences with Pearl Farm audiences also reported that Filipino audiences at Pearl Farm were far more critical and unappreciative than international audience groups. One dancer reported, as an example of the worst Filipino audience behavior, a domestic tourist refusing to participate in the final interactive segment of the performance when the dance to be learned was the national dance. The tourist communicated this refusal to the dancer using a gesture and vocal expression that were recognized as both crude and discourteous.

According to the company members, while foreigners generally responded by clapping politely or enthusiastically after each number, domestic tourists were unresponsive or in some cases openly hostile or rude during performances. Audiences who belonged to the same "Filipino" category as those who had repeatedly praised the company's performances at nontouristic, municipal venues were the ones who, ironically, expressed the most negative sentiments at Pearl Farm. As far as the Peña company members were concerned, the only "ugly tourists" at Pearl Farm were their fellow countrymen and women, "mga Pinoy," as they called them in this context, using a popular slang nickname.

Heidi, for her part, gave no credence to the negative responses of the Filipino tourists at Pearl Farm. She did not interpret the response as indicating inferior performance skills on the company's part. From her perspective, the domestic tourists were simply not living up to their assigned roles—roles she had grown accustomed to seeing enacted by other Filipino audiences on Samal Island, roles that were assumed with patriotic as well as civic and personal enthusiasm in her experience in relation to her own dancing. In emphasizing that they should be "the first" to applaud, Heidi made it clear she had very specific expectations of Filipino audiences, expectations based on her extensive experience as a Filipino folk dancer.

Identifying herself in this context as another Filipino citizen, Heidi watched the domestic tourists at Pearl Farm as critically as she and her company were being watched by them—returning the tourist gaze with a national one that was its equal, if not its superior. It was in this respect that a contestation of identities was being played out at Pearl Farm, a contestation of national and glocal identities brought into conflict through the touristification of the company's "cultural" dance choreographies.

For Heidi, dancing at Pearl Farm was thus generating a negative stereotype concerning domestic tourists, the "mga Pinoy." Domestic tourists were understood as an inferior class of arrivals who were badly mannered and who exhibited a diminished capacity to appreciate high quality performances of "their own" culture. Neither Heidi nor any of the other Peña company members attributed this circumstance to any influence on the part of the resort itself—the utopic landscape was not understood as being a factor in this regard. Responsibility for the conduct was placed on the tourists themselves, who were seen to be choosing it of their own free will and expressing their collective character in so doing. The idea that Filipino tourists might be acting under the influence of Pearl Farm's narrative of utopic exoticism, and, so, in contrast to the foreign tourists, were experiencing disappointment when they were confronted through the company's performances with "Filipino" as opposed to "Other" exotic cultural productions, was not suggested. Heidi did acknowledge, however, that perhaps the negative reactions of Filipinos were in part due to the fact that, for this category of tourists, the dancing contained no novel elements.

Heidi and the Peña dance company members were not alone in using categories of nationality—which carried strong racial and cultural associations—to define different types of resort guests at Pearl Farm. Other members of the tourate as well, the frontliners in particular, also spoke in these terms about their experiences interacting with visitors. Observing the practices of paying bills, ordering food, and requesting services provided the Pearl Farm frontliners with numerous opportunities to compare patterns of conduct among the guests and form such generalizations. The negative stereotype of "Filipino" tourists in relation to foreigners emerged in a very similar manner for other frontliners as well. One waiter, for example, described Filipino tourists as tending to be unfriendly, secretive, hard to please, full of complaints, demanding, self-centered, and elitist. He contrasted them to American tourists, who were seen to be relatively "frank" and "unpretentious," and to Japanese tourists, who were seen to be generous with gifts and tips. Filipino tourists, in his view, were also observed as displaying a competitive, "crab mentality"[25] that contrasted most strongly to the supportive collective attitudes demonstrated by Chinese (mainly Taiwanese) tourists.

Different types of international tourists at Pearl Farm also were observed by the employee tourate as having various admirable qualities in their own right. Europeans were described as the most open-minded and curious. They enjoyed exploring Adecor and sometimes even other Samal Island communities as well as the resort's "natural" landscape—weather and roads permitting—and were most open to trying unfamiliar foods. Australians were noted for their love of birds. Japanese and Taiwanese were seen to be respectful of the natural environment and particularly enthusiastic about the whale and dolphin watching expeditions organized by the resort. Filipino guests, in contrast, were observed as tending to focus on shopping as their main entertainment, a diversion that was not regarded highly by the tourate, given their indoctrination into the resort's eco-tourism and cultural tourism narratives. Pearl Farm's landscape, in this regard, had served as an idyllic international observatory of sorts for its frontliner tourate, who tended to generalize from the utopic touristic behaviors and attitudes they witnessed at the resort, to an array of "real life" national character types.

Heidi's and other frontliners' experiences indicated that in a number of contexts the Pearl Farm experience was tending to produce a degradation of "Filipino" identity as it was coming into play with the utopic tourist persona that had been designed to inhabit the resort's excessively glocal landscape. The "Filipino" tourist emerged as the tourate's bête noire, the character unable to appreciate the "paradise" experience other tourists seemed to find so appealing, the character who acted out in inappropriate ways, rejecting its narratives of perfectly egalitarian (*and* perfectly hierarchical) tourist-tourate relations, and refusing to adopt the gracious manners of either its authentically global guests or its effectively glocalized tourate. In this regard, the resort functioned, more or less inadvertently, to create an arena in which a relatively inferior "second class" character was emerging for individuals not identified with either international tourist or glocal tourate cultures, from the tourate point of view, even while those who identified with the resort as either glocals or globals were assigned a "first class" character. The domestic tourist—the nonlocal/nonglobal tourist, the tourist identified with the Philippine homeland—was emerging as the Pearl Farm counterfeit, the figure who didn't "really" merit admission to the landscape.

Heidi and her company members, through their tourist-focused experiences at Pearl Farm, were actively choosing on a number of levels to "go glocal"—to identify with the utopic spirit of the resort and become partners in its world class enterprise. To the extent that they did so, their "Filipino" identity was being supplanted by what looked to be a more prestigious, more advantageous glocal one, one that, although it was markedly local in design, allowed them literally to join hands with what appeared to be a relatively humane and supportive world of foreigners, and leave their (inferior) fellow citizens happily behind. The denigration of the Filipino tourist, as well as the idealization of its global counterpart, reinforced the understanding that a national-cultural identity was inferior to those that might be generated from within the tourism matrix itself, whether for clientele or for employees.

Leonora Tan Virata

While Father Chico and Heidi both had extensive ties to Samal Island, neither was a tourate member living in Adecor. Neither presented a viewpoint embodied by the resort's most deeply invested tourate, the tourate whose dwellings and livelihood were most dependent on the resort's success or failure. Leanora Tan Virata, however, was just such a person.

Leonora Tan Virata was the Adecor Barangay council secretary. I met and interviewed her in her own home on February 7, 1996. She was a native of Adecor, born in 1945, and a citizen who had been particularly active in the barangay's civic life. Mrs. Virata's perspective on Pearl Farm reflected an understanding that was somewhat different from that of either Father Chico or Heidi Toledo, particularly as far as Pearl Farm's complex relationship to Adecor was concerned. It was not a perspective that was particularly representative of the majority opinion of Adecor's tourate, at least not insofar as our survey work had come to approximate that larger consciousness. It was an important perspective, nonetheless, voiced by an individual who had, perhaps, more than any other, a right to call Adecor "home."

Mrs. Virata summarized her perspective on Pearl Farm in much more succinct terms than did either Father Chico or Heidi. In part, this was because her contact with the resort, despite its proximity, had been indirect over the years. She was not and had never been an employee at Pearl Farm, although a number of her close relatives were. Her personal experience with the resort management and its tourists had been far less extensive than Father Chico's or Heidi's. What she knew of Pearl Farm's landscape and narratives was largely second hand. She was among the extended family members left unemployed by the resort—the tourate who had been targeted by the micro-enterprising initiatives. She was among the majority who had not responded to the initiatives. In her case, however, this was not due to passivity on her part but because she was already fully occupied with other businesses. Indeed, it was quickly apparent from her interview responses that Mrs. Virata's personality was about as far from "passive" as anyone could have imagined. She was, in fact, the antithesis of what Adecor non-residents tended to identify as the "villager" or the "native," the stereotyped character whose activities focused on "waiting for the coconuts to fall." Leonora Tan Virata was no such individual.

She lived with her family in a small wooden cottage on stilts, of a size and design standard for the barangay, built a short walk away from the resort's north entrance gate. Despite the modest nature of her domicile—particularly in relation to the cottages of Pearl Farm—there was nothing "small scale" or "quaint" about Mrs. Virata's discourse. She had a quick memory for names and numbers and commanded a relatively large array of facts. Her understanding of Pearl Farm was conditioned by a detailed knowledge of the barangay's existential characteristics.

Despite her more distanced relationship to Pearl Farm, the resort's paradise narrative—the luxurious story it told with such firmness and certainty about itself—was not lost on Mrs. Virata. At the same time, the impact of Pearl Farm's world class status was modified and muted by her awareness of a much longer history of local development, consistently nonlocal in character, to which she and her ancestors had contributed and born witness. While she was a native of the barangay who had never left the provinces of Davao, her vision of the local reality had never been insular. She was not an atypical resident of the barangay in this particular respect. I encountered no resident of Adecor whose worldview stopped at the edges of the barangay.

On her mother's side, Mrs. Virata was related to the barangay's largest family, the Pedro clan. The Pedros, as it happened, were the only landowning family that maintained a presence in the barangay. Mrs. Virata's grandmother, Josephina Balibug Pedro, had been the first to arrive on the island sometime around the beginning of the twentieth century. She was not yet a Pedro, however, when she came from Caraga and what was now Adecor was still virgin forest. Josephina Balibug, her name before she married, had arrived to become a caretaker for the well-established Miquita family, who were "old from this place" (*karaan gyud na ang Miquita diri*), in Mrs. Virata's words. The Miquitas had held titles to public office in the vicinity since the Spanish era, and, along with another absentee landowner family, the Corinas, had owned most of what was now the barangay of Adecor. Josephina Balibug had been granted a small plot of three hectares or so after her arrival. She had later married Vicente Pedro from Bohol Island, another newcomer, and they together had been responsible for clearing some of the forest to plant the coconut trees that now surrounded the residences along Adecor's shoreline.

Josephina and Vicente had eight children (Mrs. Virata recalled all their names). Seven had eventually married and started large families of their own (Mrs. Virata knew how many children had been born to each—a total of 45). The children now had grown children of their own. A sizable minority of Adecor's 2,000 or so residents were fourth, third, or second generation Samal Island Pedros. Mrs. Virata reported that, of Adecor's 760 registered voters in 1995, 160 were of the Pedro family; they constituted the largest voting block in the barangay. They played an influential role in selecting the leadership as well, and had a decisive hand in determining the composition of the barangay overall. The tourate Pearl Farm was recruiting and cultivating from "the village" of Adecor was to a significant extent one that was being supplied to it by the Pedro family.

On her father's side, Mrs. Virata's family history could not have been more different. Her father was not only an outsider, he was not even a Philippine native citizen. "Mr. Tan," as Mrs. Virata referred to him in our presence, had come from Amoy, China, at the age of sixteen. He had arrived in the Philippines during American rule, joining relatives who had established tire recapping and hardware businesses in Davao City. Mr. Tan spoke none of the Philippine languages nor English, even until the present day. He had lived in Adecor since marrying Mrs. Virata's mother, Julietta Pedro, before the end of World War II. He was something of an outcast, limited severely by the lack of a common language with other residents. At the time of the interview, Mr. Tan was one of Adecor's oldest residents, a foreigner but also recognized by his younger neighbors as a pioneer in the community.

Mr. Tan, although he had in no way been connected with the resort's renovation, turned out quite by coincidence to be the one representative of a foreign presence on which Pearl Farm, in its present incarnation, had expanded. The resort had brought into the community a small stream of Chinese tourists, mainly from Taiwan. This coincidence had had some extraordinary consequences for Mr. Tan, as Mrs. Virata recounted. Her father now regularly encountered tourists who spoke his first language and occasionally gave him newspapers and magazines they had brought with them or sent him Taiwanese periodicals on their return home. For Mr. Tan the introduction of tourism had been quite the opposite of the stereotypical scenario. Far from losing his traditional lifeways in the presence of foreign visitors, he had fortuitously been reconnected in a most personal way with his lost homeland. The industry had enabled him to re-establish his original cultural identity in encounters with other Chinese natives that would have been otherwise impossible. Tourism was, in this individual case, having a regenerative if somewhat ironic effect, as it drew to Mr. Tan a steady trickle of visitors who were themselves intent on escaping their homeland for an exotic leisure locale.

Mrs. Virata could easily remember the days of early Philippine independence in the 1950s—long before the Floirendos arrived, even before the original pearl farm had started up—when the forest still surrounded the shore and only three houses had been built along the edge of what was then known as Balon, or "place of the deep well." Japanese soldiers had dug the well during the war when they were hiding on the island after the return of the American troops. Somehow the name had stuck, a mark of yet another episode of nonlocal development in the settlement's early history.

When she was old enough to attend school, Mrs. Virata had had to leave Balon during the week and stay at a boarding house in the municipal center of Peñaplata, a seven-kilometer walk away. The pattern of weekday boarding had continued during high school and then college, until she graduated from the University of Mindanao in Davao City. During these years Mrs. Virata experienced a miniature version of a migratory life, although the weekly movements between school and home played out a more regular pattern of mobility than the previous generation in her family had experienced.

Mrs. Virata returned to live permanently in Adecor in 1972, when she married. By then the settlement was being called by its present name and the Aguinaldo Pearl Farm was established, having started up in the mid-1960s. Her husband was not a native of Samal Island but, rather, an Ilocano who had left his familial region to become a company guard for the Aguinaldo Pearl Farm. Mrs. Virata had lived in Adecor with him ever since.

For much of its early history, as Mrs. Virata summarized it, Balon had been an out of the way place. The growth of the Pedro clan from a single nuclear family to a large extended family over the course of the twentieth century had contributed significantly to the steady enlargement of the settlement. The Aguinaldo years, from 1965 to 1980, had been a period of significant growth for the settlement as well. Laborers had moved in to work for the pearl farm, and also to work the land, planting it with coconuts more and more extensively. Some had come from other places on Samal Island, like Anonang and Kaputian's población, but others had come from more distant places, like Camotes Island in the Visayas.

While a rather elaborate family history was on the tip of her tongue, Mrs. Virata did not appear to be one of those individuals given to living in the past simply because she knew she had one to live in. On the contrary, she was progressive in her general outlook on the future of the barangay. "Progress" was a term she mentioned repeatedly in her interview, and it was her progressive view, in her opinion, that put her in the minority with regard to her fellow barangay councilors. "As far as I can see, they aren't thinking much about what's in the best interest of the barangay," she remarked resignedly, speaking of her colleagues on the council.[26]

On the central issue affecting the community—the relocation plan to move the residents inland—Mrs. Virata had taken a pragmatic stance, recognizing that if the water became unfit for swimming and fishing due to overpopulation and unsanitary subsistence practices, the community's main source of financial stability would certainly be threatened. She realized that her own home might have to be sacrificed eventually, to sustain the tourism development. She was ready, though not eager, to take this step. However, the majority of her colleagues were opposed to the plan, wanting to stay on the shoreline where their alternative forms of livelihood would be immediately available. "They were against it," she recalled, when speaking of the deliberations around the inland relocation initiative. She elaborated:

They really reacted negatively. First and foremost, they didn't want to move their homes because they were accustomed to their way of life here, at the shore. But if you really think about making progress for the barangay, then they definitely ought to move, because once the barangay is developed, the whole area will also develop. That will also help them. Their standard of living will improve greatly.[27]

Mrs. Virata echoed Father Chico when discussing the barangay more generally in this regard as well. "They are always on the negative side," she commented, speaking about the general response to the livelihood projects initiated to spark tourist-related micro-enterprises.[28] "Out of 200 residents, only 5 might be interested."[29]

With regard to the benefits of tourism development, Mrs. Virata not only shared Father Chico's perspective, but was able to elaborate upon it in some detail. She made a direct connection between her own ability to send her children through college and the work opportunities provided by Pearl Farm. "Oh it makes a big difference—the income [from Pearl Farm] is really a great help," she emphasized, commenting, "You can send your children to school. It would be difficult to send children away to school if you were depending solely on the income from the land."[30]

Mrs. Virata had witnessed firsthand as well the generosity of individual tourists coming to the resort, whose donations to Adecor's elementary school had been substantial, she reported. Tourist donations had paid for a new paint job on the school's roof, the construction of a toilet, and hot meals for children. "They have already been a great help with the school," she commented,[31] referring in particular to individual Taiwanese tourists visiting Pearl Farm.

Regarding all nationalities of tourists who ventured across the resort's northern boundary to visit Adecor, Mrs. Virata confirmed what many Adecor residents asserted regarding the relations Pearl Farm tourists had established with local residents. She reported no problems with prostitution, drug dealing, or illegal activity of any kind affecting the community. In her view, tourists had been well behaved and surpassed her expectations. She recalled as an example some incidents of Taiwanese tourists who had interacted with her father on several occasions.

Sometimes Taiwaneses tourists would go to his house. They would stay for a long time and ask for some young coconut to eat . . . He never intended to charge them for them, but they would return and give him 200 or 500 pesos all the same—depending on how large [the groups were].[32]

Tourism, by Adecor resident accounts, had not resulted in a degeneration of community values among the youth or any other segment of the barangay population. It had not brought with it an increase in alcoholism, nor had it seduced the barangay's work force into remunerative but unskilled forms of labor, such as massage, face painting, or handicraft vending. The few tourists who did venture into Adecor were generally accompanied by a Pearl Farm frontliner, and they tended to keep a respectful distance from the residents. Floirendo family members, it was widely reported, had communicated to the barangay leaders that they wished to "maintain their reputation" for conducting an elite class business at Adecor, and this had been understood by Adecor's families to mean that they did not want prostitution or any of the more lowly regarded aspects of touristic experience to have a visible, let alone prominent, role in the resort's vicinity. Adecor, being the tightly knit, extended family community it was, was able to monitor and support its residents in this regard as well, so that some of the more typical adverse affects of tourism's arrival in other communities had not in fact occurred. In residents' perspectives the consequences of tourism had so far been extraordinarily benign on an interpersonal level. Mrs. Virata had noticed that some children in the barangay had learned to ask for money from tourists, but she did not characterize this as a particularly worrisome trait. Other children still said simply "good morning" when they encountered tourists, she noted. Interactions with tourists were limited in scope, and small in number—ideal conditions that gave Adecor residents, Mrs. Virata included, a relatively positive experience of their presence in the barangay.

To judge by the overall cast of Mrs. Virata's comments, nonlocal economic development, touristic or otherwise, was a familiar cultural process that had always been a given in her experience of Samal Island, although, in the form Pearl Farm was currently undertaking, it did of course possess some unique and novel aspects—the majority of them positive. The presence of Mrs. Virata's immigrant father in Adecor and his response to the touristic influx from Pearl Farm revealed strikingly that, despite its tiny size and clannish make-up, Adecor was not an isolated, homogeneous community. Most of its households were connected through family and work to networks that spanned the Philippines at least, if not reaching Asia, Europe, and America. Mrs. Virata also had a sister, Violeta, who now lived in Los Angeles, making her own immediate family tri-continental in scope. The tourism that had arrived with Pearl Farm was not some harbinger of an unknown world of modernization, but rather a well understood next step in a history of development that spanned several generations on Samal Island.

Conclusion

The three perspectives recounted above, while they only begin to sketch in some of the more salient details of Pearl Farm Beach Resort's cultural and touristic profile, nonetheless clearly indicate that its various processes of touristification were producing both continuity as well as change in the everyday lives of its tourate. They also show that the influence of tourism development at this point in time was far from absolute. From a normative perspective, Pearl Farm was neither a simple nor a "classic" example of either a worst case or a best case scenario for tourism development. The more catastrophic scenarios, in particular, however, failed to capture the resort's cultural consequences, particularly in its more "progressive" forms.

Pearl Farm was not conceived in simple normative terms by anyone I met or interviewed who had had sustained contact with the resort. It was never characterized as an omnipotent evil force that had voided all good things in its path, forcing itself upon an isolated, pristine "real" paradise so as to sell it off, either by the inch or by the pound. The resort was never spoken of as an immoral or even amoral institution. Despite its luxury class aspirations, Pearl Farm was not seen to be drawing its tourate into the more indecent and brutal sidelines of the tourism industry, those that tourism establishments elsewhere were well known to be doing. While its "business" ethics may not have always echoed those of the "grass roots element" or their advocates, and, while its guests and hosts were not always perfect in their treatment of one another, Pearl Farm was generally understood to operate on a more human scale than tourism development worst case scenarios depicted. From its uppermost tier of owner/managers to its bottom rung of rank and file, the faces that animated Pearl Farm's landscape tended to be regarded, at least by those most regularly on the premises, as individual faces, belonging to specific people with "real" lives and families and homes that were known to all, and which made a difference. The relatively small scale of the establishment and the fact that it was privately owned and identified with a single family contributed significantly to the overall character of the resort.

This is not to say that the touristification of Adecor, or the resort's commuting personnel, was occurring in some kind of perfect harmony with Pearl Farm's utopic narratives—without contestation, loss, or even trauma. The "eyesore" label debated inside the homes of Adecor, the contested understanding of Adecor's residents as "passive" persons "impeding growth," the habitual manifestations of "shyness" in the presence of global figures and contexts, and the emergence of the "ugly Filipino" tourist stereotype even in the best case scenario of Pearl Farm's "first class" dance productions, all evidenced the fact that disturbances to collective identities at multiple levels of domestic life were occurring as part of the glocalization of Pearl Farm's vicinity and its tourate. On a more existential level, while the displacement of Adecor's main coastline settlement still appeared to be a matter of community choice as opposed to corporate power in 1996, the arrival of tourism nonetheless had presented that decision-making process to the barangay's residents in an abrupt and, if not calamitous, generally distressing manner. The decision-making process related to this relocation initiative was understood to be causing, or at least intensifying, divisions in the community that might not otherwise have manifested. Limits to the influence and control of the tourism industry and its utopic narratives over the practices of everyday life were still prevalent in Adecor, in most respects in 1996, particularly where they involved long established patterns of household and community subsistence, maintenance, and growth. However, the awareness that virtually any aspect of ordinary life was subject to impending change was also widespread. Of course, this represented nothing particularly new to Adecor's migrant-descended residents.

Its upheavals notwithstanding, Pearl Farm's process of touristification also evidenced the degree to which continuity of cultural practice could be sustained and in some cases enhanced through the operations of the tourism matrix. Father Chico's pseudo-priestly responsibilities, Heidi's pseudo-traditional/Philippine choreographies, and Adecor's real-life growth in preexisting patterns of economic and subsistence activity, not to mention its enhanced material and social existence, which remained as fundamentally aligned with the forces of modernity as it always had been, all demonstrated the general tendency of Pearl Farm's renovations to accommodate to and allow for deformations of a relatively integrative kind—sometimes even against its own design. In these instances, the boundary between touristic and nontouristic cultural practices could become particularly difficult, if not impossible in some cases to distinguish, for better and for worse.

The ultimate consequences of the resort's excessively fixed glocal landscaping efforts, as well as its narratives of luxury, perfection, and "Mindanaoness," were still incomplete in 1996, still largely undetermined, given the resort's relatively brief period of operation. That they were changing lives was certain, but to what extent and in what actual directions was still in most cases unresolved. Certainly, with respect to the re-appropriation and internalization or rejection of its utopic narratives, Pearl Farm's tourate had only just begun to set these processes in motion. Regardless of the specifics of the actual outcome, however, the current strength of Pearl Farm's reputation alone indicated that its influence was only beginning to exert itself upon the local community, and that it would continue to develop this influence, both integratively and disruptively, for years to come.[33]

Chapter 6
The Flagship Destination:
The Samal Island Tourism Estate

Not far from Pearl Farm Beach Resort, only a few kilometers and barangays to the south, there was another, very different, manifestation of the tourism matrix underway on Samal Island. This development, which even after several years of preparatory activity had yet to begin construction when I left in 1996, was named the Samal Island Tourism Estate. Unlike Pearl Farm, SITE, as it was known in local discourse, was not a private, family-backed development project. Neither was it by any measure small in scale. It was, however, like Pearl Farm, imagined as an international destination, with portions of the estate set aside for luxury landscapes comparable to Pearl Farm's. There were certain underlying similarities in the utopic narratives of the two locations. But the expression of tourism manifesting in the name of SITE was conceived within a culture of nations as opposed to families or provinces—in particular, of the ASEAN nations and their governing personalities. SITE was imagined and planned as a "Filipino" tourism development first and foremost. Its proposed tourate was being understood, and was coming to understand itself, in terms of this identity category as positioned within the networks of ASEAN. There was nothing particularly "home-spun" about the narratives or the imagined landscapes representing SITE, in somewhat marked contrast to Pearl Farm.

As its various narratives foretold, SITE was intended and understood to be the Philippine government's "flagship" tourism initiative. In this chapter I will recount the history of that flagship, the imagined landscape planned for SITE, and the local consequences of its initial phases of implementation. These were the phases in which the creation of the neutral gap and the voiding of the destination's designated spaces were taking place. There was admittedly "nothing" going on in the way of actual tourism, and no tourists were yet in sight, but the project development provided ample evidence that the consequences of the tourism matrix were occurring far in advance of the destination's opening day. The chapter that follows provides perspectives on SITE gained from four individuals who were lifelong residents of the barangays where the project was underway, and whose communities, homes, families, and individual lives were most dramatically and traumatically altered as a result of the project.

The Flagship

SITE was considered by Davao-based interests to be *the* tourism venture of the decade for the southern Philippines. It was a top priority initiative of the Ramos administration, launched officially in 1992, when a United Nations Development Plan study was undertaken. As a result of the study, the areas identified for the estate on Samal Island were officially determined to be "viable" for tourism development.[1]

The original impetus for the United Nations Development Programme study already had become a matter of urban legend as early on as 1996. A number of narratives provided differing accounts of the project's origin. The most appealing, in my view, was one told to me by a lawyer, whom I chanced to meet during a reception following the blessing of Davao City's first Mail Boxes, Etc. office. According to this individual, who belonged to the social circle that included all the key personnel overseeing the development, the idea for the estate had begun with a visit to Davao City by the prime minister of Malaysia, Mahatir Mohamad. This had occurred sometime during the beginning of "the 90s." According to the lawyer, the prime minister apparently had seen in the Mindanao region a landscape that reminded him of his home region in Malaysia. Because of this shared identity, he had been agreeable to entering into a partnership with the Philippine government in order to construct a tourism destination here. This became the SITE project.

Whether the project actually started first with Mahatir or with someone on the Philippine government side, the origin narratives generally placed the conception of the project in the early 1990s and in a transnational context. It was associated with the dawn of the Ramos era, the moment when the initial recognition of Davao City as an ASEAN gateway city of premier importance to the entire nation had begun to crystallize. While the Philippine government's interests loomed considerably larger than those on the Malaysian side, the project officially had been undertaken jointly by the Malaysian and Philippine governments from its inception. On the Malaysian side it was in the hands of the Ekran Berhad corporation, a private corporation led by Prime Minister Mahatir.[2] On the Philippine side, the Department of Tourism (DOT) was the primary agency involved, representing the Ramos administration.

The Ramos administration—not a wildly popular government at its outset in 1992—pledged itself from the moment of its election to a new era of progressive and democratic commercial prosperity throughout all twelve regions of the Philippines. The administration's liberal rhetoric, which focused on the "4 Ds"—devolution, decentralization, deregulation, and democratization—placed a high priority on regional development. This platform, along with real growth in domestic commercial enterprise over its initial years of government, generated widespread support for its projects. In 1995 this support was evidenced in midterm elections that threw substantial additional power into the administration's camp.

By 1996 the Ramos administration was considered by the network of professionals and entrepreneurs I had come to know in Davao City's middle and upper classes to be a success story for the Philippines inside its own borders. The transformation of Subic Bay, the return of electric utilities to functional status throughout the archipelago, and the release of the telecommunications industry to open market development were only a few of the cases frequently mentioned supporting this view on the national level.[3] With regard to Mindanao in particular, a marked increase in the region's gross domestic product, an increase in government infrastructure spending to a level nearly three times that during the Marcos era, a 30 percent rise in exports since 1992 and a 40 percent average annual growth in its regional loan portfolio since that year, along with substantial increases in telephone lines, building permits, and energy consumption, all stood as local evidence of the Ramos administration's having made good on the initial stages of its electoral promises.[4] The administration's ambitious future plans for the island—which had already entered the "Second Stage" of a fifteen-year master plan for Mindanao in 1995—included upgrading multiple air- and seaports to international standards, developing "open sky" and "passportless" travel policies for EAGA partners with Davao, and, by the year 2010, tripling the gross regional domestic product (from 132 billion to 465 billion pesos), doubling per capita income (from 9,000 to 20,000 pesos per year), creating 3.9 million new jobs, and reducing the poverty from 47 to 15 percent. By all accounts—or at least all those that came my way—the SITE project appeared to be one of the bolder among many initiatives on the Ramos administration's part designed to achieve this promised narrative of success, with its stated ultimate goal of making Davao "globally competitive" in the Asia Pacific region.

Aside from Mahatir's alleged personal attraction to the locality, the SITE project's geographical situation in the Davao Gulf made a great deal of objective sense in relation to the changing political and economic dynamics of the region. With the fall of the Berlin Wall, and the disintegration of the Soviet Union, the threat of communism—previously a driving force behind policy-making for Mindanao at the national level—had severely diminished. The incentive to minimize contact across the Philippine-Indonesian and Philippine-Malaysian borders, which had been viewed as danger zones since the onset of the Cold War, suddenly evaporated in the 1990s. At the same time, the Asian economy boomed at a seemingly unstoppable pace, and international trade between the Philippines, Indonesia, Malaysia, Singapore, and Brunei accelerated rapidly through all existing corridors. Growth brought with it pressures to create additional routes to assist the flow of goods and services across borders—routes that would maximize trade between subsectors of the ASEAN sphere previously isolated from one another and linked solely to national centers. As strategic interests in the region reversed themselves and maintaining unpassable boundaries gave way to developing fluid commercial "links," the absence of suitable "hub" destinations for enhancing transnational regional economic activity, particularly throughout the triangular rim of island arcs that centered on the Celebes Sea, became glaringly apparent. The weakness was evident not only to the Philippines but to its ASEAN neighbors as well, Malaysia foremost among them.

All the nations occupying positions on the Celebes Sea triangle were busily engaged during the mid-1990s in various stages of upgrading their regional ports. At the westernmost edges of the rim, on the island of Borneo, the towns of Kota Kinabalu in Sabah and Kuching in Sarawak—both Malaysian centers—had been "targeted" for development. Likewise, the towns of Samarinda and Pontianak, in East and West Kalimantan respectively (the Indonesian provinces on Borneo) were undergoing analogous developments. The tiny but wealthy center of Brunei, also on the island of Borneo, was caught up in its own, particularly well-funded wave of development. Moving eastward on the rim, to the Minahasa peninsula of North Sulawesi Island, the adjoining Indonesian ports of Manado and Bitung had already begun to develop themselves as international reef diving destinations in coordination with other local commercial developments; finally, at the northern edge of the triangle, on Mindanao Island, the ports of Zamboanga and Davao City, among other smaller port cities, had become main foci for growth initiatives in the Philippine sector.

Of all these candidates for transnational development centered around the Celebes Sea, Davao's circumstances were in a number of critical respects the most impressive and promising. Davao was the logical choice to become *the* ASEAN regional center in the area. Davao was poised near the east-west center of the triangle, making it geographically a maximally accessible location for regional interaction. More important, however, Davao's resources, human as well as material and agricultural, were by a large margin the most extensive and the most capable of undergoing rapid expansion. Davao already had a labor force approaching a million people. It had large and expandable ports, both air and sea. Perhaps most vital, it had a fertile land mass, which offered lumber as well as foodstuffs in magnitudes unmatched by other regional centers. Davao, in sum, was without serious competition to become the premier destination in what every indicator was signaling to be a major new commercial sector of the Asian-Pacific region. As long as the Philippine government did a reasonable job of managing things, Davao was more or less destined to be an international success story in the ASEAN sphere.

Figure 7. Map of BIMP-EAGA region.

The SITE project was an outgrowth of ASEAN-inspired policy initiatives, which had identified Davao City as the Philippine "back door" to a wide array of target development sites in the immediate international vicinity. The three ASEAN neighbors governing these sites, Brunei Darussalam, Indonesia, and Malaysia, along with the Philippines, after a series of state visits and preliminary activities in 1992 and 1993, inaugurated in 1994 the BIMP "group" (the initials standing for Brunei, Indonesia, Malaysia, Philippines), which from then on began to operate as a subgroup within the ASEAN umbrella. The group designated the transnational triangular rim of islands centered on the Celebes Sea the East Asean Growth Area (EAGA), formally drawing its boundaries from Mindanao Island at its northern tip down to the southwestern tip of Borneo in the southwest and—encompassing Sulawesi Island and the Moluccas—extending to the western edge of Irian Jaya on the island of New Guinea in the east.

The BIMP block, its origin, rapid evolution, and particularly the imagined transnational community conceived within its EAGA triangle, played a definitive role in the operations of the tourism matrix that were, throughout this period, in the act of constructing SITE. SITE's function was generally conceived as being auxiliary to the mainstreams of commercial activity EAGA would produce. It was intended to enhance and enlarge the flow of arrivals coming into Davao City, in part by providing some conference and seminar facilities that could be used to serve the work of international commerce. However, its main role was to develop an extensive array of recreational facilities that would support recuperative activities accompanying the influx of commercial work and serve as an additional lure for attracting transnational business to the city.

Given this scenario, it was taken for granted in the discourse generated by the project in Davao City during "the 90s" that SITE was a test case. It was an experiment that would gauge how safe an investment the southern Philippines actually was for international as well as domestic nonlocal interests. With Mindanao's political problems of the 1970s and '80s apparently now under control, SITE was expected to be a key predictor of how profitably the island's provinces could grow into productive locations for ASEAN-oriented commercial activity, given adequate multinational assistance. SITE was also a test of the Ramos administration's capacity to attract and maintain venture capital from its relatively rich neighbors—Malaysia and Brunei—and keep them coming back with more, on terms that were more advantageous to the Philippine state and economy than had ever before been negotiated by a Philippine government. Whether Ramos and his key personnel could actually deliver such goods—material, financial, and human—to its ASEAN partners, whether they could live up to their end of the specific bargains that had to be made in the course of a large scale development project *and* keep their own public and private sectors healthy and happy, was quite visibly on the line with the development of SITE. The project thus had a larger significance for the character and integrity of the Philippine government than its specific benefits, themselves not trivial, might have warranted. So important was the tourism estate's development to the national interests at stake that the negotiations for the project directly involved the highest levels of both governments. In a few instances, they carried the personal stamps of both Ramos and Mahatir as well as a number of their elite staff members.

The Landscape

Even though no ground had actually been broken in 1996, the landscape that was to be produced in the name of SITE already existed, both on paper and as an imagined reality. By 1996 the destination had been refined by its planners, working through the local offices of the Philippine Tourism Authority, into an elaborately detailed blueprint and lengthy "Master Plan" document.[5] Access to the plans was limited, of course, to those actively involved in the planning process. However, many of their vital statistics and outstanding details had been made public knowledge by 1996 through periodic reports in the local media.[6]

The landscape was not designed, as with Pearl Farm, to realize a single, coherent image of perfection—a world consistently conforming to one utopic agenda. Rather, the plan for SITE followed a more eclectic logic that corresponded to the magnitude and diversity of its imagined tourist market. The tourism estate was envisioned on a colossal scale, with arrivals projected to be coming, not only from ASEAN locations, but from Australia, Europe, and the United States as well, with a wide range of income levels, ages, and touristic preferences. To accommodate such global masses, the SITE plan situated the estate on 6,000 hectares of land at the southern end of the island, all located in the municipality of Kaputian (see Figure 8). The total area was roughly one-fifth that of Samal Island as a whole and half the total land area of the municipality of Kaputian.[7] The projected upper boundaries of the estate ran across the island east to west several kilometers south of Pearl Farm, also south of the municipal center or población of Kaputian proper. From its northern boundary, the estate was envisioned as encompassing all the municipality's southern area, down to its southernmost shores. In this regard, the plans included precisely the area of the municipality that was the most isolated and undeveloped of all its generally undeveloped territory.[8] The 6,000-hectare spread was divided between 4,000 hectares on Samal Island proper and 2,000 on Talikud Island, roughly one-fifth the size of Samal Island and several hundred meters off its southwestern tip. The estate was to consume more than 75 percent of Talikud's land area.

Four barangays of the municipality's eleven on Samal Island were to be dedicated to the estate—Pangubatan, San Remigio, Libertad, and San

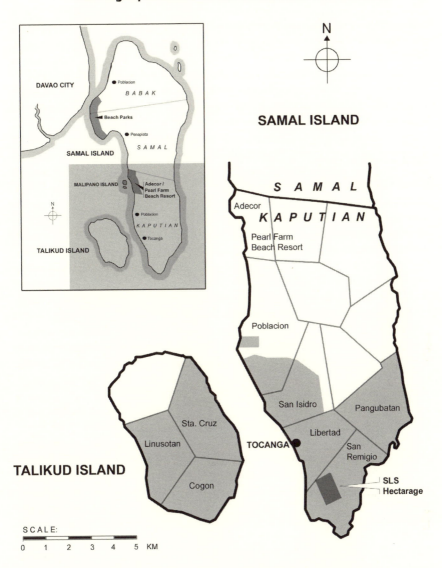

Figure 8. Map of planned territory of the Samal Island Tourism Estate.

Isidro—along with three of the four barangays on Talikud Island—Lino-sutan, Santa Cruz, and Cogon.[9] Approximately 3,000 households were situated in these barangays, with a population of roughly 18,000 in 1995.[10] This figure represented roughly two-thirds of the municipality's entire population and one-quarter of the combined population of Samal Island's three municipalities.[11]

The seven barangays had been previously developed primarily as coconut plantation lands. They had few roads, even of the dirt and coral variety. They had no public electricity or plumbing facilities or telephone lines, and they were reported to have some of the highest rates of malnutrition in the province of Davao.[12] It was onto this impoverished rural plantation landscape that the SITE project plans projected radical changes. After basic support services for water, power, transport, and sewers were put in place, an ambitious total of 3,835 "rooms," or accommodation spaces, of various categories were planned for construction. The construction process was envisioned as happening in stages, but the initial stage and the opening of the first destination service facilities to tourists, were expected to be finished in 1996—a plan that did not in fact come about.

A variety of structures were imagined in relation to the estate's 3,835 rooms, envisioned primarily in terms of economic class. In the estate's most expensive areas, "villa" and "condominium" accommodations dotted the landscape. In areas where high volume and a mix of touristic uses were anticipated, "hotels" equipped with seminar and convention facilities had been located. In less expensive territories, "bungalows," and "pensions," had been imagined, sometimes clustered into "villages."[13] While the separation of economic tourist classes loomed largest in the plan's design, the English terminology employed in the master plans also reflected vague associations to highly developed, long-established touristic locations on the order of Monte Carlo, Las Vegas, and, somewhat closer to home, Hong Kong.

Indigenous culturally or nationally coded symbolism was absent from the plan's depictions of its 3,835 rooms. The accommodations imagined were cosmopolitan as opposed to explicitly "Filipino" or "totally Mindanao." Even the physical construction of the accommodations was planned as a largely nonlocal, nondomestic operation. Imported prefabricated components were selected for the construction process. In high contrast to the Pearl Farm landscape, the kind of dwelling planned for the government-backed estate addressed itself on both material and symbolic planes to the most advanced versions of a "global village" clientele. This clientele was understood as desiring to identify itself by no markings other than those of membership in a relatively functional sector of the global economic order. The accommodation designs assured such arrivals that what could be expected from the SITE destination, above all else, was an experience of feeling and being at home in the "First World," in a utopic landscape of "development," regardless of the specificities of geographic location.

To some extent, the details of SITE's landscape followed a theme park model. The estate was subdivided into a number of different realms, each internally consistent and designated for a different kind of utopic play. Each employed its own variety of masquerade, ventriloquy, or magic and created a different arena for narrative production. Movement between the realms was conceived as an integral part of the touristic experience and was represented on the plan designs by an array of sweeping arrows that indicated which realms were likely to produce a flow of arrivals on various routes inside the estate. Visiting the estate was in this way envisioned as a choreography of multiple utopic performances, orchestrated movements that could be seen to create variety in and among themselves, as tourists roamed throughout the estate's several regions, enhancing and prolonging the overall touristic appeal of the destination as a whole.

The parameters used to conceptualize variety and oppositions in utopic experience were several. They included a low/high energy axis, which correlated with an old/young age spectrum, as well as a local/global, a nature/culture, a low/high cultural, a low/high density, and, most important, a low/high economic class axis. These were used in contrasting combinations throughout the estate. One subterritory, for example, which used the local/global and low/high cultural axes, was designated "Folklore" and was situated on the northwestern rim of Samal Island. "Folklore" was planned as a mini-destination showcasing local life and intended to offer activities such as fishing and boating, promoting them as amusements illustrating a traditional, low culturally marked "folk" way of life. A native style village and several bungalows were planned as accommodations in this relatively inexpensive area of the estate. On the southern tip of Samal Island, an area labeled "Exclusive" would work along the opposite ends of these axes, using some of the most impressive beach-front property anywhere on the estate's shores. Yachting was the imagined activity listed for this section of the estate, along with elegant night life in the shoreline condominiums that were the sole accommodations planned for this area. The "Exclusive" region combined the global, high cultural, low density, high economic class ends of the estate's utopic axes.

Other subrealms were equally contrasting in their designated themes. The "Action" area of the estate, a coastal destination featuring both hotels and pensions and designed for high energy, globally popular aquasports, was planned to share a boundary with the "Relax" region, an inland, inexpensive, high density landscape intended to support a retirement center and a golf course in addition to selected "family"-oriented leisure facilities. On Talikud Island the opposing realms of "Glamour" (high density, high energy, high cultural, global "funlife") and "Isolation" (low density, low energy, local, nature-focused, ecotouristic villages) were placed side by side. The only region that was relatively isolated from the others (although arrows connected it to the "Action" and "Folklore" regions) was that designated "Exotism." This region alone was to be located on Samal Island's eastern shore, the shore facing into the Davao Gulf away from Davao City. The rugged topography and remote coast were envisioned as setting the stage for various adventure-coded forms of high energy, globally popular touristic play designed to explore the natural environment.

The range of landscapes the estate intended was broad, matching the activities and clientele imagined. Golf courses, swimming pools, tennis, basketball, and squash courts, jogging and hiking trails, fishing, sailing, and diving schools, shopping boutiques and specialty markets, discotheques and casinos were all planned along with the variety of accommodations, strategically placed for maximum consistency within the various regions. A hospital was included, giving the sense that the estate was to be entirely self-contained and self-sufficient, a utopic totality set apart, as theme park landscaping often worked to suggest. Nonetheless, the landscape envisioned differed from classic theme park designs in certain fundamental respects. Most prominently, the estate did not envision the extreme degree of fantasy-oriented transformation theme parks typically achieve. No reconstruction of "Old World" tourist destinations, such as the city of Paris or the Egyptian pyramids, were put forward. Nor was space devoted to more technologically advanced forms of amusement such as elaborate roller coaster rides or magical animation machinery. The regions envisioned relied on the natural givens of the preexisting island environment to a great extent to achieve their utopic appeal. Thus the estate's imagined landscape fell somewhere in between a beach park destination and a theme park in its overall design.

The Philippine Tourism Authority was optimistic in its imagination of the influx of visitors the 3,835 rooms would attract, boosted in this effort by everything else Davao City had and would soon have to offer the BIMP-EAGA commercial sector. The PTA projected over 300,000 holiday arrivals to the resort for 1996, increasing to 900,000 annually by 2010, with receipts projected to increase from 1.2 billion to 3.4 billion pesos. The lower 300,000 arrival number represented more than ten times the local population of the municipality, which in 1995 was just over 27,000.[14] The higher number was nearly fifty times the total 18,000 population of the seven barangays involved in the plan. It was no exaggeration to state that the plan envisioned a demographic takeover of sweeping proportions, inundating the municipality with tourists and reconstituting the area's population in tourist terms.

The good news for barangay residents, at least from the plan's point of view, which would result from this anticipated flood of tourists and the development needed to support them, focused on employment. The plan projected 7,000 initial jobs in both construction and tourism service sectors. Employment needs were anticipated to increase as the development was gradually completed, ultimately to a grand total of around 18,000 tourism sector jobs by 2010.[15] In 1995, with the seven barangays' adult population hovering at around 10,000 and unemployment in the municipality estimated at about 13 percent,[16] these figures were indeed remarkable verging on miraculous. In effect, the development ultimately promised twice the employment opportunities the current population might require, even if all the current forms of employment, which were limited primarily to farming corn, bananas, or coconuts, raising chickens and pigs, or fishing,[17] were discontinued once the estate was in place.

The utopian character of the development was not envisioned as resulting simply from its landscaping or in relation to its tourist clientele. It was also envisioned as a utopian development with regard to its tourate population. SITE was expected to produce a more or less complete transformation of working life for the whole of the locality's labor force, wiping out unemployment and creating new, more cosmopolitan jobs for virtually every person in the barangays who might want one.

In the Philippine government projections, the financing and actual construction of these facilities—the initial phase of which was estimated to cost 2.3 billion pesos[18]—as well as their management over the longer term, was to be left largely to the private sector. Ekran Berhad had assumed the premier role as a private sector partner in this regard. At the Prime Minister's direction, it had committed itself to developing the first 1,700 rooms, in the form of a large hotel complex on 250 hectares in the "Action" region of the estate, the only area that as of 1996 was actually under the estate's control. Ekran Berhad's initial investment toward this first phase of construction was approximately 50 million pesos.[19] The government expected that other investors would soon appear to follow Ekran Berhad's lead once the development was underway.

For its part, the government committed itself financially and operationally only to the development of the estate infrastructure—primarily a road and a water system—and to "assisting" the consolidation of the lands targeted for development. These were to be made available to investors on a subleasing contract basis from a "tourism estate management company" organized by the government. The government also made itself available to "fast track" other community organizing activities related to the development of the existing local resources.

In this respect, the project plan set up a partnership for development between partners of widely varied status—the local landowners, Ekran Berhad, and the Ramos administration, working through DOT. The Philippine government was to assume minimal risk in this venture, while maintaining ultimate control of the developed territory.[20] The plan, while it was presented as beneficial for all partners, created a particularly advantageous situation for the government, or at least for those elements of the Ramos administration operating through DOT. Nonetheless, in the ambitious model of "sustainable development" the plan articulated, all partners involved were afforded exceptional opportunities to share in the estate's eventual benefits.

What actually happened as a result of the plan's partnership fell far short of the ideal envisioned. In particular, the "assistance" Davao government officials had and were in the process of giving to the occupants of SITE targeted land created a social drama of major proportions in the municipality of Kaputian, with consequences involving the whole of Samal Island. As the plan moved toward reality and various imperfections, costs, and limitations in its design began to become evident, the development process, and the understanding of tourism that was integral to it, also began to take on a different, more complicated character, particularly from its burgeoning tourate's point of view.

The Development Process

Even before the estate area was declared viable for development by the 1992 UNDP study and the master plan drawn up, a number of activities on Samal Island initiated by the government were paving the way for tourism. An extensive series of planning meetings and seminars began in 1991 between tourism and other government officials and barangay representatives. Their goal, as one municipal official who had attended some 79 of these meetings later characterized them, was to begin to prepare residents for government-sponsored tourism development. Lengthy dialogues addressing concerns and negative reactions from residents were conducted, with the result that, by the time the SITE project in particular was realized, tourism had become a well-known, much-debated subject to virtually every barangay resident in Kaputian. The imagination of the industry, its landscapes, its tourists, and in particular its tourate, was well underway. Narratives of Samal Island becoming "the next Hong Kong" in the Philippines had begun to circulate on the most local levels.

When the time came to deal with the specifics of the SITE development, a commission composed of barangay and municipal leaders was initially put in charge. The commission was charged by the provincial government to represent the interests of the local residents in meetings with Ekran Berhad and DOT. In what were later characterized as an intense, short series of meetings, this commission negotiated the land-lease price agreement with Ekran Berhad representatives, acting in coordination with officials from the Department of Tourism. The agreement arranged for payments to be made by the developers to the landowners in roughly equal amounts in two forms: in cash and in shares in the holding corporation that would ostensibly own and manage SITE.

The rate of payment eventually settled on at the conclusion of these meetings fell far short of the agreement for which the commission's members had hoped. The eventual price set by the negotiations represented roughly 50 percent of the rate multinational agribusiness companies had been paying for land use on Mindanao Island. These agribusiness rates had themselves been criticized by a wide range of sources known to the commission members for being far below what comparative international standards might have deemed a fair rate. However, despite the compromises entailed, the commission succeeded in establishing for the local residents on Samal Island a permanent role as a partner in the development process and procured a substantial ongoing income for the barangays as well.[21]

The source of what local points of view considered to be the major consequences of the SITE development by late 1995 and early 1996 emerged in 1993, when the land-lease agreements reached by the Samal Island commission for the estate were actually instituted. This occurred, not in relation to the entire 6,000 hectares identified by the plan, but to a relatively tiny subsection, a 250-hectare area on Samal Island spread between three of the four barangays involved: San Remigio, Libertad, and San Isidro. The appropriation of this property as the initial development area was spurred by several factors. It was centrally situated with regard to the planned estate as a whole. Its shoreline provided an excellent location for the estate's first jetty, which would efficiently link the estate areas on Samal and Talikud Island, as well as the estate as a whole to Davao City. Perhaps more important, however, the property was already in government hands, a coincidence that at least on the surface made its transition into the SITE project much more feasible.

The 250 hectares until 1989 had been part of a single coconut plantation, nearly a thousand hectares in size, established in the early decades of the twentieth century. It was known as the Fernández Hermános plantation, in recognition of its owner, Don Carlos Fernández Hermános, a Filipino of Spanish descent from Manila who was said to be one of the incorporators of the San Miguel Brewery.[22] The plantation's commercial name was the Compagnie Maritima, and some local residents referred to it as such. In 1989, before the SITE project was conceived, the property had been taken over by the Department of Agrarian Reform (DAR) to become part of the Comprehensive Agrarian Reform Program (CARP). This program, an initiative of the Aquino administration, was designed to redistribute the lands of large plantations to the families who had tilled their soil, often for generations. The program involved first the purchase of the land from the owner, and then its subdivision and transfer to tenants, who after establishing their occupant status could file with the DAR for a grant of ownership. While the CARP program had not lived up to its stated objectives nationwide in terms of the numbers of tenants its program was intended to benefit, the program during the later years of the Aquino administration had proceeded with the purchase and redistribution of some lands, and the Fernández Hermános plantation was among these.[23]

When the CARP initiative occurred and individual tenants were allowed to file for ownership in 1989, many of the plantation's farmers applied for titles to the land they had cultivated over the decades, as did their children, who in many cases had grown up to become farmers alongside their parents. Other tenants, however, fearing they would lose the pension benefits they had earned while working for the plantation, or suffer some other form of retaliation, did not file, waiting for some clear signal from the plantation management that they should proceed with their claims. It was into this delicate and complex process of land transferring that the SITE tourism development project intervened.

Before any land had actually been granted to any individual tenants, the DAR, which had been responsible for acquiring the plantation, agreed, at the direct request of President Ramos, to allow the DOT to take over the management of the land redistribution process.[24] The DOT, finding the prospect of negotiating land-lease agreements on behalf of private sector estate developers with a large number of individual farmers infeasible, transformed the redistribution of the lands from an individual into a collective affair. It ordered the consolidation of the CARP beneficiaries into a single cooperative landowning organization and endowed that organization with the authority to lease land collectively to private sector tourism developers through the offices of the DOT under the direction of SITE project officials. With this new institution in place, the Philippine government officials were relatively certain that the local residents who had so recently been given claim to the land, and who had become partners in the development process, could be dealt with as a single block. Transnational negotiations involving the local landowners would be simplified to a manageable degree. The government, however, did not anticipate the difficulties that would emerge in this consolidation, given the incomplete status of the CARP land transfer.

The cooperative body that the DOT "fast-tracked" into existence when it took over the land transfer process from the DAR was named the SLS Cooperative (for the San Remigio, Libertad, and San Isidro barangays). The SLS Cooperative members were identified as the same persons who had already applied for CARP transfers in 1989, some 332 beneficiaries. An initial board of directors for the cooperative was put in place by 1993.

To the SLS cooperative's board of directors fell the task of managing a 27-million-peso cash payment made to it by its first private sector partner, Ekran Berhad, through the Philippine government.[25] The SLS board was also charged with representing the cooperative on the tourism estate's holding corporation's board of directors. It was responsible as well for managing the farming of the plantation lands now held in collective trust but not yet slated for tourism development, and with overseeing the transfer of the cooperative's membership from homes situated in the hotel construction area to new homes being constructed in a designated relocation area.[26] In sum, with the creation of the SLS Cooperative, the DOT set in place in Kaputian a powerful new institution whose relationship to the existing political and economic institutions in the municipality was to a large extent undefined.

The SLS Cooperative, when my research in the barangays was taking place in 1995 and 1996, was managing some 20 million pesos in its capital accounts. This sum far exceeded the resource base of any other cooperative on the island and was more than the individual beneficiaries had ever owned or expected to acquire.[27] The money represented a remarkable opportunity for its members, presenting what would heretofore have been considered an incredible prospect for rapid upward economic mobility. The cooperative had been handed a collective pot of gold by the SITE developers.

This extraordinary good fortune, however, entailed a set of equally extraordinary problems that were threatening to destroy the cooperative during the time of my visits to the barangays. Most serious was the problem of defining the coop's membership. A group of 53 individuals not on the CARP lists had come forward claiming eligibility for membership. These claimants identified themselves as tenants who had not participated initially in the CARP proceedings, afraid of retaliation from the plantation management. Their claims had been denied by the SLS board, causing considerable tension and resulting in a lawsuit filed in Davao City, which in 1996 was still working its way through the courts.

A series of disputes having to do with the management of the cooperative's various farming and livelihood activities were also adding to a general climate of ill will in the SLS barangays. Complaints were growing about a number of issues: who had and had not been allowed to continue farming SLS cooperative lands not immediately targeted for tourism development; unfairness in management of SLS member resettlement; ineptness in management of cooperative dividend disbursements; corruption in hiring and compensation of cooperative employees, including its board of directors; and, finally, incompetence in running the SLS store and storehouse—a large concrete block building at the SLS headquarters in Tocanga, a settlement in Libertad, whose construction had been completed sometime in 1995. All these responsibilities fell mainly on the chairman of the SLS board, whose actions were subject to the informal scrutiny of the members involved and those who knew them—in short, to everyone in the barangay communities.

In late 1995, when my research in the barangays began, the SLS cooperative was in crisis. A leader capable of maintaining the support of the membership had not emerged over the cooperative's first years of existence. Claims of mismanagement had haunted the board continuously from its inception. The cooperative was losing money on its store, which was selling goods at prices far above what members could afford. It was paying out only a tiny sum in dividends to its members, who were becoming increasingly dependent on this income for their survival. Its resettlement initiatives had generated much anxiety among the individuals who had moved to the designated lands inland and who were subsequently unable to farm or fish but were also as yet unemployed by the tourism estate from which they had expected jobs. Perhaps most disturbing in the face of the membership's worsening financial situation, however, was the fact that the cooperative was spending its capital at an alarming rate to meet its payroll, most of which was going toward the salaries of its board of directors.

Complicating the cooperative's problems severely was the circumstance that its partners in development, Ekran Berhad and the DOT, had not followed through according to schedule on their own plans as set forth in the development negotiations. Ground-breaking ceremonies for the initial phase of construction had been scheduled initially to take place in 1994. But the construction phase of development had been repeatedly deferred, brought on by a series of unanticipated complications in the details of the infrastructure projects that constituted the first phase of actual construction. In 1996 the estate itself still was not yet under construction, much to the consternation of the cooperative's membership. The members had expected an immediate transition into employment with the estate's new establishments, and many had taken out loans from the SLS cooperative in partial payment for government-sponsored training seminars in which they had enrolled, seminars designed to prepare them for the new types of tourism work. This left the membership jobless, no longer able to farm, but not yet able to work for the estate.

The sense that the cooperative's vast fortune was being unnecessarily lost due to mismanagement had become widespread, and feelings of resentment and disappointment, not to mention panic, were developing in the barangays. During the period when my research was taking place, violence erupted with a night attack on the cooperative store. Rumors were circulating of an armed takeover of the warehouse and a snap election of new officers for the board of directors. The situation was so troubled that the current SLS board chairman was taking steps to bring about the dissolution of the cooperative and divide the capital among its members—an outcome bitterly opposed by the as yet nonmembers seeking shares in the organization, as well as by the members who could foresee that their best chances for long term prosperity lay with collective investment and growth, not with their own individual shares of the capital.

It was into this unhappy and unstable predicament that I entered upon my arrival in the barangays, in hopes of learning something first-hand about the cultural consequences of the SITE project and the understanding of the tourism matrix in the locality. The flagship initiative had articulated a progressive and ambitious model for a grand scale sustainable development project, designed to meet the basic human needs of the local population and ensure their integration into the development, not only as a labor force but as a partner in the estate's corporate management and ownership. But the actual implementation of the project had created a situation verging on cooperative failure. From local points of view, this outcome was due largely to the prolonged "preconstructed" situation of the estate.

The SITE development even in its preparatory phases was already generating some profound cultural consequences in the barangays. Both its prolonged process of creating the vacant land on which its landscaping was still planned to emerge, and its cultivation of tourate identities and narratives—which was proceeding unimpeded by practical delays and setbacks—were producing a variety of changes. Barangay residents were rethinking their relationships to each other, to their community leaders, to the national government, and even to the world beyond the Philippines. Despite its "on the verge" status, despite the fact that there was as yet nothing to describe in terms of an actual utopic landscape, and despite the fact that there were no tourists yet to accommodate, the tourism matrix already had a quite lengthy history in the barangays by 1996, as both an imagined industry and an actual social force. It was to that history, and the understandings of the cultural present, future, and past that it produced, that my research with individuals in the barangays was addressed.[28]

Chapter 7
The Samal Island Tourism Estate:
Tourate Perspectives

Between October 1995 and March 1996, I collaborated with a nongovernmental social services organization (NGO) based on Samal Island to conduct a series of interviews of people who were residing on or farming the 250 hectares of land that had become designated as SITE property. This survey occurred as a sequence of, for the most part, randomly selected interviews. The method assumed that an open and honest form of exchange between unknown participants could and would take place.[1]

Given the troubled condition of the communities involved, setting up such a "standard" interview process—locating the appropriate persons and constructing the contexts where a straightforward question could be asked of interviewees and answered meaningfully and personally by them—was anything but straightforward. I had been uncertain how to proceed with the research in this respect, or whether it was even feasible for a newly arrived foreigner like myself, with no identity other than that of a "researcher" visiting from the U.S., to undertake such a politically sensitive project. By July 1995, when my focus had turned directly to the SITE development, I was not optimistic about finding any means of learning first-hand about the most local forms of understanding produced by the development. Whatever the "local point of view" might be, it appeared to be beyond my grasp.

In contrast, I had already found it was an entirely straightforward matter to document the official perspective on the development. The "top down" understanding of SITE was available in English and filed accessibly in the air-conditioned offices of the DOT, conveniently located in downtown Davao City. This narrative I could learn from individuals well equipped to convey it articulately, using the results of a variety of empirical research. The documents representing the official narrative were tailored for delivery to international social scientists such as myself. Moreover, the tourism officials of Davao were authorized and prepared to deliver them in person, which they did cordially whenever I happened to pass by their headquarters. The residents of the SITE-designated land on Samal Island were an entirely different story.

Had I stepped off the plane in 1992 and used international credentials to organize a survey of the area—relying on the approval of the DOT and a couple of Tagalog-speaking research assistants provided by them, perhaps—I might have located the same individuals and communities that I eventually worked with in the SITE interview project that I did conduct in 1995 and 1996. However, the exchange would have occurred on a completely different footing. Given that the interviews would be focusing on an intensely contested topic, the possibility that people occupying the most vulnerable positions in the tourism power structure would present unauthorized candid views seemed extremely remote. Neither, however, were they likely to espouse any official utopic line, given the current crises. Had I gone the prestige-driven route for the project, I would have found Kaputian to be composed of a large number of unlocatable, unavailable persons—people adopting the only safe strategy for dealing with the kind of no-win predicament I'd have been forcing on them, "coincidental" non-participation.

There were two alternatives to this top-down method and its unproductive scenario. On the one hand, I could have taken up residence in one of the barangays near the SITE property. My research time frame, however, was insufficient to establish a trustworthy rapport. The other possibility, a far less likely one, was to locate a research partner who might be able to establish much more quickly a position in the SITE barangays analogous to the one I desired to occupy. Knowing that this latter course, problems notwithstanding, was the only viable one for my situation, I began to search for such a partner.

This search drew on all my understanding of the contemporary social and cultural structures and organizations of Davao society, as well as on a set of accidental circumstances that put me at what turned out to be the right series of places at the right times, for reasons that were manifestly not the wrong ones. It entailed an interwoven series of chain reactions involving a diverse array of key individuals: social workers from several different agencies, a few Jesuit missionaries, one theater organizer, three mayors, a couple of choreographers who were also in the resort business, at least one college professor, and an array of relatively uninvolved but trusted friends who formed a backdrop of good faith on which all my activities in Davao depended. The most central chain, critically, did not include anyone working for the DOT.

To give the briefest sketch of this methodological odyssey, the search began with a social occasion that was part of my usual round of participant-observation activities in Davao City, a beauty contest held as the climax of the recently established annual "cultural" festival of Davao, the Kadayawan festival.[2] There I chanced to see a dance company perform whose work intrigued me, and, through a friend of my hostess for that evening I was able to make contact with the director. It came out during our first meeting that a former member of his company was currently the director of an NGO based on Samal Island, an NGO that had the capability to undertake the interview project I had in mind.

The theater director put me in touch with the NGO director. At our first interview, I realized that I had found an individual who fit the profile I'd been seeking. He was the son of the island's only lawyer, a former activist himself, and a cooperative development worker whose primary concerns currently revolved around the development of low cost housing, sustainable irrigation technologies, and livelihood cooperatives. He was known all over the island as a "grass roots" professional, a civic-minded resident of the most progressive and effective type. His name was Ben Oducayen.

Ben's NGO office was located on Samal Island at the far end from the SITE project, and most of the projects it supervised did not involve the residents in the area affected by SITE. Ben was in this respect an outsider to the SLS cooperative, although his knowledge of the project was extensive. He and his staff were interested in collaborating with me to undertake the study. Their understanding of what was happening on the island in the name of SITE had given them cause for some concern about the communities involved.

On Ben's advice, we began a series of official visits, a small crusade of a bureaucratic sort, down through Samal Island's local power structure. We started by visiting each of the island's mayors, carrying a letter requesting approval of the project. Each granted this on sight—of Ben. It was clearly Ben's reputation on which the mayors were relying, even though he always presented the interview project as a joint undertaking.

After the mayoral visits, we proceeded to the barangay level, speaking with the barangay captains in Kaputian who were involved with SITE. Again, Ben's presence framed the proposed research in a favorable light. With these agreements in place, we went to the SITE area itself, to the 250-hectare area under the control of the SLS cooperative, to discuss the interview project with the cooperative and barangay leadership. Here again, and by a similar logic, we were granted permission to proceed.

This process of introduction into the local chain of command would have been unimaginable, not to mention impossible, without Ben's experience and reputation. Each individual officer had to be located in the appropriate order of status, and approached in a particular manner according to his schedule and preference for formal or informal styles of interacting with foreigners and with new developments inside his district. It was a complex and unforgettable journey on which I was taken—and which I never could have made myself. It was marked by countless benevolent signs and gestures—innumerable exchanges of soft drinks and snacks—countless formal conversations during which very little information actually changed hands, but in which power was subtly revealed, conveyed, and transferred. A misstep on this preliminary journey would have created ill feeling, I later realized, and would probably have eliminated any chance of the project going forward. A good first impression was essential at every phase. As it happened, Ben's approach worked flawlessly, and I became in this way identified with his agency. In joining forces with the Samal Island NGO, and forgoing formal linkages to the more powerful Davao-, Manila-, and U.S.-based organizations, I dissociated myself to a certain extent from more globalized forms of authority that I might otherwise have been compelled to wield overtly.[3]

For this extraordinary entree and the conversations it made possible, which in retrospect I am certain could not have been brought about in any other way, regardless of the time frame, I had Ben to thank. On his side, the benefit of having an international collaboration under his supervision, a collaboration that gave him good reason to present himself anew to the island's political leadership, was considerable.

So it happened that I collected a total of thirty-nine interviews on Samal Island between October 1995 and March 1996, on and around the SITE designated property, with individuals who had not been authorized, formally or informally, to present their perspectives on tourism development. The people Ben and I engaged had received no official narrative on the subjects we addressed—nothing they could pass on to us in the guise of personal understanding. The exchanges that took place, in the end, approximated much more closely than I would have believed possible "standard" survey interviews—standard, that is, for a relatively enabled, "developed" middle class in some relatively serene, First World locality—which the SITE barangays, most definitely, were not.

Tocanga

The majority of the interviews conducted for the study of the SITE project— and three of the four summarized in this chapter—occurred in the *sitio* of Tocanga,[4] the tiny settlement that was the location of the SLS cooperative. At the time of the interviewing, Tocanga consisted of a scattered collection of about one hundred single-family dwellings. It occupied some prime coastal territory on Samal Island, at least from the SITE developers' standpoint. It was situated on the northwestern edge of the 250 hectares of plantation land that had been turned over, first to the Department of Agrarian Reform, and then to the Department of Tourism and the SLS cooperative. It was located just about midway between Kaputian's población district and the island's southern tip (see Figure 1). Tocanga's haphazard string of waterfront homes looked out toward Talikud Island, whose eastern coast was easily visible from Tocanga's shores.

As Talikud was separated from Samal Island by only a few kilometers at this point, Tocanga had been chosen as the first place at which to construct a wharf for the tourism estate. Ekran Berhad's initial 1,700 room development was also planned for construction near the settlement, necessitating the eventual displacement of the entire community once ground was actually broken. In the meantime, however, the SLS cooperative had established its headquarters in Tocanga and built an office/storehouse building at the edge of the beach atop a stone foundation constructed just north of the sitio's center. The current chairman of the SLS board resided near the sitio as well. As the hub of a number of SITE activities, Tocanga was the first, and, as of 1995, the only community that had been wholly engulfed by the SITE development project. A number of its residents had already transferred their homes to the inland resettlement housing area. Knowing this about the sitio's situation, Ben and I elected to begin our interview work among its residents.

Until the advent of the tourism development project, Tocanga had been an isolated farming and fishing settlement. It became established in the 1920s, in part to house the Fernández Hermános plantation workers and their families. Coconut and banana trees still grew in abundance on and around its premises. The residents had, until the CARP developments, been either tenants or squatters. They had built modest though permanent houses of wood and light materials—neatly kept structures that were generally surrounded by either wild grass or, more often, well-fenced gardens.

Tocanga's dwellings were strung out along a couple of hundred meters of coastline, forming small clusters at various points where the otherwise sloping terrain allowed. The settlement was bounded by the water on its west and by a steep and rocky hillside on its east that left room only for a narrow north-south running sprawl of housing, usually no more than two or three houses deep. One main pathway ran through the settlement; it was never wider than a narrow lane and in most places resembled a walking path.

The sitio had one grass-and-dirt basketball court area toward the northern end. This space also served as a plaza, since it was the widest, flattest area available. A small open air stage bordered on the court/plaza as well. No other public structures or spaces had been constructed. There was no hospital or clinic, no post office or other public office building, no chapel— although a chapel had been there for many years in the past. The sitio at present consisted virtually entirely of homes, some of them equipped with small *sarisari* stores in front where household shopping could be accomplished for ordinary daily needs.

There were no public services in Tocanga—no electricity, sewers, running water, or telephone lines. Communication with the rest of the area occurred through word of mouth as people came and went, which they regularly did, mainly for work-related reasons, or by means of a small number of privately owned and operated radios and cellular phones. Adding to the isolation of the community was the circumstance that no public transportation came directly to Tocanga. There were no ferries and no jeepneys. There were not even the ubiquitous and relatively affordable "Skylab" motorcycles that were adapted to transporting passengers around the island's main roads and seemed able to reach even its most remote locations. A horse was still an important means of transportation in Tocanga in 1995 and 1996, particularly if hauling heavy goods was involved. Horses could best negotiate the hilly, rocky climbing pathways that connected the settlement to the main dirt road, which ran through the barangay on higher grounds, paralleling the island's shoreline. Without a horse, Tocanga was accessible mainly by the smallest of small pumpboats or bancas, or by walking trails.

We elected, at Ben's recommendation, to take a motorcycle into Tocanga on our first set of visits there. It was one of the best motorcycles on the island, a prize possession of Ben's NGO. To arrive by such a vehicle was to establish an image of authority equal to the highest ranks of the island's titled residents. The attempt at motorcycle entry, however, turned out to be a muddy disaster given the condition of the paths that led to the settlement, which had become soaked many inches deep in rainwater and overgrown with grasses and shrubs. We had so many near capsizings into jungle slime, and we arrived in such a disheveled state, that by the end of the first attempt I was more than ready to refuse ever to repeat the journey. However, this proved unnecessary, since even Ben's most virtuosic efforts behind the wheel did not manage to get us to the actual shoreline area of Tocanga, making motorcycle entry infeasible.

Figure 9. Tocanga Plaza.

Thereafter we traveled by pumpboat. We hired a weatherworn wooden banca with bamboo pole outriggers, eighteen inches wide at mid-hull. While it was completely unimpressive as a technological symbol, it kept us clean and dry and could accommodate four people if the owner, who was its pilot, sat on the rim by the engine. We headed out in this vehicle in the mornings from Kaputian's población beach park, about five kilometers north, the closest overnight accommodation available to us. It was a twenty-minute ride from Kaputian, if the water was calm.

The rented marine transport was not without its own foibles. Tocanga had no wharf, no harbor, no pier, and no deep water coastline or sandy beach. The reason one had to approach it in the smallest of small vessels was that one needed to be able to float on a few inches of water to get anywhere near a place to land on the sitio's coast. Otherwise, wading or being carried many meters to dry land was necessary. Even in a small banca, if the tide was low, the wade ashore over slippery, wobbly corals that covered Tocanga's tidal beach surface could take many minutes under the full strength of the scorching sun to complete. In sum, despite the master plans looming on the horizon, Tocanga at the time of the interviewing still existed as a part of a largely unmodernized private enterprise, more colonial than contemporary in design.

Tocanga's residents, however, and the narratives they generated in conversation with us bespoke a worldview that went far beyond the sitio's isolated and technologically undeveloped character. Their perspectives on the tourism estate in particular, each unique in various ways, evidenced an understanding of and identification with modernity, and with globalization, that would have seemed unthinkable, had not the whole of their lives, culturally and historically, been factored into their accounts. These lives went far beyond Tocanga.

In some ways Tocanga formed a most unlikely backdrop for the conversations we there enacted, even though it was the locus of the current tourism controversy, the place identified most concretely with the SLS cooperative, and the place where the touristic landscape planned for development was virtually palpable and perpetually present. Nonetheless, for the residents as for us, Tocanga was but one site on a geographical landscape that was understood in constant juxtaposition to many others, some of them foreign, most of them closer to home, and, not insignificantly, many of them formerly home, as often as not. Regardless, for the residents, Tocanga was currently home, or one home. This made all the difference in the world in terms of their understanding of the tourism development.

Pacifico Margoles

We met Pacifico Margoles on our first visit to Tocanga by boat, the first day we gained access to the Tocanga coastal settlement area. He was our first interviewee. This was no accident, although we were operating more or less at random at the time. We had begun the day by acting like newcomers, hanging around a storefront belonging to one of the more substantial wooden houses that bordered on the basketball court area, deciding to interview the first willing person we found inside. This turned out to be a social worker, from whom we first began inquiring generally about interview possibilities and then asked to interview. Determined to speak with us, however, Pacifico Margoles interrupted our interview attempt shortly after we had drawn up a rickety wooden bench and a couple of makeshift chairs and initiated it. He spotted us from somewhere nearby and came over to the house intent upon interjecting himself into the conversation.

Addressing us in English even though we had been speaking in Visayan, Pacifico Margoles interrupted our tape recording with several pointed questions to Ben about his NGO and its activities in Kaputian. The interrogation Pacifico Margoles launched into immediately took over the interaction, as it demanded that we defend our good will.

Mr. Margoles was a tall man in his mid-sixties. His face was weather-worn—I described him as "elderly" in my notes of that first meeting. He seemed a vigorous person by his actions, gate, and stance and there was power still evident in his speech. He moved with certainty and swiftness as he positioned himself among our little group, finding a place where he could quickly include all of us in a single scanning gaze, so as to gain and hold our collective attention.

After fielding his questions, Ben diplomatically asked if Pacifico Margoles would consent to be interviewed. He complied immediately. It seemed that he was not in principle opposed to our presence or activities, but, rather, was more intent on playing an integral role of some kind vis-à-vis them, whatever they might to be. He was determined, I surmised, to become our main contact in Tocanga, if we were going to have one. Moreover, speaking out on issues for the record was a job with which he evidently had some familiarity, and it was a task of which he clearly considered himself capable. There was no shyness in his manner, no hesitation in his acceptance. It was as though he'd been expecting such an invitation.

Once Mr. Margoles understood the focus of our study and our business in Tocanga, he launched into a lengthy discourse on the tourism project. After we had reoriented the tape recorder in his direction, he gave the topic his best effort, holding forth in a kind of miniature filibuster that went on for several minutes, prompted only by the question, "What is your name?" A small crowd gathered round to listen. He ended with the comment, "so that's it, that's all I can say." After several additional questions from us, however, he found considerably more to say. As he did so, he lapsed back into Visayan, still holding the little audience's attention for most of the rest of the interview. His manner softened gradually as we asked him more and more questions about his life and work on the island, steering further away from the more controversial topics of the present, which we returned to only at the end.

Pacifico Margoles turned out to be a rather exceptional personality. He was forthright, yet, after the initial opening salvo he fired, amicable. He seemed to feel entirely at home engaging us in conversation, as he did on that first occasion, and on virtually every opportunity that presented itself thereafter on the days of interviewing that followed. We would see him in passing as we were wading to and from shore, at our work day's beginning or end, when he was too busy with his own chores to stop and talk. He always had at least a smile and a wave or a good natured word or two for us, however, even though his interest in our project waned soon after his own statement had been documented. On occasion he supplied us with food—fresh chicken or fish—when we found ourselves short at mid-day, and once, when we were caught in a downpour, he gave us the shelter of his backyard porch, until a break in the weather let us cast off for Kaputian. He still lived in the sitio near the beach, although he'd reserved a lot in the relocation area for himself and his wife. Like a number of other SLS members, he was delaying his move, preferring to maintain life as usual until circumstances compelled him to do otherwise.

Mr. Margoles had been an active presence in Tocanga for several decades, since his arrival from Southern Leyte after "the independence day," as he put it, in 1949. His high-school education having been severed by the war, he had set out afterward to seek his fortune as a single man and had arrived on Samal Island at the time when the plantation's second group of *sakada* workers had just been hired. Sakada were workers recruited from Luzon, who had agreed to leave their families behind with a lump sum prepaid by the company, and travel alone at company expense to the plantation, in hopes of earning the money needed to bring the rest of the family along eventually. At that time the Fernández Hermános estate was small but expanding, employing about thirty-six laborers. Eventually it grew to support more than 500 families, Mr. Margoles reported.

At the time when Pacifico Margoles had made Tocanga his home, he had already left more than one home far behind. His original family home in Leyte he returned to only twice during the many decades he spent in Tocanga—once fifteen years after his departure and once much later, in 1991, on retiring. His relatives in Leyte had never come to visit him on Samal Island. They had been afraid, he said, of the island's "natives" as well as its "Muslims." Neither of these groups, he reported, had ever presented any real cause for fear, although they had certainly been in evidence in the early days. The Muslims, he recalled, had engaged in fishing; the "Samaleños," as he referred to the "natives," in upland farming. His relatives, however, had also been afraid of being infected with malaria, he reported, which he did not characterize as an unrealistic apprehension. In any case, the move to Tocanga had been a costly one in terms of the loss of his family of origin. He had been unable to be with either of his parents at the time of their deaths—he'd learned of their passing long after the fact on his second visit home—a loss that still saddened him. Tocanga, in Pacifico Margoles's perspective, was a settlement composed of persons like himself—a settlement of hardworking migrants willing to pay such personal prices—upwardly mobile people who had left home behind for the sake of employment and the opportunities it afforded. Now the same situation was coming true for his own family, as various of his children departed for jobs elsewhere, in the Philippines and beyond.

As his initial conduct with us had indicated, Pacifico Margoles had had some personal experience of what it meant to occupy a position of leadership. He had risen through the plantation ranks to the position of assistant overseer for the plantation after many years as a timekeeper and a laborer before that. He had earned 2,000 pesos monthly at the height of his career in the 1970s; he had been in charge of some 48 workers of the plantation's "Block 3." Several of the older residents in Tocanga had once been his subordinates. Tocanga had been a company town for most of its existence, complete with bunkhouses for the single men, he recalled.

Mr. Margoles had married Virginia Garcia, the daughter of a "cowboy" sakada, after a couple of years working on the plantation. Eventually we interviewed several members of the family, which consisted of himself, his wife, and nine children, all married. Three sons were still living in Tocanga. Another was in Saudi Arabia working as an electrician. There were also numerous grandchildren, one of them already starting a family in Tocanga as well. Through the circumstances of the family, Ben and I began to get a picture of family life in the sitio, which while not a wholly representative one was nonetheless illuminating of some general values and circumstances.

The Margoleses were a relatively enterprising and well-educated family. Pacifico Margoles had used his salary in part to send his children to school, placing a priority on obtaining education for his descendants that many of his neighbors expressed as well, although in many cases they could not realize it to the same extent. When told during the interview that he still looked quite healthy, he replied, "My job, because I had a little education, was to do payroll," he commented, speaking of the advantage education had given him in his own working life on the plantation. "That was my job for fifteen years. I just stayed in the office."[5] When asked what he hoped for as an outcome of the tourism development for his community, his first thought was that "the younger children will have a better life . . . they can send their children to school because they have jobs."[6] Among his sons in Tocanga were two high-school graduates—one who hoped to become a SITE security guard and the other a cook—and one college graduate in education from the University of Mindanao. This second generation, now raising children, were struggling to keep their own dependents in school. College education, of course, entailed leaving the sitio, one reason it was particularly difficult to finance.

As with many other multigenerational households, the awareness that times were much harder now for "the children" of the plantation sakadas was quite evident for the Margoleses. High-school graduation for Pacifico Margoles's grandchildren seemed possible but unlikely, although it was still recognized as a key factor in getting reliable employment. College, while greatly desired, seemed financially beyond the family's reach. Links to family and in-laws who were working abroad (America, Saudi Arabia, and Malaysia in the Margoles case), or in other areas of the Philippines (Surigao and Manila) were multiple and important in terms of supporting the extended family. Education was now the outcome of a transnational network, all of whom shared the realization that education brought with it the means of a better life. This global effort had not been the case in Pacifico Margoles's younger days. He had belonged to a generation in Tocanga when a hardworking couple could manage to send at least one, if not several, of their own children away to school themselves.

Mr. Margoles was a strong supporter of the SITE project, as were his sons. He announced this spiritedly in his initial English language remarks of the interview. "We are very happy now that our place belongs to a tourism area," he stated. He did, however, express sadness over the conflicts that had developed between those who were currently cooperative members and those who were not. He knew personally of many cases of former workers who had claims to beneficiary status but who were currently being denied membership. "My laborers," he referred to them. "[They thought] maybe the owner of the land will be angry because they are still working, so they did not apply to be a member of CARP." He understood the workers' reasons for delaying. The transition to cooperative status was by no means going perfectly in his view, and he did not deny that there was much unhappiness over the development. Like many others in the cooperative, he was concerned and frustrated, he said, about the current management of the SLS cooperative accounts and activities, and the fate of the 200 families already displaced who were no longer able to farm. However, despite the community tensions the formation of the cooperative had produced, Pacifico Margoles remained staunchly in favor of the DOT's general strategy.

He emphasized two main benefits to the project as the basis of his positive stance. In the first place, and most important, he believed the project would bring jobs and return prosperity to the location for his children and grandchildren to enjoy. "I believe," he commented, slightly more than midway through his opening speech,

Because this place is [becoming] a tourist spot . . . and we are also [being] given a place in [it], which we are given a relocation time. That's the time that we will [be able to] live here for many years. Maybe because . . . our children will be the workers for the investors in our place.

Pacifico Margoles was not himself anticipating employment in the establishments to come. His income currently came from a social security pension.

He had suffered a stroke in 1991, which had necessitated his retirement. He foresaw no change in his retired status, as it was his understanding that jobs in the tourism estate would be given to the young people in the coopera- tive's households primarily, those between the ages of twenty-one and forty. For the younger generations, however, he was optimistic that the SITE pro- ject would reestablish something like the good life that he had himself enjoyed for so much of his own time in Tocanga—when the plantation had been growing, unowned land had been available and cheap,[7] and the island's resources plentiful. Just as he had succeeded in being promoted up the ranks of the Fernández Hermános establishment, so he hoped Tocanga's current working class would be able to progress on the tourism estate. A continuity of employment practice was assumed in his optimistic outlook. At the end of the interview, he summarized this outlook when asked about his vision of the development's future, commenting,

I believe that this place will be developed and the people living here will have an eas- ier time because they will have employment. We—those of us who are already old— would be happy if the investors would come in sooner rather than later because then we would [also] be able to see the improvements they are going to make. We would just like to have a view of these, because the place will be beautiful if. . . . It really will be beautiful.[8]

Digressing to dwell on his own history, he recalled the days when the forests around Tocanga had still been in existence. The abundance of the forest environment dominated his memory of these times. "Before, it was a very forested place" he recalled, referring to the time when he had first arrived in Tocanga, prior to the days when the 889 hectares that constituted the entire Fernández Hermános property had eventually been planted with coconut trees. The plentiful food supply the forests supported came up repeatedly in his interview comments. "Monkeys and wild pigs came regu- larly to the seashore because there were few people who were living in the place," he stated. Later on in the interview, he elaborated,

The wild pigs here were still abundant. Also seashells on the shore, wild monkeys, pythons. For every five hectares we could easily find a snake. Sometimes they were nine meters in length. Often we found the *bagtak* [snake]. They would just lie in a coil because their stomachs were usually full—they had eaten already. . . . In those days, we still didn't eat them [snakes], because there were still other [sources of food] . . . there were fish.[8]

At another point during our question and answer period, he summarized his memories of the abundant food supply, remarking, "At that time there were a lot of fish here; a lot of shellfish and fresh fish. That's why the low pay was still OK because there were fish and also food from our farms—we had more than enough to eat from the farms."[10] The profuseness of the food supply emerged as a central theme in his characterization of his earli- est times in Tocanga. In the plantation's early days, a worker's salary could go mainly toward purchasing land or other long term life improvements, if he chose to spend it that way. Most basic needs were met without cost by the island's natural resources. No one ever thought of going hungry.

Pacifico Margoles had lived through several decades when these supportive environmental conditions had been enjoyed by the plantation workers in Tocanga. They had gradually deteriorated, however. By the 1980s the forests had been logged, the soil was depleted, and the population had more than doubled, outgrowing the dwindling natural resource base. By then, he recalled, there were no more pigs, no monkeys, no fish, and the coconut trees, now senile, produced less than half what they used to, as did the rice and corn. Now land was selling for a million pesos per hectare, impossible to buy even if it could have been farmed.[11] Now, he acknowledged, people were suffering. "The price of commodities now is relatively high," he observed, noting that these increases had prevented some of the families who had already opted to relocate from finishing the construction of their new homes. "The people here—we are really having difficulties,"[12] he reported at the end of the interview, noting that, in particular, those who had already left their farms to relocate inland but who were still waiting for the promised employment were in serious trouble. He saw the situation as an obvious outcome of the delays in the project:

Why wouldn't we be in bad shape when we have no more plants and farms since we already left the 250 hectares? About 200 families are in the relocation site. They are waiting for the investors so they will have jobs. They have no more farms so they can only go fishing or just work as laborers. That's why it would be good if the investors would come right away so that the people will not be experiencing any more hardship.[13]

Listening to Pacifico Margoles's narratives, both during his interview and in the days following, it became evident that there had actually been "good old days" in Tocanga, and they were well within his memory. His comments contained no trace of nostalgia, just facts that indicated the once plentiful natural resources available in the area were now gone. In the best days of operation, the plantation had maintained rotating harvesting strategies, harvesting coconuts continuously throughout the year, 35 to 40 tons a month. It had developed a policy of produce sharing that had enabled the workers to prosper, when the soil was still able to support them. The plantation had paid the laborers 250 pesos for each tree planted on plantation land—a handsome sum in the postwar era—in addition to the 2.50 peso daily wage. Those days, however, were gone. Pacifico Margoles had no illusions about the agricultural times changing for the better at any point soon.

Now, in the present moment, with that plantation history in mind, he saw in tourism a new industry capable of replenishing the exhausted economy, bringing with it new forms of livelihood accessible to Tocanga's younger generations. "My wish now is that my children will be able to find employment in tourism,"[14] he admitted, when Ben asked what his hopes were for the community now that it was involved in the tourism development. He praised the DOT in this regard, remarking in his opening English language comments that recently

our children were invited by the DOT to have seminars in Davao. So we are proud enough that, before the [arrival] of the investors, our children will learn something [about] what is actually going to happen when Ekran Berhad comes here. Because [of this training] it is they [our children who] will construct the motor pool, the hotels and everything. So, we are proud.

One of Pacifico Margoles's sons, with his strong encouragement, had been involved in the DOT-sponsored training programs, taking out a loan from the cooperative to pay for his share of the expenses. Again, education—this time in the form of vocational training—was perceived as the key to successful integration into the new economy. The DOT's provision of this training was taken as compelling evidence of its intention to make good on its commitments to the SLS cooperative.

Pacifico Margoles mentioned Ekran Berhad by name several times during the interview and expressed some familiarity with the company's plans for the estate. The firm clearly had become a household name to him, one with positive associations. He was by no means hostile to or unfamiliar with the idea of nonlocal investors developing the area. This had been the case with the Fernández Hermános plantation, and he had done well in that operation, enjoying the experience of increasing financial gain and company authority and responsibility. There was in his view no reason to doubt that the new investors, albeit somewhat more foreign this time than before, would prove any less viable as employers. "All members are quite proud and very happy that this place will be cultivated by the foreigners," he stated emphatically in the opening segment of his interview. The project did not represent an unknown form of takeover or the dismantling of some once-local enterprise or livelihood. Rather, it appeared as an enhanced renovation, a contemporary upgrade, of a long-established means of doing business and creating employment.

Along these same lines of enhancement, the second major benefit Pacifico Margoles perceived in the tourism development concerned the arrangement negotiated by the DOT with Ekran Berhad that had established the SLS cooperative as a partner in the holding corporation which ostensibly owned and managed the estate. This granting of partial ownership to the cooperative membership offset any sense of foreign domination in Margoles's view, and the value of its occurrence for him could not be underestimated. Midway through his opening interview comments, he made this point, remarking,

this land now is owned by the actual laborers and this was supported by the DOT in negotiating [with the] foreigners as an investor. That's what produced the 47 million. And it so happened that this land was fully paid [for] by the members of the coop. [It was] because of the money which was given to us by Ekran Berhad, which they will [use to] cultivate this place.

Again, as he concluded his initial interview monologue, Pacifico Margoles reflected on what might have happened had the tourism estate not come to pass, asserting that ownership would not otherwise have come about. "As long as I have lived here," he posited, "we have been living a hand-to-mouth existence, because we are just only tenants." The "just" in his comment was conspicuously placed. Its inclusion signified as well as reinforced the inferior status "tenants" held in his perspective, a status that destined the community to a life without security. "But now," he continued, "we are the owners of the land," and he put a stress on the word "owners" in a way that expressed both conviction and triumph with regard to how extraordinary that change in identity was in his opinion.

There was no doubt, on hearing him utter these words, that this transformation from tenants to owners represented for Pacifico Margoles the single most important effect of the tourism development, and that it was a development of truly fundamental benefit to the community in his view. He could not have been more in earnest in his manner of making this point, his tone of voice having had the ring of a man making a case before a disinterested party, completely convinced of his argument's merits. With this thought, he brought his own initial statement to a close. He returned to the idea, however, in the question and answer portion of the interview, when we asked him about his dreams for the future, assuming the development was a success. "I would never have believed that Samal could become like this [so much improved],"[15] he replied, framing the development once again in positive terms. He then returned to the ownership theme, as he continued, "During all my time living here, I have never been able to buy a good-sized piece of land for myself. . . . Nothing at all. I only have acquired some land now . . . through CARP."[16] Having been a tenant all his working life in Tocanga, he placed the greatest value in the ownership that had been transferred to the occupants of the SITE project as a result of the cooperative's establishment.

Pacifico Margoles's perspective on the tourism development emphasized both parallels and contrasts between the conditions he had experienced in his work with the Fernández Hermános plantation and those envisioned for the tourism development. On the whole, he expected to see positive developments unfold with the Ekran Berhad investment: new jobs, new opportunities, new prosperity. With the added benefit of ownership, the status of the new generation of employees would be transformed from one of subordinate occupants to one of landed equals in his view. This contrast to his own working situation created a significant advance for Tocanga's current generation of workers and signaled social progress to him. The terms in which he evaluated and understood the tourism estate were thus derived from the practices of the former plantation in which he had participated for the better part of his life.

Clarita Dugno

Nearly two weeks after the interview with Pacifico Margoles, on October 25, 1995, Ben and I interviewed Clarita Dugno. The interview took place during our second visit to the SLS cooperative's residence relocation area. The area was still in a largely preliminary phase of development, with only about seventy of the several hundred households ultimately scheduled to transfer there as yet having begun the process of doing so. Nonetheless, we decided that we should try to do some interviewing there, in order to get a sense of how the estate development was perceived by people who now had actually been displaced. Mrs. Dugno was one of those individuals.

The plans to interview at the relocation site did not work out well for a number of reasons. First, the hike into the area, up the only trail, was not an easy one. The small road that started it out went up very steeply, through largely unshaded bush. It was so steep that not even a motorcycle (not even Ben's motorcycle) could traverse it. On our first assent, I heard Ben starting to sing "Climb Every Mountain," when we were about halfway up, after the road had become a narrow coral pathway. For my part, I wondered how whole houses might possibly already have been built in the area above, if this trail was the only access route. There seemed to be no means of getting equipment, let alone large pieces of furniture, into the area. The general impression I gathered from the few visits we made to the area was that the occupants were indeed exhausted. It was not an ideal atmosphere in which to pursue discussions of tourism, to say the least.

Even more difficult than the problem of access was the more general social environment we encountered at the site. The settlement consisted at this point of nothing other than a patchwork of small, 10 or 20 by 30 meter lots, some dotted with small wood plank houses and others vacant. These residences—the only built environment that as yet existed—were strikingly unlike the sitio's homes, mainly because of their recently finished, or as yet unfinished condition. They stood in the open sun, their galvanized iron roofs unsheltered by any trees that might at some point be planted for that purpose. They were trim and uniform in structure, with no makeshift additions or ad hoc constructions complicating their split level boxlike designs. In contrast to the sitio's dwellings, around which distinctive clutters of useful and enjoyable objects had long since formed—pots, toys, tools, odd pieces of cement, wood, netting, clotheslines, and so on—the relocation area's houses had only the barest minimum, or literally nothing, in the way of exterior furnishings, which gave their freshly painted and well-built facades a stark, institutional appearance. Their gardens, neatly laid out and cared for, were as yet composed entirely of new plantings. Carob-colored,

Figure 10. Relocation route.

bone-dry top soil was all that was visible on many surfaces. The garden's' split rail boundary fences were bare of any covering as well. No ornamental graces except an occasional flower bed softened the area's structures, again in stark contrast to the sitio, where orchids and bougainvillea cascaded from available niches and various kinds of large-leafed bushes were placed strategically around buildings so as to mask their louvered windows, whether wooden or plastic, from the heat.

The cumulative effect of all these features of the relocation area dwellings was offputting. Establishing fundamental necessities was obviously still the focus of the residents' activities. It was not a relaxed environment in which people could take time off to pause and reflect. Also, aside from the condition of the homes themselves, there was nothing like the plaza/basketball court area of the older sitio to use as a gathering place. There were no sarisari stores with benches set out to accommodate passersby. There were no shaded tables or rattan-fashioned rest gazebos built to accommodate trade or a collective meal. There was no unowned no-man's-land for general use. There was no hint, in other words, of any kind of life other than that of the minimized domestic spheres. It appeared as a more or less lifeless settlement in this collective regard, like a ghost town, strikingly different from the shoreline, where a certain amount of circulation and neighborly interaction was more or less in constant process. The people who were in

Figure 11. Relocation homes

residence in the relocation area remained inside their houses, encamped on their tiny properties, generally preoccupied with various ongoing construction projects, or just tending to their own housekeeping as best they could.

After a few visits to the area, it became clear that the chances of worthwhile conversation with residents were much greater if we met off the site in more congenial contexts. Nonetheless, a half dozen interviews did result from our forays up the trail—and Clarita Dugno's was one of the most informative of these.

We spoke inside Mrs. Dugno's house, for lack of a viable outdoor alternative. She and her husband had been assigned a 10 by 30 meter lot, the exact location determined by a raffle in which all the cooperative members relocating had participated. The house was built of dark, rough wooden planks on a cement foundation with a galvanized iron sheet roof. It consisted of three square rooms designed in an L shape, each room around three meters on a side with a ceiling four meters overhead. There was one room for cooking, an elevated room for sleeping, and a front living room with the main door. We sat in the front room, on a low wooden bench—the only piece of furniture in the room that day. Clarita Dugno sat on the small set of stairs that went up to the sleeping room in front of a curtain that served as its door. The rest of the room was empty, except for a dusty television on a makeshift shelf in one corner, a lamp, and a wall clock. Two calendars decorated the otherwise bare walls. Yellow curtains hung from the single wood-shuttered window, which was open. No one stopped by to listen and no crowd gathered as we talked. We conducted the interview alone with Clarita Dugno, whose opinions about the tourism development project were in many ways diametrically opposed to those of Pacifico Margoles. She expressed them, however, with equal certainty, clarity of detail, and conviction.

Her life history was in some ways parallel to his. She was sixty-six years old—another member of the Philippines's Commonwealth generation. Her husband, who was eighty-two, had lived through even more of the period of American rule. They had come to Samal Island, however, only in the era of independence, in 1956, slightly later than Pacifico Margoles, by way of Manila. The Dugnos had met in Manila shortly after the end of the Second World War, when the city was still in ruins but employment was available. They had started a family and remained in Manila for several years. Neither was from Manila originally. Like Pacifico Margoles, they were from Leyte, but Clarita had spent many years as well in Surigao, on Mindanao Island's northern tip. Like many other residents of Tocanga, the Dugnos had set up homes in several places in the Philippines, urban and rural. Eventually they moved to Samal Island in search of the opportunity to farm. Here, however, they had not moved on. They had prospered and been able to raise seven children, all now married and still in the Mindanao region. Three of the children had moved to other lots at the relocation area when the family farm had had to be vacated.

Clarita Dugno's earlier living situation had been somewhat different from Pacifico Margoles's in that before the SITE project the Dugno family had not been based in Tocanga proper—"at the shore" as she phrased it[17]—but had occupied plantation lands inland. Clarita Dugno recalled the plantation's previous decades much as Margoles had. She described the abundance of the plantation[18] and the times when her family had lived in comfort, with her married children occupying lands adjacent to those she and her husband had farmed. "The owners were not strict," she recalled, speaking of the plantation's management of the tenants.[19] Tenant farmers had not been expected to pay the company a share of cassava or bananas they harvested on land they themselves had cleared, even though it was company land, and they could even harvest coconuts off company trees for their own use. The Dugnos had planted some of the original coconut trees on the plantation, under a general agreement that Clarita Dugno still considered to have been fair and advantageous to all involved. The company had never exacted any dues from them. "We had a good life then, that's true," she summarized, "We raised livestock, poultry and hogs. It was very easy. We also raised cattle. . . . No one could say that we struggled."[20] Her estimation of the plantation existence was, if anything, more positive than Pacifico Margoles's, even though she had occupied a relatively vulnerable and dependent position in the plantation economy. It was that position, however, that in the current transition would become the main source of her difficulties.

The loss of their farm, with the abundant produce and livestock they had been able to raise there for so many decades, weighed heavily on Clarita Dugno's mind. Unlike Pacifico Margoles, she had never entered "retirement," and all she had worked for since she had moved to Samal Island was still actively tied up in the farming she had done. There was currently no possibility of farming at the relocation area for the Dugno family, or for any one else there. Their lots were too small even to raise chickens, let alone pigs or cattle. "Even if you raise poultry here, you won't benefit since there are so many neighbors," she commented: "They would just go lay their eggs just anywhere. I used to have a small chicken here. . . . It just went everywhere. It laid eggs but the chicks died later. That's how our situation is here. Difficult. We are really hard up here."[21]

Their only cultivation project now was raising flowers, which she had taken on in hopes that this would qualify her for work as a gardener on the tourism estate. She had heard this was the only type of work the older cooperative members might obtain at the new development. The flowers blooming around her house represented her main hope of future employment for herself and her husband. As for the present, there was literally nothing she could do to contribute to the household income. "Nobody has a job yet. The promise was that jobs would be available, but nothing has come of it yet," she reported, and added, "This is the situation here; you can ask anyone—it's the same for everyone."[22] This assessment was indeed borne out by the other interviews we conducted.

Unlike Pacifico Margoles, Clarita Dugno entertained a strong interest in contributing to the family's income through continuing to work—she had no pension to contribute, and she and her husband had given the money they had been paid by the cooperative for their last crop to their children as an early inheritance. This left them in need of further income, but with no resources to do so. "Here we have nothing left," she summarized, and then added the question, "How could you make a living here? That's our situation here. Really. We can only wait for somebody to give us work." To express the insult she felt directed specifically at her age group as a consequence of this disabling situation, she added bitterly, "The elderly will eventually be made into canned salmon . . . or maybe a coconut milk dish. It might be possible to cook [us] with coconut milk—that's how our life is here, that's the truth."[23]

The absence of any opportunity to generate income from farming was particularly difficult for Clarita Dugno to accept, given that the farm she and her family had vacated was not currently under development and so was in the same condition as when they had stopped working on it. She reported this to be a source of complaint generally among those in the resettlement area, and, again, our research bore her out. The lands they had vacated were not yet being developed by the government, but they were also not being made available to their previous occupants to farm. "The first chairman told us," she reported with some frustration, "'if you relocate, even if you move to the relocation area, you still can make copra; you can still harvest food—bananas—even if you were already paid [through the disturbance fee] for the plants, because the land is not as yet being developed.' But now, it's not happening."[24] The coconut trees the Dugno family had for so many years managed on their former farm had become the property of the cooperative, and the current SLS chairman had decided that other members of the cooperative would have the opportunity to harvest them. Complaints had arisen over who had been chosen for this purpose, as the lucky ones included many members of the chairman's own family. One of Clarita Dugno's sons also had been fortunate enough to have been granted this privilege and to continue harvesting some of their land. However, the share of produce given to the cooperative was much larger than that taken in the old days of the plantation—more than 50 percent of the harvest. Even more disturbing, the cooperative collected everything produced initially, supposedly to repay the laborers on an installment basis, which in her son's case had not in fact occurred. In this regard, the tourism development project had resulted in a consolidation of profits from the lands of the previous laborers into the hands of the cooperative leadership.

Unlike Pacifico Margoles, neither Clarita Dugno nor her husband had risen up the ranks of the plantation work force. Their farming had been their entire livelihood, and their stake in the use of the land was thus even greater. The delay in construction and the contrast in management styles between the plantation management and the SLS cooperative loomed much larger in her perspective on the tourism estate than they had in Margoles's, and, while the details were much the same in both narratives, they led to a much more negative evaluation for her than for him. She understood herself to be further from ownership than ever before, as she was forced to watch property she had long managed as her own, property she had even been able to turn over to her children, being granted to others. "Our way of life was really good," she said, summing up her own life as a laborer. She continued:

We had plenty of livestock then, since my own children were our neighbors. . . . Our occupation? twelve hectares of land. . . . Not really [that large] since we divided it among the children. We gave each of them three hectares . . . . That was really our situation then; it was more comfortable than here.[25]

When discussing the details of the relocation process, Clarita Dugno's comments made it even more painfully clear how the transference of residence had taken a negative toll. On the surface the compensation for households vacating their farmlands looked generous, but it was proving to be inadequate, given the current absence of tourism sector employment. A "disturbance pay" of as much as 40,000 pesos had accompanied a construction allowance set at 30,000 pesos for every relocation area household. In order to avoid depleting these payments while waiting for jobs, some younger family members were now traveling into Davao City and nearby areas to look for employment opportunities. Other families, Clarita Dugno reported, were living off the interest or the capital of what was left over from their resettlement payments. Others had had to shift over entirely to fishing in order to generate income. The lack of employment was everyone's main concern, and it was a problem to which she returned again and again in her interview, in contrast to Pacifico Margoles, who had barely touched on the issue. "If you interview others, you will find this is really the situation," she said at one point, "Work is what is needed here—truly, what I'm saying here is that work is really the important thing."[26] Again, her assertion proved generally accurate.

The chairman of the cooperative, according to Clarita Dugno, had at one point promised to start projects for members to raise poultry and pigs on cooperative lands, giving them some control over their food supply. He had also promised to deliver a sack of rice to each family every month until employment was available (Margoles had mentioned this promise as well). But none of this had happened, she reported. Instead, the chairman had criticized the members for having spent their disturbance pay improperly, buying home entertainment equipment instead of saving the maximum amount against future uncertainties. The chairman blamed them in this way for their own hard times, she reported. "The chairman actually said, 'you bought karaoke and TV sets—you didn't manage your money properly,'" she remarked midway through the interview, her incredulity over this statement plainly evident.[27]

The most local level of management related to the tourism development dominated Clarita Dugno's outlook. While Pacifico Margoles had virtually ignored the chairmen and their activities and focused on the institutions involved in the tourism estate, the different SLS cooperative chairmen's individual roles in the tourism development were characterized as highly significant and reported in detail in Clarita Dugno's comments. She was particularly resentful of the present chairman's criticisms, given what she viewed as the unequal distribution of the cooperative's resources, and the intrusive, patronizing attitude toward household decision-making processes that they represented.

The house built by the Dugnos had cost 35,000 pesos to construct and included only the barest necessities. Although the materials used were not the cheapest, they were of modest quality. In addition to the 40,000-peso disturbance pay and 30,000 in construction assistance, they had also been given a "bonus" of 10,000 pesos in December 1994, which was the only payment they had used to buy their TV (they had no karaoke). Regarding this purchase, she pointed out that they knew they could resell it if they needed to.

They were living on the interest of 35,000 pesos they had deposited in the bank while they waited for the SITE project to come through with its promised employment opportunities. In Clarita Dugno's view, there had been no mismanagement of the payments they had received. Neither was it the role of the chairman to pass judgment on their interest in acquiring some of the electronic equipment so commonly associated with good fortune and prosperity. "If I'd been there [when the chairman made his reproachful comment], I would have told him, 'It's none of your business what we do, because the money belongs to us!'" she stated emphatically.[28]

Concerning the management of the cooperative's capital, she not surprisingly expressed many more doubts than had Pacifico Margoles. "The year is almost over, yet we still don't know what our share [of the cooperative's holdings] amounts to, how much interest our money has earned—we don't know where he [the chairman] has it deposited,"[29] she complained at one point. Her sense of shared ownership in the cooperative's assets was as certain as Margoles's, and she spoke of the twenty-two million pesos reportedly on deposit for the cooperative as "our money."[30] At the same time, she was far more concerned about the actual value of this capital than about the symbolic advances of ownership it had represented so importantly for Pacifico Margoles. The rumors of a plan to divide the capital among the members had reached her, and she was in favor of this strategy, if an audit accounting for all subsequent expenditures could be conducted. "[It is better] than if only one person benefits,"[31] she reasoned, referring to the chairman's current activities.

Clarita Dugno suspected that several million pesos of the original capital investment might have been misspent and wanted a complete report of the expenditures before accepting that the amount left was the only source from which she was entitled some share. She interpreted the resistance of some of the cooperative leadership to the plan to divide the capital as suspect in this regard. She speculated that they wanted to avoid dividing the capital so as to continue drawing from it for their own enrichment. "They will make [the capital] their milking cow," she stated. "Haven't they been milking it already? There are those on the Board of Directors who wouldn't agree to divide the capital. They don't want it divided because they want to milk it."[32]

Clarita Dugno also had formed no optimistic scenario of a sustainable partnership for development in the long run between Ekran Berhad, DOT, and the SLS cooperative. She was not yet convinced that such a partnership, or such a development, was actually ever going to come to pass. She had not translated the plantation's prosperous collective past into the tourism estate's supposed future as Pacifico Margoles had done. When Ben asked her to describe her own vision of tourism, what she imagined when she thought about the industry in general terms, she summarized her thinking about the project and the ambiguities it presented without a concrete response. Instead, she answered by returning to her theme of unrealized employment: "What I can say about tourism is that it's for the best, for the best for the people. This is because it will provide employment. However, now it's not yet happening."[33]

Ben pressed the issue of tourism's character further, asking her to describe the distinctive features or "form" ("porma") of tourism. To this more specific inquiry, however, she responded, "We don't really know. Nothing. . . . Not yet, really nothing yet. . . . It's only something that will be in our best interests . . . that's what we were told."[34] She returned to this idea at the end of her interview as well, when Ben asked her for a closing statement. She replied, "Nothing. We don't have anything to say about the project because we don't know what it is."[35]

The logic of the planners' choice of location for SITE was also not apparent. When Ben asked why the tourism project had been located in the area, she replied, "We don't really know the reason why,"[36] and verified that no reason for constructing the project, other than that it was for the welfare of the people and would give them jobs, was ever mentioned by anyone involved. The BIMP-EAGA landscape had yet to become a salient part of her own worldview, which, as her interview comments generally indicated, was still oriented around the Philippine archipelago, independent of other regions and countries. Clarita Dugno had not acquired the sense of the ASEAN growth triangle that was so much on the minds of the DOT and the

Ramos administration. Without this vision of the region's transformation, SITE's location remained more or less a mystery, an arbitrary choice. Her faith in the eventual success of the project was far from certain. From her relatively "local" point of view, the motivation for SITE's presence and the rationale for its success were not evident, let alone compelling.

The alternative to a division of the cooperative's existing capital, in Clarita Dugno's perspective, was thus not necessarily a prosperous future sharing the profits from the tourism estate. The much more likely alternative was to continue watching others in the cooperative profit unfairly at her expense and the expense of the membership, until ultimately nothing was left. Particularly galling were the board members themselves, as their salaries were several thousand pesos a month each—enormous sums compared to the meager earnings of the members, who were reduced to going without rice or fish for days at a time, living on cassava and bananas, while waiting for some means of generating income. Clarita Dugno characterized the chairman's cost to the cooperative in harsh but accurate terms:

> He [the chairman] grabs all the jobs. As a result, people are reacting against him sometimes. His workers are his children. . . . As chairman, he receives 7,000 pesos salary—5,000 from the cooperative and 2,000 from PTA [Philippine Tourism Authority]. . . . That's why people are complaining. They are thinking that he might already have made a provision for himself, [in case] the money is divided.[37]

As she was commenting on the actions of the current chairman, she noted that he had arrived in the area many years after she and many of the plantation workers had, and was a relative newcomer. He had occupied no land in the barangay and had never planted anything. "He always lived by the shore," she observed. "He bought lumber and produced charcoal."[38] Yet, she continued, he had been included as a CARP beneficiary on an equal footing with those who had cleared and planted the land. She questioned the legitimacy of the chairman's status in this regard. Despite the fact that the cooperative membership tended to have a mobile residence history that was occupationally driven, there was still a sense of community among the residents, she believed, which derived from their shared history of working the land for a period now spanning several generations. This was a history that Pacifico Margoles had not identified in his comments, even though he had been deeply concerned with the idea of ownership as a benefit for former tenants. There was a local identity assumed in Clarita Dugno's comments, defined not in terms of the presence or absence of legal property ownership but rather in terms of a continuity of labor.

For Clarita Dugno, in sum, life at the relocation area was nothing other than a deadly waiting game, whose end, given the arbitrariness of the development, was more than likely to be negative. In contrast to Pacifico Margoles, she felt that she and others had been foolish when they gave up access to former farm lands, since access to a farmer—tenant or not—

meant everything. The promises of employment were far from trustworthy, and the lack of current employment and unfair profit sharing canceled out any benefit of titular "ownership" the members supposedly possessed. Tourism had not yet proven itself a worthwhile venture. Far from it, its promise had been all but completely extinguished by the hardships and losses of the present situation. When Ben asked her overall impression of the tourism development, she responded without hesitation, "The project has been a disturbance for the people."[39] Even if the most recent schedule for development were adhered to and a resort opened in a year's time, she didn't see any way to survive the interim on the existing resources. Toward the end of her interview, she summarized her outlook, again emphasizing employment as a vital necessity:

Certainly, the main need of the people is work. Nothing else. It is work that people are really waiting for. If the tourism project does develop, and they can just get work, everything will be good. People won't be so hungry. But if this goes on until next year, we won't make it. Really, nothing will be left. . . . [We'll be] dead. That's when people will go over to Davao to work—in a different place where they can get something [to provide] for their families. That's our situation here.[40]

Clarita Dugno's position as a former farming tenant on the plantation, with the dependence on season to season productivity it entailed, had generated a pessimistic and highly "local" perspective on the tourism estate. The limbo of the present moment had undermined any basis for good faith about the future, regardless of the past.

Paolo Lopéz

In the generation of "the children" of Pacifico Margoles and Clarita Dugno, in the generation born in the era of pre-Marcos independence—the "Magsaysay babies"[41] as it were—the most knowledgeable individual we interviewed in Kaputian regarding the SITE project was Paolo Lopéz. He was thirty-nine years old in 1995 and a native of Kaputian. His name was first suggested to us by one of the SLS barangay captains, but Ben recognized it immediately as well from some earlier interactions with the cooperative and agreed that we should definitely seek him out.[42]

Paolo Lopéz's family history was similar to those of Pacifico Margoles and Clarita Dugno. He was one of eight children born on Samal Island to a couple, now long established, who had migrated from elsewhere in the central Philippines. In his case, however, the family was not from Leyte but from Bohol Island, off Leyte's southwestern shore on the northern border of the Mindanao Sea. Bohol was close to Leyte geographically, as both were to northeastern Mindanao, but ethnically and linguistically it was quite distinct. Several parts of its landscape, both on its coasts and in its interior, had already been appropriated by the tourism matrix as well. Its inhabitants, which the guidebooks unfailingly described as "friendly," often humorously referred to themselves as "the Texans of the Philippines," in recognition of their extraordinary sense of regional pride and their history of resistance to Spanish colonial rule. Paolo López's parents had moved to Samal Island in 1937, a few years in advance of its main migratory waves and, critically, before the Japanese occupation. They had arrived during Davao's "time of abaca," and had done well for themselves, eventually acquiring more than 35 hectares of land under legal title in Kaputian, in addition to working land on the Fernández Hermános plantation. They had never raised abaca, however, and never suffered its loss. Their farms had produced coconuts and corn—the coconut trees grown from Fernández Hermános seedlings.

Paolo López, now married and with five children of his own, was helping manage the land for his parents as they grew older. The property now stood to be divided between more than twenty descendants on the parents' death. The first time we tracked him down to request an interview he was emerging alone from one of the family cornfields, leading a large beast of burden, appearing in no respect different from the many farm laborers we had encountered around the island's interior. He was no ordinary farmer, however. He had been a key player in SITE's early history and was a former chairman of the SLS cooperative board.

We spoke with Paolo López on two occasions at his Kaputian residence, which was located inland, at the intersection of two main barangay roads and across the street from a large elementary school. It was a busy place at a center of rural yet modern life, far upland from Kaputian's isolated shoreline. Tocanga's relatively depressed landscape and its SLS cooperative troubles seemed a distant memory here, and certainly only one of many current events transpiring in the locality. The noise of the school and the road traffic created a more or less constant din throughout the conversations and served to distract our attention, along with a couple of dogs and a chicken that occasionally passed through the front room where we sat talking. Most distracting for the interview, however, was the swarm of more than twenty children, evidently on recess, who pressed in at every aperture of the house to witness the occasion of a foreigner having a conversation with their neighbor. The children as well as the house animals periodically needed shooing away (invariably ineffectually), whenever the web their bodies gradually formed became too oppressive. Paolo López attended to this task, although only when the situation reached extremes that made concentration completely impossible and then with the mildest of gestures. He presented quite a contrast to Pacifico Margoles in this regard, relatively unassuming and unassertive in his general conduct and demeanor.

The house was weatherworn but in solid condition. It was obviously many years old and not built of the most durable or expensive materials. Its walls were of dark rough wood and it had a smooth cement floor. It was furnished to the full extent it could be—in striking contrast to the relocation area home of Clarita Dugno—with wooden bookshelves, tables, and chairs. There were no high-tech entertainment appliances in sight—no karaoke stations gathering dust. Several calendars adorned its interior walls, and seashells, a clock, a guitar, and some plants, drawings, and dishes were stacked, hung, shelved, and otherwise placed on almost every available surface. The house had had ample time to accumulate its fair share of modest belongings. They had reached a density that gave the building the appearance of a longtime family home.

Paolo Lopéz's perspective on the SITE tourism development project was unique. Having served in a leadership position during SITE's earliest years, he had participated in the initial negotiations in 1992 with the Department of Tourism officials and their associated personnel. His experience of all the forces at play in the development project—local, national, and foreign—was personal. He had himself reviewed the baseline and topographic surveys and the master plans for the project. He had sat face to face with the representatives of Ekran Berhad and the Ramos administration. He remembered the exact figures of the lease agreements he himself had signed. He remembered the telephone call "from Malacañang" that had ultimately pushed the negotiations through. He was capable of discussing the project employing the same development models the government officials in charge of SITE were using, but he was far more acutely attuned to the specificities of the municipality and its barangays. He knew the list of cooperative members more or less by heart, the names representing familiar faces and characters to him. He had dealt on a day to day basis with the cooperative membership, the barangay officials, and the municipal government. They had all been a part of his life for as long as he could remember. He also knew the resettlement area intimately—he could describe how it had been divided, exactly how many lots it contained, and where its road (already surveyed, he reported) was supposed to pass whenever it might be built. His expressed views on the tourism estate were heavily charged with a sense of his own role in the project and of his responsibility to his home community.

Paolo Lopéz's personal history also added to the uniqueness of his perspective on the tourism estate. "I am used to being poor" (*Anad man akoy ug pinobre*), he remarked at the end of his first interview, but his record of achievement contradicted this statement in any but the most material sense of the words. He was one of the island's tiny minority of homegrown college graduates, holding a bachelor of science degree in marine technology. He had been trained in community organizing and grass roots agricultural development as well; thus he was not only a scientist but an experienced social worker. Like Pacifico Margoles, he placed education in the foreground of his comments. He was the only interviewee who went so far in his thinking as to link an educational agenda directly to the tourism estate itself, expressing a desire to see the SLS cooperative develop a scholarship program for its membership with some of its capital. He was acutely aware of the atypical nature of his education vis-à-vis his home community, and he repeatedly raised the issue of the municipality's low levels of educational attainment in his interviews, which he described in percentage figures that generally matched those of provincial surveys.

Paolo Lopéz had not filed as a CARP beneficiary at the first opportunity, although the small amount of land his family had farmed on the Fernández Hermános plantation had qualified him to participate. He had applied late, on the request of some people in the municipality who were at that time intent on making him an officer in the cooperative. Seeing this as an opportunity for community organizing, he said, he decided to get involved. Unlike those of many of the other late applicants, his application had been accepted and he had become an SLS cooperative member without complications. He viewed the cooperative membership as problematic in this respect and noted, much as Clarita Dugno had done, how diverse the situations of the individual members actually were. "Nearly 60 percent of those [who benefited] were not longtime residents of this place," he commented. "They were just lucky because during the time CARP was implemented, they were already there [on the plantation lands]."[43] He reported that eventually he himself had been branded a newcomer and cast as an intruder by some of the people in the cooperative, despite his having been a lifetime Kaputian resident.

The misrepresentations and denials of local identity generated by the opportunities of the government programs were not trivial insults to Paolo Lopéz or those he had initially represented in the cooperative. They were egregious assaults on personal character traits and familial history, unjustified and injurious. His initial involvement had been an attempt to prevent this kind of misrepresentation from causing tensions in Kaputian. He had, however, been unsuccessful in the long run and had fallen prey to such accusations himself.

His narrative of the tourism estate, set in the context of the municipality's history, differed significantly from those of his neighbors in both detail and conception. Perhaps most striking, he did not see the development project as existing primarily in opposition to the Fernández Hermános enterprise. The two-era history other residents had spontaneously generated—the plantation days followed by the tourism project—was not conceptualized by Paolo Lopéz. Instead, looking back, he located SITE along a double-helix-like historical continuum conceived in terms of twin spiraling strands of social and economic progress and regress. The occupational history that had loomed so large in other accounts was replaced by an awareness of growth in the municipality's civic life, which had happened in his lifetime in more or less five-year cycles and spiraled steadily upward. "The population was really tiny; the school only went through the fourth grade," he remarked in his first interview, speaking of times from his earliest memory. "It was during the 1970's that a full elementary school was established, which occurred along with an increase in the population."[44] Changes had gradually occurred in Kaputian, with various infrastructural improvements following in the early 1980s and stabilizing "peace and order" efforts in the late 1980s. These had brought about an end to the shootings and other forms of violence characteristic of the late Marcos and early Aquino administrations. Now, the early 1990s had presented once again a new cycle of progressive change.

In somewhat ironic juxtaposition, however, Paolo Lopéz presented an economic counter-narrative that formed the other, in his view downwardly spiraling, strand of Kaputian's history. Along this continuum he charted the devaluation of commodities sold by local farmers, as prices for supplies and services had risen periodically over the decades. He quoted the changes in the price of transporting a sack of copra the three kilometers from his barangay to the municipal port as an illustration of the problems small farmers in that local industry had faced. He himself had diversified into a charcoal business in order to generate more income, but this option, he knew, was not available to all. The result of the twin strands of social upgrading and economic downgrading was a kind of ironic stasis. "A reversal is happening now," he commented:

> The school is close but it's not possible [to attend] because there is no money. In earlier times, the schools were far away, off in Davao City, but it was really possible to support attending them—if there was really an interest. The only problem was that it was difficult to find a place to stay there.[45]

Families that had once lacked schools and transportation but not the means to send their children away for education now had the institutions and infrastructure in place locally, but could not afford to use them, needing the labor of the children to survive in the present economy. Life remained difficult (*kalisud*) in Kaputian, in Paolo Lopéz's viewpoint, but it had always been so. The sources of the difficulty had simply shifted.

A similar intertwined vision of economic, political, and social factors organized his comments about the present status of the tourism development as well as its future. SITE presented an opportunity for economic growth in his view. He gave one example of SITE's positive consequences thus far, describing the case of a locally managed tourism destination he had planned for development in coordination with the larger international estate. "Take for instance the tourism site in San Isidro," he said: "The plan to develop [the site for tourism] is beautiful because there is a really pretty creek there. . . . The people themselves will be the ones to develop it. This will make it all the more an attraction to visitors."[46] Tourism definitely had the potential to transform Kaputian's landscape for the better, and residents could be in charge of this, in Paolo Lopéz's view.

He was painfully aware, however, that the SLS cooperative was currently in serious trouble. "Its condition is pitiful,"[47] he stated in his first interview, after a detailed discussion about the current lapses in financial accounting and reporting procedures. His concerns about the current management of the cooperative echoed those of Pacifico Margoles and Clarita Dugno. They were voiced primarily in terms of the economic problems now being visited upon the members, particularly those already relocated in the settlement area who were not being allowed to farm the as yet undeveloped land, and those who had undergone the training programs but as yet had no employment, or had left the area in search of it. Having participated in the initial negotiations for the development, he was well aware that the small scale livelihood projects had been identified as part of the benefits for the cooperative in order to ensure that Ekran Berhad would not become the sole source of employment for the membership. He was also aware that as of yet nothing had happened. In his first interview, he commented:

It is in the agreement [with Ekran Berhad and the DOT] that the people here (or SLS) will already be directing [enterprises] that will supply the tourism industry [with additional goods or services]. However, now it happens that they haven't yet started. It will be too late to begin these once the tourism project has already arrived. They should be starting them now, so that when the project does happen, they will also be able to begin operating right away. If they were able to begin now, while the project is not yet operating, it would be possible for us to deliver our products to Davao. They are very much in demand already. The people need this now. . . . This has to be planned well so that people will know what they should be doing.[48]

For Paolo Lopéz another source of concern about the present situation stemmed from his understanding of the political context of the development. Here he spoke in terms of abstractions rather than individuals, as Pacifico Margoles had done, but his analysis was negative rather than positive. He had witnessed an ongoing lack of coordination between different sectors of government. At the most local level, the cooperative appeared to be working on its own, without consulting municipal officials. "In my observation, there is now something of a gap between our local government and the leadership of SLS," he reported.

Because what I see is that the SLS leadership is not cooperating with the local government . . . . They should [cooperate] with all the various agencies, and not focus their attention only on the Department of Tourism. That's really how I see it, however—they are fixated only on them, they will have nothing to do with other agencies or groups. Perhaps they have forgotten. It is really too bad.[49]

As a result of this fixation, some of the plans the cooperative was making with the DOT were duplicating those underway in municipal offices. This lack of integration was generating confusion.

When envisioning the future and the long term benefits to Kaputian he still believed the tourism estate could produce, Paolo Lopéz's comments again focused as much on civic life as they did on private gain and emphasized a gradual shift from transnational dependence to local autonomy. In describing a best case scenario for the tourism development, he sketched a sequence of economic developments growing outward from the construction of the transnational resort, which would first bring employment to construction workers and later hotel frontline personnel; as tourists arrived in greater numbers there would be more independently owned auxiliary businesses, such as souvenir manufacturing and ecotourism attraction developments. With time, people would come to realize that their own initiative could make an enterprise attractive to tourists. Even their backyard garden activities, Paolo speculated, could be transformed into tourist attractions with the appropriate awareness and design. "What was the purpose of having the [relocation area] lots be as big as 20 by 30, that is, 600 square meters? If they can manage those lots for backyard gardening, that is tourism, isn't it?"[50] He then went on to suggest that other "unrelated" enterprises such as reforestation and municipal park development could become tourist-supported businesses as well. "You could reserve a mini-forest to keep the area cool, then develop sites underneath the trees," he suggested, adding, "That's tourism, it's too bad [it's not happening].[51] There was virtually no enterprise that could not become profitably linked to the tourism industry in his perspective. Speaking of another of his own initiatives, he illustrated this theme, recalling,

I initiated a plan for a livelihood program that included an agricultural component, agricultural technology, one for [land] contouring. I planned that one. It could have become an attraction for [tourists]. . . . It was designed as a preparation for raising goats. When the land was contoured, it would have supported the growth of feed plants so that goat-raising would have followed. After a while the area would have looked beautiful. But that is all lost. Nobody remembers it now.[52]

Paolo Lopéz's idea that raising fodder for livestock might be a prospect for tourism development seemed unlikely at first hearing. But in his opinion even this could attract the tourist gaze if developed creatively. His concept of tourism included the recognition that the actual content of the utopic landscape was less essential to the success of any attraction than the narratives and activities developed in relation to it.

With the emergence of autonomous secondary local tourism enterprises, the community's long term economic prosperity could be ensured, in his view. The ultimate symbol of the success of this ideal process was not an image of wealthy local residents. Instead, he envisioned the growth process culminating in the municipality's being able to construct its own college. He put forward the following scenario in his first interview:

During the construction period, 1,000 [jobs] would be a conservative estimate. If the construction happens all at once, 1,000 would be a small number. . . . 1,000 more or less [would be needed] because it is such a big project. There are swimming pools to be built, and how many units will there be at the sea? There is a hotel; also many ballrooms. If those are all going to be built at the same time, many will gain employment. . . . After the construction work, they [the tourism establishments] will be open, so there will be other kinds of employment: chambermaids, roomboys, bellboys. As [the estate] will already have everything it needs, they will be able to start operating right away. At the same time, if a lot of people have ended up there, a lot of workers, they can then become involved in business. Small-scale ones. A demand will develop for recreation—for the people. At the same time, there will be tourists wandering around, here in the vicinity, wandering around with nothing to do. Of course, these tourists wandering around here, they will buy [things]. Those [living] here would be able to make money. Some would be able to make a living making souvenirs. This was one of my plans . . . we already conducted a training program here in making bamboo novelties with DTI [Department of Trade and Industry]. Some T-shirt printing as well. . . . That's what I'm saying: if these people are ready for it, especially if the young people prepare themselves for the arrival of the project, they will be able to develop sidelines that will generate a living. And perhaps at that time, if many have come here, perhaps then it will also be time for Kaputian to have a college of its own here. Because if there were a college here, the children would be able to go to school; at that same time as they were working here, [they could be in] school. So the standard of education would become higher.[53]

The sustained economic growth in the private sphere would ultimately express itself in the establishment of a civic institution. In this regard, Paolo Lopéz's perspective reasserted an awareness of the need to integrate commercial and civic interests. His vision depicted resources, both human and material, being reinvested in an evolving local community, in high contrast to the present moment, when more and more neighbors and family members were compelled to leave the municipality in search of resources and opportunities elsewhere.

Putting the best case scenario aside, however, he saw the more likely outcome for the cooperative in much bleaker terms. "Sayang," he said at several points in the interviews when summarizing his general impression of the situation. The Visayan term epitomized a sense of loss that occurs whenever an opportunity meets unexpectedly with misfortune and so comes to nothing. The greatest loss, in his view, was the loss of a chance for community autonomy, a theme he stressed repeatedly and one for which he held the cooperative membership itself responsible. When Ben remarked during the first interview that, in our own observation, it seemed that most of the cooperative members perceived the tourism project purely in terms of finding employment with Ekran Berhad, he agreed immediately, commenting, "That's how I see it: that they really focus only on employment."[54]

The vision of autonomous development on which he had placed such a high priority when he was active in the cooperative management was no longer prevalent among the membership or the leadership in his view. A plantation mentality of sorts, with its dependence on nonlocal ownership and management, remained resistant to change—much as had been the case with the attitude of Pearl Farm's tourate and the new Floirendo management policies. This disheartened Paolo Lopéz, particularly when he assessed the long term consequences of such a passive stance vis-à-vis development in general. He anticipated that the lack of foresight, within one or two generations, would lead directly to homelessness and displacement. In the first interview, he elaborated:

I have been with these people for a long time. Their thinking is truly very limited. . . . I can see that they [look] only one or two steps ahead and, then, after that, nothing. That's why I sometimes think I have problems, but because of my commitment—we have made a commitment . . . sometimes I am sick about the situation. I would ask myself, "What can I do? How can [I get] these people to realize what kind of future they will have? They have children. Where will their children end up if they understand things only on this level? We would only be employees, laborers. Better our positions would be those of executives. But no, we would only become laborers—what a pitiful outcome! Then, these laborers, if they marry and have children, how will they make a place for their families? how will they support their children?[55]

Paolo Lopéz was aware of the plan to disband the organization and believed that the opportunity the development had represented would be largely lost if this happened. He expressed regret and some anxiety at this possible outcome, remembering the efforts that he and others had made on behalf of the cooperative and wondering what would befall the membership. "The latest I have heard is that they want the money to be distributed to all the members," he reported in his second interview, speaking of the cooperative membership[56] and returned to the subject at a later point:

I heard only yesterday about the plan. It makes me sad to think about it. If the money is divided, according to my estimate, it amounts to 23 million pesos spread over 332 [members]. That's more or less about 60,000 to 70,000 pesos for each. Within how many months will that money run out? After that, where will we be? . . . That troubles me; last night I did not sleep. When I learned about this turn of events, I could not help but think to myself that the efforts that we made had gone to waste; after the people saw a greater gain [from dividing the capital], now, that's all that they will do with their money.[57]

Paolo Lopéz was, however, considering proposing an alternative cooperative arrangement to the membership, one that would allow those who wanted to pursue the original plan to remain members, while those who wanted their share paid to them in full could withdraw permanently. In his second interview, he explained:

I have a plan if this happens. I would suggest this condition: that whoever takes their share had better sign an agreement that they are cutting themselves off completely from the cooperative. Those who do not take their share will remain members, since these are most likely the people who understand the real value of money to the cooperative and the future.[58]

Under this arrangement the cooperative could go forward with a smaller membership pool, which would include only those members who genuinely believed in the cooperative plan. Despite all the problems generated by the project, the accusations of corruption leveled against himself and other leaders, the frustration over mismanagement of the cooperative store and farm lands, and the fears and disappointments related to the delays in construction and employment, he continued to believe that the community's best interests lay in some form of collective participation in the development project. Toward the end of his second interview, he again argued:

> The cooperative has been a great disappointment. Speaking as one of the cooperative's members, however, my stand now is that the cooperative should not be closed down. I would like to see the cooperative to continue to operate, because it is part of a larger process—it can still be a kind of stepping stone for the people here.[59]

Paolo Lopéz's connection of the cooperative's involvement with a sustainable economic future for the community led him to remain strongly supportive of the continuation of the organization, and of tourism development more generally, even at this tumultuous point in its operation.

Genorosa Duarte

Genorosa Duarte was living in the coastal settlement of Tocanga when we met. We interviewed her at a wide spot in the trail that passed through the main cluster of houses along the shore, where our paths had crossed by chance. When she heard what our project was, she agreed to stop for a while and be interviewed. As it turned out, she had been involved in similar work herself in the past; she was willing to take the time out to assist us, I inferred, knowing what this kind of a survey took to be successful.

Genorosa Duarte was well informed about the needs of the barangay. She was currently a volunteer social worker in Tocanga and was very involved with this work, although it took her away from her home far more than she thought normal. She had a long history of such community service and had been involved in family planning efforts when she had worked as a Barangay Social Projects Officer (BSPO). She previously had taken part in community action research as well, doing household survey work.

Genorosa Duarte was also one of a small group of respondents to our survey whose local roots reached back before the time of Fernández Hermános. Her mother was a member of the island's indigenous cultural group (or relatively indigenous, as migratory records would have framed it). She referred to her mother's people as "Samaleño," or belonging to the Dumaan group. The name "Samalnon," however, was more commonly recognized by government census takers to represent her ethnolinguistic group as well. This group, which had given the island its name, comprised roughly only 12 percent of the total population in 1995 and 1996.[60] It was currently an almost invisible minority in the locality, although this situation was relatively recent. As Pacifico Margoles had recalled, it was scarcely more than a generation ago that *natibos*—as the Visayan immigrants referred to the Samaleños—were easy to distinguish from the immigrant labor pool. Their habits of dress and grooming were then clearly recognizable, their filed, beetlenut-blackened teeth being the most prominent mark of cultural difference. Now the Samaleño "population," extensively intermarried with the immigrant pool, no longer stood out in any obvious way from the rest of the island's inhabitants. Rituals and ceremonies were still performed sporadically, which were of considerable local interest to Visayan as well as to Samaleño islanders, but these had yet be incorporated into the tourism landscape in any obvious way. On the whole, the minority indigenous population was a subtle, largely assimilated presence that intermingled peacefully with the now-majority Visayan culture and society.

Although her mother had not practiced Samaleño "traditions," as she put it,[61] Genorosa Duarte could still speak a little and understand well the dialect spoken by the island's pre-plantation era inhabitants. She identified her father as a "Muslim" from Davao Oriental who had met her mother while staying on Talikud Island during the Japanese occupation. Aside from his Muslim ancestry and faith, however, he had another identity that carried an entirely different and, in the current context more beneficial meaning. He was a "veteran"—one of those fortunates whose activities against the Japanese during World War II had actually been recognized by the American armed forces. He was still living and was collecting a veteran's pension from both the United States and from the Philippine government. Genorosa Duarte's family background, although peculiarly distanced from the more prevalent Spanish influences that had infiltrated along with the Visayan immigrant population,[62] reflected nonetheless a diversity of cultural legacies, themselves also global in derivation and scope. Even for *natibos* like herself, local life was far from purely local, much less "traditional" in character, at least not for the present generation.

Genorosa Duarte was born in 1952 and had lived all her life on Samal and Talikud Islands. At forty-three, she was the mother of seven children and had just become a grandmother. She had lived in Tocanga since 1976, when her second husband, eleven years older than she, went to work for Fernández Hermános. He was "relieved" of work as she put it, in 1991,[63] and turned to fishing and farming. He cleared and tilled a three-hectare plot on the company's land, on which he planted corn. It was this farming that qualified him as a member of SLS. The family had always kept a house in the sitio and were still living there. It was their base of operations for fishing, on which they were now entirely dependent. Fish were becoming increasingly difficult to catch, however, she reported. The trials of the resettlement process were yet to come, and at the time of the interview, they did not seem to be looming large in her view. Not much about the tourism project was definite, in her opinion.

Genorosa Duarte's general view of the SITE project was ambivalent. She was not sure if the development was going to offer any benefit to the community or not. "My opinion about tourism is that it is confusing," she stated, when asked what her general perspective on the project was. She elaborated upon the remark as follows:

> Is it good or not? I don't yet believe in it as a good thing—I'm not really sure. . . . It's because we still don't know if they will manage it well here. Because they say that this Malaysian Ekran Berhad, they say that Ekran Berhad, [pause] I'm not yet convinced [about them]. I cannot rest easy yet.[64]

Her ambivalence stemmed in part from her perception that the development agents were foreign. But it was also based on the fact that no action had yet been taken on the development. When asked how she would feel if the future development were managed well, she replied, "OK," but repeated several times that she was not at all sure that this would be the case, that there were conflicting forecasts about how the project would go forward.

Although she was not without hope of finding employment for herself, Genorosa Duarte's narrative stressed the consequences of development, positive and negative, with respect to her children. "I am concerned that they manage it well because I have children," she stated at one point in the interview, and a few moments later added, "All I would ask for is that my children would be able to get jobs."[65] She assumed—as had Pacifico Margoles and Paolo Lopéz—that the significance of the tourism project lay first and foremost with a generation other than her own—not the generation currently in charge of things. It was a transgenerational, long term perspective that many other interviewees shared.

Much of Genorosa Duarte's understanding of the development project stemmed from her participation in one of the tourism training programs sponsored by the DOT. This was not her first experience with training programs. She had been sent previously to a Basic Health Worker training program at Davao Medical School by another cooperative of which she was a member. In the tourism case, she had attended a three-week program composed of several "modules," focusing on cooking, housekeeping, food and beverage service, and other hotel services. She had been in the second "batch" of six groups of trainees, as she termed them, all cooperative members who had applied and been approved by the cooperative leadership to undergo the training.

The training programs she described were engineered by the DOT in coordination with the Davao Tourism Association (DATA). They had been brought to Davao City, however, by a Manila-based company, the Asian Pacific Tourism Training Institute (APTTI). The director of APTTI was none other than Narzalina Z. Lim, head of the DOT at the time the initial SITE negotiations had been made. Having personally overseen and approved the SITE master plan while holding government office, Lim was ideally positioned, after leaving the post, to design the private sector business that could provide the training the SITE plan envisioned for local residents. She also had the political network in place to ensure that the services her firm offered would be considered favorably for government contracts.

APTTI was established in Quezon City less than a year before it arrived in Davao. Although the firm was not developed specifically for the SITE project, Davao was its first venture outside Manila—its first effort to "go national" as the Davao programs were described in APTTI's first newsletter in August 1995. In Manila, its training programs included courses in restaurant service, housekeeping, bartending, and hotel front office operations, as well as courses in "occupational English" for workers in multinational hotels, computer applications for tourism (Word 6.0, Excel 5.0, Powerpoint 4.0, and Access 2.0), and travel agency and tour operations. While the curriculum for these courses was drawn in the main from international tourism training programs, APTTI reportedly "customized" modules for the Davao project in seven different employment areas.

Genorosa Duarte, however, reported that in her experience the training program had not been particularly effective. "We learned only a few things," she stated, when asked to describe the outcome of her training.[66] When asked to elaborate, she continued:

> What I really liked [learning] was housekeeping but the instruction was done in a very direct, one-time-only style that we were not able to keep pace with. . . . The teaching really ran right along and it wasn't possible to go back [and review lessons] because the next lesson followed right away. . . . The next day it was more difficult still; they would give a test. They would give a small test and sometimes I would get only six correct answers from a total of ten. Learning nowadays seems to be different from the way we were taught in school before. I felt like I was a newcomer.[67]

She had found the food and beverage service materials in particular very difficult and unfamiliar. Housekeeping had been a more enjoyable topic, and she had decided to apply for housekeeping jobs if any became available.

Genorosa Duarte's main problem with the training involved the instructors, despite the fact that she assigned them a general "OK." They were the ones who had elected to teach the training modules in English, and this language choice had diminished the learning experience significantly for Genorosa Duarte. It had created even more problems for her classmates. When asked if she had been able to understand the English instruction, she reported that she had been able to understand some of it, and informed us that she had finished two years of high school in Davao. However, for others in her group the English language training was a major difficulty. "I noticed in my group that my classmates had difficulty [understanding what the trainer was saying], because they had elementary school educations only."[68] When asked what she would recommend so that the instruction might be more effective, she responded immediately with one thought: that it should be given in Visayan (*Bisaya unta*) or at least in Tagalog.

The training programs were evidence to Genorosa Duarte and her fellow trainees that what was coming to Kaputian was a kind of business that had already established itself elsewhere and already had its own set of practices. It was an industry that was arriving in a pre-packaged, "modular" condition, even with respect to its relatively human dimensions. The foreignness of this packaging was concretely communicated in the APTTI training sessions. At the same time, the fact that this foreignness was not utterly beyond the reach of the local community was also made evident. The legacies of American colonialism suddenly became influential in this regard. Genorosa Duarte had been able, albeit marginally, to pass the APTTI test, a test given on Manila-based terms in the "world" language of English, and she had done this on the very first attempt. Her less well prepared neighbors, for their part, had not been left behind entirely. For all the residents who were fortunate enough to have become qualified to apply for jobs "inside" the tourism matrix through the APTTI training program, there appeared to be at least some real possibility of making the transition into actual tourate positions, if not immediately, then within the foreseeable future. The APTTI experience carried with it a somewhat mixed message in this regard, of both foreignness and possible incorporation.

Summary

The four perspectives above, taken as a group, are in many respects representative of the collective we interviewed. In terms of educational achievement, the sample is somewhat skewed, presenting a slightly over-educated profile of the interviewee pool.[69] In terms of ethnicity, the pool was somewhat more diverse than the sample, although it was, loosely speaking, "Visayan" to the same degree. That is, all but one interviewee claimed some form of Visayan ancestry, and the ethnic identities mentioned in this regard included those of many ethnolinguistic groups scattered throughout the western, southern, and central regions of the Visayan Islands: Samar, Leyte, Bohol, Surigao, Cebu, Negros, and Camotes Island specifically. Mixtures of non-Visayan ancestry included Samalnon and "Muslim," as Genorosa Duarte's case illustrated, but also Chinese, Mansaka, Ilocano, Tagalog, Batangeño, and Dabaweño. The pool's diversity reflected once again the island's—and especially Kaputian's—history as a kind of rural hub for migrants of many different sorts. They had arrived from all over the nation—although generally speaking from no points further beyond—and had made the locality their second, or third, or perhaps even their fourth home. It was a distinctly Filipino immigrant mix, ethnically speaking.

Regarding the parallels, as the profiles documented indicate, we worked with men and women in roughly equal numbers (twenty-one interviewees were male, eighteen female). We worked in the main with an older population—particularly in relation to the island's demographics.[70] Only two of our interviewees were under twenty-five and twelve (almost one-third) were over fifty. Sixteen had been born on Samal Island, and thirty-one (roughly 80 percent) had lived on the island for more than twenty years. The pool's collective experience and identification with the area was extensive, as it was with the four individuals reported above. The earliest immigrant in the pool had arrived on Samal Island in 1937, the same year as Paolo Lopéz's parents. Three had arrived in the 1940s, as had Pacifico Margoles; seven had come in the 1950s, as had Clarita Dugno and her family. Six others had arrived in the 1960s. Only three interviewees had lived in the area for less than ten years.

The general understanding we gained of Kaputian's would-be tourate, in this last regard, was that its members, while they were not in most cases living on anything like ancestral homelands, nonetheless, had their familial roots firmly planted in the local soil. The municipality was by no means a transit labor station, even though it was constituted largely by migrants and their descendants. The most frequently mentioned adverse effect of the tourism development, in fact (mentioned by twelve interviewees), was the necessary relocation—imagined or actual—of residents outside the barangays. With the price of land in the barangays escalating to between one and one-and-a-half million pesos per hectare, the interviewees were well aware that their households were no longer secure. The worst case scenario put forward by interviewees, as Clarita Dugno's perspective illustrated, prominently foregrounded the loss of home through forced relocation as the single most distressing consequence of the development—not just individual homes, but also the cultural institutions that had developed in relation to the practice of establishing a home altogether.

Most of the other general findings of the survey are also represented in the views of the four individuals documented above. With regard to Kaputian's past, everyone who addressed the topic in any length (fifteen did so) emphasized that, well before the advent of SITE, residents in the locality had fallen on increasingly difficult times. The most important factor noted in this regard was the depletion of the soil (*umaw na ang yuta*), which was conceived of as an act of nature for which no one was directly to blame. From the general point of view, the tourism industry could not have arrived on Samal Island at a more opportune moment, since the general understanding that agriculture was failing was already widely disseminated by the early 1990s and a pattern of out-migration had already begun in response. The Kaputian barangays were in this sense "ready" for tourism and for assuming a tourate identity to the extent that it meant an identity as an employed population. They were already accepting of and even hoping for a change in their livelihood alternatives. Given the bleak agricultural scenario, tourism was viewed, not as a competitive industry, but as a substitute for farming. As one interviewee put it, "Our land is really meant now for tourism. Its future is tourism. Agriculture is out. Tourism alone is our hope for the future."[71]

Likewise, with regard to the present and future, the majority of inter-viewees looked at the arrival of the tourism industry as at least potentially positive. Twenty-seven interviewees expressed favorable opinions of the industry, seeing it much as Pacifico Margoles, Clarita Dugno, and Genorosa Duarte had done—as a new source of employment. If the government made good on its policies, and if priority were in fact to be given to local resi-dents, it was generally believed that opportunities for work would open up, especially for the youth, and the general standard of living would increase. Paolo Lopéz, moreover, was also not entirely alone in his awareness that the benefits of tourism extended beyond employee roles. Six respondents also noted additional developments of the kind he identified—including improve-ments to the local infrastructure, and additional business opportunities for local residents—as being a possible consequence of the SITE initiative.

Given the changing sense of place occurring in the locality, the arrival of tourism was not considered in and of itself to be destroying any essential character of Kaputian's identity. When imagined in the best case scenario, tourism was understood, in fact, more as a *preservational* or rejuvenating force, extending the life of the barangays for the majority of families cur-rently living there. For them the locality, after all, had never been under-stood as anything other than a place for employment—a place to come to in order to find work. The best case possibility of tourism served to con-tinue that foundational local sense of place and even to present the possi-bility of enhancing it. The transition, viewed optimistically, was seen as a catalyst for the kind of progressive industrial and social development that had always been desired for Kaputian. Tourism, and the tourate identity it entailed, were thus understood to be bringing a change of industry but not necessarily a change of culture. The hope of sociocultural continuity, and the deferred realization of a progressive vision of modern life, sustained the generally optimistic outlook on the tourism industry per se, even while there was abundant evidence that the industry's actual manifestation in the locality would fail to produce a best case scenario.

Like Genorosa Duarte, however, few interviewees looked at tourism in such best case scenario terms exclusively. Worries over forced relocation were only the most frequently cited among a host of fears, all of which together conveyed the general sense that tourism was an uncontrollable industry[72] and a potentially catastrophic form of development. Seventeen interviewees spoke to this theme, several expressing, as Genorosa Duarte did, uncertainty over the question of whether or not the industry would in fact bring employment locally. One interviewee had already observed a case where local workers had been passed by when a private resort near the SITE project had started construction, and outsiders had been brought in to fill construction jobs. Two others commented that tourism developed by outsiders could actually become competitive with existing or planned businesses and preclude management and ownership opportunities for local residents. Concerns over the impact on the local fishing industry were also voiced by four interviewees.

The potential loss of community control precipitated by the loss of collective action and bargaining, and with it the loss of personal autonomy, took on grave proportions as many interviewees looked ahead. The concept of "slavery," even, was brought up by two interviewees when describing the extent to which the industry might go in debasing the local standard of working life.[73] And, of course, the problems with the SITE project itself fed uncertainty about the industry's presence in the locality. Pacifico Margoles was literally the only interviewee who characterized the SITE development in generally positive terms. Everyone else who was willing to comment on the situation (twenty-seven did so), characterized the project in predominantly negative terms, citing the same litany of managerial shortcomings, and often reporting, as Clarita Dugno had done, that it had disturbed the peace of the locality (*nadisturbo gyud ang mga tao*).

The understanding of tourism that SITE participants were developing was quite different from that of the Pearl Farm tourate, whose exposure to tourism had been through a relatively small scale enterprise that had not altered so dramatically the tourate community's established sense of place—on local, national, or international registers. While the SITE participants had not yet been confronted with the realities of tourism once its utopic manifestations were operational—the "eyesore" and "shyness" traumas and the "ugly Filipino" or other stereotyping had yet to come into play—nonetheless the changes and general sense of disturbance the SITE interviewees reported experiencing in the pre-utopic phase of the development far exceeded those of Pearl Farm's tourate. The SITE project, in effect, had introduced a colossal multinational power structure into Kaputian's southern barangays that was playing out its highest levels of social action literally in the backyards of Kaputian's citizenry. Pearl Farm's tourate had yet to cope with anything of this magnitude.

When comparing the two situations—Pearl Farm so excessively private in conception and design, SITE so exuberantly public—I was struck by both the congruencies and the contrasts in the perspectives on tourism in the two cases. In terms of the general outlook—what families and communities wanted—Pearl Farm's tourate and SITE's would-be equivalent appeared to have much in common. Both populations had been confronted in the recent past with the loss of a certain form of livelihood. Both had been receptive to alternative forms of employment that would foster and possibly enhance the visions and realities of modern life, public and private, that had remained relatively unchanged despite the unfortunate sequence of events. Indeed, the more optimistic comments of the SITE interviewees presented a vision of continuity not unlike that which was being actualized, albeit imperfectly, among Pearl Farm's tourate. Adecor had in fact received some of the infrastructural benefits of development that Tocanga's residents desired—electrification in particular. Adecor had seen the growth of its educational and economic institutions, albeit not as extensively as Paolo Lopéz hoped for in relation to SITE. Adecor's children were indeed being sent longer to school, although this did not seem to be preventing them from leaving home to any noticeable extent. Adecor was in many respects actually moving down a progressive pathway similar to the one Tocanga's residents hoped to be taking via SITE. Even the resistance to autonomous parallel development that Adecor's residents had exhibited—the "passivity" shown in response to Pearl Farm's micro-enterprising programs of which Father Chico had spoken—and the preference for sustaining the previous status quo in management/employee relations, even these found close parallels in the employee mentality Paolo Lopéz had found so problematic among the majority of the SITE cooperative membership. In sum, the desire for a continuity of place and employment practice, for better or for worse, enhanced by the technologies of modernity, appeared as fundamentally similar orientations with regard to the tourate identity the residents of both locations were intent upon cultivating.

Unlike the consequences of Pearl Farm for those whose lives had become linked to it in one way or another, however, the influence of the SITE development on its would-be tourate was imagined and experienced as being far more extreme—closer to absolute. While Pearl Farm's tourate had retained a relatively stable sense of their own community, and particularly of Adecor's standing vis-à-vis the resort management's attempts at environmental innovation—attempts they had successfully resisted on occasion—those affected by the SITE project had already accepted a far more sweeping set of transformations that stood to alter essentially every aspect of their communities' lives. Prominent was the project's threat to existing individual and familial identity via its construction of a tourate home community and utopic landscape—something that had not occurred at Pearl Farm. Only one or two SITE interviewees spoke about themselves and their loved ones as if they were anything more than a cooperative member number and a relocation lot (if they were even that) in relation to the SITE master plans. Nothing was represented of their current identity and none of their currently employable capabilities appeared to be valued in the imagination of SITE's realities. The sorts of qualified continuity experienced by Father Chico and Heidi Toledo at Pearl Farm Beach Resort did not appear as a possibility on the SITE tourate horizon. Moreover, not only the individual residents but their own officials as well—their barangay officers, their mayor—faced analogously severe losses of identity and agency in the development's emergence, as the DOT, with the Ramos administration behind it, took charge of government projects and initiatives. The development had already forged new and far more divisive alliances between separate factions of Kaputian's government than had occurred in any of the interviewees' recent memories. In sum, the consequences of SITE were dramatically different from those of Pearl Farm. Whether they ultimately would be disastrous or beneficial, a great deal more was at stake, given the sheer scale and force of the industry's capital investment in the locality and the fact that the power behind it was not under local control.[74]

It is important to remember at this juncture, however, that even at the crisis period when the research took place, no sense that either the scale or the design of the project was somehow fatally flawed was ever explicitly stated, or even indirectly indicated, by any of the SITE interviewees. Likewise, no desire to isolate the SITE barangays on principle from such relatively large scale "flagship" projects was ever suggested. Globalization—or meta-localization, at any rate—was still playing relatively well as a modus operandi among the interviewee pool, as far as tourism in particular and community development in general were concerned. If anything, it was the "grass roots" level of operation that had become more suspect through the SITE experiences.

The culture of nations in which the development had been conceived retained a relatively positive image. The DOT, specifically, was not perceived as an oppressive, exploitative, or corrupt agency or as an essentially unacceptable partner-in-development by any of the interviewees. Similarly, Ekran Berhad was not seen as an inherently dishonorable or unacceptable partner or as an organization somehow too foreign to establish a sustainable relationship with the cooperative. The SITE project appeared to have sustained and perhaps in some cases even strengthened a general belief in the flagship model of development in the abstract. The people who were understood to be manning the flagship's helm, and the basic structure of the vehicle itself, were not held accountable for the problems the development had thus far actually generated. Indeed, they appeared more than ever to be the most trustworthy sources of solutions to these difficulties. The interviewees as a group were still prepared to get on board the flagship and to identify themselves with the culture of nations—to "go global" as it were—espousing the idea that the barangay communities' best chances of survival were more likely to result from voluntary integration into the larger economy, rather than from open resistance to it.

Ultimately, then, SITE's potential was understood in optimistic terms by the SITE interviewees. Their responses, though perhaps highly guarded and using somewhat forced optimistic terms, were basically positive nonetheless. Finding themselves caught between the "rock" of a failed agricultural base and the "hard place" of competing in an unfamiliar global industry, the SITE interviewees had elected to wait and see how the latter would develop, doing what they could in the meantime to prepare for tourism's arrival. They were trusting, to the extent that they could reasonably do so, that their own adaptive capabilities and their modern worldview, along with those of their new "partners," however foreign or powerful, would somehow see them through to better times.

Whether the residents and their families would in fact survive the tidal wave of development due to break upon their shores was a question that could not be answered in 1996. I was reasonably certain, however, that nothing was likely to come about as a result of the development that bore any great resemblance to the existing master plan. Nothing had so far. The survivors of the estate development, in my estimate, were most probably going to be those residents who were able to find or create benefits in new and unlikely circumstances, or who were possessed of exceptional capabilities of one kind or another. This was not a particularly pessimistic perspective. The more I had learned about Kaputian's southern barangays, the more I had come to realize that they were made up to a considerable extent of both of these kinds of persons.

In any case, the uncertainties and ruptures generated by the tourism estate had yet to fully emerge. While the consequences of the preliminary phases of development were already extensive and profound, they appeared to afford only the barest glimpse of how the tourism matrix might eventually come to envelop the existing cultural landscape and its narratives within tourism's global operations.[75]

Part III
Local Amusements

Chapter 8
The Home Away from Home: Marjorie's Inn

Middle class hotels in Davao City, while they did exist in the early 1990's, were not particularly easy to come by. It was a striking, definitive feature of the locality. The Lonely Planet's *Philippines—Travel Survival Kit* in its 1991 edition listed only "Top End" and "Bottom End" classes of accommodations for Davao City, with nothing in between (1991: 375–76). Tourists who fell into the middle class found themselves in something of a bind.

On the top end, there were two large "first class" hotels designed for professionals traveling on international-size corporate expense accounts and staying for a few days to a few weeks in the city.[1] On the bottom end, there was a considerably larger array of some two dozen lodging houses designed for travelers who wanted or needed to stay, for a few days, perhaps, but just as likely for a much longer span of time, even months. The first class hotels charged 1,200 to 2,000 pesos a night for a double room. They provided everything from air-conditioning, cable television, refrigerators, and international telephone service inside the rooms, to swimming pools, well-manicured grounds and gardens, tennis courts, discos, international restaurants, luxury boutiques and galleries, and business centers on the premises. The low-end "inns," "lodges," and "pensions," as they tended to be named, were charging around 300 pesos a night for their version of an air-conditioned double room, and offering little more than a bed, a bathroom, and a cantina or makeshift cafeteria/food stand.[2]

Hotel size also evidenced the persistent gap in middle class accommodations. The two first class hotels consisted of 153 rooms and 105 rooms respectively in 1992. All but three other establishments had fewer than 60 rooms, with the average only 28. If an average of the top end (roughly 130 rooms) and bottom (roughly 30 rooms) size was calculated, the resulting "standard" size—roughly 80 rooms—was not represented anywhere in the city.

The gap in the middle—that elusive 500-1,000 peso a night "experience" that promised more than just a simple bed and bathroom—was not completely empty, however. A few intermediate standard class hotels and four or five more expensive "economy" class inns and pension houses did exist in Davao in 1992.³ However, they seemed few and far between for a city of a million people.

It was to one of these more recently constructed, smaller establishments that I eventually went and registered, after exploring both ends of the discontinuous spectrum of accommodations in the city. The place became my main residence until my final departure in 1996. My hotel, Marjorie's Inn, had opened in 1991. The inn's beige concrete exterior was still free of blemishes, with no ornamentation other than its own large neon sign. It had been designed according to the latest local standards of modern urban architecture, solidly engineered, four stories high, with clean straight lines and small, white-trimmed unshuttered windows. It was located on one of the city center's main streets, walking distance to the main downtown offices, shopping centers, and jeepney pickup points—an urban tourist's best case scenario.

The building was far too new and respectably constructed to belong to any "low" class category. It was also kept immaculately clean by an ever busy staff. However, the twenty-one rooms, located on the building's second and third floors, were far too inexpensive and modestly furnished to suit a "luxury" category either. There was no marble, no old-growth wood paneling, no gilding, no velvet or satin, no material trace of wealth anywhere inside. The furniture was made of painted rattan and wicker for the most part, with the occasional vinyl cushion. There was only one slightly contradictory feature, a wood (as opposed to linoleum) floor on the inn's second story—a feature that tended to impress foreigners primarily. This was the inn's only nod to a higher-than-economy-class accommodation, and I later discovered it was actually an unplanned byproduct of construction, not an intentional upgrade. The lobby was in every respect "economy." A tiny space directly behind the building's main double doors, it was just large enough for a two-person counter and standing room, with rattan furniture seating for two squeezed along one mirrored side wall, and a staircase landing wedged into place along another.

The inn had no elevator, only a narrow wooden staircase with a thin red carpet. The only restaurant, located on the ground floor beside the lobby, fell into the "coffee shop" category. Its floor, like the lobby's was a practical white tile. It contained eight or nine linen-covered tables seating two to four guests each, and a small bar along the rear wall, seating two or three, with a portable television at the far end. On the inn's top floor was a large open room, the "function room," with a seating capacity of around fifty. The room could be used for meetings or parties, or, as I was eventually informed, as a place for bodyguards and other extensions of a paying guest's household to sleep. There were no grounds or patio areas connected with Marjorie's Inn, no sports facilities, no business center, and no boutiques. The building stood at the end of a concrete driveway that it shared with half a dozen other establishments. It faced another concrete building that was its virtual twin and sat next to another. No landscaping of any kind softened its facade or that of its neighbors.

In sum, there wasn't much more to Marjorie's Inn than a well built structure and a clean, functional interior, with convenient food and basic hotel services. Rather like a motel, were it not dislodged from any automobile-based transportation network, the inn's character was fundamentally passage-like, as opposed to place-making. Its dwelling-ness approximated in quality the durative, syncopated characters of pausing, not residing, and this predominantly mobile orientation did not allow for the collection of elaborate identity markers.[4] It proved to be a wise, relatively sociable choice as far as I was concerned. A wide array of friends and acquaintances visited me there: teachers, artists, housewives, maids, students, politicians, businessmen, missionaries, and NGO workers, among others. They came and went, generally without comment. Individuals of radical and conservative orientations, male and female, young and old, wealthy and poor, foreigners and native sons or daughters—no matter the "walk of life," no one ever remarked on anything being particularly off-putting or attractive about Marjorie's Inn. I was reasonably certain, after a few years of visits to the inn, that it was probably a more neutral and so more inclusive choice of residence than anywhere else I might have landed in the city. Meetings and conversations took place there, narratives were generated there, that would probably not have happened anywhere else.

I had no idea in 1992 that Marjorie's Inn and the one or two others in its class represented only the first small crest of a much larger wave of development, a wave inspired by visions of tourism, albeit of a hybrid business-oriented kind. The number of intermediately priced and sized hotels in Davao City increased markedly between 1992 and 1996. By the time of my departure, they were appearing on nearly every block of the city center.

These new hotels announced the arrival of the tourism industry in Davao City more substantially, ton for concrete ton, than any other single indicator in the city's built environment. Similar to Pearl Farm Beach Resort, they were financed and constructed, and more often than not designed and managed, by individual families. Unlike Pearl Farm, however, the new hotels were in many cases being developed by Davao's "pioneer" families—families that were already established in the city's pre-independence periods. Family names well known in Davao City's oral history—Garcia, Nograles, Lizada, Montemayor, Robillo, Santos, Gonzalez, Villarica, and Dakudao—stood behind the new standard class of establishments. While the hotels included the same general array of features—fully air-conditioned rooms, 24-hour color cable TV, baths with hot and cold water, meeting/function rooms—each bore the distinctive marks of its individual owner's taste and touristic vision. As with Pearl Farm Beach Resort, the families developing the hotels were in most cases new to the hotel business and the tourism industry. The hotels were just one component of a much larger complex of family enterprises, one sideline in a more complicated, generally multigenerational mosaic of family life and enterprise.

I came to understand the pristine and growing collection of small hotels in Davao City that developed with such speed and industry between 1992 and 1996 as the touristic expression most representative of the city's local society. This wave of development was understood as the economic opportunity of the given moment in the city, the local way by which Davao-based elites were "getting into the act" of tourism, as upper classes everywhere of the world were wont to do.[5] It evidenced the limits of these families' financial strengths, their building power, as well as their touristic sensibilities. It also evidenced the appeal the tourism industry had acquired for these families, who were now eager to partake of the industry's benefits, design its venues, and control the local production of its narratives and performances, as they had controlled the lion's share of the city's social and economic performances in the past. From a global perspective, this kind of development was set up largely for Philippine consumption and was operating in a more or less un-self-consciously Philippine style. However, it was also, at precisely this time period, making initial contact with the transnational tourist industry and learning how to integrate itself sustainably into larger flows of capital, commerce, and touristic activity.

Culturally salient as they may have been from my perspective, the hotels were not overtly or self-consciously "cultural" in conception. They did not advertise themselves in terms of distinctive local charms and were not designed for recognition as exotic destinations. Only one of these establishments, the Mandaya Inn, appropriated the name of an indigenous minority cultural group. None of the hotels featured "Davaoeño" architecture, artifacts, costumes, or native style services—all of which would have required elaborate reinventions of tradition to reconstruct and authenticate.

The new class of hotels were set up to feed into the emerging small scale "seminar" tourism market in the Philippines and its large scale and increasingly transnational counterpart, "convention" tourism. These essentially urban forms of touristic enterprise combined various professional and commercial business meetings and training programs with travel and vacation incentives. They were forms of business/tourism travel fast becoming a mainstream element of working culture throughout the Philippines for all types of professionals. They marketed a form of tourism that was inseparable from a mix of nontouristic travel and commercial activities and which existed as part of a business-and-pleasure itinerary that attempted to enhance a nonleisure environment with enough touristic allure to produce a competitive destination appeal.[6]

The emergence of the business market itself was a direct consequence of the prosperity and stability of the Ramos years. It did not require, and in some ways actually benefited from the erasure of "cultural" fantasy symbolism—itself too completely playful to serve all the purposes at hand.

Figure 12. One of Davao City's new standard class hotels.

All the same, the business tourist market did entail certain forms of touristic practice. It did serve to generate touristic narratives and it did, perhaps most significantly, situate its business within a certain type of utopic landscape.

In sum, the new class of tourist accommodations evolving in Davao City, while it was not meant to provide an escape into paradise, was integrated, albeit incompletely, into the tourism matrix. Contrary to the landscapes of Samal Island, however, the small hotels were engaged in producing the resorts' utopic counterparts: relatively unremarkable, unexciting, home-away-from-home landscapes. The slogan, "Home away from Home," was, in fact, itself occasionally featured in some of the advertising for the new establishments. The small hotels were intended to perfect the regular as opposed to the extraordinary, and the familiar as opposed to the strange, in their utopic narratives and performances. A touristic "take" on the most mundane forms of domestic life was thus emerging in the city's new wave of small hotels.

One of the oldest, most modest, and on several levels most original of these homes away from home, as it happened, came to be my own. Although it had emerged slightly ahead of the trend, the utopic home Marjorie's Inn constructed for its guests was broadly representative of the touristic construction of home that was being produced more widely by the standard class hotel industry in Davao City. In this chapter, after a brief sketch of the inn's employee tourate, I will recount one of more influential narratives that I witnessed and co-created about Marjorie's Inn, one that contributed to the general perspective I developed on the small hotel boom and its cultural consequences for Davao City. This narrative illuminates the utopic construction of home from the perspective of its tourate producers—the managers and owners who made the hotels operational.

The Tourate

The staff at Marjorie's Inn was small and changing. At any one time there were no more than around fifteen employees who divided between day and night shifts. They were a younger group, in their twenties for the most part, except for the cooks, who were in their thirties if not older. In terms of education, one desk staff member I knew of had graduated from college with an education degree; another was dating a man with a mechanical engineering degree; a third had two sons in college. None of the college-educated individuals had yet found jobs in their professional fields. While college was by no means an unknown phenomenon, neither was it a guarantee of professional opportunity. The staff at Marjorie's Inn were doing better than Tocanga's would-be tourate as far as educational attainment was concerned—although they were not in the same league as Pearl Farm's—but the professional consequences of higher education were as yet largely unevidenced.

The staff were not themselves without touristic experience. Their discourse at the inn regularly included accounts of their own travels to other parts of the Philippines, especially to destinations in the south, where they themselves would assume roles as "visitors" or "guests." I never heard of any staff member, however, who had international touristic experience. Neither did anyone mention experience in the overseas labor market.

Even though my interaction with the inn staff was more or less constant during my visits, I never met their families, I never learned their life histories, and I never accompanied them anywhere outside the inn, except in one case to a market a few blocks away. I did acquire a collection of biographical fragments pertaining to them. There were times—when someone got pregnant or someone brought a child to work—when the private side of life spilled over into the tourate side we shared. I learned in this way that the chief desk clerk in 1992 was a widow with four sons in school, her husband shot to death in Cotabato by the military during the Marcos years. I learned that one of the security guards was a native of the coastal town of Mati, on Mindanao's eastern coast, but that most of the staff came either from Davao City or from towns nearby. One of the room staff happened to be an intern with the APTTI program from Samal Island. Most of the rest of the staff, however, had worked for families who knew the owners of Marjorie's Inn and had come by their jobs in that way.

From details such as these, I gained the general impression of the staff as belonging to a relatively insular middle class. They were not yet directly integrated into any international economies in their working lives, not even as pawns, much less full-fledged players. Their movements and activities were internal to the Philippine context, registering on provincial and national scales. They measured the successes and failures of their employment, as well as charting the course of their career opportunities, largely in relation to provincially defined structures, organizations, and companies. With regard to these frames of reference, they were doing reasonably well, with decent jobs and good chances for future progress, should the times "inside" the Philippines remain good.

In this very regard, however, the staff at Marjorie's Inn belonged to an economic sector on which the current ASEAN-driven economic boom stood to have, perhaps, its most significant cultural impact. The staff represented a Philippine-produced generation of would-be managers and entrepreneurs, a class who had never before been tapped by commercial interests in such a professional style on such a massive scale, given the nation's record of underdevelopment prior to "the 90s." Now, however, these entry-level individuals were among the "frontliners" of upward mobility. Their lives stood to change the most dramatically of any economic sector in the Philippines, if the resources and opportunities promised by the Ramos administration's "4-D" policies became available and they were actually allowed to move beyond the employee or laborer positions in businesses owned by provincial elites they currently occupied. They had the vision, the will, and in many cases the education to do so. The staff at Marjorie's Inn, in this regard, exemplified a generation and an employment sector currently poised on the brink of corporate life, waiting for the right doors to open. They understood that such doors would be ASEAN-engineered, transnational doors, if they were to materialize at all.

In part, the limits to the rapport I was able to establish with individuals on the staff of Marjorie's Inn were due to the turnover of employees from year to year. While this was never absolute, on every return visit I would typically encounter a new cook and several new desk clerks, new room service staff, and new security personnel. In contrast to Davao City's top end establishments, whose staff tended to be lifetime employees, Marjorie's Inn supported a fluctuating cast of characters. However, in addition to the turnover, there were also unspoken principles for respectful behavior that worked to preclude the staff's taking any initiative to form anything other than a working relationship to guests as well, myself included. We all respected those unspoken rules. I was no more inclined to transgress them than I was to become a bother to the inn's guests. The unarticulated code of conduct created barriers for all but the most assertive staff members as a result, and the contrast to a full-fledged tourism context was striking in this regard. In the more classic touristic locations in the ASEAN matrix, it was not unusual to hear an entire life history and an invitation to participate in it on some ongoing basis in the course of single afternoon with a driver or bartender. Staff members in more developed touristic contexts, I'd observed, tended to discover that within the "roomboy" or "waitress" job position there were opportunities for staging independent operations with tourists of a fairly elaborate scope. At Marjorie's Inn, however, the closest I came to this was when, after two years of arriving and departing had gone by, a couple of the restaurant and room staff laughingly announced one day that they had decided they were becoming my luggage on the next trip back to the States. Once, at the very end of a visit, one of the restaurant staff made a half serious inquiry about whether I had a maid already in California. However, this was nothing like the hard sell pushes to become a broker in the souvenir market, or a diving equipment supplier, or an informal sales representative for the resort trade, that I had encountered in tourist meccas elsewhere.

What I came to know best about the staff individually and collectively was their style of working, the way they fulfilled the tasks that I grew, over the years, to know extremely well. This conduct, more than anything else, was what gave Marjorie's Inn a culture of its own. It was a manner that, along with the inn's material givens, defined its ranking in the high economy class. While it was embodied by the staff, it was not designed by them. Rather, it was set on them, scripted and choreographed for them, by the inn's management. The staff performances never lacked individual nuances, to be sure, but to understand the general principles of their conduct, I was compelled to focus my attention on the inn's management and the influences that were currently at play in its activity field.

The Tourism Management Keynote Address

I attended a seminar event for tourism owners and managers held in Davao City in 1995, accompanied by the owner of Marjorie's Inn. It was one of the most important occasions that I was able to witness during my research in Davao City, one of the few occasions where I was able to observe first-hand the global tourism matrix actually at work, disseminating a narrative of what utopic tourate conduct should entail and how it should be perfected in Davao City's new array of standard class hotels. This was a chance to observe an actual instance of globalization, to watch the tourism matrix engulf a locality. In this context, the matrix's operations worked smoothly, producing a seemingly effortless consensual procedural style and a cordial and dignified manner of incorporation. This was accomplished through a certain, increasingly popular speech event: the seminar.

Seminars, while they were social forms that grew out of a long history of related practices, were at least conceptually a somewhat recent development in Davao City. The term had been all but lacking from Davao's English vocabulary in 1992. However, by 1993, it had infiltrated the discourse of the city's professionals to the point that I made notes about the fact that I was hearing it everywhere. In 1995, "seminar" had become the prestige term used for a wide range of meetings and collective occasions a few hours to several days in length. It defined an occasion when some form of valued information exchange was planned to take place. All kinds of institutions and organizations that took their missions in life seriously sponsored seminars. Churches held them, as did businesses, NGOs, and government agencies. The term carried a certain cachet as an up-to-date, Ramos-era phenomenon. It gave whatever took place under its rubric—lectures and other sorts of presentations, as well as group discussions and exercises of various kinds—an aura of contemporary significance.

A great deal more than serious learning generally happened within the seminar event. It was an opportunity to reinforce and enlarge the network of one's social and professional connections as much as it was a chance to learn new skills or obtain current information on the field or topic addressed. The more social aspects of seminar events could in some cases even outweigh the educational ones. Nonetheless, to attend a seminar was to participate in a transformative process that served to elevate, however subtly, one's status as a knowledgeable person on the topics at issue. The seminar format marked a certain change of consciousness with respect to the ways in which expertise was recognized and disseminated throughout Davao City's society. By 1995, no one who was or wanted to be a participant in the social and professional networks the various seminars represented failed to attend them.

The particular seminar I attended was sponsored jointly by the Davao Tourism Association, the Department of Tourism, and the Technical Education and Skills Development Authority of the Department of Labor and Employment. These were the main forces governing tourism development in the city at this time. The seminar was designed so as to make some general guidelines for tourism development explicit, and to convince the owners and managers of the city's tourism establishments that they merited acceptance and application. It was a "top down" vision of tourism development, which the sponsors intended to have internalized and reproduced throughout the city. It foregrounded the rise of EAGA and the regional opportunities it represented for the Philippines and anticipated the arrival of the global tourism industry in the provinces of Mindanao on a scale never before contemplated.

The seminar was entitled "Davao: The Lead City in Quality Tourism Service." It drew about forty members of the top echelon of the tourism industry in Davao City, the owners, CEOs, supervisors, and general managers of the city's tourism establishments—the "key players" in the words of the seminar presenters. It was held at an elegant meeting room, the Orchid Room of the Apo View Hotel. The fee for attending was 500 pesos—high enough to discourage all but the top end of the tourism sector, or their chosen representatives and associates, from participating. As I entered the room, I recognized among the several round tables set up for the attendees junior members from the main hotel-owning families, supervisors from the Davao City Philippine Airlines office, and representatives from a number of other businesses—restaurants and orchid gardens—that had a stake in the tourism industry. Pearl Farm's management was represented, as was Apo View's. The seminar had been effective in gathering a broad sample of the Davao tourate leadership.

Among the seminar's featured presenters was Margarita Moran-Floirendo (now president of DATA), Catalina Santos Dakudao from the DOT, and, in the keynote position, Narzalina Lim, former secretary of the DOT and founder and director of APTTI. I recognized, as did all the participants, that the messages at this gathering were being delivered by the most influential figures known to the city's tourism entrepreneurs. Throughout the seminar, their speeches were received accordingly, with the deferential acceptance that was standard for such semi-public occasions. No overt resistance or critical response to ideas was typically voiced in such a context, nor was any voiced on this occasion. It was not a moment for debating the material, despite the fact that all the seminar leaders called repeatedly for a "cooperative effort," in which they wanted, "to hear the views" of the participants and to conduct an "honest," "candid," and "open" dialogue about Davao's touristic "problems." The seminar, however, was an occasion to get on board, not to rock the boat. On this particular occasion, it fell largely to the keynote speaker, Narzalina Lim, to communicate to the seminar participants precisely what that meant.

Lim's half-hour keynote address was made in English, as were all but one of the day's several presentations. It was preceded by a shorter speech by Catalina Santos Dakudao, devoted to describing the current booming climate for tourism development in Davao City (the "400 percent" growth statistic was again prominently featured), and the challenges that climate posed for the assembled body. The keynote address was followed, before and after lunch, by a series of more narrowly focused talks, which gave more details of the content and organization of programs APTTI, DATA, and the DOT were developing in their efforts to upgrade and expand Davao's tourism sector, and, even later, by discussion sessions engineered to articulate the views of the participants themselves in relation to all these subjects. It was in the keynote narrative, however, that the utopic landscape envisioned for the city and the tourate character to be performed inside it were most vividly depicted and defined. Moreover, the keynote address was designed to give the assembled body a set of paradigms in which they could come to terms with their present identity and tourate status as well as the desired utopic identity—an identity explicitly defined in universal terms. Delivered by the highest ranking official in attendance, it was the only narrative that served as much a performative function as an informative one, moving its audience with authoritative certainty into a new conceptual space where connections to a transnational network of tourism professionals who "spoke the same language" were accessible and where the assembled body was expected to rethink and reinvent its touristic practice according to the Philippine government's master plans.

Narzalina Lim did not cut a particularly striking figure in the Orchid Room, given the elite field of affluent professionals she faced on that morning—all dressed in various male and female renditions of the developed world's "power suit." Lim was relatively ordinary in appearance. Margie Moran-Floirendo and Kiling Dakudao—both of whom were referred to by their nicknames on this occasion—were many years younger than she. However, whatever director Lim may have lacked in glamor, she more than made up for in personality. She described herself at one point in the keynote as someone who "did not hold her punches," and, nothing she did or said in the course of her keynote address on that morning belied that description.

The director began her address with a token transgression that effectively sent the message throughout the room that she was a person who was used to making, as opposed to obeying, the ground rules of any event in which she was inclined to participate. Taking a position at the front and center of the room, she refused to use the lectern provided for her, which Kiling Dakudao had vacated only a moment before. "If I talk from there, I don't think you'll listen," she told the group, demonstrating her in-your-face style of interpersonal conduct at literally the first opportunity. "And you'll get bored," she added, with a slight trace of humor in her voice. The crowd responded politely, with a few subdued rueful chuckles, sending back a respectful acknowledgment of the bravery this small but nonetheless slightly risky opening gesture evidenced.

She used her relatively unprotected standing position at the front of the group to reinforce immediately the presenters' intentions to conduct a "candid and very open" workshop. She reiterated these intentions from this stance, demonstrating that the stated intention was made in earnest and that she would back it up with the whole of her person if need be. The crowd settled quietly into a collective listening mode, aware now, if they had not been before, that the officer currently in charge was evidently capable of confronting any of them at any time and for any reason. Had there been any doubt about this, the director erased it when, in the midst of a few minutes of opening comments describing her APTTI organization, she broke off in mid-sentence to request that all the cell phones in the room be turned off. The phones had been ringing more or less continuously throughout the morning, and one particularly loud one had just rung during her previous remark. Wasting no words on the subject, she instructed the cell phone users to take their calls outside, commenting in a voice that was both sincere and edged with impatience that it was very distracting for "the speaker" when phones were constantly in use. The group honored the request. The director resumed her speech, her control over the seminar now firmer than ever.

Regarding APTTI, Lim emphasized one, and only one, feature of the organization. "We are *accredited*," she stated, after having given a few details of the locations of APTTI's centers and the design of its courses. "And that's a very important word," she added, specifying that APTTI's accreditation had been bestowed on it by the morning's two national sponsors: the DOT and the Technical Educational and Skills Development Authority. Elaborating on APTTI's accreditation, she made it clear that the utopic landscape she envisioned developing in the Philippines—and in Davao City in particular, should the seminar's participants decide to get on board with her program—was one that would conform to the tourism industry's established global parameters and that this would be verified through the instrument of accreditation. No interest in originality or transgression was evident in the director's outlook on this issue. She did not play fast and loose with the development of the industry. She elaborated:

Now why were we accredited? We were accredited I guess because we meet certain standards in training. We have our own center. We have training rooms. We have 22 computers. We have a lot of films which we have ordered from abroad. Unfortunately there are no films, training films for hotel and travel made in the Philippines, so we have to rely on films from abroad. I brought three of them just to show to you over lunch what sort of films we show in our training programs. We invest in manuals, we invest in books, et cetera. So there is a big investment on our part just so that our training meets certain standards. And again that is a very important word which you will encounter during this day's seminar. What are the standards that should be met in training and what are the *standards* you should meet in your various facilities so that you offer quality.

Lim's comments indicated some dissatisfaction with the currently marginal status of the Philippines in the formulation of industry standards. She found it "unfortunate" that the Philippines was not yet producing its own tourism training films. However, the emphasis on meeting "standards," a concept that was repeatedly voiced throughout the keynote and its follow-up presentations, was never qualified by any Philippine-identified concepts— or those of any other nation or region for that matter. Industry "standards" were assumed to be uniform worldwide. The seminar participants were being put on notice in the keynote's opening moments, in this regard, that such standards—whatever they might actually be—were now a presence inside their own borders, not only their national borders but locally as well.

The term "quality," with which the opening segment of the address ended, served as the focal concept of the director's utopic vision. "So—let's talk about *quality* customer service, or *quality* tourism service," she continued, segueing deftly into the main portion of her talk. "Quality" was the prestige term for the entire seminar. It encapsulated the desired character of both the tourist landscape and the tourate conduct occurring within that landscape. "Quality" in this discourse carried no evaluative neutrality. It did not represent a continuum of possibilities ranging from low to high. It had been reduced to the status of a purely positive indicator, imbued with goodness alone. "Quality" was either present or absent, a tourate or a landscape either had it or it didn't. If it had "quality," the keynote promised, then good things would happen for the participants' "Bottom Lines." If it didn't, then tourists would go elsewhere.

A universalist, global perspective was again assumed in this concept of "Quality" tourism service. There were no cultural variants acknowledged with regard to Quality, no "foreigner" or "Filipino"—much less any "Davaoeño" styles of Quality mentioned. The Japanese "Quality guru" Ginichi Taguchi was cited repeatedly in one of the follow up presentations, and his model of the "Three Rings of Value" in "Quality Production"—a formula for generating "optimal quality within the bounds of commercial viability and success"—was presented as unproblematically applicable to the Philippine tourism industry as well as any other. "Quality," in sum, defined a perfection disassociated from any cultural, ethnic, historical or national specificities. Its nearly absolute abstractness gave it the widest possible breadth of evaluative industrial range.

To give the audience a definition of "Quality Tourism Service," Lim sought the aid of a text which she referred to somewhat inexactly as "the Australian hospitality manual for service excellence." If anyone in the room

registered the irony of this description, given the predominance of Australian clientele in the Philippines illicit sex tourism market or "hospitality
industry," it was masked completely. The definition was presented on a slide
and read aloud twice for emphasis before she asked for a discussion of its
"key words." She read:

Quality Tourism Service: When the Customer's Perception of the Service Experience Consistently meets their Expectations.

Despite the repetitions, the definition failed to strike any kind of obvious
responsive chord among the participants. Only a short silence greeted its
presentation. The "key word" request did not meet the director's own expectations either, as the only word initially suggested by the group, somewhat timidly, was, "perception," and this response stopped the director
short in her flow of speech. A gap in understanding became apparent in this
moment. The participants and the leader were obviously not yet talking the
same tourism talk, not yet playing the same language game where tourate
conduct was concerned. It took less than a second, however, before Lim
rallied and came back with a strategic, integrative response. Faltering ever
so slightly, she answered the suggestion with another question, asking *whose*
perception was at issue. It was only then that she received the term from
another audience member on which she evidently had prepared to dwell:
the Customer. "It's the *Customer's* perception," she responded emphatically,
back on track once again. She went on with a spirited elaboration of this
theme:

It's turning things around. It's not from *your* point of view, but it's from the *Customer's* point of view, and it's the perception. All right? So, let's look at this, look
at the elements of Quality Service, of Service Excellence. . . . It is defined from the
Customer's perspective. All right. It's not from *you* the manager or you the owner's
perspective but from the *Customer's* perspective. It's very, very important. That's a
change in mindshift in service. OK? It centers around what the *Customer* perceives. It
does not matter whether you think you're giving good service, if the Customer does
not think that you're giving good service, then it's not, for him, Quality Customer
Service. OK? So it matters not if the service provider feels that she delivers Quality
Service if the Customer does not see it that way.

The "Customer," a being unmarked by age, sex, nationality, ethnicity, or
any other distinctive feature—a contingent character, defined only by the
presence of spending power—this Customer, overlooked by the seminar
participants in their initial scrutiny of the definition, became the determining agent of a "Quality" landscape, in Lim's definition. With this concept,
she stripped the assembled body of its most basic touristic agency—its power
to define and realize touristic perfection or, in her terms, "Quality Service."
While she gave passing mention to the importance of creating a memorable
"Experience" through tourate service performance, and while she focused
momentarily on the need for "Consistency" in service performance as well,

it was to the role and the relative power of "Customers" vis-à-vis the owners and managers of the city's tourism establishments that she returned repeatedly in defining "Quality."

In this way, the keynote rhetoric dislodged what was to become the main indicator of utopic presence from the seminar participants' direct control. Davao's tourism establishments could not own "Quality," no matter how much of Davao's prime real estate they might have possessed for however many generations. Neither could they produce Quality, naturally or culturally, entirely on their own, no matter what their influence over their subordinates or fellow citizens might be. "Quality," the magic of the tourism landscape, was asserted to be inherently unreal in any empirical sense. There was nothing essentially "Quality" about Davao, or the Philippines, or its populations, from the director's point of view. The presence of "Quality" was understood to be essentially imaginary and dependant ultimately on the mindsets of "Customers" or tourists. Lim's utopic vision, with its highly abstract, universal, and psychologically oriented model of Customer-centered "Quality," made a radical break with preexisting discourses of power and distinction, whether traditionally, locally, provincially, or nationally grounded in their frames of reference. "Quality," now, was grounded only in "Customer" satisfaction.

Apparently Lim understood that persuading her audience to accept this vision, given the status it assigned to them, was likely to be something of an uphill battle. She gave her Customer-centered comments everything she had, in this regard, in terms of evidentiary weight. The Australian definition was followed by several negative examples of the current absence of "Quality" in a number of Davao's existing (though here unnamed) hotels. The cases in point were no less convincing in their identification of flaws in tourate performance for having been framed as "constructive criticism" in the introductory comments. One example focused on the lack of a "Do Not Disturb" sign in one hotel, a second pinpointed the absence of a telephone/fax number listing inside the rooms of another. These were cited as "basic, basic things" that indicated a lack of "Quality" in Davao. She summarized her indictment of the city's touristic status quo, arguing:

> If these expectations are not met, then you're not even meeting the basic service, much more Quality Customer Service. You know these are small things, but these are things that *customers* look for and which *you*, the establishments are not providing, OK. Because you are not thinking from the Customer's point of view.

She drove home the consequences of this predicament by shifting her focus to the future, closing this segment of the keynote with her strongest globalizing comment yet put forward:

> Davao is no longer just a domestic destination, visited by people from Manila, Cebu and other places in the Philippines. It has become a *regional* destination, and

very soon it will become an *international* destination. . . . So far you only have Borac Airways Manado-Davao. Very soon Air Palau is coming in twice a week. They have booked 60 rooms in this hotel, I understand, per week. Malaysian Airlines is flying KL, Kota Kinabalu, Davao. All right? So that's another addition of Malaysians. And then Silk Air is planning to come here eventually, et cetera et cetera. Even Hansen Airlines from Darwin in the Northern Territories of Australia. Before you know it, international tourism is in Davao. And as Kiling rightly said, are *you* prepared for it? You cannot even service a Manila customer looking for a "Do Not Disturb" sign or looking for "what's the number of this hotel? I can't even find it anywhere in this room." OK?

With this withering barrage, Lim proceeded into the remaining half of the keynote address, in which she informed the participants of the components of Quality Service. "Service," again, as it was found to be defined in APTTI's international sources, contained two "dimensions" or "elements"—"Personal" and "Procedural." The Procedural dimension, she explained, established methodical systems of service delivery, guaranteeing consistency and efficiency. The Personal dimension imbued procedures with positive affect, embodied them in appropriately responsive attitudes and behavior, and conveyed them with communicative competence. Another, even longer story of flawed performance exemplified the definitions, again an incident personally witnessed by Lim at an anonymous Davao hotel. This time, a lengthy check-in process overseen by an uncommunicative cashier formed the substance of the narrative.

By the end of the story, and in the remarks that followed, one main premise of Lim's vision was strikingly clear. Quality Service, while it might be generic in virtually every respect, needed individual subjects to manifest it, and it needed them in a very personal, even emotional way. Quality was not simply an affair of mass production, although it was certainly that, or at least it was intended to be that once "standards" were put in place and enforced. Quality, the director repeatedly stressed, was just as dependant on the Personal as it was on the Procedural. A high degree of individual internalization of the Quality doctrine was essential for the success of any tourism establishment. Moreover, this was essential not only for the owners and managers, the "key players" in attendance, but also for the tourate employees, the "rank and file" as the seminar's presenters termed them. My thoughts turned to the staff at Marjorie's Inn as I took in this portion of the speech, wondering how they would react to this news.

To develop this point, Lim illuminated a series of four slides that graphically depicted, one by one, the possible combinations of good and bad Personal and Procedural service. The first slide, named "the Freezer," exemplified the worst case scenario: poor Procedural and Personal service combined. Much to the group's amusement and perhaps relief, Davao's establishments were not selected as illustrations of this combination. The director instead shifted her gaze to the national level and identified two domestic monopolies, both notorious for their inefficiency and their abusive treatment of their clientele: Philippine Airlines and the Philippine Long Distance Telephone Company. The shortcomings of these companies had long been the source of jokes and urban legends, both in the city and throughout the country. The examples drew a hearty laugh from the audience as soon as Lim announced them, employing, as all regular users did, their initialized nicknames. She could not have chosen more effective targets from a pedagogical standpoint, as the applicability of the Freezer category was immediately understood and accepted by everyone in the room. Through the unambiguous initial examples, the participants were confidently initiated into the practice of conceptualizing the domestic tourism industry along the lines Lim's international paradigms established.

A slide named "the Factory" next appeared, which illustrated the mixed combination of good Procedural but poor Personal service. Here Lim chose a transnational, ASEAN-oriented example, citing the entire city state of Singapore. The response was less enthusiastic this time, the participants seeming less certain about the meaning of the example. The director filled the void and simultaneously reminded the audience of her own personal familiarity with the ASEAN circuits of the global tourism matrix, elaborating, "I think Singapore is like that. They're very efficient. Everything works like clockwork. But I think the people are being trained by their government to smile and to be friendly. Even that was to be [pausing] ah, processed." This assessment again emphasized that, in the director's perspective, the Personal element of Quality Tourism Service could not be embodied mechanically. It demanded more than the superficial "processing" of a script or a memorized behavioral repertoire that might include smiling and friendly discourse. The Personal element involved a more profound and holistic subjective involvement for a top Quality rating.

The third slide presented the other mixed good/bad combination of the two dimensions of service: poor Procedural and good Personal service. This slide was entitled, "the Friendly Zoo," a phrase that drew an immediate reaction from the audience. The room erupted in a ripple of knowing laughter—the first really spontaneous display of collective affect all morning. Lim ignored the response, however, and passed on quickly to the final slide, which she introduced as "what we all came for," the slide depicting "Service Excellence," showing good ratings on both Procedural and Personal dimensions. "This is where we all want to be—I *hope*," she concluded, introducing a note of anxiety into the final word. She engaged the room then in a rallying cry, adding, "I hope that you agree with us and that this is not just Margie and Kiling talking. Do you agree that this is where we want Davao to be?" The group, alerted to the change in speech act by the previous change in tone, were ready by the time the question had been fully articulated. Without hesitation, an enthusiastic, collective "Yes!" filled the Orchid Room, moving Lim to answer back, "All right. Great!" She then proceeded with the penultimate phase of the speech.

After a slight pause, which served to create a suspenseful effect, Lim posed the first of what she intended to be the most memorable set of questions to the group. "Having seen these three," she said, indicating all the slide combinations except—for what she evidently assumed were now well justified reasons—Service Excellence, "where do you think Davao falls?" The response was again unhesitating. "Friendly Zoo!" came the answer, amid much supportive laughter. Here the logic in her previous avoidance of the category became clear. She had intended for a revelation along these lines to occur during this, the climactic moment of the presentation, not earlier. Lim identified the respondent, whom she knew already by name, and said to the crowd, "Are you a Friendly Zoo here in Davao? Do you agree with Francine?" In order to reinforce what it was now evident had been her own category choice as well, the director went back to the other possibilities, the Freezer and Factory slides, and elicited a collective "No" to each slide from the crowd in turn. She returned one last time to the Friendly Zoo slide and asked, with a clear note of jubilance in her voice:

So you, you think Davao's not there, ha? [pointing to the other slides] So what about this? Francine said a Friendly Zoo. Are you a Friendly Zoo? You are very hospitable, charming, friendly, smiling, but you really don't know what you're doing. Right? What? Is that where Davao is?

Much laughter accompanied these questions. The group had now become a "crowd," riding its own collectively generated wave of humor, brought to life by the unanticipated consensus that the slide had evoked throughout the room. "Yes!" came a spirited collective response, as soon as the string of questions ended. "What?" Lim chimed back, her timing echoing the rhythm of the room, her own vivaciousness heightened by her evident success in energizing the audience. The woman she had recognized as "Francine" again responded, this time to such laughter at her own table that her words could not be heard beyond it. "Pardon?" Lim said, and Francine repeated her response, this time so that it also rang throughout the room. "That's why we're here," she called out, in a tone that expressed the smallest trace of genuine suffering, but with such a self-amused spirit accompanying it as well that the entire gathering burst into laughter yet again, the strongest expression of it yet.

The director was plainly delighted. "Oh, that's why you're here," she echoed, and added, "Good—to tell me the truth." Something in her manner suggested to me that she believed what had just occurred in the room was itself slightly extraordinary, that things had gone beyond a seminar's normal communicational expectations with regard to the very openness and honesty she herself had called for at the outset. She was moved to adopt something like a testimonial mode in response. She repaid the audience with a true story of her own, recounting her recent history within the inner circle of the government's tourism leadership, speaking now in subdued and earnest tones: "When we were doing an analysis about training needs of Davao, we were working with DATA and with the DOT and with TESDA, this was our analysis. Davao falls here [she indicated the Friendly Zoo slide]. And I'm glad that, Francine, it came from you."

Then, as if she had somehow gone too far in her own self-disclosure, Lim began to change her affect, expressing a somewhat uncertain assessment of the situation, both immediate and collective. Ignoring the room's uproarious behavior of only a few seconds past, she continued:

> I don't know whether the rest of you agree. OK? So we have to strengthen maybe the procedural. But also some of the personal, OK, the values. Values, attitudes, behavior, and communication skills. And that's why we're here today, as we said, because this is Day One of going forward together for making Davao a Quality Tourism Destination. Margie will explain to you in a while how we wish to achieve this but this afternoon we want to hear from you directly *how* we can do this together because it's no use for us dictating to you what we should do, what kind of training you have. We have to hear it from you directly because you are the owners.

With this contrite, conciliatory appeal, Lim prepared to bring her presentation to a close. She showed the group a final slide, listing "reasons why" her vision of "Quality Tourism" was imperative for Davao's local establishment to adopt. As conciliatory as her tone had become at the end of the previous segment, now the Director returned with equal intensity to her a more authoritative manner. She closed the keynote address with two assertions, both calculated to alert the assembled body to the magnitude of the impending changes coming to their locality and to compel them to reflect soberly upon their own responses to it.

The first assertion focused on the newly designated rulers of the tourism matrix, the Customers. In this regard, Lim emphasized the global consciousness of these generic beings, placing for the first time especial emphasis on a "tourist" identity to drive home this awareness. She stated:

> People nowadays, customers nowadays, *tourists,* are no longer content with just one or two, there are many choices. They have become *very* sophisticated. They have become *very* knowledgeable. Information technology has made the *world* very small. They see how it is done in other places. You can look at your CD-rom for example and see what hotels in other parts of the world look like and what service they give. So customers, tourists nowadays are very, very sophisticated and they *choose* and they *expect.* Not just the minimum, but Quality, top service, OK? So there is that expectation, a verified expectation.

In her second focus she pulled out all her rhetorical stops, identifying—again in globalizing terms—an even more threatening element in the contemporary domestic tourism matrix: "Competition." After acknowledging the current "seller's market" in Davao City, which she warned would not "last forever," the director stated:

There are threats to you, OK. Now you may be enjoying 80 percent occupancy but once a new hotel comes in and *gives* the service—all the things that I've been pointed out . . . but I guess no amount of me talking and telling you will convince you, you have to feel it. But why wait for that day? Let's prepare *now* and face the competition. Now, who is Davao competing with? Have you ever thought about it? Who is Davao competing with? Who are your competitors? Outside and inside?

Members of the audience responded initially with the names of provincial cities in the central and southern Philippines, which Lim accepted but quickly challenged by asking about "external" competition, identifying EAGA in this respect. Malaysia, Brunei, and a variety of destinations on Borneo and Sulawesi were identified, which prompted her to launch into her final pitch. She ended with an admonition:

So, you're competing not only with cities in the Philippines who are aiming for that Quality Service. You're competing with the region as well. And internally, you are competing with new players who want to put up hotels here. And I know this for a fact . . . *Serious* people, who will give this service. If you don't get your act together now, once these people come in, you're done for. I can tell you that because the customer will *choose*—an efficiently and professionally managed establishment, that provides service. So the competition is there . . . competition is very, very, *real.*

With this final warning, Lim gave a brief description of the seminar's presentations to come and then closed her keynote to substantial applause with a simple "Thank you very much."

After I left the seminar, and in the weeks and months that followed, Lim's remarks stayed with me, as I expected they did with the other seminar participants. I had many opportunities during this time to observe the gradual application of the Quality model to the city's tourism landscape, and, in most specific detail, to the tourate scripts and choreography of Marjorie's Inn. To be sure, the seminar's influence was far from all-pervasive, and there were several respects in which Lim's understanding of the landscape and its tourate seemed to be somewhat out of touch with existing reality. Her "basic" assumption that every hotel had a fax machine, for example, was still ahead of the times, as was the assertion that guests typically had access to CD-rom technology. However, her understanding of what the seminar's participants had been "ready" to hear regarding "Quality Tourism Service" more generally, and what they were prepared to implement into their own managerial practice, had on the whole been much closer to the mark. The ripple effect of the seminar, while it was impossible to quantify, was substantial. The event had been one of those seminal moments when the imagination of touristic reality had changed.

The "Friendly Zoo" category, in particular, was destined to produce a lasting imprint. Davao City, in actuality, of course, had no zoo, friendly or otherwise. The concept, as with "The Freezer" and "The Factory," was a token of a once-foreign, now-Philippinized discourse of modernity. Yet, the

Friendly Zoo metaphor, its colonial origins notwithstanding, had captured the seminar's collective imagination with regard to the local tourate predicament, encapsulating in a mildly humorous manner the historical circumstance that the new Standard class of tourist accommodations in Davao City, such as Marjorie's Inn, exemplified. Still in their initial years of learning how to cope with the various procedural challenges of hotel operation, they ranked themselves low on the Procedural dimension. At the same time, a general sense of the Personal attitudes, values, and behaviors already cultivated among their respective tourates was also apparent and widely felt. Producing such "Quality" personal performance was not the unfamiliar territory that organizing functional procedures had turned out to be. In sum, the Friendly Zoo model, employing its own globally oriented terminology, had served to reinforce and articulate a common sense, already present in the tourism establishment, that training in operational procedures for tourism services was needed, but that the tourate was several steps ahead of the global tourism game with regard to the development of interpersonal conduct. The closeness of the metaphoric fit eased the process of reimagining the local tourism industry in global terms, comfortably positioning Davao's tourism establishment, if not at the top end of "Service Excellence," then certainly not in the lowest position of "the Freezer."

Returning to the specific case of Marjorie's Inn, I could also understand from my visits over the years, how and why the metaphor of the Friendly Zoo was seen as applicable to the inn's general style of tourate practice. The Friendly Zoo label did capture a combination of characteristics evident at the inn. On the Procedural side, some of these were manifest in material form: toilets that often failed to shut off and whistled softly day and night, lamp bulbs that worked so infrequently I made a note of it when they occasionally did turn on, and telephones that clicked incessantly when not in use. The coffee shop had menus that quoted prices long since raised two or three times. Other imperfections were manifest in tourate performance: room rates once or twice misquoted, room charges once or twice doubled, room reservations once or twice lost, along with wake-up calls, phone messages, and mail. Meals at the coffee shop occasionally took more than half an hour to appear when a banquet was in progress. Getting change back from a restaurant bill could take even longer than getting a meal at any time, as there was a perpetual absence of change at the front desk. There was also a perpetual absence of information at the front desk, which struck me as particularly non-tourate-like in character. The desk staff rarely, if ever, were able to field a question about life outside the hotel, even something as close range as where to find the change they themselves seemed never to have at hand.

The inn owner/manager (whose responses to the announcement of the Friendly Zoo category had been as animated as those of any of the other participants there) was very much aware of a need for "strengthening the procedural side," as Lim had ultimately phrased it. When we were discussing the general tourate situation at the inn one day, she recounted an incident that seemed representative of the inn's "Zoo" predicament. A group of DOLE officials recently had come and inspected her hotel, she said. She was informed by them that she would have to pay 10 percent more to her night shift staff. She had agreed, but had then told the staff also that they would now have to stay awake during their night shifts, and if she caught them asleep three times they would be fired. After a short time, she reported, the staff requested not to be paid the extra 10 percent. The story sparked a memory of one of the few times I had arrived at the inn alone after midnight, when I had walked past the sleeping security guard, lifted my room key from its slot inside the front desk counter as the clerk lay asleep in her chair, and walked upstairs without provoking so much as a change of snoring pattern from anybody on duty. In sum, what the Australian manual characterized as the "Procedural" side of Marjorie's Inn was existing, pretty much across the board, in a state of mild dysfunction. Even by the Director's exacting standards, however, it would never have ranked anywhere near "poor." The level of competence was always only one or two small steps below the standards overtly set, not lagging greatly.

The applicability of the other side of the Friendly Zoo metaphor, the Personal dimension, was not difficult to justify as well. The inn's tourate, to a person, went about their business with an earnest good faith, a sympathetic energy that would without doubt have fallen into the much-praised "hospitable" attitude category. When Lim had summarized excellence on the Personal side during the seminar, she had done so with one concept, "care." In true Quality Tourism Service, she had informed the group, the "message" sent to Customers was, "We *care* and we deliver." If there was one thing I became convinced of over the years of visits to Marjorie's Inn—long in advance of the seminar and its Quality model—it was that the staff and the management were indeed adept at sending such a message. Whenever some mishap did occur, a long-faced, humble apology quickly followed. When things were running smoothly, a buoyant, enthusiastic, slightly triumphant good humor typically prevailed. Examples of what the seminar's model would have recognized as the "friendly" and "caring" character of the inn reiterated themselves countless times a day in the hotel's most ordinary practices. Luggage was delivered to rooms with bright-eyed enthusiasm, no matter what the hour, as was laundry, particularly on special request. If a desk clerk actually did have a piece of information to impart on occasion, such as where to find a particular jeepney stop, or where was best at a certain time of day to flag down a taxi, the news was generally voiced as such, as *news*, as a not insignificant contribution to the exchange, which was gladly and freely given.

The most memorable example of the "Friendly" dimension of the staff at Marjorie's Inn, in my experience, was embodied by one of the waiters,

Freddy. Freddy was one of the relatively permanent staff members who had worked at the inn all the years I visited there. Over the course of the time I knew him, Freddy became something of an institution in his own right at the inn. I never saw Freddy take an ordinary step while he was working in the coffee shop. He literally sashayed his "friendly" way around the restaurant, both when he was taking orders, and also when delivering trays full of food to tables. He imbued his "Procedural dimension" with all the vim and alacrity of a competition square dancer in mid-call. When unencumbered by a tray, he would move around the room with his head down, his arms tucked in, and his whole upper body inclined slightly forward, his legs working furiously underneath, arriving at some table with a burst of energy, arresting himself so suddenly and so completely as he reached it that the Road Runner cartoon image came to mind watching him. Freddy's intensity might have been offputting, had he not been able to change his manner abruptly once he was standing still, smiling so broadly and inquiring after the guest's order with such a disarming, soft-spoken, light-hearted voice that it was all but impossible to believe it had been he who had just dashed pell mell across the crowded space. "Chipper" did not even begin to do him justice. Neither did "friendly," really, since he always, despite his enormous smiles, and exaggerated physical antics, maintained a fairly formal interactive way of speaking when dealing with the inn's guests. He sprinkled his discourse liberally with honorifics of whatever sort were applicable, and whenever he was asked a question by a guest—about a menu item, the hotel, or the city more generally—he always treated it with the same intensity that was apparent in the more solitary aspects of his service work. Freddy, I was certain, would have passed even Lim's most discriminating tests for the Personal dimension with flying colors. His signature performances, however, constituted only one of the more flamboyant versions of the inn's generally "Quality" staff conduct.

What the model characterized as the Personal side of Marjorie's Inn, while it was manifest in an individual manner by every staff member, was also to a considerable extent a product of leadership. The owner/manager of the inn set the example in this regard—"Ma'am" as she was known to the staff, or "Jerry," as I eventually came to call her. Jerry was both the heart and the mind of Marjorie's Inn. She was there daily, often closeted for hours in a tiny second floor air-conditioned office with her bookkeeper. From this nerve center, she managed everything. It was she who oversaw the inn's finances, signed its checks, decided its future. It was she who hired and fired its staff, formulated its staff policies, conducted staff meetings, and dealt with staff emergencies. It was she who cared for the inn's appearance and condition, approving or vetoing all its countless minor upkeep upgrades and adjustments in decor and furnishings. The staff might occasionally suggest a new practice or procedure, offering a "special meal" to single customers, for example, or changing the kind of flowers on the coffee shop tables. I remember one occasion when the desk staff were invited to select from three alternatives Jerry had identified for a new uniform type. None had the slightest interest in the "Filipiniana" option that was presented. All wanted an urban look and chose a tailored suit variant, despite Jerry's comment that the Filipiniana style would be "cooler." The staff held firm, and Jerry went along with them in the end. It was Jerry, however, who made the final decision. All in all, Marjorie's Inn was Jerry's baby, her brainchild. She set the tone and she modeled the roles.

I came to know Jerry fairly well over the course of my visits to Davao, although we did not become close personal friends. Her father had been a guerrilla "all over Mindanao," as she put it, during World War II, after which he'd bought land around the city at bargain prices and moved from his native Pampanga to Davao. Jerry did not speak Visayan, but Kapampangan, Tagalog, English, and, through her Zamboangeña mother, Chabacano. She had been an AFS exchange student in Pasadena, California as a teenager, and had made a Greyhound bus trip all the way across the United States on that visit, which had included one memorably long ride between New York and Florida. One of her own children became an exchange student to the United States during the period of my visits, and she was also hosting a Rotary Exchange student from Connecticut at the same time. The inn's foreigner guests were by no means the only transnational presences in Jerry's life.

As it was Jerry who supplied the problem-solving responses to the various situations that arose at the inn, it was she who most meaningfully defined the "Friendly"-ness of the Inn's particular Friendly Zoo for the inn's clientele. Always ready with a smile in greeting and a laugh to offer at the first possible chance, Jerry was endowed with a seemingly fathomless well of patient, resourceful sympathy. "We care" might well have been tattooed across her forehead. She was the most dependably hospitable person I ever came across in the tourism business, with a world class gift for the "Personal" dimension of service delivery. Whenever I came forward with questions or requests, which tended to happen several times a week, they were invariably met in a "Quality" spirit. One morning a few weeks after my first 1995 arrival, for example, I asked Jerry if she knew of an orchid garden where I could go and spend the day reading. She thought of one that I had already seen mentioned in the tourism literature and ran upstairs immediately to call a friend to get the phone number. She came down a few moments later with jeepney instructions and the names of the cantina manager and the garden's owner's daughter. She then went upstairs again and handwrote a note of introduction for me to the owners. This incident took place many weeks before the seminar. I had expected Jerry only to tell a desk clerk to put a flyer in my hand and send me on my way. Instead, something like the stuff of a tourist's dreams had transpired. However, these were the lengths to which Jerry frequently went in her everyday managerial practice at the hotel. They consistently ranked off the scale of "caring" on the Personal side of Service Excellence.

In all the ways mentioned above as well as a host of others, the tourate practice at Marjorie's Inn conformed to the general features of the Friendly Zoo metaphor. Yet the globalizing metaphor ultimately failed to do justice to the inn, obscuring rather than revealing the most significant aspects of the establishment's cultural and historical character. The "Zoo" label, with its institutional connotations, assigned to the inn an essentially public conceptual space, a space where forcibly displaced animals might be imagined to be finding a "home," but which, for its human tourist occupants, was a space that had no domestic associations whatsoever. The "home away from home" dimension of the inn was not represented in this stereotype, nor were the cultural traditions and institutions from which the utopic "home" landscape was in historical fact derived, and to which it was at least in part still connected. The metaphor failed to represent the way the inn's practices resulted in a particular sense of "home"—to some extent a utopic, touristic version of home, but also a home whose foundations, symbolic if not material, still lay wholly outside the tourism matrix.

Davao City's local society prided itself on high standards of "hospitality," a term I heard frequently in the city's discourse, in part because, as a visitor to the locality, I was constantly provoking the practices to which "hospitality" referred. The interactive practices of welcoming and entertaining amicable nonresidents, whether such visitors were allied through kinship ties or not, were transgenerational. They had been passed down through so many generations that they had become a part of folklore and were consciously recognized as belonging to "Tradition." While I was tempted to read into them—particularly their English language variants—a legacy of colonialism and its subordinating "Yes, sir" mentalities, the traditions of hospitality were more often regarded as precolonial in origin, understood as a part of the nature of an indigenous "Filipino" or "Davaoeño" or "Visayan" spirit. Indeed, a mild ethnically oriented rivalry existed in relation to them, which left it open to question which ethnic group in the Philippines, or in the city, for that matter, in reality was truly the most hospitable among them all. In any case, the understanding of the value of hospitality was regarded as distinctly Filipino. I once heard a group of Davao's Rotarians, themselves in the act of welcoming home a friend who had recently returned from an extended vacation touring China, deride the entertainment standards of an American branch of the organization because of the "celebration" that branch had organized in honor of the arrival of an international contingent of fellow Rotarians. The Americans had not come close to meeting the group's own standards of hospitality, even on such basic grounds as the presence of an appropriate excess of food and drink. Being "hospitable" was a way of being cultural in a popularly, broadly Philippine-identified manner. It was a culturally marked way of accruing prestige as well.

In this respect, the "friendly" aspect of the city's new class of "Friendly Zoos" tapped into long-standing cultural institutions of receiving visitors. The city's history of hospitality and its traditions of practice, as they had been elaborated and enhanced by the city's most prestigious "pioneer" families over colonial and post-colonial periods of residence, explained to a great extent why the tourate currently emerging in Davao was already more than up to par on the Personal dimension of Service Excellence. The global models, however, were entirely inadequate in representing the distinctive historical and cultural record of hospitality in the city, a record that had been manifest for the most part in private and domestic spaces.

I had on so many occasions been witness to extraordinary acts of generosity in Davao in the name of "hospitality," acts made specifically to welcome "guests" of so many various kinds, that by the end of my research period I had come to believe I understood something of what the local standards of hospitality entailed. They were a demanding set of standards, which in extreme cases could necessitate permanent sacrifices on a hosting family's part, if, for example, it was perceived that a guest might be moved to gratitude by a gift from an unreplacable family collection of some kind—of books, or artifacts, or consumable goods, perhaps. More often, however, the tradition demanded more temporary losses, the displacement of family members from their normal working routines so that they could be present to welcome a new arrival or the expenses of a special meal, often organized without advance notice, which had to go well beyond everyday practice in its presentation of both local "delicacies" or transnational, "First Class" extravagances. In this highly exacting social climate, Jerry had stood out to me as a model of what a gracious hostess, Davao City style, ought to be. Her success in the Personal dimension of the hotel business was no coincidence, nor was it the result of some excessive commercial ambition that had moved her quickly along a steep learning curve of touristic "Friendliness." Rather, it was the product of a lifetime's practice in cultural spaces—her own home and in her parents' home as well—where such a concept did not even begin to represent the range of humane and "caring" conduct that was possible, let alone expected, of a person.

An episode in October 1995 epitomized Jerry's unique brand of "Quality Tourism Service" and also illustrated where the Friendly Zoo metaphor fell short of aptly characterizing the hotel's actual cultural predicament, poised as it was between global models of commercial touristic performance and models extending from "middle class" or mainstream Davao City society. The incident illustrated the hybrid character of the inn as a home away from home, both utopic and otherwise. It was, perhaps, a unique, "unrepresentative" event, one that would have happened only with and to

the particular individuals involved in it, myself included, with their particular histories of interaction. However, its one-of-a-kind character, in and of
itself, indicated the partial nature of the inn's incorporation into the global
tourism matrix.

I had arrived at the inn at seven o'clock in the evening, returning from
several days on Samal Island interviewing SITE project participants. I had
developed a pattern during this phase of the research of leaving the inn for
Samal Island during the week, giving up my room, and returning on the
weekend for a day or two, to run errands in the city or attend some tourism-
related event. Usually the strategy required little or no planning, as the
inn was almost never fully booked. On this occasion, however, I returned to
find that there was no room reserved for me. The staff, for once brimming
with information, let me know that there were no rooms to be had in the
whole city either. A huge convention of some kind was going on throughout
the weekend and every space was booked. They gazed on me in no little
consternation as they imparted this news, the possibility of some kind of
dramatic response clearly troubling them, although by now I had established a lengthy track record of avoiding such responses. They knew, however, as did I, that this was a situation in which the consequences were more
serious than any we had previously confronted. The tension behind the
desk was running high on this particular evening.

Tired and in a somewhat disheveled, unpresentable condition, the news
that there was no available room at the inn, while it was hardly worthy of the
catastrophic rating the staff's affect was indicating, did produce a reaction
of visible disappointment on my part. It was intensified somewhat by the
fact that I felt I was in part responsible for my own predicament. I had not
reminded the front desk at my departure several days previously that I was
coming back on this Friday. I had given them the month's entire itinerary
at the beginning of the month, and I had told Jerry and one of the room
staff at my last checkout that I was returning this Friday. The front desk,
however, I had neglected to remind, and they hadn't held a room. I had felt
some apprehension during the ride into town that the lack of reminder
would turn out to be costly, and indeed it was looking as though that would
be the case.

Jerry's husband André was at the desk when I arrived. He reported that
the desk had sold "my" room just five minutes before I had appeared—a
"double" room with two twin-size beds, at the far end of the third floor that
I had booked regularly enough to have earned for it the designation,
"mine." Unfortunately, however, designations aside, the room was let to
another traveler and there was no going back on that agreement. The inn's
Procedural dimension was already strong enough to have made that option
unthinkable.

Jerry arrived at the moment André finished his report. She was, true to
form, very sympathetic hearing of my plight. At the end of the story, her

response was unhesitating. She said that if I couldn't find another room in the city I could stay as a guest in her house that evening. At this point Jesus (one of the room staff) came downstairs and held a brief conference with Jerry. There was an empty room in the inn, saved supposedly for someone whom Jesus and Jerry were sure wouldn't use it. This room was given to me, and I was happily checked in.

Jerry's decision that night transgressed the boundaries of a hotel manager. She chose instinctively to go beyond the call of Service Excellence in issuing her invitation. In that spontaneous utterance, she assumed the role of a homeowner, not a tourate CEO. She offered support to a stranded unfortunate without considering its impact on any "bottom line" or Procedural side.

As grateful as I felt toward Jerry on that occasion, and as much of a relief as it was that no such imposition would in fact be necessary, there was also a little piece of the back of my mind in which a small voice commented, "This will never last." The "this" referred to the historical moment in which a hotel owner in Davao City might be willing to assist a customer, even an unusual one, in such a genuinely friendly way. Nonetheless, at least for the moment, in "the 90s," this mixture of the Davao City hostess and the hotel entrepreneur could and did exist, not just at Marjorie's Inn, but throughout the new wave of standard class establishments more generally. In this regard, these businesses made good on the claim to be "homes away from home" to a far greater extent than their advertising could ever indicate. They proved through countless actions, large and small, that the "Friendly Zoo" classification was still, on the whole, inept, still ahead of the times. Like a private dwelling place as opposed to an institutional space or establishment, Marjorie's Inn was made *livable*, not dysfunctional, by its "we care, whether we deliver or not" style of working conduct. Its domestic aspects still provided a constructive foundation for its practice of everyday commercial life.

Conclusion

As the above incidents indicate, Marjorie's Inn functioned in many ways more as an extension of a family household than as a commercial enterprise, although it was in fact a cross between the two. The particularly trenchant division of labor separating staff from management, especially with regard to decision-making and information management, the fact that management and ownership were embodied by the same individual, and the relatively modest size of the establishment, all combined to produce the impression that the inn operated more like a household than a business with regard to its tourate culture.

However, the inn's *habitus* was in the process of outgrowing this evaluation, shedding its domestic status, and heading on to the bigger leagues of

"Service Excellence." It was this very process of growth that defined the cultural moment for the city's emergent standard hotel tourate. It was a moment of initiation, of construction, when the hotel industry was undergoing a transformation at the bidding of the national government, metamorphosing from family-style businesses, conducted along family lines, into globally accredited, "Quality" tourism establishments, striving to conform to practices designed at distant centers of tourism commerce and industry.

In this transformative period, it was the position of "manager" or "general manager," more than those of the staff, that became key as an indicator of how far the tug of war between familial and transnational had progressed, how deeply government-sponsored policies had actually permeated into the tourism establishments' consciousness and practice. The actual integration of local and global orientations was occurring at the managerial level, as managers constituted the link between the interests of owning families and the demands of the tourism industry. A manager was an authority figure in the hotel system, but he or she ultimately answered to the owners as well. If managers were enmeshed in family dynamics that defined their motivations and interests (such as reinforcing the family's elite social position by snubbing hotel customers), these would be reflected in the hotel's practices, for better and worse as far as the tourism matrix was concerned. In these cases, something other than Quality Tourism was likely to result.

All in all, in the mid-1990s the influence of owning families was still the governing influence in the main, and tourism policy was relegated to the status of an enhancement to family style business management, however that might be expressed in a given establishment. Managerial positions were still typically filled by members of an owning family, as was the case in Marjorie's Inn. Here there was no mediation between family interests and touristic operations, as there stood to be should the growth of the industry require hiring additional managers from outside an owning family. Managers embodied the family presence and culture in the hotel, and they were treated by the staff in a manner generally identical to the way household "helpers" or domestic workers treated members of the households in which they were employed. Whatever conflicts of interest might ensue between the goals of Service Excellence and those of being a successful family member, they were conflicts generally being worked out within a single person, not between some ambitious non-family professional manager and an owning family member. The culture of global tourism was not yet endowed with autonomous agents in the standard class, on the whole. The process of transformation was still in an initial stage in this regard.

In the case of Marjorie's Inn, the family- and tourism-governed orientations were not presenting any major conflicts during the mid-1990s. Instead, the new transnational discourse was integrated into the existing household style of operation, beginning to improve its operating practices without altering substantially the role of the owner/manager as it had heretofore been constructed. I noticed the impact of the new policies as my bills became uniformly correct and communication services improved. Jerry, however, remained as all-pervasive a presence as ever. Jerry remained the only person who knew how to give directions to guests to places nearby, to tell them where to buy medicine, or whether there was yet an internet cafe up and running, or the schedule of Davao's festival events, or who to go to for travel information or tickets for a direct flight to Singapore or Hong Kong. Jerry remained the only person who had the status, as an owner, to call on other businesses and inquire details from or make arrangements with them. Jerry, in sum, remained the only professional in the inn's tourate who had experience dealing with other businesses in the city that a guest might need in order to deal with them as well. Tourism discourse and practice entered into Marjorie's Inn only so far as Jerry welcomed it, and she was no slave to the global market—as yet. She was beginning to learn, however, how to think about that prospect in much more specific terms.

It was this balance of power, which was only beginning to tilt away from family-governed business practices in the direction of the global tourism matrix, that defined Davao's small hotel cultural predicament in "the 90s." It was this balance that constituted the "Friendly Zoos" as they were now identified, on their way to Service Excellence. Davao's journey toward becoming a "Quality Destination" for urban tourism had only just begun, and the internal impact of global tourist practices on the local power structures of commercial life were yet to be registered in full.

Chapter 9
Local Expressions of Leisure:
Beach Parks

Little has been said thus far of the tourists who were residents of Davao City itself. They did exist, in the same contingent, temporary manner as elsewhere in the world, although in fewer numbers. They were a minority segment of the population, somewhere between 5 and 10 percent of Davao City's total, but still tens of thousands strong.[1] They included the most modest fringes of the local version of the middle class on upward, those segments of the city's population that had managed to attain modernity, or at least the occupations that most closely conformed to it. They were the city's company employees as well as its managers and professionals, its technicians, high school and college students, service providers, as well as its executives, entrepreneurs, and administrators. Such relatively prosperous residents of the city were likely to take on the tourist identity upon occasion, taking themselves away from their homes for playful reasons when time permitted or occasion dictated and enacting the leisure dimension of their working lives in touristic fashion.

The utopic landscapes designed for Davao City's tourists entailed far more modest excursions than the transnational journeys heretofore described for the city's incoming visitors—except, of course, those marketed to the city's tiny upper, upper class of jetset residents, whose travels were as global in scope as those of jetsetters anywhere in the world. The tourist journeys marketed to the local population, however, tended to be journeys in miniature. These were billed as lasting hours or days, not weeks or months. They involved the use of buses, automobiles, or pumpboats, not airplanes, trains, or ocean liners. All the same, these journeys were essentially touristic in character and motivation. They involved utopic spaces, enhanced forms of social life amid strangers, services provided by a tourate, and acts of relaxing and otherwise enjoying time off from work in playful, idyllic environments.

For residents fortunate enough to engage in tourism in Davao City, the most popular forms of touristic practice took place at beach park resorts. There were several dozen of these establishments in operation in the city's environs. Many of them were located to the south of the city center, along the coastline, from a suburb named Matina on the southern outskirts of the city to the beaches of the nearby town of Toril, some fifteen kilometers south. There were more than twenty such establishments scattered throughout this area. In addition, another dozen or so beach park resorts were located on Samal and Talikud Islands, concentrated along the coastlines closest to the Davao City port areas, some only a few minutes from the city's shores by pumpboat.

The coastlands on which these parks were situated did not present world class sandy stretches. Neither were the coral reefs and marine shelf just offshore of any extraordinary merit for recreational diving. The vast expanses of white powdery substances that had achieved such renown for other parts of the archipelago, and the underwater coral gardens and caves for which the Philippines was famous in the diving world, were nowhere present on or off the beaches of Davao Gulf. What sand there was was yellow, moderately coarse, and often covered by small corals that made wading treacherous at high tide. What diving there was was of a more standard variety as well.

However, while there was nothing approaching Bali's Kuta Beach, Hawaii's Waikiki strand, or Palawan's reef cultures, numerous natural sandy stretches

Figure 13. A beach park on Talikud Island.

on a much smaller scale could be found along the coasts around Davao City and Samal Island, appearing amid coral bluffs that otherwise formed the coastlines. These areas were sheltered by the gulf's geography from high surfs, hazardous marine life, and ocean storms that caused problems in other locations. This made them feasible, relatively safe tourist destinations.

The resorts that had cropped up on a few dozen of the more attractive of these modest beaches were privately owned establishments, not parks in the full sense of the term. They did not exhibit the character of sanctuary that is commonly experienced in public parks, whether colossal or tiny in scale. Aside from their non-public status, however, the resorts were park-like in most other respects. They defined areas known for their natural scenery and saved from the forces of industry, preserved for the purposes of recreation. They bore no great resemblance to theme parks in this regard and remained *real* in the sense that they were oriented around preexisting natural givens. Whatever interventions they made on their environments, it was for the purposes of enhancement, not erasure. The parks were all variations of what Jane Desmond (1999: 176-216) has characterized as the "in-fake-situ" model of touristic landscape development, similar to Pearl Farm Beach Resort in this respect.[2] As such, they staged "the natural" of the very sites that had existed prior to their own construction, occupying a kind of middle ground of touristic reality. They fell somewhere between actual nature preserves and parklands, on the one hand, and amusement destinations constructed entirely out of previously nonexistent elements, on the other. They integrated to differing extents the found and the made, so as to transform the natural into a utopic vision of itself.

The practices engaged in at beach parks were not invented out of whole cloth either, although there was no preexisting tradition of beach-going in Davao City's cultural background. The *dagat* or beach had no history as a site for any practices that might be considered touristic precursors. The beach had been culturally defined as a place of work not play, where fishing and perhaps other forms of industry might take place. There was no obvious precedent in local cultural practices for beach park tourism. The touristic activities at the beach parks were not imitations of European or American beach culture either, with their emphasis on sunbathing and beachcombing. Beach park practices were instead the outgrowths of celebratory practices with longstanding nontouristic histories.[3] A number of the most popular had emerged out of the "party" concept, an English language notion, probably a survival of the American colonial period. Parties were held in honor of birthdays and other anniversaries, gatherings for special friends and special guests, reunions of all kinds, from the most momentous, involving the most far-flung, to the most regular, involving the most intimate *barkada* (close friend group) associates. Parties, typically day-long, privately sponsored festive occasions, were the cultural source of many beach park tourism practices.

The beach parks were also a venue for the public equivalent of parties: festivals or fiestas. Privately owned parks were by definition incapable of staging authentic reconstructions of such practices, since both the fiesta and its more recent secular analogue, the festival, necessarily took place in the public spaces of the communities sponsoring them, but the parks nonetheless lent themselves to the touristic equivalents of such gatherings. They were typically sponsored by a collective of some kind, governmental, commercial, professional, or nonprofit. Activities—contests, games, feasts, pageants, ceremonies, sports, diversions, and other such entertaining fun— were organized along lines virtually identical to traditional fiesta/festival formats. These pseudo-festival or -fiesta gatherings formed the other end of the spectrum of beach park touristic occasions.

Beach parks, in accommodating this full spectrum of celebrations, provided the most popular environment for the forms of tourism in Davao City's local social networks. They were culturally significant destinations, evolving widely used models for utopic practice in relation to which the newer, larger scale transnational tourism industry was to be understood. The parks were not a great distance from Davao City's homes, but they were nonetheless understood as getaway kinds of places, basically analogous to those being developed at the Samal Island Tourism Estate and Pearl Farm Beach Resort. While the routes leading to them were relatively short compared to some ideal tourist's journey, they were still routes away from home, as were the routes bringing arrivals from Taiwan, Japan, Germany, and America. In sum, the beach parks functioned as the kinds of un-homely destinations tourism sought everywhere to produce. Not "abroad" in the full-fledged sense of the term, they were certainly "afield," allowing their clientele to experience themselves as "out and about" for the purposes of leisure. They were mini-escapes, whose usage illustrated the types of touristic identities, values, and behaviors that were becoming embodied by the city's residents.

In this chapter, I first give an account of the development of one of Davao City's most popular beach parks, in order to illustrate the manner in which the parks evidenced a local form of tourism development—a form that had evolved more autonomously than any other in Davao City. Beach park development was motivated by a complex array of contingent historical circumstances, not all of them, or even most of them, economic or transnational in nature. I then recount a "party" celebration that illustrates the ways beach park tourism was integrating itself into the more private end of the continuum of celebratory practices of Davao's tourist population. As with other consequences of other touristic forms and landscapes, the findings in this regard were mixed, and they involved a combination of disruptive and conservative influences. On the whole, however, the mixture, in the case of the beach parks, was relatively conservative in nature. It brought more into the tourism matrix and took less from it, in this regard, filling tourism's utopic spaces with familiar, longstanding habits of celebratory life.

A Model Resort: Fantasy Isle Beach Park

Fieldnote Entry: June 21, 1992, First Visit to Fantasy Isle, Samal Island

Late in the afternoon around 4:30, I asked the manager at my resort to tell me the way to Fantasy Isle, and I was given a small boy, Aries, as my "kauban" (companion/guide). He led me to a locked gate, which we climbed over, and then went down a path to a guard post inside the resort, where two security guards with large rifles were placed. One started in on me in English, asking my purpose coming to the Philippines in what I thought were hostile tones. I wondered if I had just stumbled into a genuinely life-threatening situation. Fighting hard to maintain an air of normalcy in the face of the guard's aggression, I told him I was studying tourism and asked him what he thought about it in the Philippines. He wasn't enthusiastic, despite his present occupation. I argued with him about the U.S., when he characterized it as a wealthy country, saying many poor lived there also; he couldn't accept it. He was in law school at the University of Mindanao, one of 25 children (three different mothers, same father), the only one in college. He proudly asserted he was "pure Davaoeño." He said he had once dreamed of going to the U.S. to make money and return wealthy, but now was not so obsessed with the plan. I said it was the Japanese who would be calling the shots in the Philippines, not the Americans. He and the other guard, who listened quietly, agreed to that.

It was quite a tense interview for me, a strange introduction to the most popular tourist park on the island, but at the end I decided I had just misread the guard's curiosity and interest in practicing English for hostility—the rifle had really given me a turn. His tone was not friendly either, one question following another in a barrage, "what is your purpose here, what is your purpose in researching here, why research tourism, why tourism in the Philippines," very quickly and without much heed to the response. The second guard was gracious, went and found change for my entrance fee, counted it for me, and let me pass easily. Of the two, I grew to like the difficult one more; he gave me a smile toward the end and let me take his picture.

I walked down to the beach area somewhat shaken. There were still a few tourists left and I avoided them, wandering toward the cabins, where I met Inday, a very hospitable young woman, who reported that the cabins sold for 350 pesos a night, as did those at the Costa Marina resort next door. She liked her job and had been there two years already. Tourists came at vacation time: December, April through May (mainly students); foreigners of all types stayed there; no one group was more frequent than any other.

One beach park, Fantasy Isle Beach Park, stood out from the others in terms of both design and patronage. It was the oldest and, by a considerable margin, the most popular of the Samal Island parks. It was also the most actively engaged in a continuous process of reinventing itself, the most invested in keeping pace, if not setting the pace, of ongoing development in this particular sector of the tourism industry. Fantasy Isle was a leader in its field, defining trends for what was occurring in the name of beach park tourism. I lived next to the park for several weeks in 1996, visited it occasionally throughout my research process, and interviewed its manager/owners, who belonged to yet another of Davao City's well established families, the Laguna family. The more I learned about the park, the more I came to understand it as a particularly illustrative example of what the beach park establishments were all about, in terms of the kinds of transformations they were staging in the realm of recreation and the manner in which tourism was emerging out of long established practices of entertainment.

The park itself, only about a hectare of beach front land initially, was part of a sixteen-hectare plot purchased by the Laguna family during the early period of American rule. It had started operating only in 1980, originally as a joint venture between the Laguna family and the Davao Interconti-nental Insular Inn. Insular had leased the property and coined the park's name, using the beach front exclusively for day parties for its own guests, whose transportation and food service it organized. Fantasy Isle was in this regard essentially foreign and touristic, although on a very limited scale. It was initiated as a mini-destination for foreigners, at a time when the for-eigners were mainly Germans and Australians who were in Davao City for the purposes of visiting penpal girlfriends.

The Laguna family had not been motivated to enter this arrangement by any desire to jump onto some tourism development bandwagon such as was present in the mid-1990s, although these were also years when Imelda Marcos's Ministry of Tourism loomed very large in the national conscious-ness. The family was instead attempting to find a way to deal with the un-wanted presence of military personnel on the property. The military had been stationed on Samal Island in the 1970s, ostensibly to deal with the activities of the communist New People's Army, who were moderately well established on the island during that time. The Fantasy Isle property, near the border of the Samal and Babak municipalities, was politically in a kind of no-man's-land and thus somewhat vulnerable and unprotected in terms of governance. The property had attracted the attention of the military, who had formed the habit of occupying the beach for their own purposes without asking permission of the owners. The owners, choosing to avoid forcing the issue in a direct confrontation, banked instead on the idea that a beach park would bring foreign civilians to the property and compel the military who were using it for free either to pay for their time on it or leave it alone. In this respect, the tourist enterprise that began on the beach was a diversionary tactic, not an outgrowth of a tourist industry in motion. It was instigated to defuse a volatile political situation by commercial means. The tactic was to prove not only effective in the short run, vis-à-vis the infor-mal military occupation, but highly consequential for the development of the local tourism matrix in the long run as well.

It was at this time, in 1980, that what came to be Fantasy Isle's most dis-tinctive feature, its shady grove of beach-side *talisay* trees, was developed. The manager of Insular had overseen this planting project in partnership with the senior head of the Laguna family. They had selected the talisay variety from a wide array of possibilities, knowing that it grew well in salty water. The trees had flourished over the years. By the 1990s, when my visits began, they had long since become large enough to provide generous "natural" cover for the dozen or so rows of picnic tables along the shore of the park. Their presence, a triumph of landscaping ingenuity unequaled elsewhere in the vicinity, served to convert the property from a "wilder-ness" into a bonafide "park." The dense canopy of green waxy leaves made it possible for the resort's entire guest population to sit comfortably at the water's edge, even in the hottest part of the day. The development of the talisay grove was the first genuinely utopic transformation occurring at the resort, the first development that created a distinctive reputation for Fantasy Isle as an extraordinary landscape and defined its status as an authentic destination.

Fantasy Isle became independent from Insular in 1981 and was run until 1985 by a daughter, Felicidad Laguna, who at that time had just returned to Davao from Madrid, where she had been studying culinary arts. During this early period of development, the resort remained small, catering to parties set up with tables and chairs under the talisay trees on the beach. There was no electricity, no running water, and, despite the worries about the NPA and military, no security. The boats used to ferry guests across were so small they could only make the crossing at certain hours of the day. Water had to be hauled by boat from Davao in containers that were manually emptied into a rudimentary reservoir on the property. The entire operation was staffed by three women and twelve men, all residents of Samal Island who had worked for the Laguna family previously harvesting and producing copra.

Felicidad personally trained the small staff for food service and resort work and organized some training in English for the employees, so that they could communicate with foreign guests. She described this training process in an interview with me as a long one, involving mainly the staff's learning to imitate her example in every detail of resort maintenance and operation. It was a strategy that had involved her constant presence, as well as much hard work on everyone's part. The training process had been highly individualistic and identified specifically with the Laguna family, in contrast to the APTTI approach. The early training scenario illustrated the more general fact that the Lagunas were personally involved in managing every detail of the resort's growth and operation, much as had been the case with Jerry at Marjorie's Inn and the Floirendos at Pearl Farm Beach Resort.

The clientele for the resort changed significantly during this early period of independent development. At first the guests remained mainly the elite Insular clientele, who came by the tens on weekdays and might peak to a small crowd of fifty or so on the weekends. Once Felicidad began to contract the services of independent local boatmen, however, and establish a regular ferry service from the city to the Fantasy Isle dock, the park's clientele began to include a broader middle class spectrum. By the end of Felicidad's tenure in 1985, the tourists coming to Fantasy Isle had shifted from being almost entirely foreigners to being around 80 percent Filipino. The clientele slowly increased over these years, until by the late 1980s arrivals averaged around 150 on Saturdays, and 250 on Sundays. It was during this period that the local beach park tourist industry began its emergence in earnest.

Felicidad encouraged the development of this middle class tourist market in two main ways. She advertised in places frequented by middle class residents and kept the entrance fee low (7.50 pesos at that time). The park made its profit mainly on the food it sold, now in an à la carte, rather than banquet style. Felicidad also instituted an item-specific payment system that allowed for a hierarchy of patronage to develop, with some customers spending only for the transport and entrance fee, and others for additional amusements, food, and accommodations. In her interview, Felicidad compared the resort's amusement experience to that of the local movie theaters, which also appealed to the middle and working classes in the city as well as the elite, and which had sliding cost scales whose lower ends involved approximately the same amount of money.

Broadening the park's tourist base was a conscious decision on Felicidad's part, based on an interest in increasing the overall volume of customers, which she perceived the resort as needing in order to make a profit. In so doing, she had focused on creating a park that would be "welcoming," in her words, to "all kinds" of people, a place where everyone who arrived would feel at home, from those who could only afford the entrance fee and brought their own fish and rice to eat on the sand, to those among the wealthiest in Davao, who could afford to rent the picnic tables and order the most expensive dishes on the menu. The creation of such a socially heterogeneous space, not in the activity-based context of a cinema, but for the purposes of social gathering per se, set in place the foundations of a touristic experience. Felicidad's inclusive, profit-driven efforts produced an environment in which sharing an enhanced utopic space by otherwise unfamiliar, disconnected persons was made attractive and commodifiable.

Felicidad's lasting contribution to the resort was the à la carte menu she developed, whose standard items were still, in 1996, being prepared according to the recipes she had instituted. She had gone all over Davao City collecting recipes from the best restaurants for the Fantasy Isle food service. A cook from Insular was also recruited to train the cooks on the island. Given her own recent training in cooking, Felicidad was able to set a high standard for the food service at the park, which was to become her legacy in the years ahead.

While Felicidad's management saw the beginnings of a highly localized popular touristic experience on Samal Island, it was a constrained development process nonetheless. Given the political problems of the 1980s, which included clashes between the communist New People's Army and the military and a variety of crimes staged by what were commonly known as "sea pirates," the resort's guests were not allowed to remain at Fantasy Isle overnight. All tourists were transported back to Davao City by five o'clock in the afternoon. There was no attempt to develop overnight accommodations or elaborate the park's utopic space to draw crowds from distances that would require a stay longer than the daytime hours.

Political unrest also played a role in Felicidad's eventual decision to cease managing the resort. She began to receive threatening letters, demanding money for her life, and she left Davao City for Manila in 1985 primarily to escape them. At that time, Fantasy Isle was turned over to a sister, who ran it without significant change until 1988, when she married and moved to San Francisco. The park was then given to a younger brother, "Cacoy," who had remained the manager through 1996 and under whose management the park was converted into a full-fledged, nationally competitive tourist destination.

Violence and other forms of unlawful conduct continued to be a major concern during the early years of Cacoy's management. He reported in his interview that he had seen his own name appearing as number 10 on a kidnaping list that had fallen into his hands, the only "non-Chinese" among a group of wealthy Chinese-Filipino Davao City residents, he commented. In response to the perceived threat, the park started to employ armed security guards, who were stationed at its entrances and used as bodyguards for the management while on the premises. The guards were maintained into and through the mid-1990s and added a somewhat defensive character to the resort's otherwise idyllic appearance. Their presence signaled, as the presence of armed guards did everywhere in the city, that a powerful boundary existed between what was believed to be a dangerous, chaotic public space, and a peaceful, orderly private realm. The guards and their automatic rifles were living testimony to the fact that the business occurring on the park's premises was a valuable one, that the interests at stake were worth defending, and that those who patronized the resort would be safeguarded, at least while in the act of participating, although they might have to deal with the consequences of their involvement when they returned to the outside world.

Cacoy did more in response to the political turmoil, however, than arm the resort. He was aware during his early years as manager that, despite the guns and guards, the NPA was continuing to monitor closely the resort's activities under his leadership. In response to the NPA observation, Cacoy encouraged and promoted various forms of profit-sharing, projecting a liberal image to the park's employees in so doing. He assisted in the development of autonomous businesses on the park's grounds and expanded the already independent pumpboat business, which had from its start been organized by a cohesive Muslim community free from any associations with conservative or elite political affiliations. *Merienda* (snack stands) and seashell souvenir stalls were established inside the park's premises, whose earnings went to local vendors and for which Cacoy provided the capital. Cacoy also participated in the creation of charcoal production and banana leaf harvesting businesses, which he guaranteed would receive the park's business. Not all the touristic elaborations made to Fantasy Isle during the early period of Cacoy's management were sparked by commercial interests.

Many of the park's developments were politically motivated and designed to counteract the perception that the park was nothing other than a product of established capitalism.

Cacoy, like his sister Felicidad before him, took over the management of the park on arriving home to Davao City after a long period of absence. He had been working for Timex Corporation in the Mactan Export Processing Zone in Cebu City as a production foreman supervising more than five hundred employees. Twenty-one years old, he had recently completed an industrial engineering degree. His experience with a "U.S." company, as he described it, had made a strong impression on him, and he applied at Fantasy Isle many of the lessons he had learned with Timex. The ways the resort was to develop under Cacoy's management reflected strong transnational influences, although they were also strategies that bore the stamp of a member of one of Davao City's well established local families. Cacoy continued a pattern initiated by his father, who had collaborated with the European management at Insular on the park's landscaping, and maintained by his sister, who had integrated Davao City's most successful longstanding recipes with European culinary skills.

The most important lesson Cacoy learned with Timex, he reported, was that cleanliness always reduced unnecessary waste and increased productivity. I had never, on any of my previous visits to Fantasy Isle, made conscious note of the establishment's cleanliness, but when Cacoy brought this up in his interview his words immediately rang true, and I realized that the park had indeed succeeded in producing this effect, in a utopic, touristic manner—imperceptibly, in a way that created the illusion of a "naturally" clean environment. The park of course was in reality anything but naturally clean—by Cacoy's account and Felicidad's as well. Given the lack of utilities, maintaining even a minimal standard of cleanliness had always been a challenge. Garbage accumulated in the inland area of the property despite concerted efforts to stay on top of its disposal.

Cacoy had applied the Timex lesson to Fantasy Isle's waste disposal problems with obsessive intensity, he said, setting a standard far above any previous one and enforcing it with meticulousness. He commented that the staff, even now in 1996, were amazed by his ability to spot trash and litter floating on the sea or lying on the beach. He cited a *Reader's Digest* story of an entomologist in New York City who had been able to discern cricket noises on the city streets on a busy day, a feat that had amazed his companions until he himself dropped a handful of coins on the pavement, which everyone around managed to hear quite clearly through the din. Convinced that sufficient interest and determination went a long way in developing any project, Cacoy had called on his own personal resources to lead his Fantasy Isle clean-up efforts. His strategy—including assigning staff constantly to clean both the water and the sand—had transformed the park's environment. Regardless of the size of the crowds, Cacoy's crews maintained an extraordinarily unlittered status for the sand and water by local standards.

The quality of purity that Cacoy's clean-up efforts produced foregrounded the sense of natural beauty and comfort the talisay grove originally had been designed to cultivate. This quality, in Cacoy's perspective, came to be recognized as one of the main attractions of the resort. In my own observation, the rigorous attack on waste had achieved a Disneyland-like magic about the park. Many tourists could gather and, through the labor of the clean-up details, enjoy the illusion that the park was all but free of human occupation and its more unsightly, telltale trappings. Fantasy Isle's upgraded environment, while at first entirely natural in effect, was in reality an indication of a productive transnational corporate mentality at work. It was the aspect that, more than any other, transformed the meta-natural park landscape into a genuinely ultra-natural utopic space. It was "Service Excellence" in beach park form.

In addition to his clean-up campaign, Cacoy applied himself to increasing the park's popularity, pushing it further into a touristic mode of operation to attract a larger and larger volume of visitors. He expanded the resort's circle of influence far beyond known networks of clientele. One of his strategies had been to make the park "Big," as he put it. This concept he described in nationally and ethnically marked terms, saying that he believed "Filipinos" in particular liked to be in places that were "Big," and that businesses arranging either leisure or working seminars—a main source of the park's business at that time—would have more respect for Fantasy Isle and be more interested in patronizing the resort if it were "Big." Working along these lines, Cacoy expanded Fantasy Isle from its original one hectare to ten hectares over the first three years of his management, using sections of family-owned land that had lain idle. On these new grounds he had developed lawns and gardens, using local grasses adapted to the beach environment and planting the hardy, replantable *duranta* plants for hedges.

Cacoy worked on increasing tourist arrivals that could be generated at the collective pseudo-festival as well as the "party" end of the touristic practice spectrum. He sponsored one or two attention-getting activities every year, including an Oktoberfest, a Mr. and Miss Fantasy beauty pageant, Ati-atihan celebrations,[4] and a triathalon. Domestic tourists, Cacoy commented, responded enthusiastically to these kinds of "gimmicks," as he described them. The special events had worked well, achieving a level of patronage that approached what Cacoy characterized as a "saturation point" for the park. They were its most explicitly touristic experiences, spectacles that were miniature versions of Davao City's own public festival events. These special occasions drew local participants into the closest approximations of pseudo-public forms of festival tourism.

With the profits generated from these new developments, Cacoy in 1991 had been able to add electricity to the park. In 1992 he developed running water. In 1992 and 1993, he began to develop two dozen "native style" cottages, making the park's first bid toward a transnationally viable tourist accommodation. These latter buildings were modeled after some developed at the main Philippines international beach tourist mecca, Boracay Island, which Cacoy had studied and copied. Air-conditioned versions of the cottages were being completed in 1996.

In 1996 Cacoy was also looking again to increase the electrical capability of the park, buying a 300,000-peso generator to serve as a backup in case of brownouts, which at the time were a regular problem. The staff had increased more than tenfold, and Cacoy was managing over one hundred employees. They had become an organized tourate, divided into specialized roles as cleaning crews, food service providers, gardeners, cooks, lifeguards, and security guards, among other jobs. Most staff were still hired locally, many having been fishermen before coming to work at the resort, but the DOT was now beginning to help with training, feeding them into the accredited APTTI programs with their standardized training formats. The evolution of the park was following a pattern similar to that of the small hotels in this respect, shifting from a family/household-oriented form of management to a corporate one. This was due in large part to Cacoy's individual corporate background, however, rather than to initiatives of local government offices.

The tourist clientele had also increased by tenfold in 1996, with around 250,000 arrivals annually, 90 percent of them Filipino by Cacoy's estimates. Fantasy Isle was at this time a successful destination, with a thriving tourist population. What had begun as a private exclusive beach party enterprise staged for political reasons had been transformed over the years into a full-fledged recreational park for a wide range of tourist clientele, complete with ping-pong tables, roving musicians, water sports, souvenir shopping, children's playgrounds, food and bar service, deluxe overnight cabins with electricity and running water, and even a "mini zoo" with native birds and reptiles—the only aspect of the park that merited the "Friendly Zoo" label. The local economy supported the resort almost entirely, and practiced tourism "Davao City style" on its grounds.

Looking forward, Cacoy remarked in his interview that his dream for the future was to put up a hotel on Fantasy Isle, a move that would transform the resort into a more predominantly nonlocal touristic establishment. He was waiting, however, to see whether Ekran Berhad would follow through with its plans for the Samal Island Tourism Estate. Cacoy viewed a hotel development at Fantasy Isle as dependent on the development of the larger estate. Such a large scale project was necessary to make a name for Davao as a tourist destination, in his opinion, a reputation on the coat tails of which hotels like the one he imagined could ride. Without intervention of that magnitude, Cacoy believed the tourism potential of the locality already had been fully realized and that beach parks such as Fantasy Isle had reached their peak in terms of growth. He forecast no rise in tourist arrivals to Davao resulting from increased publicity of its existing attractions to the ever-friendlier ASEAN neighbors. The destination itself would have to change before a next stage of tourism growth could be attempted, the stage in which Davao might become "Big" in global numbers of arrivals and gain the respect of international partners.

Fantasy Isle found itself on the brink of entering the global market, although lacking the means to move ahead autonomously. The resort's predicament illustrated that of the beach park tourism industry in the mid-1990s in general. The parks managed to conduct a relatively small scale daily business with sustainable success. As they did so, they supported a culture of tourism that disseminated touristic identities and experiences more widely into the local population than any other enterprise currently was able to do. Fantasy Isle in particular was without question a defining force in local understandings of what tourism was all about. If the average middle class resident were to have a chance to "play tourist" in Davao, this endeavor would most likely take the form of beach park tourism, in either its party or festival modes. Making the next move into a bonafide transnational market was currently the stuff of dreams, even while that imagined reality was daily growing more and more clearly defined.

Beach Park Practices: The Father's Day Party

This event occurred so soon after my initial arrival in Davao City that I had little idea of how to interpret it at the time. In hindsight I realized that it illustrated most if not all of the key features of two forms of party-making in their more or less classic modes—the *barkada* drinking party and the family style guest-reception party. As the occasion was held on the premises of a tourist resort, it also exemplified how the transition of these forms from their traditional contexts, homes and neighborhoods, into touristic utopic contexts was beginning to occur.

My host and hostess for this occasion were Mr. and Mrs. Morada, whose acquaintance I had just made on the evening before the party took place. Mrs. Shirley Morada directed a dance ensemble I had gone alone to see perform at Insular. She also happened to be the owner of a beach park resort I had been intending to visit. When I met her and told her of my plan to visit her park unaccompanied, she responded with an invitation to ride over to the resort with her on her pumpboat the next morning and attend a party at the beach park in honor of some friends who had recently returned from a trip abroad. I accepted, not realizing how mandatory and, as it turned out, inconvenient the invitation had been for Mrs. Morada. By local standards of hospitality, my blunt announcement of my plans had left her no other choice than to extend the invitation or risk appearing unwelcoming to a lone visitor of international standing. I had no idea at the time of the position in which I had placed her and was merely grateful for the opportunity to observe how life at a resort was carried on from an owner's viewpoint.

Mrs. Morada and her driver arrived at around 8:30 the next morning in a Mercedes sedan and we set off. Before leaving the city, however, we stopped at three different open markets to buy fruit and vegetables for the day, a preparatory process that I later came to recognize as a standard feature of the beach park party form, as was my having been incorporated into the "picking-up" process. Guests rarely traveled alone to beach parties, but rather collected into groups to organize their efforts. It was not unusual for some form of private transport to be used, for one or several family cars or jeeps to be requisitioned. The amount of baggage that always accompanied such an expedition was considerable—numerous odd-economy-sized Tupperware containers full of rice, noodles, and desserts; thermoses and cases of Coke and other soft drinks; the knotted pink, or yellow, or green and white striped plastic bags carrying ant-attracting sweets or greasy hunks of *lechon* meat (if a whole roast pig was not also part of the menu); rattan mats, inflatable rafts, swimsuits, T-shirts, shorts, and towels for the afternoon bathing; the boom boxes, books, toys, and games that filled in the rest of the non-eating party times. The paraphernalia required for such a trip made having a vehicle at the party's disposal a definite asset. Usually someone in the gathering was able to borrow or beg one from a friend or extended family member, if nobody happened to own one. However, jeepneys and, less frequently, taxis, could also become the chosen mode of the pre-party subconvening process, and the lack of a private vehicle seemed to have no impact on the amount of baggage taken. My ride on this occasion was several steps above the average, but its use and practice were of a fairly standard variety.

The purchase of some kind of special food on the way to the beach park location, such as was the agenda for my portion of this particular morning's journey, was also generally undertaken in such party events. Although food was for sale at the beach parks, most tourists still brought at least some of their own. It was a matter of economy for many. However, tradition in combination with taste preferences contributed to these pre-party shopping sprees as well. Party givers typically wanted to celebrate whatever the occasion was with the best the city had to offer, to the extent that they could afford it, and to have such specialty foods, whether fruit, fish, breads, *lechon*, or other delicacies, arrive in the freshest possible condition. This meant making side trips to favorite vendors and marketplaces, where unique products were for sale, while on the way to the beach park. The custom of *pasalubong*, of bringing home to one's friends and family the specialty products of other locations that one had just visited, had some influence as well. If a party was celebrating the presence of visitors or returned friends, these guests would typically have brought something to the party for consumption.

Food was a main source of social gesturing in this cultural context. It formed the substance of the balancing acts of gift exchange that stabilized and enhanced the longest of long term personal and social relationships. Beach parks had not developed to the point where they controlled the food supply on their premises, and in many cases the owners were themselves sympathetic to the food exchange on their premises. They tolerated and expected such practices, even assisting in some cases, if the foods brought, such as a raw *lapulapu* fish or an uncut *nangka* fruit, might require it. This gustatory aspect of the beach park experience was still governed by non-touristic practices transported into the beach park environment. They were played out in these touristic contexts much as they might have been in someone's home.

The number of stops on the way to the park, I learned over the years, indicated roughly the importance and size of the gathering. A two-stop journey usually was the minimum for a party destination. A four-stop affair, such as the Morada party turned out to be that morning, was somewhat higher on the scale of elaborateness, although for a major event one could expect many, many more. The concept of "one-stop," or "express" routes was a long way from entering into the beach park party experience from the tourists' side of things. It was not a convenience-oriented endeavor.

The pick-ups and subgatherings also served to produce a gradual building of social momentum for the party. By the time the final tourist destination was reached, the party had already, at least in part, begun, and begun in relatively private nontouristic contexts. The tourist location did not contain the whole of the social experience in this respect, although it was still the primary context for it. Instead, the general effect of the intermediate stops made to pick up fellow guests and purchase special food was to give the arrival at a beach park party a quality of indirectness and complexity. Even though the parks were only minutes away from the city center when direct routes were taken, the preparatory practices of beach parties generally made them hours away in "party time." The complication and social enrichment of the travel served to heighten the ultimate arrival moment and make the destination seem somewhat further from home than might otherwise have been the case.

On the morning of the Morada party, all the markets were in full swing as we passed through them. Their countless makeshift stalls were bulging with all types of produce, from green oranges and calamansi limes to prickly red-skinned rambutans and spiked durian fruits. The lines of lean-to, tarp-draped fruit stalls displayed whole walls hung with what at first sight appeared to be tapestries of bananas, interweaving hues of brown, green, yellow, and orange. Mounds of neatly stacked smooth-skinned fruits were piled atop boxes, carts, and tables—palm-sized golden mangos, huge avocados and papayas, and soccer ball-shaped dark green watermelons. Piles of yellow pomelos, themselves about the size of cannon balls, were everywhere, as were curtains of dark purple mangosteens—Christmas-ornament-like orbs hanging in column after column after column. Even an occasional binful of waxy red Washington State apples could be found at these market stands. I had yet to learn on this morning that Davao was widely known for its plentiful, cheap, high quality fruit, and that its produce, particularly the durian fruit, was destined to become a key symbol of the tourist landscape. On this bright morning I was simply impressed by the reality of the fruit market itself and took note of the fact that so many stands were offering such attractive goods. Their presence made party-giving an activity that had to be orchestrated on the shortest term basis possible, since I guessed this highly perishable produce was likely to be a featured component, as it was on this occasion.

Mrs. Morada did all the marketing herself and was clearly a well-known figure to the vendors. She chatted with them warmly, if quickly, as she selected her purchases, and left each with a friendly smile that was returned in kind. I learned later that she had been dealing with these local businesses for many, many years. She was a native of the area and came from a well established family on Samal Island, the Morales family. The family had bought a large two-hundred-hectare property there in the 1920s. The senior Mr. Morales had been the first principal of the Babak school and a mayor of the municipality after that. Mrs. Morada had herself made a bid for mayor on the island many years previously, during the Marcos regime. She had long since retired from politics by the 1990s, however. Currently the farm and the beach resort were her primary interests. It was Mrs. Morada, along with her husband David, who now managed the Morales property, growing cashew and mango trees among a variety of others. Mrs. Morada knew her fruit as well as she did her market vendors.

We drove out to the Samal Island pumpboat dock with the Mercedes fully loaded. The entrance to the dock road had none of the trappings of a tourist stop—no souvenir stalls, no hawkers, no soft drink stands. We were apparently totally outside the tourism matrix at this point, or so I gathered. However, the dock was, as I was to learn, the main loading site for the island's beach park tourists. The fact that hundreds of thousands of tourists passed this way throughout the year was in no way obvious in the scene that emerged as we left the main highway. A long cement road, turning into pot-holed dirt and gravel, marked only by one large fine-print sign, led down-hill away from the main road. Clearly a service road and nothing more, it passed by large Caltex fuel storage containers on one side and vacant property on the other for several hundred meters. The tourists using this dock were engaged by no surplus tourist businesses. Similarly, there had been no effort to gentrify the dock entrance, or even to publicize it much. I was later to learn that most people gave directions to this main dock by reference to the fuel storage tanks rather than any tourist signage.

The dock's beach itself was small and muddy, entirely lacking in beautification. Mrs. Morada informed me that their beach park had three pumpboats that docked here, which could be rented for thirty pesos for a ride to the island. The boats going to her resort carried a maximum of ten passengers. Adapted to the more traditional collective traveling strategies, the Morada boats charged not by individuals but by boat loads. Boats from several other resorts also left from here as well. These others, Mrs. Morada explained, were more profit-oriented and charged four pesos a head—a surcharge since the resort owners collected fifty centavos a head from the pumpboat pilots.

As we emerged from the Mercedes and helping hands appeared from all quarters to begin loading the bundles of fruit and other goods purchased before my pick-up aboard one of the Morada's vessels, I could see the pumpboats out on the water at various stages of the route to Samal Island. They were an impressive sight, a small fleet scattering themselves across the inland gulf passage like a train of gigantic skaterbugs, some white, some pale green, many distinctively orange in color—the hallmark hue of the Fantasy Isle beach park resort. That morning they glided along smoothly, skimming the surface of a calm sea like great insects, without even a wobble. They were virtually noiseless out on the water. At most I could hear a faint "tuktuktuk" from the engines. Often there was no sound at all when a large boat docked.

The wooden boats were around thirty feet in length, their bamboo outriggers equally long. Canvas tarps were hung tent-like above the passenger area, those from Fantasy Isle printed with enormous "Kodak" labels—the only evidence of transnational investment in the enterprise that I observed anywhere on that occasion. The boats were designed to seat people in half a dozen tiny rows of three or so passengers at the vessel's center, at about the water line. This endowed riders with a faintly regal quality as they made the crossing, particularly on that day since the water was glassy and the ride across completely undisturbed.

The dock's beach was busy with people that Sunday morning. There were many loading boats. Children waiting to board were scampering about, their shouts and laughter carrying over the air that was already filled with many kinds of noises, mostly shouted instructions of both crew and passengers. The tourist market in action at the dock was closely focused on the transport service. I saw no other Mercedes or anything comparable—nor did I ever on my subsequent visits to the beach park dock. People were being dropped off by a varied array of jeeps and small economy cars in various stages of dilapidation, or they were arriving by jeepney or some other form of public transport. Likewise, there were no signs of international tourism. The tourists who were here knew their way about and were clearly experienced with the process. This was not the kind of touristic system whose clientele was comprised by uninformed strangers who might be exploited in various ways and who had their own ideas about what their destination entailed. Instead, it was tourism in a hometown style, where the tourate were conducting a business at little if any variance from their standard ferrying routines—even though most of the people using their services didn't actually know them or each other.

Once we had loaded and boarded, the crossing to Samal Island took only a few minutes since the seas were calm. We arrived around 10 A.M. I was taken immediately around the resort for a quick tour. The property included a short stretch of coastline, around a hundred meters I guessed, and extended back to the island's perimeter road, some hundred and fifty meters back. Several hundred tourists on a peak day might comfortably inhabit its grounds, which took the form of a flat grassy plain running the length of the coastline atop a short bluff that banked steeply upward only as it neared the road at the property's inland boundary.

The main feature of the Morada resort was a floating restaurant pavilion seating around thirty people. It had been built out over the water and was connected to land only by a walkway around twenty meters long. In addition to this seating area, small covered tables were located on the small sandy beach that ran beneath the bluff along the waterline. Atop the bluff's edge, larger picnic tables were sheltered by nipa roofs. Beside them several "native style" cottages of rattan and nipa were perched over the water's edge. Behind the tables were a swingset, a small stage, a cantina, and further back another eating area. A few meters behind that sheltered pavilion stood a row of concrete block air-conditioned units with a series of large water tanks along their southern end.

The general appearance of the park indicated that it was not designed for accommodating a maximum capacity crowd, nor one that expected an ultranatural environment. It was more farmlike than parklike in design and had been developed the way farms tend to be, haphazardly, with buildings constructed in the service of one specific project after another, rather than conceived and built all at once according to a master plan. As the years passed, I came to understand this particular resort, which I visited repeatedly over the years, as the antithesis of Fantasy Isle. It defined the conservative end of the spectrum of development strategies, staying close to the farm or plantation property models that had emerged in colonial eras, while Fantasy Isle defined the progressive corporate, transnational end.

I deposited my bags in one of four "native" bamboo cottages, making the only glocal tourist choice available. Then I made my way back to the floating restaurant, where at long last I joined the beach party of Mr. Morada's friends. I stayed with them until the party's end, at around 3:30 that afternoon.

The party was already in full swing when I arrived. The guests of honor were a couple I gauged to be in their fifties, Mr. and Mrs. Go. Mr. Go I'd met already, at one of the local golf courses while I'd been making a tour with its owner. He was a quiet man compared to the others present. He was in the hardware business and had done very well in it. Mrs. Go, was the only other woman at the table once Mrs. Morada excused herself to supervise the kitchen activities. The Gos lived in a large home in prestigious San Pedro— one of the older upper class housing developments in Davao City. Mrs. Go's parents, like Mrs. Morada's, had moved to Davao in the 1920s and prospered, as had her husband in more recent times. The Gos were surrounded by half a dozen or so friends, men in roughly the same age and income category, most of them with business connections to Mr. Morada.

The similarity in age among the guests and the lack of children at the party seemed atypical to me at first. However, as I later recognized, this party fell somewhere in between an all-male *barkada* drinking party and a family party, both of which were common beach park party types. In the *barkada* the participants were generally homogeneous, male friends of the same age and social class. The family party included a more diverse array of family members and friends—the more diverse the party, the more festive the occasion. *Barkada* parties tended toward transgressive forms of amusement, sanctioned by drunkenness, in contrast to family parties, where displays of talent and wit often formed the main source of entertainment. My inclusion at this particular party somewhat shifted the balance from the *barkada* toward the family format, although events had progressed far enough that a complete shift in that direction was no longer possible.

During the party we ate continuously. The table on the south corner of the restaurant that had been designated as ours became the center of our temporary universe. I knew when I saw this arrangement, no different in design from what it might have been at a private residence, that I was not participating in a global beach tourism event, where the sun, surf, and sand were the main attractions. At this party food would come first, last, and in between. The table was the party's social anchor, not so much a fixture for the placement of individual guest settings as a platform for supporting all the food set out for consumption. The guests made themselves at home around the spread, and left and returned to it for various periods of time. No one was expected to eat in synchrony with anyone else; rather, people "tried" foods as they felt inclined to do so. The table in this way provided an element of stability balancing the fluctuations of the group.

The array of food served for this occasion was particularly spectacular, given the wealth of the participants involved, although it was standard practice to bring an excessive amount of food to any beach party (enough "to feed a barangay," an American Jesuit priest had once remarked, at his eightieth birthday beach party celebration, which had included fewer than a dozen guests). On this day the table was loaded with *kinilaw* (marinated raw fish), *pancit bihon* (a noodle dish), *bangus* (an enormous grilled milkfish), *lechon*, *lapulapu* fish, seaweed salad, fish soup, an enormous calf's liver, an assortment of sweet rice cakes (also bought at the market), and fruits: three kinds of durian (Thai as well as local), rambutan, mango, mangosteen, pineapple, and banana. The main item of consumption, however, was a large bottle of Johnny Walker Black, which the men were drinking. It was a duty free windfall brought home by Mr. Go. The return voyagers' *pasalubong* was the party's main source of entertainment.

Conversation ranged over various topics and formed the primary alternative to eating for most of the party. No one was interested in testing the gulf waters on this occasion, although many other beach park guests—those pursuing family-style party modes—already were floating on plastic rafts and inner tubes around the restaurant as well as nearer to the beach's shore. Bathing (actual swimming was virtually nonexistent) was usually done wearing T-shirts and shorts. It was more popular among children and teenagers than adults.

Mrs. Go, my main partner in conversation, initially focused her remarks on the topic of safety, or the lack thereof, in the city. She reported that a child of the well-known Wong family had recently been kidnapped and held for "millions" in ransom. However, after pursuing this subject as far as it would go, which was not very far since I had no stories to tell in return, she spoke with me mainly of her recent travels with Mr. Go. She had found China most impressive, especially the Great Wall. They had also toured Latin America, visiting Mexico City, Guadalajara, Panama, and a few other Central American spots.

Among the other guests was a Mr. Gaiona, who sat alone at the end of the table. He was obviously a man who liked to eat, and he likened Filipinos to modern day Romans because of their "glutton"-like eating habits. He led the banter and joke-telling that were ongoing throughout the party. Father's Day was mentioned in this regard, with the joke that only the men should be allowed to eat. The most popular joke for the day concerned the food, which was characterized as "a see-food diet: what you see, you eat."

I assumed the joking was a response to my presence, since I noticed that as soon as I managed a conversation with Mrs. Go the men shifted to a discussion of the recent election, using Visayan mixed with Tagalog. The English joking was only used with me. All the same, the pace and fluency of the joking, the bursts of laughter exploding instantaneously in response to a punch line, the reiteration of the punchline occurring with almost mechanistic smoothness, I took to be evidence that it was well practiced. I guessed that my presence was serving to exaggerate an aspect of the *barkada* style of party-making that was probably always present. It served more generally to break the ice at the beginning of such a gathering, and to sustain the good humor of interactions after drunkenness had made more complex forms of discourse increasingly difficult.

Mr. Gaiona acted the clown's role until the end of the party, when he got up to talk to Mrs. Morada about her farm and the new crop she was planting. He then dropped his jester's facade entirely and spoke quickly and directly about the kind of seed and planting process she was employing, proving himself to be a concerned observer in this area. As he changed characters before my eyes, it became evident that the party context definitely had its own set of assumable identities that were donned for its specific purposes and could be quickly abandoned when the context changed, provided not too much alcohol had been consumed. The difference between a person in "party mode" and out of it could be extreme, as was definitely the case with Mr. Gaiona. While the beach park tourist context had not generated the jester identity, it was providing an additional context for its performance.

The first moment of serious conversation for the group as a whole came soon after the initial spray of jokes, when Mr. Gaiona, learning of my occupation, broached the topic of anthropology. He was joined by the others in an impromptu quiz session that started with his asking me if I thought that "the first man" was black or white. Somewhat taken aback but nonetheless intent on staying engaged in the exchange, I answered that the first hominids were probably black, since the earliest fossil finds were located in Africa (this seemed to be news). Next, I was asked if I believed humans were actually descended from the apes. I outlined the "common link" genealogy currently accepted in hominid evolutionary theory, but was not fully successful getting the model across. Next, I was asked how Adam and Eve could be reconciled with Darwin, and questioned on my religion. My response—that the Bible and natural selection were not necessarily contradictory—was met with blank stares and rejected quickly, and discussion moved on to another question, whether the Philippines could be the site of ancient occupation. I answered that linguistic evidence suggested it was possible, and this was received with some interest. However, my comments were soon countered with the report that there was evidence of limestone deposits on nearby Mount Apo, indicating submarine origins of the archipelago that seemingly ruled out early habitation, and no resolution was reached on the issue. I was asked about the Tabon caves, if I'd heard of them, and I responded I had, confirming their importance in the archaeological record for the region.

These exchanges, I was to understand in hindsight, were also a standard part of the party agenda, one that could be somewhat more competitive in *barcada* parties than in family style ones but was likely to appear in both. The questioning and answering served to integrate visitors into local discourses. Party participants would attempt to find subjects over which visitors had some authority and then direct the conversation to include local referents, particularly those that could highlight important or prominent local features that the visitor would then be invited to admire and appreciate. The twenty-question kind of interchange used in my case was a rite of passage, more *barkada* than family style, by which my knowledge and identity were grafted onto the local scene, showing the scene off to its best advantage.

The conversation, however, did not always result in the locality coming out on top. Mr. Julio, for example, arrived a little later from Tagum, the gold mining district, took a seat at the table, and joined the party. When talk turned to politics, Mr. Julio turned to me and said, with a candidness that seemed somewhat surprising at the time, that the results of the recent election had made him ashamed to face a foreigner like me because the process was so corrupt. When I responded that I'd seen progress with regard to elections since I'd arrived in the mid-1980s, he conceded that. "Rome wasn't built in a day," he acknowledged, but emphasized that "the Filipino's hatred of losing" presented an impossible obstacle to really democratic elections. Mr. Morada remarked at this point that he'd observed three ways electoral cheating had gone on in the most recent election: polling places switched, voters' names not being listed outside, and votes cast for voters without their permission. In addition, he knew of people being bought at one hundred pesos a head to stay home from the polls. A survey had been taken before the campaign, he reported, in which most of the questions had been apolitical, but the last had asked people's mayoral choices. Mr. Morada believed the survey had been used by the incumbent later on. In this exchange, local processes were described as inferior to "foreign" ones. Visitors were taken as tokens of their respective homelands, both for better and for worse. Both the twenty-question and the self-deprecating comparison types of visitor discourse became common in my own party-going experience.

Perhaps the most memorable character at the table that day was Rudolfo Roxas. He was in the import business, raising rubber trees for wood. What made him memorable was not his business per se, however, but the travel experiences he had pursued through it. He had made yearly trips to the west coast of California between 1974 and 1990. He knew the freeways and the small towns throughout the state far better than I did, a fact that clearly amused him. He described attending a Lion's Club convention in California, noting with proud exuberance that the badges he had brought to represent his home branch of the Lion's Club were larger than those of the Texans, whom he described as arrogant (the Texans, however, had brought thousands of badges, he noted somewhat sadly, while he had only fifty or so). He compared Lion's Club hospitality in the U.S. and the Philippines, finding the American style stingy and disappointing—one drink as opposed to gallons of free booze, as he summarized it.

When the party proceeded to its post-eating phase sometime after noon, Mr. Roxas insisted on leading the company into another standard party activity: singing. Singing, particularly with the aid of videoke, was a popular form of entertainment for all kinds of parties. Often it was performed in a series of solos, but singing along with one's neighbors or the video was also a common strategy. Again, recognizing the presence of a visitor, Mr. Roxas began with a song in my honor, the "Star Spangled Banner." He sang this a capella over the videoke microphone, in near-perfect tune. He followed this with "My Country 'Tis of Thee," again a capella, at what seemed a ponderous, almost funereal tempo. Even though the two selections took him what seemed an eternity to complete, he was about to follow up with "God Bless America" when the rest of the group intervened. He then switched cultural references and sang the "Beer Barrel Polka," complete with the introduction, his intonation on this melody perfect and his phrasing masterful. There was no doubt he was an accomplished singer. His recollection of melodies and lyrics matched his geographic memory in its accuracy and detail.

Mr. Roxas's choice of repertoire was clearly transgressive from his party's point of view, and at my expense, since he compelled me and no one else to sing the songs he chose. He had not made these choices simply because they were in English. Neither had he made them in an overdone gesture of international respect. He sang them to demonstrate his own mastery over them and what they represented, and to indicate the level of investment he had made in America. This intent was evident from the force, pace, and style of his performance. He sang in a swaggering, almost taunting manner. I interpreted the behavior as a "been there, done that" approach to establishing a transnational identity.

The rest of the restaurant sat quiet during this spectacle. It was a key moment when the touristic context brought its own dimension of meaning to the party. Although I couldn't read the looks on the faces of the other customers, I saw no smiles. I wondered if the crowd of strangers had served to exacerbate Mr. Roxas's transgressive behavior, raising the stakes of his offensiveness and egging him on, or to constrain it, forcing him to obey his own party's requests to cease his U.S. flag waving more quickly than he might otherwise have done. It was impossible to say which might have been the case, although the reaction of the other Morada party guests to curtail the performance clearly had been undertaken in recognition of the whole crowd gathered in the restaurant. What was most certain, however, was that the drunken spectacle Mr. Roxas had made of himself and of me was not a purely private affair, even while he was a member of a private party on private property. The touristic setting had changed the meaning and interaction of the traditional transgressive drinking scenario.

There followed a period of videoke singing, most of which was in Tagalog, although one tape of Sinatra songs (featuring "Didn't We" and "Begin the Beguine") was used as well. Several of the group took turns singing with the videoke. The video images, which appeared on a small portable television on a shelf beside the Morada party's table, where only its guests could view it, were taken mainly from beach resorts in Manila and Cebu. The footage was filled mainly with women in bathing suits posing in different ways on the unmarked stages of the utopic landscapes. The visual discourse objectifying women's bodies was completely embedded within touristic frames of reference. The sequences were expressly designed to accompany *barkada* forms of party-making.

The party broke up when the Gos got up to leave and all followed suit. There were no long goodbyes, just a brief farewell as a pumpboat was made ready and boarding ensued. I left the gathering convinced that the rapport I had begun to develop with the group was a deformed one. It had been warped by very influential stereotypes. Only time and chance were likely to alter its now badly twisted course. As it happened, nothing did. I never saw the majority of the party's guests again.

The party, despite its initial shocks, later stood out to me, not so much in terms of its rhetorical content as for the form of its process. The motivation—a friend's return, an arrival of some significance—was one that I learned to recognize as a standard one that merged neatly with touristic practices. The presence of a special guest was a typical trigger for such a gathering. The role of conversation was defined by the guest's presence as well. It was designed to bring a guest, particularly a person visiting for the first time, into the local sphere, to make the person feel more at home there, welcome and among friends. Eating, begun immediately and continued unceasingly as the main form of entertainment, was the single most important gesture of hospitality offered for guests' enjoyment. While eating was interspersed with other activities such as videoke singing, also a standard feature of such parties, eating and drinking were more typically the primary organizing activities for such beach parties. There was no bounded "mealtime." Food was a constant presence.

While this party did not constitute a standard form of tourism, tourism was never far out of the picture, and actually intervened to influence the course of events at its peak moment—when Mr. Roxas's Americana songfest was curtailed. Tourism was also the reason for the honored guests' departure and return. It was a main subject of conversation at the party for Mrs. Go and myself. Tourism was foregrounded as well in the videoke images accompanying the singing.

The tourism matrix, in sum, infiltrated the entire day's affair in various ways, even while the guests were not assuming tourist identities per se. While the basic agenda and enactment of the event were nontouristic practices, the frame of tourism was serving to modify and appropriate these practices, shifting them into its own stages and landscapes. The Morada party, even while it preserved intact the traditional private party form, also subjected itself to touristic influences, particularly with regard to the diminishing agency of its hosts in determining the course of events, in response to the loss of autonomy the touristic space produced.

Conclusion

The beach park industry, like the small hotel boom, was a product of local networks of commerce and industry, although the beach parks had preceded the hotels by a decade or two and had proceeded on a much smaller scale of investment. Unlike the hotel development boom, there was nothing "top down" evident in the emergence of the beach park industry. There was no high level government attention given to the establishments. No special seminars were held to indoctrinate owners on "Quality" ways of developing the parks. The beach parks had come about somewhat more autonomously in the overall social scheme of things. They were economic sidelines that the families owning coastland properties suitable for such enterprises had developed in response to changing economic and, as with the case of Fantasy Isle, political contexts. Their emergence had dovetailed neatly with transnational development projects, but their origin and evolution had been for the most part independent of them.

Given the autonomous nature of the development, the tourism emerging out of these establishments, even while it was in many respects echoing the transnational industry, nonetheless exhibited a high degree of continuity with longstanding nontouristic social practices—more than was the case with other forms of tourism developing in the locality. The contrast with

Figure 14. A "farm" style beach park on Samal Island.

Pearl Farm Beach Resort, which had instituted house rules designed explicitly to prohibit local styles of beach tourism (no guests were allowed to bring their own food onto the resort's premises, for example), was particularly striking. While Pearl Farm went to great expense to design a utopic space that edited out all but elite international social practices, albeit amid the adornments of a "totally Mindanao" artificial/natural environment, the beach parks welcomed and supported time honored celebratory practices of the locality, putting available resources into sustaining them to the extent that their establishments could profit from so doing. This was the case with the entire spectrum of social practices, from family to festival style.

Despite the continuities evident in the beach park tourism scene, however, it was also apparent that these establishments were arenas for staging the more playful aspects of globalization, such as these were infiltrating into the middle and working classes of the tourist population. The parks were preferred venues for nonlocal encounters, places in which special guests and visitors from abroad belonged most fittingly, and where they could be introduced to local networks. Transnational visitors in particular, whether they were *balikbayan* cousins from California, consultants from Toronto, long-lost classmates home from Singapore, or overseas workers returning from Saudi Arabia or the Netherlands, all these types could be made to feel at home in the utopic neutral gap constructed at the beaches. The parks

Figure 15. A beach park party event on Samal Island.

served in this regard as a social threshold for receiving and sending off such persons, as places for entertaining visitors as well as genuine tourists when they were actually passing through the area.

In addition to such hybrid instances of transnational encounter, tourism in its more classically developed form was also emerging at these beach parks. The parks provided a stage, not only for the entertainment of visitors, but also for the contemplation of possibilities for leisure experiences elsewhere. They produced settings conducive to the discussion of touristic endeavors: vacations one had taken previously, vacations one would like to take, vacations others had taken. The exchange of knowledge on touristic topics and destinations was a common form of discourse occurring at the parks. Utopic elsewheres loomed larger on their premises, and in more appealing, approachable forms. In this regard, the parks played an important role in the cultivation of tourism amongst the city's local residents. They served as tourism think tanks of a playful sort, as well as touristic stepping stones, where sojourners could practice on a miniature scale, and in the most familiar terms available, touristic identities that later might be assumed in more expansive utopic projects.

In sum, the parks were a touristic spawning ground from a local standpoint. While they were moving toward a commodification of hospitality along transnational touristic lines, they still preserved many elements of a neighborhood park or home experience. They still lacked the dominant sunbather, beachcomber population that defined globalized beach tourist destinations elsewhere. For those bonafide global tourists who did arrive, however, the basic elements of a tourist market were in place. Tickets were for sale, souvenir vendors could be found, beach-side nipa cottages with running water and western toilets had been constructed, chairs and lounges for sunbathers had been built. The parks did indeed stand prepared to receive at least the opening waves of global tourists predicted by the ASEAN pundits, in addition to the steady stream of actual transnational tourists that already passed through the region and had been doing so for some time. In this regard, they formed Davao City's touristic frontline, as far as actual and potential international arrivals were concerned. Their very hybridity— their culturally conservative utilization combined with their globally oriented aspects and potential—defined a conservative transitional landscape in the city's development boom. As a result, a relatively sustainable, slowly moving process of tourism development was being constructed at the parks from relatively local private interests on relatively local terms.

Chapter 10
Conclusions

This study calls for three conclusions, one methodological, one theoretical, and one ethnographic. Regarding method, as the volume's introduction indicated, there remains the question of how useful the standard ethnographic method of "rooted" participant/observation can be in the current era of globalization and particularly in relation to "glocalizing" phenomena such as tourism. Regarding theory, there remains the issue of "home," its relationship to tourism, and the general understanding of tourism as a utopic, consumption-producing, landscaping matrix. Finally, there is the question of what Davao City's investment in tourism during the boom years of "the 90s" contributed to the locality's cultural and historical record. I will address these issues beginning with the latter, proceeding backward, so as to give the final word to method.

Davao

Looking at the range of touristic landscapes operating and under construction in Davao City and its environs in the mid 1990s, it is difficult to form a general conclusion about the cultural consequences of tourism for the locality, engaged as it was in the larger process of developing from a provincial Philippine port city into a transnational ASEAN hub. In the main, this is due to the variety of touristic enterprises operating in the locality and the unfinished condition of many of them. However, from a historical perspective, a general role for tourism development did appear to be emerging in relation to the city's cultural life at the end of the twentieth century. It was a leading role, and historically unique in a few respects, although on the whole it conformed to a larger pattern of cultural-historical change.

Davao's history since its emergence in the late 1800s had involved a series of fairly radical shifts in local and cultural identity, from a fledgling Spanish colonial settlement to a thriving Japanese colony under American rule, to a booming multiethnic, immigrant Christian Filipino metropolis. Each new period of the city's history, from the time of the Spanish to the time of abaca, bananas, the Marcos, and so on, had brought with it entirely new populations, radically different cultural practices and traditions, new languages and lingua francas, and new industries of production. The city had remade itself from its cultural foundations on up several times over the course of its history, and the extent of the transformations in each successive historical phase was remarkable. Little hard evidence was left of the Spanish or American presence, even less of the Japanese. Davao in the mid-1990s existed largely in its present postcolonial moment.

In sum, cultural continuity was not and never had been a distinguishing feature of Davao City's abiding—or unabiding—cultural-historical character. Neither was cultural homogeneity. Instead, even for the families that had survived in residence in Davao over the course of the city's existence, disjuncture, impermanence, and heterogeneity dominated the record. If there was anything that was unchanging where the big picture of Davao City's cultural identity was concerned, it was the continuous series of new cultural arrivals, groups that had each in their turn intervened and, albeit temporarily, come to dominate the city's cultural life before the next wave of foreign interests appeared on the horizon. This was as true of the Filipino groups arriving in the city as it was of those coming from more distant shores. Davao was a settler colony and neocolony even for its Filipinos, who still in the main identified ancestral homelands elsewhere, whether on Luzon Island, or throughout the Visayas, and who identified Davao in futuristic terms, as a "land of promise"—a phrase Manuel Quezon had used to describe the whole of Mindanao during the 1930s[1]—rather than as a site imbued with cultural longevity, let alone antiquity.

The rise of ASEAN and the institution of the East Asean Growth Area, with its contingent of Southeast Asian forces and agents, appeared in this regard as simply the latest foreign influx to redefine Davao City's character. The prominent role played by tourism in this process, while it represented an industrial shift, did not produce an altogether new historical moment. The broad spectrum of deformation that was in the process of emerging in the mid-1990s through tourism development could be understood as only the most recent of a long sequence of analogous interventions and reinventions of Davao's cultural landscape. What was most unusual about it, in fact, was the relatively conservative and partial character of its disruptive effects, and the fact that its emergence was not preceded or accompanied by massive political and demographic changes.

As the various perspectives and narratives documented throughout this study have evidenced, tourism development was bringing continuity as well as change. Even with regard to the Samal Island Tourism Estate, the most disruptive of all of the cases examined, tourism development was not producing an absolute rupture with the identities or practices, or the people and institutions, of the plantation culture that preceded it. While tourism development was hastening the end of agriculture, at least as the small scale farmers displaced by the estate had practiced it over the last several decades, and while it introduced a new Malaysian array of "partners" at the highest levels of the estate power structure, the development was also attempting to preserve the local barangay communities, however imperfectly, and to integrate them into the development process with as little social, let alone cultural trauma as possible. The estate was without doubt deforming many local institutions. Local government, subsistence practices, and educational opportunities were foremost among them. It was also altering the sense of local identity by inserting Samal Island into a commercial transnational network of East Asean tourism destinations. The transformative effects of the development, however, were not all-encompassing. The local communities caught up in the project were not, or at least not yet, wiped of the island's map. Local social networks and organizations, while strained, were still operative. Neither was the development, at least at this point, demanding any fundamental change in the residents' understanding of themselves as Filipinos—as modern citizens of the Philippine nation state, however peripheral and disadvantaged they may have been. The development was not currently asking the residents to reimagine their ethnic or religious identity. Neither was it presenting them with conditions—or the prospect of conditions—that would compel them to do so. Many aspects of cultural life were left unchanged by the tourism development, and they did not appear to be subject to change, even when the project became fully operational— although this was, of course, impossible to predict with any certainty.

As was the case with Pearl Farm Beach Resort, which had sustained and even reinforced a variety of economic and social aspects of everyday cultural life, the cultural consequences of the industry's development of the Samal Island Tourism Estate, while significant and bound to become increasingly so, were ultimately incomplete. This was particularly true in comparison to the development of the now dying plantation culture, which had occurred in the context of various waves of colonization. The development of plantations in the locality had brought with it a new way of life in virtually every regard, as well as new populations of inhabitants. Tourism was bound to be something of a different story, relatively speaking.

This is not at all to say that Davao's cultural life and identity were remaining fundamentally unchanged. Nor is it to suggest that the potential of the tourism industry to deform virtually any aspect of cultural life in Davao was somehow inherently or unconditionally limited. Even in the relatively subtle and conservative instances of the tourism matrix's proliferation in Davao City, in the waves of small hotel and family owned and operated beach resort development, the influence of the industry was evident in some of the most important and intimate practices of everyday life. The reinvention of "home" in the city's new Quality-oriented business hotels was providing new models of conduct and new consumption-driven values for the entire spectrum of middle class domestic practices. The deformations of familial and communal celebratory traditions occurring along with their transplantation into touristic landscapes were no less fundamental.

While it had not yet brought with it more than a tiny influx of new persons—an increasing trickle of foreign and domestic arrivals—tourism development had nonetheless introduced a new array of partial or contingent identities for virtually every class of resident present in Davao City, from its *massa*—its masses—to the most powerful members of its elite. These identities, however, both tourate and tourist roles, were not replacing older ones entirely. Rather, they were generally being inserted into those that already existed. The personnel officer role was grafted onto a priest/counselor', the cultural entertainer onto a folk dancer, the estate gardener onto a tenant farmer, the frontliner onto a domestic helper, and so on. Likewise, the utopic "tourist" identity was being inserted into the preexisting roles of the businessman, seminar leader, student, host or hostess, returning or departing friend, and even such an extraordinary character as a beauty pageant queen. Such inserted and grafted partial identities were occasional, negotiable, and largely transcendable as they were being assumed and discarded in the mid-1990s in Davao City. All the same, the touristic identities complicated the picture of all it could mean to be a resident of the new "Gateway" to East Asean, enlarging the cultural repertoire of personhood via utopic commercial additions.

In sum, tourism development, as it was occurring with increasing momentum in Davao City in the mid-1990s, was engaged in a relatively gradual but nonetheless pervasive process of redefining the cultural landscape yet again. It had given a new dimension of identity to Davao City itself, as well as creating new contingent identities for its residents. The industry was producing new utopic landscapes, designed for new arrivals, whether foreign or domestic, to consume. It was also changing the understanding of what a productive landscape could be, what "work," which had generally been understood in terms of heavier industries and agribusinesses, could entail, as well as what practices and identities "play" might be encompassing within it.[2] Despite the partial and additive nature of its interventions, despite the fact that many cultural practices and aspects of everyday life had yet to be incorporated into the operations of the tourism matrix, tourism developments were fast becoming an integral element in Davao City's contemporary cultural character.

Tourism

To return to the implications of this study for the general understanding of tourism, the cases documented here in several respects have served to illustrate in specific detail the distinctive features of tourism identified in the introduction. However, they also illustrate the operations of the tourism matrix in a developmental, unfinished condition, illuminating the character of certain features in emergent rather than fully operational forms. In addition, they specify some limits of the tourism matrix's influence and reveal the manner in which its operations could themselves be deformed when they were brought into contact with other interests, identities, practices, and institutions.

As regards the general utopic character of touristic landscaping, in every case here documented, the fundamentally utopic character of the landscapes developed for tourism is clearly evident. Each landscape, or planned landscape, was fully engaged with the production of perfection of some kind. Perfection, whether in the form of "Paradise" or "Quality Service," dominated the narratives associated with every tourism enterprise. The foci of this utopic production varied considerably, as did the performative tropes employed to actualize it. In the case of Pearl Farm and the other beach resorts, the perfection of the natural landscape was the main utopic production attempted, with masquerade being the premiere trope used. In the case of the new hotels, the "home away from home," the cosmopolitan domicile was the interior location slated for perfection. Ventriloquism was the primary performative trope brought into play in this case, as the tourate were being trained to internalize and reproduce the doctrines of Service Excellence. With the Samal Island Tourism Estate, the perfection of vacationing itself in all its "Developed" forms was envisioned.

The range of utopic subjects apparent in Davao City's touristic spectrum indicates that the capacity of the tourism industry to capitalize on different elements of an existing landscape was extremely flexible. Nothing appeared inherently inappropriate for development. This utopic flexibility may have appeared particularly evident in Davao City, given the early stages of the tourism matrix's development. The potential condition of the industry sparked the imagination of a particularly wide range of possibilities and landscapes. Paolo López's idea of creating a utopic version of goat fodder cultivation and my friend Grace's interest in turning her handicrafts factory into a tourist destination were two of the more imaginative possibilities raised along these lines in my presence. Both of these touristic visions challenged even the reliance on "worklessness" in touristic utopic landscapes, as either might have been developed into a destination where tourists were invited to play at working, either with the crops or on the factory line, should that appear to have had some additional "hands-on" participatory appeal.[3] The utopic flexibility of tourism, as it was emerging in Davao City in the mid-1990s, appeared to have few limits, even with regard to work in industrial and agricultural contexts.

Tourism itself had taken on something of a utopic aura in Davao. The utopic realm of possibility also seemed to be orienting itself in a few specific ways, however. What the oldest and most successful of the destinations—Fantasy Isle—suggested is that touristic utopics, if they are to prove sustainable, must tap into longstanding narratives and practices. They must appropriate subjects and sites for their utopic play that both tourate and tourist clientele have already recognized as extraordinarily meaningful. Ironically, it is precisely what the groups involved might deem inappropriate for touristic utopic development that is most likely to become the desired focus of such development.

As regards the tendency of tourism's utopic spaces to impair the ability to distinguish between the real and the unreal and constantly blur the boundary between the two, little evidence of such dissociative disordering came to light in Davao City. Heidi Toledo's remark about approximating the practice of a "real" Muslim in the dance performance at Pearl Farm Beach Resort did give some indication that, for the tourate as well as the tourists, fantasy/reality blurring could be a consequence of involvement with touristic utopic sites, particularly the more elaborately developed ones. However, in the main, and, again, perhaps because of the emergent, largely incomplete nature of the tourism matrix, episodes and narratives indicating the experience of touristic hysteria were few and far between. Whatever the disorienting effects of the matrix might be, they were still to be determined.

The reasons apparent for the limited utopic effects varied from establishment to establishment. In the case of Pearl Farm, the village of Adecor's presence at the edge of the resort, as the resort management's initiatives to "clean up" the settlement indicated, appeared to be quelling tourists' abilities to extend the resort's utopic landscaping beyond the boundaries of the resort property itself. Tourists literally could not get past Adecor when scanning the horizon for further touristic possibilities on Samal Island, beyond Pearl Farm itself. Adecor's residents, for their part, suffered no confusion about the differences between the fantasy "villages" Pearl Farm constructed and their own community.

Similarly, with regard to the beach parks and city hotels, many analogous "reality checks," in the form of individuals, institutions, and practices operating partly or even entirely outside the tourism matrix, were positioned or occurring in close proximity to these establishments. These inhibited fantasy/reality substitutions to a great extent. The manager of Fantasy Isle and his beach park tourate, for example, had no illusions about the unnaturalness of the resort's utopic beachfront environment, since they spent many of their working hours sustaining the conditions for it. The staff at Marjorie's Inn, for their part, exhibited no confusion about the fact that they were not working in a home of any kind. In this respect, in fact, their conduct indicated that they had not yet fully made the transition to understanding themselves as being incorporated into the tourism matrix. The matrix itself, as the hotel "Quality" seminar episode evidenced, was still under construction. On the whole, the staff at Marjorie's Inn had no misapprehension that any of the guests were personal friends, or that they might be so possessed by some utopic identity to think or act as if they were.

No such identity play was as yet operative at Marjorie's Inn. No tourist culture of this type had yet emerged.

With regard to the production of touristic hysteria, the tourism developments in Davao City appeared to indicate that such disorders tend to be associated with the consumption of tourism rather than its production. For the tourate, the boundaries on the whole between fantasy and reality tended to remain apparent. Also, however, the general capacity to produce hysteria within touristic landscapes may be something that occurs and evolves only with the passage of time and in destinations where the matrix has established a relatively great degree of control and influence over the locality in general. In the emergent context that Davao City provided, the hysterical consequences of the utopic landscapes being developed were not in most cases apparent or significant. They could be read into the design of the landscape as theoretically present or potentially of consequence, but this was the extent of their influence. Basic operations had not moved very far in this direction.

That said, the emergence of tourism did appear to be producing a variety of forms of contestation, with the struggle to define "home" foremost among them. In the case of the Samal Island Tourism Estate, this struggle was emerging in the most material and costly manner, as it involved both the actual residences and farms of barangay residents and their ways of earning a living and the relationship to the natural environment, both land and marine. In the case of Pearl Farm, the contestation was somewhat less all consuming, at least in the immediate term. It appeared as well to be occurring between parties who were on a somewhat more equal footing. Those who were not completely incorporated into the tourism matrix's development had been successful in preventing their own displacement from the shoreline and the loss of the lifestyle that went along with it. They had also been largely successful in rejecting the "eyesore" identity the resort had asserted with regard to the general condition and appearance of Adecor's homes. The definition of what a home was—where it was, what it contained, what made it beautiful or ugly, what occurred within its walls that made it a home—was still largely in the hands of Adecor's residents. Nonetheless, what a home *could be*, and what the Floirendo family's understanding of home actually appeared to be were also set forth in concrete detail, confronting Pearl Farm's tourate, whether they liked it or not, with a model very different from their own.

With regard to the other examples of tourism development, the redefinition of home occurring in response to the growth of the tourism matrix was not one that was occurring in the main against the will of those engaged in it. The small hotels and resorts staged what were on the whole voluntary, self-selected opportunities to play with new forms of home-making, and home-leaving, for both tourate and tourists alike. The family-run resorts and hotels could be seen to situate themselves along a spectrum of deformation with regard to the ways "home" was commodified and consumed in their narratives and practices. Some invoked relatively few features of domestic life, some virtually all of them. The redefinition of "home" was explicit in the case of Marjorie's Inn, as the impersonalization and professionalization of the many aspects of domestic dwelling the establishment attempted to provide under its roof were overtly developed for what they were, unmasked by any pretense of being some other kind of commodification. Moreover, the small size of the inn, and the limited clientele it supported, approximated the conditions of a domestic household in many existential respects. On the other hand, Fantasy Isle made few claims to be creating a home-away-from-home and invoked no narratives of home in its own publicity rhetoric. It set itself up as a destination for a public that it managed and provided for in relatively generic terms. Yet even this type of un-homely destination changed the understanding of what a domestic place of residence could mean by providing an alternative site for practices that had previously been associated closely with homes.

In various ways, the tourism developments in Davao City were bringing about a new understanding of what one's familial household, one's private domicile, one's own place could be and mean. Each kind of development tested the limits of what was still beyond the reach of the tourism matrix's operations of commodification and commercialism in this regard—what was still inalienable for "real" homes outside the matrix. In various ways, they played with home's distinctive features. In the main, the gains appeared to be outweighing the losses in this process of redefinition, even when the "play" was occurring in its deepest, most serious forms, gambling with the identities and domiciles of entire communities. The more permanent consequences of the play involving home, of course, were largely to be determined.

In reviewing the many kinds of deformation that were occurring in conjunction with the development of tourism in Davao City, one of the general understandings of tourism that emerges for the industry is the character of its operations as forms of *subjection*. Subjection, to borrow from Foucault,[4] defines a certain mode of creating relationships of power, one that operates less overtly and abruptly than the relatively direct forms of domination and exploitation that tend to emerge with imperialism and colonization, either internal or external. Subjection does not entail the excessive use of force, nor does it involve the rapid dismantling of existing power structures in their entirety and their replacement with entirely new structures and agents. Subjection was a concept Foucault developed to characterize relatively gradual processes of takeover and control, processes in which the new relationships created are not wholly involuntarily constructed on anyone's part and in which preestablished structures and organizations are not wholly transformed.

The tourism matrix, at least in its initial phases in Davao City during the mid-1990s, tended to create such new relations, "partnerships" in which the application of power was relatively attenuated. While the operations of the tourism matrix contained the power of global economic forces, the industry's dependence on a relatively wide range of human faculties and resources for its functioning also tended to compel it to restructure relationships indirectly, in ways that would sustain certain habits of operating while simultaneously altering them. Tourism's cultural consequences, in this regard, were difficult to understand in terms of cause and effect. The matrix's activities, and the continuities and changes brought about in relation to them, were rarely if ever undertaken independently. They tended to occur in concert with a much larger multiplicity of interests, some of them ongoing, others newly emerging.

Method

I now leave the subject of tourism to focus on a general methodological concern. Tourism, of course, is only one of a number of contemporary subjects that have challenged the viability of cultural anthropology's most distinctive feature, its use of long-term participant/observation as its primary method of study. The ethnographic study of tourism, in part because of the industry's peculiarly vexed cultural and historical relationship to anthropology, casts in particularly high relief this challenge and the consequences of succumbing to it. It is for this reason that I include here, in closing, this final methodological commentary.

I have endeavored throughout this account to remain attentive to questions of method, to tracking the manners in which a "means was found" to go on in the tourism matrix, and to make such means and their consequences explicit. To turn a phrase from Evans-Pritchard (1969: 261) somewhat on its head, if I am accused of describing facts as exemplifications of my *method* in this ethnography, then I have been understood. Method has been a main interest throughout this research, in part because it has always seemed to me that cultural anthropology is united on the basis more of its method than its theory, and in part because, given the ways the world at large is changing, the validity of the standard ethnographic method seems ever more open to question.

Regarding the aptness of the ethnographic method herein employed in relation to the subject of tourism, then, along with the general appropriateness of relying on relatively "planted" forms of participant/observation to conduct culturally focused research in a world that seems no longer to be exhibiting this method's once-assumed standard objects of study (discrete, deeply rooted, stable "cultures," their abstract character notwithstanding), I put forward here a somewhat unlikely suggestion, one that Clifford Geertz suggested some time ago. The suggestion is this: that anthropologists, as Geertz observed, have "been speaking Wittgenstein all along" (1983: 4).

Throughout his writings, Geertz has presented a number of key insights from Wittgenstein's later writings that combined to serve him as a philosophical rudder in navigating the interpretive "turn" for cultural anthropology.[5] While interpretive anthropology, to be sure, has outgrown Geertz's original vision, and while the world itself has changed substantially since the initial charting of the interpretive ethnographic turn, the subdiscipline of interpretive anthropology nonetheless remains set on a philosophical course that is closely aligned with the work of the later Wittgenstein, particularly in relation to Wittgenstein's understanding of the role of method in relation to theory in philosophical investigation. To the extent that it does so the rooted participant/observation method remains viable for ethnographic research, even, perhaps, indispensable.[6]

The decision to persist in the participant/observer ethnographic method, in other words, is justifiable, and, perhaps, can only be justified, as a philosophical decision. Contemporary empirical conditions as well as predominant theoretical discourses are insistently calling for, even dictating, the application of very different methodologies. The Wittgensteinian philosophical foundation, however, redeems the ethnographic method as an inherently and relatively *thoughtful* way of investigating the human condition of any given situation, even "postcultural" ones. It is thoughtful not only in the sense of being intelligent (literally "full of thought"), but also in the sense of being considerate of others—of all that remains "other" to the anthropologist, for whatever reason, during and after the course of his or her research. In so doing, the philosophical orientation sustains the method's legitimacy, even in a moment when postmodern crises of representation and ongoing eruptions of culture wars and cultural critiques define the discourse of interpretive anthropology as well as those of its most closely related disciplines, and even when "culture" and its empirical referents are quickly transforming beyond all recognition.

It is this philosophical foundation and the justification of the ethnographic method as "thoughtful" that it provides that I seek here briefly to elucidate. The ethnographic account just given hopefully presents some evidence of its validity.

Wittgenstein at times summarizes his entire philosophical project as the attempt to work out a new method for philosophical study, one that entails a new relationship between method and theory. While he never articulated any synthetic overview of this method—and, in fact, indicated that such a programmatic statement of it would be fruitless—certain hallmark characteristics do become apparent in his later writings. Basic among these, and the main feature operative throughout ethnographic research, is the principle that theoretical propositions or *theses* should not dictate methodological design in philosophical inquiry. In fact, something like the reverse should generally be the case. Conduct itself should become the organizing basis for, and the emergent structure of, studious practice. Practice ultimately should govern processes of learning and thinking. "In the beginning," wrote Wittgenstein, "is the deed." Wittgenstein's philosophical project shifted philosophical study away from beginning—or ending—in thesis-makings to beginning—and continuing—with reasoned deeds, to *practicing*, in the humblest sense of the term, all that might be meant by gaining an understanding.[7] As this practicing gradually acquired an understandable character of its own, it became recognizable as reasonable, considerate, and thoughtful.

The reversal of the roles played by method and theory was justified by Wittgenstein in pragmatic terms, as part of what has been characterized more generally as a "realistic spirit,"[8] toward the complexities of both philosophical investigation and the human condition. It was in fact his recognition of the complexity of the subject matter, a subject matter that has only grown more and more complex in the time since he wrote, that motivated his development of this alternative philosophical role for method. Studying via thoughtful deeds proved itself as a way, as *the* way, of avoiding the confusions, paradoxes, fallacies, misrepresentations, and other "nonsense" as Wittgenstein sometimes typified the problems, that were otherwise unavoidable and ultimately insurmountable in thesis-driven modes of investigation. Thesis-making, because of the compulsion to generalize that was always already inherent in it, invariably proved to oversimplify and thus misrepresent the picture of whatever human subject was at issue, to render it less thoughtful, less considerate of the intelligence that existed and was growing beyond the philosopher's own.

In sum, the consequence of espousing the primacy and the ultimacy of methodical practicing is that one commits oneself to an inherently unfinishable process of learning-by-doing. Its price is to give up on, or at least to perpetually defer, the project of producing an ultimate mastery or knowledge over a given subject of study. Its alternative is to substitute the desire for mastery with an interest in the cultivation of methods designed to continue a gradual increase of understanding, and to find meaning ultimately in the unending work of practicing understanding.

The parallels to the ethnographic method of interpretive ethnography are obvious.[9] James Clifford has characterized ethnography in the contemporary moment in such terms, as a vast array of error-prone activity—never undertaken in isolated privacy—that constitutes what Clifford has identified as the "process of living one's way into an alien expressive universe" (1988: 36). Clifford rejects the attempt to formulate a "master narrative" or general thesis of cultural history as the predominant contemporary objective of ethnography, replacing it with an interest in presenting partial, conjunctural truths (1988: 14). The discipline of cultural anthropology thus emerges as a "hybrid activity . . . a mode of travel, a way of understanding and getting around in a diverse world" (1988: 13). Such ways and processes count throughout the whole of ethnographic study, from its most alienating to its most integrating moments, as the method of figuring out how to live on as well as can be expected under whatever may be the given circumstances, while not living alone in a culturally unfamiliar place. Interpretive anthropology casts cross-cultural ethnography as largely constituted by such ways and processes, thoughtful activities unhinged from stabilizing general outlooks or conclusions. These tend to appear as "pointless" or "blind" method from a theory-driven perspective, method-making that cannot "speak its own sense" in general terms, at least not until a considerable amount of practice has occurred. When it can, it tends to become the substance of an ethnographic account.

This generative as opposed to instrumental role of method in interpretive anthropology arises from an awareness of the complexity of the subjects at issue, as well as from the anthropologist's assumption that there is really no telling just how much he or she doesn't know about the unfamiliar context encountered in his or her "field." The field itself, in fact, is largely delimited in precisely such terms, as the place where "knowing-ness" is embodied by "others" and where the ethnographer personifies non-knowing-ness to an extraordinary degree. Nothing in the field necessarily goes without learning for the ethnographer, even as far as the simplest, most basic practices of getting through an ordinary day are concerned. All knowledge previously gained outside the field becomes suspect and ungrounded. From this initial assumption of potentially absolute non-knowing-ness, the anthropologist goes on and on, acting in consideration of what others are saying and doing, practicing learning, taking nothing for granted except not knowing. The ethnographic method emerges from this recognition.

Despite the changing character of the fields of ethnographic study, such an understanding of the ethnographic predicament and its resulting role for method nonetheless remains useful in the context of contemporary globalizing phenomena. Given that the degree of complexity of the subject matter has only increased, and that the environments in which the anthropologist works require even more careful attention to understanding what organizing assumptions are at play, the assumption of the initial "non-knowing-ness" of the ethnographer and the character of the deep but blind method that follow from it do not lose their appropriateness. On the contrary, it is in this regard that the ethnographic method, so defined, remains viable, even preferable, as a way of working on cultural subjects—even in an age when the subject of culture itself appears to be becoming all but obsolete.

To bring this discussion back home, I did not go to Davao City to prove any preconceived thesis about the place or its tourism. I went believing that I could learn how to get along with people, and that, being human, I could probably improve in that capacity over time. I took as given that when I arrived in Davao, I would not be in a position to know anything, that I would be finding myself in a highly irregular, abnormal set of circumstances, and that I would be largely atypical in my experience of the place in that regard. When I stepped off the plane, I knew I would experience radical discontinuities of time and place and find myself in a situation where practices of displacement and encounter would play defining roles in my life.[10] I assumed that I often would be in a position, to follow Wittgenstein, to articulate "an expression of giving up the attempt to know my way about" (1970: 393). In sum, I expected the classic field situation to confront me in Davao. To a large extent this was by my own design—I was dealing out this ethnographic deal to myself so as to embody a certain disciplinary practice of thoughtfulness.

"Method," then, meant that I was to start from scratch figuring this position out, working my way back through misunderstandings. If I engaged in rule learning, it was in order to learn how to make the sorts of mistakes that would indicate to any local witnesses charitably inclined to notice that I was teachable. I then made a habit out of failing to disappoint such people, cultivating what Rabinow (1996:xiv) has termed an "emergent rationality" along the way. Interaction by interaction, move by move, I created an unfinishable and collective dwelling, a virtual place of dwelling-in-understanding through flawed but gradually more learned practices and self-disciplines.

This is the method I have tried to make explicit in this text: the moves from "scratch" toward positions of ordinariness in the generally fallible applications of practicing understanding, the understanding of tourism. The tourism matrix, a human construct however deformed, can also be defined for all those who enter it as a field of such emergent methodical practice. In this regard, the human condition of tourism remains what it has always elsewhere been, complex beyond knowing and changing continuously. The ethnographic method, while nonetheless an outgrowth of an older modernity, remains one particularly thoughtful approach to understanding it.

The cultural consequences of tourism in Davao City for both the locality and its residents indicates something more general as well about the character of contemporary cultural life and transformation. Cultural realities, in this era of globalization, must be understood, not only in terms of partial truths, but as ontologically un-whole themselves. They must be understood, in other words, *by degrees*, as aspects of a given human totality. They cannot be assumed as wholly present or absent in their various manifestations, but rather as realizable in relation to something like sliding scales of identity, narration, and practice. Cultural identity, in particular, is made evident at present, not simply by participation or a lack thereof in an established tradition of some kind, whose ever-stable enactments allow for such "in" or "out" commitments to be made. Rather, cultural identity emerges in the way in which participation is *qualified* by some factor or set thereof in a whole variety of practices—not all of them having cultural, or the same cultural sources. It is evident, not by the understanding of certain clusters of dominant symbols alone, or the presence of such symbols in a person's life. Rather, it is evident by such things as the degree of proximity that a person or group maintains in relation to such symbols, and to varying clusters of them, and by the extent to which these become central or peripheral, habitual or extraordinary, exclusive or combinable, or inalienable or negotiable in an individual or a collective form of life. Cultural practice, as well, is currently constructed more in terms of trends that develop rather than as a consequence of perpetual conditions that exist. It, too, manifests as choices made amidst heterogeneous options, rather than as the fulfillment of a given destiny. It becomes apparent in the manner in which arrays of practices are manipulated, rather than in the way in which a given array is adopted or espoused, or not.

In sum, cultural realities cannot at present be studied as homogeneous webs of meaning, spun in different corners of the world. Globalization is pulling apart such constructions, drawing out separate strands of them and entangling them with one another, sometimes cutting them off from their original sources and incorporating them into fundamentally different structures and designs. One must tease the cultural out from such heterogeneous "glocalized" entanglements. With tourism, as with other such supercultural matrices, such a process may never produce a perfect representation of any one cultural entity. However, it will serve as testimony to the complexity of the human condition, now as always.

Notes

Preface

1. My father served nearly fifteen years as chair of the commission, service that eventually won him a term as the town's mayor in 1988. He finished the term four years later, at the age of ninety-two, in the same year that my research for this book began in Davao City, Philippines.

2. I have written of one of these experiences in some detail. See Ness (1996).

3. Abu-Lughod (1991: 137) defines a "halfie" as a person "whose national or cultural identity is mixed by virtue of migration, overseas education, or parentage." In relation to the global tourism industry, since it is neither a culture nor a nation, nor a "part" of one, it is difficult to establish grounds for any equivalent sort of identity. However, as I have an involvement in the industry that spans most of my life and have belonged to various tourates and consumer tourist populations for extended periods of time, I invoke the "halfie" designation here as the least worst analogy available for defining a nonexternal status in relation to the industry and the global order to which it belongs. My cultural identity is certainly "mixed" by virtue of this lifelong involvement with the industry, to an extent roughly equal to those mixtures produced through the educational, migrational or familial circumstances Abu-Lughod identifies.

Chapter 1. Tourism and Culture

1. Crick (1995) estimated tourism as the largest industry in the world in dollar terms. Wood (1997: 1–3) cites Garrison (1989) and Hall (1994) in this regard as well, noting that in the year 2000 18 percent of all international tourist arrivals were expected to choose Asia-Pacific destinations. In 2001, as a result of the September 11 terrorist attacks in the United States, the tourism industry entered a sharp decline. The World Travel and Tourism Council (WTTC), in text appearing on its website in March 2002, has forecast that throughout 2002 demand for the industry will decrease by 10 percent worldwide, with a loss of 8.8 million jobs. However, the WTTC has also forecast that the decline is temporary and that the industry will regain its momentum gradually. In a media release from September 2001, also appearing on the website in March 2002, the WTTC continued to describe the travel and tourism industry as "one of the biggest industries in the world." It noted that the industry currently generates $4,494 billion in economic activity and constitutes approximately 11 percent of the worlds GDP. It currently provides 8.2 percent of the world's employment (207,062,000 jobs).

2. See Lett (1989). The tourism industry's travel statistics continued to show rapid growth from the period during which research for this study was undertaken

(1992–96) through 2000. The Travel Industry Association of America (TIA), in its March 2002 Travel Statistics and Trends web page segment, "Top Stories: International Market Updates," noted that 2000 was a year of record growth for the industry, during which time travel and tourism increased by 7 percent worldwide. The TIA also reported, however, that tourism arrivals worldwide had decreased by 11 percent after the September 11 attacks. A gradual recovery was forecast, but its details remain difficult to project.

3. ASEAN, the Association of Southeast Asian Nations, is the regional international governmental organization that includes the Philippines as well as Indonesia, Brunei, Malaysia, Singapore, Vietnam, Laos, Kampuchea, and Myanmar.

4. See Wood (1997: 1) on the growth of tourism in Southeast Asia during this time period.

5. "Globalizing," as in manifesting globalization (following Basch et al. 1994), refers to the involvement of social, economic, cultural, and demographic processes that take place within nations and localities but also transcend them, such that attention to limited local or national processes, identities, and units of analysis yields incomplete understanding of the local or the national. While globalization and transnationalism have frequently been defined in contrast to one another—globalization involving relatively universal, impersonal, abstract, less institutionalized and intentional processes and transnationalism involving nationally anchored political and ideological processes—this study follows Michael Kearney's assertion (1995a: 548) that the two phenomena can and do overlap, particularly, in this case, with regard to what Kearney defines as their "trans-statal" powers—their capacity to conflict with, transgress, or bypass the jurisdiction of host states. Transnational processes can occur—as is intimated here—as part of a larger trend toward globalization, although this is of course by no means always the case. The relationships tourism has created between distinct processes of transnationalism and globalization in the Philippine-ASEAN context is one general focus of this study.

6. "Classical" is used as it has been used by George W. Stocking, Jr. (1992: 357) to refer to the period roughly from 1925 to 1965 in Anglo-American anthropology, when ethnographic fieldwork achieved central importance in the discipline. As this practice grew more definitive of the discipline, so too did the notion of cultures as entities existing in fixed places around the world. I have avoided the cumbersome phrase "Anglo-American anthropology" in the body of the text, but it should be understood that the "anthropology" I refer to throughout is the discipline in which I was trained, a descendant of this Anglo-American discipline. By the time I encountered it, it had become an Anglo-Franco-American discipline, and in my particular experience the "Franco" loomed much larger than the Anglo.

7. Such "super"-, "trans"-, "multi"-, and "pseudo"- cultural processes have been identified and emphasized by numerous tourism scholars in this regard. See, for example, Boorstin (1964) and more recently Eco (1986) on the "pseudo"-events of tourism. Pierre Van den Berghe in his study of tourism in San Cristobal, Mexico notes the "multi"-ethnic relations developed by ethnic tourism, which he characterizes as "the last wave of exploitative capitalist expansion into the remotest periphery of the world system" (1994: 10, 16). Essays in Lanfant et al. (1995) and Rojek and Urry (1997b) emphasize the importance of mass mobility and supercultural practices in developing a theoretical perspective on tourism. More recently, Aviad E. Raz characterizes his study of Tokyo Disneyland in terms of the mapping of "trans"-cultural flows of "glocalization" (1999: 14). Crick (1989: 332), who notes that tourism consists of "meta-cultural" processes, and Greenwood (1989: 183) both have broached the issue of the inadequacy of classical paradigms of culture to handle tourism. Greenwood, in particular argues that "tourism challenges anthropology on

the theoretical center of its turf." Kearney (1995a: 549, 555) recognizes tourism as a particularly representative member of an array of emerging topics in sociocultural anthropology that have necessitated and signaled a fundamental theoretical shift in the discipline from "modern" to "global" orientations.

8. "Depth" is the adjective used by George Marcus, appropriating comments made by James Clifford (1998: 245) to characterize the key objective of anthropological fieldwork methodologies. The ideology of fieldwork, following Clifford, depends on "depth of interaction." The contingent identities of tourism may preclude the recognition, or even the production, of such depth.

9. See Stocking (1987, 1992, 1995) for extensive discussions of the science and profession of nineteenth-century anthropology in Europe and the United States. Regarding tourism, John Urry's definitive study (1990: 4) establishes the origins of mass tourism in mid-nineteenth-century Europe, and identifies tourism as one of the characteristics of "modern" experience. Dean MacCannell, likewise, associates nineteenth-century tourism with middle-class Western modernity and the rise of industrial society (1976: 1–16). Graburn (1983), Kirshenblatt-Gimblett (1987), Bruner (1989, 1995), and Crick (1985) all mention the fact that tourism and ethnography (and colonialism) are relatives, culturally speaking, having arisen from the same social formation of Western expansion. Jane Desmond (1999: xiii) argues for an even stronger connection, observing that tourism, both historically and in many contemporary instances, actually relies on the production of the popular equivalent of a nineteenth-century "scientific" ethnographic gaze. However, no in-depth study of the genealogical relationship between tourism and anthropology has been undertaken.

10. On tourism as a form of revitalizing ludic behavior, primarily restitutive or compensatory in nature in relation to the realm of home/work, see Urry (1990: 11) for relevant sources. My development of this idea is based on personal experience.

11. See Urry (1990: 2–5) for a discussion of the structural relation between tourism and work and the importance of this opposition in modern industrial society.

12. James Lett (1989) and Theron Nuñez before him (see Nuñez 1989/1977) have argued that this negative evaluation of the subject of tourism no longer holds, as is evidenced by the increased financial support anthropologists working on the topic of tourism have received, the increased recognition the topic has been given by leading cultural theorists within the discipline, and by the appearance of a large anthropological literature focusing on the topic, which includes entire special issues of journals such as *Cultural Survival Quarterly*. I would agree with Lett that tourism definitely has gained legitimacy over the last two decades as a serious research subject within the discipline of anthropology, particularly as the subject of globalization has come to occupy a central place in the discourse. Leading scholars such as Edmund Leach (1984), Claude Lévi-Strauss (1976), Jean-Paul Dumont (1984), James Clifford (1988, 1989, 1997), and Renato Rosaldo (1986), among many others, have come to recognize tourism as a subject of interest. However, it is my perception that the attitudes mentioned in the text still exist within the discipline to a greater degree than Lett would admit. Pierre Van den Berghe, for example, begins his study of tourism in San Cristobal, Mexico with the comment, "Judging by the smirk which the mere mention of tourism brings to the face of my colleagues, most social scientists do not take tourism seriously" (1994: 1). Nash and Smith (1991), Bruner and Kirshenblatt-Gimblett (1994), Crick (1989, 1995), Wood and Picard (1997), and Rojek and Urry (1997a: 11) note that tourism is still typically denigrated as a subject of research. While virtually all the leading late 1990s texts on cultural theory mention tourism in passing as a subject worthy of research, none of them have even one chapter focusing on it. Nor have any of the leading theorists within the discipline of anthropology given it their serious attention. Nor have major journals such

as *Cultural Anthropology* or *Public Culture* produced special issues on the subject. Crick (1989), in the same year Lett made his statement, characterized the anthropology of tourism as still in its "infancy," still lacking full length ethnographies. More than ten years latter, tourism appears to be a "hot" topic "in theory" *only*, to a considerable extent, although book length studies are now beginning to appear.

13. Crick (1985, 1989, 1995) has written the most probing accounts of the problems the tourist identity poses for the cultural anthropologist, focusing on the unwanted "overlap" the two figures share. Wood (1997: 3) has characterized the conflict here described in the most extreme terms, writing of a scholar's identification as a tourist as constituting "the ultimate disgrace." Bruner (1989, 1995) has also given this topic serious attention, characterizing it in terms of a threat to ethnographic authority. See also Errington and Gewertz (1989) and more recently Deborah Kaspin (1997) for more conservative discussions of the issue. As for the problems the industry poses for the discipline more generally, a much larger literature exists on this issue, too large to summarize here (see Lanfant 1987, 1995; Greenwood 1972, 1989; Wood 1997; and especially Crick 1989 for summary discussions). Lanfant (1995: 5) aptly characterizes the discourse focusing on these problems as the "social and cultural impact" literature, which holds tourism responsible for the destruction of cultures. See also essays in Rojek and Urry (1997b) for a contemporary response to this impact-of-tourism literature.

14. See Eco (1986) for a discussion of such hyperspaces. On hyperspace in relation to postmodernism and multinational capitalism in general, see also Fredric Jameson (1984), whose theoretical work is in general born out in the details of this ethnography (see also note 30 on Jameson).

15. See, for example, Crick's closing remarks (1989: 338) on the need for more in-depth ethnographic research in tourism studies.

16. Rabinow (1991: 59) cites Foucault (1984: 41) citing Baudelaire to define this phrase as "an exercise in which extreme attention to what is real is confronted with the practice of a liberty that simultaneously respects this reality and violates it."

17. In 1984 and 1985 I lived in Cebu City, Philippines, which is located in the Visayas or Central Philippines (see Ness 1992). Cebu City like Davao City is a lowland Philippine port. The two cities share many general cultural features, and the great majority of Davao City's residents migrated from Cebu and other Visayan locations. To the extent that an ethnic dominant existed in Davao during my residence there, it was a Visayan ethnicity. In this regard, I tended to understand my working in Davao as a return to the "same" cultural milieu, very generally speaking, that I had worked in in the mid-1980s, even working with members of many of the families that I had worked with at that time. However, as Chapter 2 elaborates, Davao City's history and cultural predicament were in many respects quite distinctive and must be understood on their own terms.

18. My periods of residence in Davao occurred during June, 1992, June–August 1993, July–August and October–November 1995, and January–February and March–April 1996. I left three different times for several weeks each over the course of my main research period from July 1995 to April 1996.

19. The chapters that follow give accounts of the array of methods used to develop the understanding presented. In many cases, the research followed methodological courses that were sociological as well as cultural anthropological. The use of small scale survey interviewing in particular, which was a well established, well respected methodology in the locality, proved important in gaining a broader understanding of the larger scale developments in the area, as well as in establishing a rapport with the best-informed individuals, most of them involved in social work themselves, residing in the area. In this regard, the "researcher" persona

I developed pragmatically during the research process was an interdisciplinary, not strictly speaking an anthropological one.

20. The argument here follows Donald Moore's (1999) more general characterization of development phenomena.

21. Marcus and Fischer (1986), Clifford and Marcus(1986), Clifford (1988), Rosaldo (1989), and Fox (1991) are the most frequently cited works articulating this critique.

22. See Appadurai (1990, 1991), Clifford (1997), Marcus (1998), Gupta and Ferguson (1997a, b,c, and essays in 1997d,e), Kearney (1984, 1995b, 1998), and Rabinow (1986 and particularly 1989). Kearney (1986, 1995a) provides overviews of the main subfields of this literature. In identity studies, Rapport and Dawson (1998: 24–28) also cite Lee Drummond (1980), Ulf Hannerz (1992), and Robert Paine (1992) as leading theorists in this regard. Clifford cites Mary Helms (1988), David Scott (1989), Amitav Ghosh (1992), and Aihwa Ong (1995), among others in this regard. With regard to the cultural analysis of tourism specifically, John Urry's work stands out as a model in this regard (Urry 1990; Lash and Urry 1994; Rojek and Urry 1997).

23. In structural geology, "matrix" refers to a relatively fluid mass that encompasses more rigid bodies. In a deformational event a rigid body in a fluid matrix is subjected to pressures, resulting in a new set of structures and fabrics in the form of foliations, faults, or folds among others. In mathematics, a matrix refers to a multidimensional array of individual numbers. A synthesis of the two definitions begins to approximate both the multiplicity and mass productions of the tourism industry and its territorializing properties vis-à-vis older, relatively rigid elements of its landscapes. Lanfant (1995: 6–7) has suggested a similar characterization of the industry, emphasizing its differences from imperialistic and monolithic powers and stressing a recognition of the agency local interests can exercise in the development and maintenance of destinations. In globalization studies more generally, as Kearney (1995a: 558) has noted, biological metaphors such as the reticulum and the rhizome (Deleuze and Guattari 1987) have been employed to foreground the decentered nature of globalized social forms and enterprises. The matrix, however, presents an inorganic nature that I have found to be more apt and less aligned with naturalism (see note 27).

24. See Crick (1989) for a discussion of work addressing the neo-colonizing tendencies of the global tourism industry. Picard (1995, 1996) has developed most extensively a theory of what I am calling the composite or external/internal character of the industry's locational operations.

25. The argument here follows Harvey's analysis of capitalist political economy. Temporal compression is one general result of the imperative in capitalism to constantly shorten the average turnover time between investment and the taking of profit. See Harvey (1989; also summarized in Kearney 1995a: 551).

26. See Chambers (1997a).

27. Clifford (1997: 25) has described the "naturalizing bias" of classical culture theory as characterizing "culture" as "a rooted body that grows, lives, dies, and so on." It is not the naturalizing of culture itself that is most problematic for my study, but rather the naturalism that is pervasive in the assumptions about the world or "field" in which such "culture" exists in anthropology's classical orientation—a more fundamental naturalism, philosophically speaking, that is a legacy of nineteenth- and early twentieth-century anthropological theory and practice. See Gupta and Ferguson (1997) and Kuklick (1997) for a more extensive discussion of naturalist assumptions operative in common sense anthropological discourse about the world and the problems entailed in such assumptions, in both historical and in contemporary

contexts. See also Stocking (1992: 342–61) for a more detailed account of naturalist paradigms in relation to other scientific paradigms that have been influential in the history of anthropology, and particularly in the Anglo-American classical period.

28. Rabinow's study of the emergence of modernity in France (1989) provides the most extensive ethnographic account of such a denaturalization process I am aware of. I am conceiving of tourism here as one modern industry that denaturalizes its given world in a manner indicative of modern industries in general, as it is of modern states.

29. The understanding of tourism as an industry centrally concerned with staged interactions is pervasive in the tourism studies literature. MacCannell (1976) is most often cited in relation to the development of this perspective, particularly with respect to the concept of authenticity. See also Nuñez (1989/1977) and more recently Bruner and Kirshenblatt-Gimblett (1994) and Desmond (1999). Bruner and Kirshenblatt-Gimblett's study, which characterizes tourism as producing a kind of *experience theater* that achieves a form of realism rather than authenticity, provides one of the most graphically detailed applications of this notion to a tourist destination. In the Southeast Asian context Adams (1993) and Volkman (1984, 1990) have also developed the idea of the stage in relation to the transformations of Torajan funerals brought about by tourism.

30. This perspective on the tourism industry, although it has developed from personal observation and reading the largely sociological literature on tourism studies, is closely aligned with the perspective Fredric Jameson developed in the 1980s (1984) on the operations of multinational capitalism in general.

31. Causey (1997: 33), who along with Chambers (1997a) has identified this tourist-centered orientation, cites Dennison Nash (1981) as a prime example in this regard. MacCannell (1976), Graburn (1989/1977), Van den Berghe (1994), Boissevain (1996), Selwyn (1996), Abram et al. (1997), and Burns (1999) also illustrate this orientation, which places primary importance on the tourists' experience, impact, and cultivation. Rojek and Urry (1997a: 11), citing MacCannell (1989) and Krippendorf (1984), characterize the predominant interpretive position taken with regard to tourism as a focus on tourism's meaning as a quest for authenticity—a tourist-centered perspective. Boon (2000) presents a similar view. Burns has also recently argued the position, claiming, "However one defines, describes or analyses tourism, it is the tourist that remains at the heart of the matter" (1999: 41). Causey's work on Batak carvers in Sumatra (1997), Michel Picard's on the touristization or touristification of Balinese society (1996), and particularly R. Timothy Sieber's study of Boston's touristic revitalization efforts and Aviad E. Raz's study of Tokyo Disneyland (1999) illustrate approaches adopting an orientation more similar to that of this study, where the production and consumption of the touristic landscape in its entirety is interpreted in (post-) industrial as opposed to consumer oriented terms. Chambers (1997) and Picard and Wood (1997) also provide a number of recent essays illustrating this general orientation.

32. Causey (1997: 30) cites Andrew Yiannakis and Heather Gibson (1992) as the authors of the tourist categories "action seeker" and "high class." Smith (1989: 12) uses the "Off-beat" and "Charter" types in a typology ranging from "Explorer" to "Charter" to identify differences in tourist numbers, goals, and adaptability to local norms. E. Cohen (1974) developed the "drifter" category at the far end of a spectrum he created to characterize variations in dependence and autonomy among tourist travel strategies. Cohen is the tourism scholar most often cited with reference to the development of tourist types and categories.

33. I mean this in a Peircean sense. See Daniel (1984) for a general introduction to Peircean semiotic theory. While even a summary statement of Peircean semeiotic theory is beyond the scope of this study, it defines the "sign" in much broader

heterogeneous terms than other semiotic theories tend to do, allowing for a virtually inexhaustible typology of signs, material as well as conceptual.

34. This term is used by Raz (1999: 14) to characterize the combination of globalizing and localizing practices that are typically found occurring at sites of transcultural flows.

35. Wood (1997: 5) makes a similar argument in regard to what has been termed "indirect tourism," noting that the "key impacts" of tourism may be experienced by people who are not present at sites of direct host-guest interaction and who never actually see tourists in person. See Richter (1989) for an account of the origin of "top down" tourism development in the Philippines and Thailand. Chambers's work on tourism development in Thailand (1994, 1997b) is also important in this regard, providing an ethnographic focus on the dynamics of local/national involvement in Thai tourism development. See also Adams (1997) for an Indonesian example of indirect consequences of tourism that are ethnically and regionally coded.

36. I adopt this term following Andrew Causey (1997: 34), who coined it in order to identify as a specific group the individuals at any given tourist destination who interact with tourists or tourism. The tourate, in contexts of global tourism, particularly those that foreground ethnically coded attractions, is generally taken by tourists as a representative subgroup of their culture, an assumption that the touristic system itself may have seriously compromised. Causey's distinction between the tourate population and the larger cultural group is adopted in this study as well, although it is also emphasized that the tourate is itself a diverse, heterogeneous, and contingent population whose practices and identities have formed in a variety of ways in relation to tourism.

37. Joel Kahn's (1997) study of Georgetown, Penang Malaysia examines specifically this process of cultivation and resistances to it and makes the important point that interests other than those of tourism can often support it. Other recent work, as well as Kahn's on ethnicity and tourism has stressed the recognition of political agency, albeit constrained agency, that tourism tends to produce in tourate groups as they engage in such cultivation processes. In the Southeast Asian context, see for example Volkman (1985, 1990), Adams (1993, 1995), essays in Picard and Wood (1997), and Causey (1997).

38. Causey cites Lousi Marin (1984) with regard to the concept of "utopic."

39. See Causey (1997: 45–54) for a more extensive discussion of utopic theory and space. Causey cites Karl Mannheim (1953), Paul Ricoeur (1986), and Louis Marin (1984) as his main sources on utopian thought and action, following most closely Marin's theory of utopic space as a textual space that tends to manifest itself between two positions of an ideological continuum, rather than in direct opposition to an ideological concept or construct. The idea of ideological inversions occurring in utopic space presents yet a third possibility, which I have taken from Crick's (1989) remarks on the ludic or liminoid character of tourist worlds. In this study I leave open the possibility of either inverted, intermediary, or oppositional utopic plays on ideology, but adopt the notion of a neutral gap or voided space as the specific foundation on which all such forms of utopic play tend to occur.

40. Causey (1997: 51) cites Marin (1984: 69) in this regard, who argues in regard to utopics, "The discourse will speak the place: the place is nothing but the place as told, recited."

41. For detailed accounts of such politics in the Philippines context, see Richter (1982, 1989). Richter views the Philippines as a worst case scenario, stating that "one finds in the case of the Philippines a microcosm of the political uses and abuses of tourism" (1989: 52). I have found the Davao City context to be considerably more complicated.

42. Causey (1997: 49) mentions freedom from materialism as one reported

experience in cases of tourists involved with ethnic tourism, who encounter groups whose existence they believe to be more authentic than those of the tourists' home culture.

43. See Bateson's metalogue "Why a Swan?" (1972: 33–37) for a discussion of the "muddling" of reality in these terms. The metaphysical "frames" of understanding Bateson problematizes in this exchange, juxtaposing the representation and lived experience of reality, are precisely those that touristic operations work to conflate or dismantle. Joseba Zulaika (1988: xxiv–xxvii) adopts the metalogue to characterize his own unstable understanding of the political violence that was the subject of his ethnographic research in Itziar, a Basque community in Spain. Following Zulaika's insight, tourists like ethnographers can experience such an unstable understanding of the landscape they encounter, shifting back and forth between metaphoric/representational and sacramental/existential interpretive modes.

44. As Elaine Showalter (1997) documents, the definitions of hysteria are numerous and contested. In this discussion I am using what Mady Schutzman (1999: 9) has identified as a most enduring definition of hysteria, one that makes connections to schizophrenia as it has been discussed in relation to capitalism, most notably by Fredric Jameson (1983, 1984), Deleuze and Guattari (1987), and in tourism studies Bruner and Kirshenblatt-Gimblett (1994). I occasionally use the prefix "quasi" to emphasize that, while I wish to draw a connection between the effects of tourist landscapes and actual illnesses diagnosed by the term "hysteria," I do not mean to conflate or confuse the two.

45. Greenwood (1989) discusses at some length the promise of ownership sold by tourist marketing as an expression of capitalism.

46. See Schutzman (1999) for a discussion of hysteria and the advertising industry in late-capitalist consumer culture. Schutzman (1999: 11) identifies five performative tropes in advertising—masquerade, ventriloquism, magic, narrative, and ritual. I have selected the first three tropes as particularly relevant in the case of tourism landscapes.

47. The analytical framework set forth here follows closely that of Bruner and Kirshenblatt-Gimblett (1994). It does not assume the same Foucaultian perspective, however, but, rather one more closely aligned with de Certeau and Wittgenstein, as the chapters following will demonstrate.

48. In the ASEAN region, Kahn (1997) has undertaken work that assumes a similar perspective, understanding tourism development and touristic consciousness in Penang Malaysia in relation to a variety of economic, social, and political influences. The need to examine tourism as one among an array of factors systematically creating social and cultural change has been argued for more generally by Wood (1997) in the Southeast Asian context specifically and by Crick (1989) more broadly as well.

49. Van den Berghe (1994), for example, defines tourism in terms of leisure, as pleasurable travel, focusing on the search for exotic attractions. Smith (1989: 19) likewise sets up a theoretical overview of tourism in terms of tourism and leisure, defining tourism as a "manifestation of leisure" and mentioning the leaving of home only in passing—a perspective that the anthology's essays adopt as well. Bruner (1995) notes that the concept of home is often not problematized in tourism theory, even when it plays an important role in theoretical constructs, such as in the case of the tourism-as-pilgrimage model developed by Graburn (Bruner's 1994 work with Kirshenblatt-Gimblett, however, employs the notion of home without problematizing it, opposing it to the "stage" or "picture" that constructs touristic spaces). Burns's compilation of tourism definitions (1999: 30–31) bears out in summary form Bruner's claim. Georges Van Den Abbeele's theoretical work on tourism and domestication

(used and cited in Morris 1993) should be noted as a significant exception here. Desmond's 1999 study as well, by emphasizing the importance of seeking *difference* from self (citing Urry in this regard) as a motivation for consumption in the tourist industry creates an analytical focus that comes closer to including the concept of home. However, Causey (1997: 41–43), whose approach emphasizes an understanding of tourism developing from the study of place, and whose ideas are in large part adopted in this work, has gone furthest in approaching the question of home directly in the ethnographic literature on tourism, problematizing home as a key construct in tourism theory, identifying touristic places as the "not-homes" of tourists and the "homes" of tourates.

50. Smith (1989) further defines the person as "temporarily leisured" and in possession of discretionary income.

51. See Causey (1998: 29) for an elaboration of this point.

52. Clifford's earlier work (1989) also suggests a parallel of the home/abroad opposition to that of practice/theory, although this latter is not a parallel that has much salience in the narratives of the tourist industry.

53. The unequal gendered relation of home (female) to travel (male) as it is symbolized in tourism's ideology and practices has been noted and discussed in detail by Wolff (1995), Craik (1997), Bolles (1997), Desmond (1997), and Jokinen and Veijola (1997). The genre of tourism where this relation finds its most extreme expression is, of course, sex tourism. See Leed (1992), Craik (1997), and Clift (1994) for recent studies of this topic. With regard to recent work on sex tourism in Southeast Asia specifically, see Richter (1989), Truong (1990), Kruhse-Mount Burton (1995), and Chant and McIlwaine (1995).

54. Meaghan Morris (1993: 271–72) has argued that this opposition, which she terms the voyage/*domus* opposition, in fact loses its oppositional significance in and after colonialism, when mobility displaces "home and family" as the primary activity of existence. In this regard, the narratives of tourism, to the extent that they continue to rely upon and make influential this opposition may be interpreted as nostalgic, denying this aspect of the histories of imperialism and their contemporary aftermaths in which the industry and its clientele in actuality are embroiled.

55. Consider, for example, the title of a promotional article for the Swiss Youth Hostel Association, which appeared in the Travel section of the December 19, 1999 *Los Angeles Times* Sunday edition, "Alpine Hostels Where Heidi Would Feel at Home." The title implies simultaneously that (1) the reader, like Heidi, would also feel at home at the hostels and (2) the reader is not like Heidi.

56. See Bruner and Kirshenblatt-Gimblett (1994) for an illustration of the discomfort occurring when this type of home/tourist landscape confusion results at the Mayer Ranch destination in Kenya. Bruner and Kirshenblatt-Gimblett discuss this condition, citing Bateson (1972), as moving toward schizophrenia.

57. Paulla Ebron's (2000) account of a U.S. corporate-sponsored "homeland tour" to Senegal and Gambia gives a more detailed example of the complexities of tourism for diasporic and particularly forcibly displaced populations.

58. Chambers (1997a: 5) has emphasized this point, as has Siebers (1997) for urban homes and home communities in particular.

59. This common sense observation has been developed at some length in the literature on home and homelessness. Peter and Barbara Berger and H. Kellner, in their classic sociological treatise on the subject, *The Homeless Mind* (1973), argued that "home"—a unified, traditional lifeworld—was *the* pre-modern cultural concept whose loss signaled the advent of modern consciousness. Rapport and Dawson (1998: 31–32) have taken issue with this argument, claiming that "home" was not lost in modernity but rather destabilized and reconceived in relation to the predominance

of migratory experiences brought about by modernity. My intention in this discussion is simply to make the point that home precedes tourism as a cultural construct, and not to espouse any theory of modernity's impact on it, an impact that I would argue is too variable in terms of individual experience to model theoretically from an ethnographic perspective.

60. The notion of home as practiced space stems from Michel de Certeau's work on space and spatial stories (1984). Mary Douglas (1991) among numerous others has made this point about the space of home in particular, defining home as a pattern of regular doings, furnishings and appurtenances, and a physical space in which certain communitarian practices are realized (cited in Rapport and Dawson 1998: 6–7).

61. This is the definition Rapport and Dawson (1998: 32) adopt in their discussion of contemporary identity, claiming that "home-making" has preserved the reality of home "even as individuals and groups lead their lives in and through movement (cognitive and physical) and refrain from finally and essentially affixing their identities to places."

62. Jackson closes his study with the assertion that, "in the end, home is not a place that is given, but an experience born of what one makes of what is given" (1995: 155).

63. Stack's (1996) study of twentieth-century African-American migrancy illustrates a class-based point argued by Karen Olwig (1998): while home may tend to assume more and more abstract characteristics to the relatively affluent members of the global economy, for those who are positioned less advantageously, home may remain largely a territorial reality—a contested space of rights and obligations—constructed through social relations as opposed to narratives of self-knowledge, and constantly threatened by relatively powerful interests.

64. Quoted in Jackson (1995: 121).

65. Jackson (1995: 87) cites Susan Sontag (1995: 1), Peter Berger, and Theodor Adorno among others in this regard. Rapport and Dawson (1998: 6, 23) cite John Berger (1984) and Trin T. Minh-ha (1994); Gupta and Ferguson (1997c: 37) cite Edward Said (1979:18). In addition to the experience of homelessness, another key condition of modernity, the dominance of the sense of sight over other senses, is also basic to touristic operations. Rojek and Urry (1997: 9) cite Heidegger's claim that "the fundamental event of the modern age is the conquest of the world as picture" (1977: 134). The landscapes of tourism produce leisure as an experience of this conquest.

66. Bruner and Kirshenblatt-Gimblett (1994) address this point in their study of the Mayer Ranch in Kenya, noting the importance of the practices—for it is only practices in this case—that separate the homes of the tourate from their tourist stages. The case study illustrates a relatively advanced stage of a tourist landscape development, where material or physical boundaries between home and tourist destination have ceased to exist and it is only practice that distinguishes the two. Oakes (1997) cites Britton (1991) in this regard as well, questioning the degree to which tourism tends to "flatten" an authentic sense of place.

67. See Crick (1989) for an extensive discussion of the positive and negative representations of international tourism in anthropological discourse, as well as those of social science more broadly. Picard (1995) reports that both types of positive and negative characterizations of the tourism industry have been offered for Bali, Indonesia, showing that even the same destination can be understood from widely varying perspectives. Chambers (1997a:3) notes that in the history of the discourse on tourism within anthropology, earlier studies—1970s and before—tended to dwell on the negative characterizations while more recent studies characterize tourism as variable in nature. Wood (1997) defines this trend as resulting in a "postnormative"

phase in contemporary tourism studies, what he has viewed as a positive development that "sets aside" normative judgments of the industry in favor of objective analyses. In the Southeast Asian context Philip McKean's work on Bali should be noted as an important exception to this pattern, as is Eric Crystal's on Toraja, which actually moves in the opposite trajectory (see McKean 1976, 1989; Crystal 1989/1977). Chambers presents a similar perspective to that given here: ultimately it is difficult to judge tourism as essentially negative or positive given the diffuseness of its cultural dimensions. Lest my own characterization of the positive view seem overstated, see Crick (1989: 328–29), who reports numerous examples of the "peace and understanding" rhetoric in both national and commercial tourism discourse, and who is largely critical of it. See also Smith (1989: 4), who reports of the Canadian government's 1988 forum, "First Global Conference, Tourism—A Vital Force for Peace," and who takes a somewhat less critical stance. Smith (1989: 6) notes that tourism, because it is labor intensive and can use "unskilled" labor, "ranks high as a developmental tool" in developing countries and takes a generally positive view of the industry. See also notes 12 and 13 regarding the literature characterizing tourism in negative terms.

68. The Preface gives some account of the particular relationships with tourism that have shaped my own life history.

Chapter 2. Davao Arrival

1. I put the term "first" here in quotations to mark the tourist's process of consumption, which necessarily involves some prior indoctrination and impression of any given destination occurring in advance of arrival. Nonetheless, the term is appropriate here without ironic qualification as well, when understood as defined in the terminology of Peircean semiotic theory. In this context, it refers to the comprehension of qualities of signification that set new precedents for interpretation, as in experiences that evoke the expression, "That was a first." Touristic arrivals, when successful, tend to evoke precisely these kinds of first impressions.

2. All these figures were presented by Philippine Secretary of Tourism Mina T. Gabor in an address delivered May 7, 1997 at the Focus on the Philippines International Conference, held May 6–8 in Los Angeles, California. Gabor cited the World Tourism Organization as the source of her statistics on tourism outside the Philippines.

3. A missionary's identity was most often assumed because the majority of Euro-American women seen regularly in Davao unaccompanied by any official entourage were missionaries. My age, manner of dress, and ways of using Cebuano all conformed to this identity.

Chapter 3. Davao Understandings of Tourism

1. See Richter (1989: 52–56) for a discussion of Imelda Marcos's role in promoting tourism development in the Philippines during the early years of martial law. Activities were particularly intense in 1973 and 1974.

2. These included the Indonesian Boraq Airlines, the Singaporean Silkair, Philippine Airlines, and its recent rival Grandair.

3. Anflocor, or Antonio Floirendo Corporation, is a conglomerate controlled by the family of Antonio Floirendo. Its businesses include one of the largest piggeries in the Philippines, as well as banana plantations.

4. Following Doreen Fernández (1996: viii), the term *palabas* in Tagalog denotes simultaneously "performance" "show" "entertainment," and "fun" as well as connoting an outward, community-oriented mode of acting. In my experience, the term can also be used derogatively, to signal artificial, disingenuous forms of conduct. As I have used it above, however, *palabas* refers positively to the spectacular nature of the social life displayed on this occasion.

5. This characterization of moro identity and cultural groups derives from a discourse that is one-sided and obviously reductive. For scholarly treatments of Islamic groups identified by the moro label, see Majul (1973), Gowing (1979), Laarhoven (1989), and Beckett (1982).

6. A *malong* is a large rectangular, or often tubular, piece of cloth, which can be worn a number of ways and is associated with the material culture of Islamic groups throughout insular Southeast Asia.

7. "Chismis" was a local slang term for "gossip."

8. It is difficult to characterize with much accuracy the many sources of conflict that produced the violence that erupted in Davao City during the 1980s—before and after the end of the Marcos regime. No historical study of this period has yet been undertaken for Davao City or the surrounding provinces (which cannot be understood in terms of the political conditions that have been documented for other areas of Mindanao). No reliable chronicles or in depth journalistic accounts exist. The subject remains at present largely a matter of local oral history. Davao City residents of this period tended to attribute the violence to different groups and conflicts, some specific to the Marcos regime, and the police and vigilante forces it fostered, some specific to more local rivalries and tensions, and others to more longstanding conflicts involving Islamic separatist organizations or the communist New People's Army. Probably there is some truth to all these accounts. In any case, the violence was widespread, frequent, and extreme enough to create what residents remember as wartime conditions during these years. Curfews were habitually in place and mobility into, out of, and within the city was highly limited.

9. The initials stand for "Brunei, Indonesia, Malaysia and the Philippines—East Asean Growth Area," a subdivision of the ASEAN network that recognized Davao as a centrally located, rapidly developable hub city.

10. *Kalakbay* is a Tagalog/Filipino term that can be glossed roughly as "tourism," although its origins are premodern. *Lakbay* loosely translated, means "journey," and the prefix acts as a general intensifier to the root term.

11. In 1996, 7 million pesos was the equivalent of $175,000. However, the average worker in Davao City was earning only around $100 a month. GATT, the General Agreement on Tariffs and Trade, was the predecessor to the World Trade Organization, which replaced it in 1996. In this regard DATA's grant, although it was administered through the Technical Education and Skills Development Authority of the Philippine Department of Labor and Employment (with the assistance of the regional office of the Department of Tourism), was of multinational origins, supporting global, as much as national, interests. The "new" WTO has been described as an agent of globalization with powers equal to if not greater than those of the World Bank, providing an institutional arena in which one nation will be able to challenge the laws of another if they are not seen to conform to the global economic order set forth by the WTO (see Burns 1999: 126, 169).

12. My research interest in Philippine dance is documented most extensively in Ness (1992). More recent publications on this topic include Ness (1995, 1996, 1997). Although my reputation as a dance scholar was well established in Manila and Cebu City during the years I was working in Davao City, only a few of Davao's residents, who were themselves especially knowledgeable on the subject, were aware of this

aspect of my professional identity. In all but a few instances, it was not a factor in my rapport with Davao's residents. I was generally known as a "researcher" interested only in tourism. However, in the relationships where this identity was known, it did play a significant role in strengthening my rapport with the individuals involved and contributed in no small way to establishing the network of trusted friends and colleagues that were essential in proceeding with the research at hand. The narrative recounted here is one example of this situation.

13. It might well be argued that a "time of abaca" should refer only to the latter American phase identified above, as this was the period when large scale abaca development and production occurred. Dabbay (1992: 35) recounts Davao City's history in this manner. My account reflects the understanding I gained over the course of my own interactions with individuals in the city, which had its ambiguities and distortions. Nonetheless, abaca cultivation was among the agricultural pursuits undertaken during the Spanish era of Davao's initial development, although coffee, copra, and cacao were also primary trade goods during this period (see Goodman 1967: 107n3; Baranera 1899; Corcino 1993: 29). Even during the more intensive American phase, the "time of abaca" was a period when both coconuts and lumber were major trade items in addition to abaca itself.

14. Davao's existence did not strictly speaking begin in the mid-nineteenth century, or as a colonial settlement, although its immigrant population arriving from the northern islands does date to this time. While the Spanish pueblo of "Nueva Vergara" (referred to as Davao after 1858) was established sometime shortly after 1848, when Spanish possession of the area was secured, the site was occupied before this time by indigenous groups and immigrant groups arriving from the southern islands. Gloria Dabbay (1992: 17–18) reports that prior to Spanish settlement, a trading center for multiple ethnolinguistic groups had been well established. Some of these groups were Islamic, migrating in from islands to the south. The population of the settlement, even fifty years after its Spanish takeover and pueblo development, remained small. By the advent of the twentieth century, it numbered only around 1,500 (1887 census figures reported in *A Pronouncing Gazetteer and Geographical Dictionary of the Philippine Islands,* U.S. Bureau of Insular Affairs 1902); Baranera (1899: 116), quoting a less reliable source, reported the population to be closer to 3,000 by the onset of American occupation. However, Davao was nonetheless described in one of the first American reports of the area, published in the *Gazetteer,* as "well laid out, with broad streets and has a number of well-built houses" (1902:497), indicating that the mid-nineteenth-century immigrants had made some progress in transforming the site into an organized settlement during the early, Spanish-governed decades.

15. This situation, however, reflected only the postcolonial tourism matrix. During American rule and the more productive phase of the "time of abaca," the abaca industry in Davao was in fact the primary feature of the city's touristic landscape. The 1931 *Manila Hotel: Tourist Guide to the Philippines* (published in Manila by the California Directory Association), for example, described Davao simply as "the center of the hemp industry" and "only interesting for being an important commercial town" (1931: 52–54). Davao, while it did merit mention in the *Manila Hotel* tourism brochure, was given only one paragraph's page space—less than a quarter of what any other provincial destination was afforded, and devoted entirely to the subject of abaca and ways to tour its production and manufacturing. Likewise, the 1931 brochure of the Southern Cross Cruises company, which included Davao City as its last stop on a 10-day excursion throughout the archipelago, described the city briefly as "the center of the hemp industry" and "a strictly commercial"city that only as "an example of pioneer commercial progress" was considered to be "well worth a

visit" (*Southern Cross Cruises from Manila to Visayan Islands Sulu Seas Moro Land*; the brochure can be found in the U.S. National Archives File 25759, document 53-D). The Philippines during this period was the world's main supplier of abaca or "Manila hemp," a product with global industrial significance in this period. The industrial image asserted for Davao contrasted starkly with that of Zamboanga for the same time period. Zamboanga was described as "a green verdant jewel," "famed in song and story," and "one of the most charming places in the entire Orient—with human interest rampant—a strange mixture of races, a most polyglot community" (1931: 50). It also contrasted with Cebu, which was cast as "the center of European civilization in the Philippines," replete with historic churches and "charming" old stone battlements (1931: 48). While other provincial sites were characterized in terms of cultural and historical features, the diverse ethnic character of Davao City at this time, particularly its predominantly Japanese character, was not played up in its touristic image, and its modern agricultural aspects were selected as the main objects for the tourist gaze.

16. Cabezas de Barangay governed under the provincial *gobernadorcillo*. See Dabbay (1992) for a listing of Davao's original government officers.

17. Spanish, or rather its local dialect Chavacano, was widely spoken in Davao throughout the American period. It remained in use as the lingua franca spoken universally by Japanese, Chinese, Tagalog, Visayan, and local ethnic groups (see Dabbay 1992: 36). It is thus not at all surprising that Donding's parents, although they lived and worked during the American regime, would still be using Spanish as a main language.

18. These statistics are reported in Dabbay (1992: 24) for Davao with the primary source given as the report on the "Fourth District" (established 1860), December 21, 1890, by Governor Domingo Gijou, who served as governor of Davao in 1890–92 (in the Spanish era, governors served usually only two year terms in Davao; a total of 23 different individuals served between 1848 and 1899). The report divides the 26,000 non-Christian count between Bagobos, Tagacaolos, Mandayas (the largest group with 8,000), Altuas, Manobos, and Samales. Magdalena (1997: 8), however, notes that the 1903 Census of the Philippine Islands already lists Davao District as significantly larger, with a total population of 65,496, of which only 20,224 were classified as "Civilized" and 45,272 as "Wild," a label that included Muslims. Goodman (1967: 31) notes that by 1934, around the time of Donding's birth (and as the Philippines neared transition to commonwealth status), the total population of Davao Province reported by the U.S. Bureau of Insular Affairs had grown to just over 200,000—increasing in exponential proportions throughout the American period. Of those, 105,071 were "Christian Filipinos," and 80,125 were "non-Christian." Magdalena (1997: 19) also reports that during this time period a total of 18 highland tribes were recorded for Mindanao as a whole, along with 13 Muslim or "Moro" groups. Davao City's population was around 21,000 at this time—many times what it had been at the turn of the century, although only a tiny fraction of what it would become less than thirty years later.

19. The list here has been compiled from groups mentioned by Davao's local historian Gloria Dabbay (1992), as well as by Savage-Landor (1904: 193), who described the number of tribes living in the region of Davao at the turn of the century as "bewildering," and by the Bureau of Insular Affairs *Gazetteer* (1902: 496). Groups mentioned by all sources are the Bagobos, Guiangans, Tagacaolos and Atas.

20. Concerning the population of the Davao pueblo itself, figures reported for an 1887 Spanish Survey, cited in the 1902 *Gazetteer*, placed Davao's pueblo population at 1,473 total. The ethnic breakdown of this population is not given in the report. The Spanish government, from as early as 1871, was monitoring, as well as

encouraging, the immigration of Christian families from the northern islands into the Davao district, on the assumption that the most effective means of stabilizing the area politically was to populate it with such migrants (see Dabbay 1992: 24). It is possible that a majority of the 1,500 as well as of the larger population of around 4,000 that was reported for the entire vicinity, which had reached 15 pueblos by this time, was predominantly Christian immigrant families. In 1899, according to Baranera (1899: 116), the population of the "capital" of Davao was 3,308 (this figure, however, may have included settlements near and around the pueblo, in addition to the pueblo itself).

21. As Dabbay (1992: 24–25) notes, when American military forces arrived in Davao on December 14, 1899 there was no armed opposition to their occupation of the pueblo. Davao transitioned from Spanish to American rule quickly, in a generally peaceful manner, although the first "quasi-civil" governor of the district, Edward Robert Bolton, was assassinated in 1906. Military administration was replaced by civil administration in the area in 1906. Davao's pueblo had already become part of a "municipal" district by this time, as of 1903 belonging to the newly created "Moro Province" of Mindanao, with municipal presidents initially being appointed by the military and later by the civil government until 1917 (long after the period when Donding's father was active), when they were elected by the citizenry (see Dabbay 1992: 28).

22. The change in population relative to the Philippines as a whole is perhaps best represented in Magdalena's study of population density for the combined Mindanao, Sulu, and Palawan region. From 1903 until 1990, Magdalena (1997: 12) reports, the population density increased in the region as a whole from 5.9 individuals per square kilometer (706,529 people, or 9.3 percent of the entire population of the Philippines) to 116 individuals per square kilometer (14, 815,392 people or 23.2 percent of the entire population).

23. For an insightful description and discussion of such popular music in the Philippine context, see Pico Iyer (1988: 151–94).

24. Mixed vegetables stewed in *bagoong* shrimp paste.

25. Caraga is located due east of Davao City on Mindanao Island's eastern coast. Surigao is located on the northernmost tip of Mindanao, and has particularly close economic and ethnic ties to the Visayan Islands. Both Caraga and Surigao are recorded in Spanish chronicles as sites of Christianization dating back to the earliest stages of Spanish rule. "Caraga" was initially the name for the whole of east and northeast Mindanao. During the late 1700s, in response to chronic raids by Islamic factions that had depopulated the entire eastern coast, the Spanish Crown ordered that Caraga be reestablished and repopulated as a military stronghold, and it remained an important center from that time onward. For a history of the colonization of Mindanao's northeastern area, as well as its role in the Philippine revolution, see Peter Schreurs (1987, 1989, 1994, 1998).

Census statistics given in the 1902 *Gazetteer* also support the comparison made by Donding and Celia for the period mentioned. Caraga's 1887 population was 8,690, while Davao's was only 1,473 (cited in Corcino 1993: 28 as well). Population statistics cited in Baranera (1899: 116) also indicate that at the turn of the century the relative importance of Caraga was still greater than that of Davao. Davao's population was 3,308, Caraga's 8,408.

The first governor of Davao, José de Oyanguren, was himself active in the Caraga district before taking up his position in Davao, and Dabbay (1992: 19) reports that the soldiers who assisted de Oyanguren in his efforts, and who became the first Spanish-governed inhabitants of the settlement built shortly thereafter, were themselves from Caraga and Surigao.

26. The earlier date mentioned, 1848, refers accurately to the year in which the "conquest" of Davao by José de Oyanguren occurred; the pueblo settlement that became Davao City's civic center, then named Nueva Vergara, was constructed; and the religious order primarily responsible for converting local populations to Christianity, the Recoletos or Recollects, arrived, established a local mission, and built the pueblo's first chapel, the San Pedro Chapel. De Oyanguren is believed to have taken over the settlement by force from a leader popularly known as Datu Bago. Historical sources provide no conclusive evidence of this process (see Corcino 1993 for a detailed summary account that mentions Datu Bago, and Schreurs 1989: 281–83 for an account that does not). In any case, de Oyanguren was given an official grant, issued by the Philippines governor general at that time, Narciso Claveria, to "conquer and subdue the Moros in the entire gulf area," which was dated February 27, 1847 (cited in Dabbay 1992: 19; Corsino 1993; Schreurs 1989: 282), making it fairly certain that the area was not obtained without some form of armed struggle. In any case, 1848 does mark the beginning of a sustained Spanish presence at the site.

Illustrations and maps of Davao drawn in 1856 and 1862, found respectively in the 1902 *Gazetteer* (Bureau of Insular Affairs 1902: 495) and in *Itinerario del Burriel: Il itinerario de la excursión hecha a Mindanao y Jolo* (see Blair and Robertson 1903–9, 53: 400), bear out the description given that Davao was not a center of any magnitude when it was initially converted to Spanish rule. The 1856 Spanish survey map of "The mouth of Davao River and its approaches" in the *Gazetteer*, for example, depicts "Vergara (Davao)" as a tiny settlement with only approximately 40 structures, most of them organized along a grid of paths, five running roughly north-south and four east-west, the southeast corner of which was perched on the northern edge of the Davao River, some 1500 yards from its mouth at the Davao Gulf. Likewise, two 1862 maps from the *Itinerario del Burriell*, "Plano del pueblo de Davao (Vergara) Cabeza del 4^0—Distrito de la Yola de Mindanao," and "Reconocimiento de 'Davao,'" which give even more detailed and virtually identical blueprint-like drawings of the pueblo, show only a triangular fort, church, "Casa del Gobernador" government house, "Galleria," "Tribunal," and two "Pantalan" as named main structures in the settlement. The plans also depict an unmarked street plan showing only three main streets running roughly north-south and four shorter east-west cross streets. Again, the maps indicate a total of only around 50 to 60 structures comprised the built environment of the entire pueblo. A drawing entitled "Vista de Davao y del Volcan de Apo tomada desde el frente de la Boca del Rio," dated December 27, 1862, also found in *Itinerario del Burriel*, depicts the pueblo in even more minimal terms, setting it amid a forest of palms and other trees that hide all but two small nipa-roofed buildings and a somewhat larger church. Indeed, as Dabbay reports (1992: 21), the development of Davao was chronically hampered, despite interest from Manila-based financiers, by a lack of skilled labor and extremely limited transport facilities. De Oyanguren was himself dismissed from his post in 1852 for failing to overcome these difficulties in his attempts to develop the settlement.

The beginning of "pioneer" family migration into the area from northern islands is somewhat more difficult to pinpoint, although it ostensibly begins in 1848. The initial 70-plus occupants of the pueblo were volunteer soldiers from Caraga and Surigao, Mindanao (see n. 25). Corcino reports (1993: 28), without citing any source, that the población's population in 1852 was 526, indicating a significant migratory influx. There is some evidence (cited in Dabbay 1992: 23) to suggest that the Spanish government was as late as 1871 in initiating efforts of its own to recruit immigrants into the vicinity, with no clear success (the population increased only to around 1,500 over the next 25 years and was reported at 3,308 by Baranera 1899:

116). Immigration did not produce a dramatic change in the population until the American era, particularly after 1915, when it reached 10,000 for the first time.

Regarding the 1910 date asserted as the beginning of Davao's larger scale development, this estimation is also accurate, although 1905 was the year when the first waves of American veterans and Japanese laborers were arriving. Only around 150 of the Americans, however, as Goodman (1967: 31) and Dabbay (1992: 34) note, remained for more than a few years. In any case, it was not until the 1910s that the development of Davao into an international site for abaca production and manufacturing gained any kind of real momentum. The 1914–18 period, as Dabbay notes (1992: 35), was the first boom period for hemp sale. Dabbay summarizes the fifty years of Spanish rule in the area as a time when "the economic condition of the people did not improve at all" and "no industry was developed" (1992: 24) Similarly, A. Henry Savage-Landor's 1904 account of Davao City—one of the few pre-1910 American accounts from this period—supports this characterization that, even after the Spanish established the settlement of Nueva Vergara/Davao, the pueblo failed to grow significantly. Savage-Landor described Davao City in 1904 as "of very little interest. An old Spanish settlement which has gone through many vicissitudes, it is now a sort of tumbling-down place, with luxurious drinking-saloons kept by American money-makers or by Spaniards . . . it is to be hoped that someday Davao may flourish again as it did some years ago" (1904: 189). The account illustrates how, as late as 1904, no large scale agricultural industry was in current operation, although some activity had previously occurred, and that Davao was still not a provincial center of any major importance. In Goodman's summary terms, "Davao in 1905 was little more than a village, typical of many scattered at wide intervals along the Mindanao coast" (1967: 107n6). Rapid, exponential growth came to the settlement only in the 1910's, particularly during 1914–18, when the first major boom in abaca production shifted into full swing and the poblacion's population increased to over 10,000 (Quaison 1993: 15).

27. Regarding the importance of the Mindanao logging industry and its environmental consequences, Magdelena (1997: 17) notes that in 1969–70 alone Mindanao produced 99 percent of the Philippines plywood, all its veneer products, and 76 percent of its commercial logs. As of 1989 Mindanao was still contributing 62.3 percent of the country's total log production. Magdalena characterizes the environmental losses of this period in terms of rapid deforestation for Mindanao Island as a whole, reporting (1997: 14) that, while in 1960 the island was still 60 percent forested (down from 75 percent reported for the turn of the century), by 1991 that figure had dropped to 22 percent—an average of 210,000 hectares of forest being cleared annually, with experts predicting complete deforestation within the next twelve years. Magdelena (1997: 22), like the participants of Donding's gathering, also summarizes the environmental history of the Mindanao region in terms of pre- and post-1960 periods, the former characterized by frontier colonization and the latter by the ultimate destruction of the forest cover as a result of illegal logging and upland agricultural development.

28. See Goodman (1967), "Introduction." Quaison (1993: 17) estimates that in the late 1930s, when the Philippine Japanese population reached its peak, 75 percent of the Philippines 19,000 Japanese residents were living in Davao City. Goodman's estimate is roughly the same, placing the 1938 Japanese population in Davao Province at about 14,000 (1967: 82).

29. The Japanese began to arrive in Davao in large numbers in 1904 and 1905. Some were already workers in the Philippines, who had worked on the Kennon road in Baguio between 1899 and 1904 (Quaison 1993: 14 estimates that some 500 workers arrived in Davao via this route; however, different estimates have been

suggested). A number of others were recruited in 1904 and 1905 by the Kobe immigrant Ohta Kyosaburu, who settled permanently in Davao in 1905, opening the town's largest department store, the Osaka Bazar. According to Dabbay (1992: 30, also Goodman 1967: 2; Quaison 1993: 17), the majority of the Japanese workers came from Okinawa, Kyushu, and western Honshu, places where the climate was somewhat similar to Davao's but the economy was generally depressed. In addition to laborers, Japanese merchants, entrepreneurs, and professionals also migrated to Davao during this period. According to Quaison (1993: 15) 60 Japanese-managed corporations were operating in Davao by 1914, although that number fluctuated over the next two decades, following periods of depression and boom (Goodman 1967: 4 places the Japanese population in Davao in 1916 at around 10,000; however, he reports (p.25) only 25 Japanese controlled firms operating in Davao as of 1932). By the 1930s, the city's population had increased to around 21,500 (Goodman 1967: 21; Quaison, 1993: 15 estimates the population at only 12,000 in 1933, but gives no source) with at least 13,000 Japanese (Goodman 1967: 26, citing a report by Japan's Acting Consul in Davao; Quaison 1993: 15, estimates only 7,000, but cites no source). Goodman (1967: 21, 31) reports that at that time 80 percent of the abaca grown in Davao was being produced by the Japanese, and the control of the Japanese over the economic life of Davao was extensive, achieved despite government attempts to keep at least titular control of the industry in the hands of American and Filipino owners. Quaison (1993: 16) estimates that Japanese paid roughly 60 percent of the domestic taxes for the province in 1937. Goodman (1967: 82) cites a 1938 memorandum from Charles Burnett, then chief of the U.S. Bureau of Insular Affairs, estimating that 90 percent of all goods sold in Davao were Japanese. Through a variety of both overt and covert corporate organizations, Japanese migrants dominated not only the hemp industry, working an estimated 50,000 hectares of land (Quaison, 1993: 15), but also the lumber and fishing industries as well as retail trade in Davao and its surrounding area. The Japanese acquired control of land during this time, not only through Christian immigrant land owners, sometimes acting as "dummy" or default "pakiaw" corporate owners, but also through negotiations and marriages directly with the Bagobos, who controlled large tracts of land, land that was not returned to the Bagobos when the Japanese were expelled at the end of World War II. See Goodman (1967) for an extensive overview of Davao's Japanese settlement.

30. Quaison (1993), Dabbay (1992), and Goodman (1967) would concur with this opinion. Japanese management was largely responsible for implementing progressive technological strategies on the abaca plantations that led to their increased production. They were also adept managers of plantation labor, attracting and maintaining work forces of a high quality whose reputation drew Filipino migrants from as far away as Luzon by the thousands (Goodman 1967: 111n101 shows evidence of 7,000 so employed by 1938). Goodman's study in particular addresses the constructive and generally beneficial character of the Japanese colony in Davao during the American period, bringing out, among other facets, President Manuel Quezon's extraordinary statesmanship in sustaining its presence until the actual takeover of Japanese troops in 1941.

31. Davao Gulf and Davao City in particular were important locations in the U.S.-Japanese conflict. As Corcino (1993: 30) notes, more lives were lost in Davao City during the end of the war than anywhere else in the country. Davao suffered extensive destruction from U.S. bombing missions, being a Japanese stronghold and a prime target in this regard. Its role in World War II has yet to become the subject of any detailed local history.

32. See note 1 on Imelda Marcos's tourism activities.

33. The role of cultural dancing in diplomatic and touristic events in the Philippine context generally bears out Jane Desmond's theory (see Desmond 1999) of the function of bodily display in such performances to attribute reality and naturalness to certain cultural differences, assertions that are then set to work in various ideological operations benefiting the sponsors of the performances.

34. "Strong" here I interpreted to mean the accentuated movements of the pelvis that were a distinctive feature of the folklorized renditions of some Bagobo dance steps as well as of some traditional Bagobo dance practices.

35. *Merienda*, a Spanish term, is used throughout the Philippines to refer to a light meal or "snack" that occurs between main meals.

Chapter 4. The Excessive Destination: Pearl Farm Beach Resort

1. Desmond (1999: xx–xxi) citing Urry (1990) explains that the tourist gaze can be divided into two broad types: the romantic and the collective. The romantic emphasizes the characteristics mentioned above in addition to invoking "solitude," while the collective emphasizes a sense of carnival. Pearl Farm clearly fell into the general category of a landscape designed to attract the romantic gaze.

2. In this regard, my perception of the resort exposed its status as what Desmond (1999: 176–216) has characterized as an "in-fake-situ" type of destination or site. In-fake-situ destinations fall midway along a "realism continuum" in their attempts to stage "the natural," according to Desmond. Pearl Farm created a utopic simulacrum of the very site on which it was built, making the realism of its landscape maximally persuasive. However, the landscape's "perceived realism quotient," as Desmond identifies it, was lower for me, given my coincidental exposure to its engineered, non-natural foundations. Desmond notes that in-fake-situ sites require complex ideological work, as they bring together signs of nature and culture "under the oscillating sign of the real/not real. In this regard, promises of extraordinary authenticity and uniqueness can be essential in motivating such work on the part of an in-fake-situ site's tourists. Such was definitely the case with Pearl Farm.

3. Statistic included in the typescript "Background Profile" for Kaputian municipality, obtained from the files of the LAWIG foundation.

4. The barangay is the submunicipal unit of local government in the Philippines. The municipality of Kaputian on Samal Island, where Pearl Farm was located, was composed of 15 barangays.

5. *Balay* is the Cebuano term for "house" or "building."

6. Reports by researchers on the Floirendo enterprises differ as to the actual size and status of the Tadeco plantation, although contacts close to the Floirendo family informed me that it was roughly 6,000 hectares. Bonner (1987: 263) reports it as "17,000 acres of public land where the Davao penal colony was located," and identifies Imelda Marcos as having made the arrangements for the expansion. However, Manapat (1991: 146), who provides a more detailed account, reports that Tadeco since 1949 had title to 1,024 hectares—the maximum amount a corporation could legally own under the Philippine constitution. In 1969 an additional 171 hectares was awarded the corporation, and in 1976 the company was somehow able to expand to 4,504 hectares. In 1979 Tadeco was again somehow allowed to increase its holdings by 25 percent. Manapat indicates that 4,758 hectares of Tadeco's land was located within the Davao Penal Colony. Tadeco was officially committed to leasing most of its total of around 6,000 hectares of land from the government. From 1969 until 1986, however, Manapat also asserts that "it was reported" by an unnamed source that the company never actually paid any rent. This would have allowed the plantation

to function much less expensively, as did Tadeco's use of penal colony inmates, who were hired at what Manapat characterizes as "exploitation rates," far below the standard minimum other plantations were compelled to pay (Manapat 1991: 146–47). While Floirendo was titular president of Tadeco it was "widely known" according to Manapat, that he was a front for Ferdinand Marcos (not Imelda); Manapat's unnamed "sources" indicated Marcos received up to 80 percent of the profits. Seagrave's account differs from Manapat's in some details (1988: 283–85). He does note, in agreement with Manapat, that Ferdinand Marcos was the force behind the development of Tadeco, Marcos being interested in breaking the grip of the two big international food houses, Castle & Cooke and Del Monte, who dominated the Philippine banana industry, and needing to develop a producer under his control in order to accomplish this. Seagrave reports, however, that the size of the plantation was 12,000 acres, not 6,000 hectares as Manapat indicates, and that all of it was inside the penal colony. Also, he claims that Floirendo did pay the government $9 an acre per year to lease the land, albeit while the going rate to planters elsewhere was $30 to $50 an acre. According to Seagrave, prisoners were hired at less than 20¢ a day per man—the going rate for plantation laborers being closer to $2 a day. Youngblood's (1990: 105) account also differs in some details. He reports that Tadeco's plantation holdings increased from 171 hectares in 1969–70 to 4,504 hectares in 1976 and mentions in addition that the corporation also was using an additional 3,480 hectares of land within the Davao Penal Colony. Youngblood (1990: 104n.7), citing a report from the Philippine Inter-Agency Research Team on the Banana Workers, also elaborates on the violent tactics, which included torture and murder, the Tadeco management used to force sale or evacuation of the lands Tadeco was interested in acquiring. These activities, which were reported to have affected hundreds of families of small farmers and Ata tribespeople, were carried out, according to eyewitnesses cited in the report, by Tadeco security guards working in collaboration with Civilian Home Defense Force personnel, the 57th Strike Force, the army of PANAMIN (Presidential Assistant on National Minorities), and Davao Penal Colony prisoners. Manapat's account (1991: 148) also includes similar information about the violent tactics Tadeco employed in collaboration with government personnel to claim additional lands, citing the ICL Research Team document, *The Human Cost of Bananas* (1980). Despite the discrepancies noted, all reports identify the crucial role of the Marcos government in assisting Tadeco's expansion far beyond legal limits, largely through the use of the resources of the Davao Penal Colony, but also by other, sometimes violent, means.

Despite the emphasis researchers have placed on the role of the Marcoses' in the Floirendo family's fortune-building, conversations with longtime local residents in Davao indicate that Antonio Floirendo, the head of the family, was seen locally not simply as a Marcos crony but as an entrepreneur who maintained close relationships with a long line of Philippine presidents, Marcos prominent among them. Floirendo had already achieved considerable success in plantation enterprises among other commercial pursuits prior to his involvement with Marcos. Local sources agreed that President Quirino was most likely his first such high level contact.

7. Quirino served as president of the Philippines from 1948, when as acting vice president he succeeded Manuel Roxas upon Roxas's death from a heart attack, until 1953, when he was defeated in his run for reelection by Ramon Magsaysay.

8. See note 6 above. Sterling Seagrave (1988: 283–84), for example, reports on the construction of a fifteen-mile road, ordered by President Marcos, that ran directly to Floirendo's private dock on the Davao Gulf where Tadeco's multinational trading partner United Brands docked its freighters for loading.

9. For more on Floirendo's relationship to the Marcoses, see Seagrave (1988),

Bonner (1987), Manapat (1991), Youngblood (1990). Accounts vary as to whether it was Imelda or Ferdinand Marcos who involved Antonio Floirendo most directly in their various dealings. Seagrave (1988: 390) reports that Imelda had hoped to marry her daughter Imee to the oldest son of Antonio. Instead, he married the Filipina Miss Universe of 1973, Margie Moran, who became Pearl Farm's first general manager. See also note 6 above.

Chapter 5. Pearl Farm Beach Resort: Tourate Perspectives

1. Ten of the interviews were conducted in Adecor and included both employees of Pearl Farm and members of their immediate families; seven were conducted with employees on Pearl Farm's grounds. The rest were conducted either in Davao City or at other locations on Samal Island with part- and full-time Pearl Farm employees. In all but five cases—the interviews conducted with Floirendo family members and two managers, which I conducted in English and in all but one case alone—I worked closely with local research associates, who acted as the primary interviewers, using Cebuano as the main language of the interview. Whenever possible, I worked as part of a team of three. These teams changed in personnel over the course of the research period. In most cases, however, the individuals I collaborated with were either well known to the interviewees or shared a number of characteristics with them (educational affiliations, hometown locations, age, ethnic and linguistic identity). In this respect the rapport my associates were able to establish in the interview process went beyond any I might have been able to achieve, and their joint presence served to create a group discussion atmosphere rather than a one-on-one interview situation, even while, for the most part, the interviewees responded to questions posed by only one research associate. My role in the process was generally to listen attentively to the questions asked, respond silently, and add a few questions of my own toward the end of the interview. Typically I voiced these in English, which the interviewee generally understood, but also had them translated by one of the other interviewers into Cebuano so as to ensure that Cebuano, and the fluent Cebuano speakers, remained predominant in the conversation.

2. Honorifics were not easy to come by on Samal Island. Few people held them. There were no PhDs or professors resident on the island, and the island had no universities or colleges. There were only two doctors, who were both working at the island's only hospital. There were a few priests and attorneys, but only a very few—less than a dozen professionals all told. Kaputian itself had only one Roman Catholic "Father" currently serving the whole municipality. Political titles were scarcely more common. There were three mayors, the highest government title holders. There were 44 barangay "captains," the largest single title holding group. All these included, however, it was still a very rare thing to encounter a person holding a title of any sort. When such occasions did present themselves, titles were used frequently in conversation, as a gesture of respect. People could find ways, I had witnessed, to insert these honorifics—be it "Mr. Mayor" or "Doctor" or "Father"—into every sentence when engaging in a conversation with a titled person. The loss of a title was not a small thing, and Father Chico had not been stripped of his in everyday life, even while officially he had surrendered it several years previously.

3. The island's interior was populated by a scattered array of tiny settlements, and these did not tend to attract migrants. Newcomers were far more likely to settle on the island's western coast, in one of the island's three municipal centers—Babak in the north, Peñaplata midway down the western coast, or Kaputian's población in the south.

4. This description to my ears constituted an exaggeration that I repeatedly attempted in vain to correct, but it was apparently a mandatory classification to my research associates, who used it, I gathered, to reinforce the legitimacy of the work we were undertaking at Pearl Farm. Eventually I came to understand the phrase differently from its use in standard American English, the "very good" indicating only an actual state of good will evident in interactions, not a particularly strong personal bond.

5. Father Chico's interview was one of the five conducted entirely in English, the language he chose to use on this occasion.

6. The general function posited here for the cultural dancing performed at Pearl Farm is one that Desmond (1999: 16–17) has also observed for the performance of hula dancing at luxury class hotels in Hawaii. Desmond writes, "Live cultural shows provide the most concentrated dose of Hawaiiana . . . the bodily presence of certain live dancers (and not others) serves as a guarantor of the authenticity of this cultural difference." This was definitely the case with Pearl Farm's "tribal" dance performances.

7. The Bayanihan Dance Company, whose history has yet to become the object of in-depth cultural or historical study, remains one of the most important and influential national/cultural institutions in the Philippines. The Bayanihan Company's choreographies were originally staged in 1958 for an international competition in Brussels. During the Marcos regime, Bayanihan—officially the folk dance company of the Philippine Women's College—became closely associated with the Marcoses' political interests, both domestic and international, and acted as a campaign tool and a body of "cultural ambassadors" abroad. However, the company's choreographies later served as authenticated sources for the teaching of Philippine folk dance throughout the Philippines, becoming widely practiced by dance groups that were organized both within the public and private school systems, as well as through civic organizations and private institutions. The popular understanding of Bayanihan choreographies, an understanding now disseminated throughout the Philippines and its global diaspora, has entailed both nationalistic and patriotic recognition of the dancing as representing "Filipino culture" and an ethnic reading of the diverse choreographic repertory as authentic but theatricalized renditions of the dance practices of highland and lowland cultural groups inhabiting different regions of the archipelago. While the Bayanihan Dance Company and its innumerable reconstructions have become an important component of Philippine-identified spaces in the global tourism matrix, the company and its choreographies are still identified in basically political and ethnic, as opposed to economic or commercial terms.

The Toledos were two of several professional Philippine folk dance choreographers based in Davao City who produced authenticated representations of Philippine cultural dancing. Sometimes such groups were hired for civic celebrations, sometimes for private events backed by a wide range of political, social, and economic interests. The Bayanihan repertory was the symbolic template for the Peña company in all its Philippine-identified choreographies, and was the original source for the cultural dancing staged at Pearl Farm. None of the Peña company members had ever interacted directly with the Bayanihan Company or its artistic directors. "Our dream," Dani Toledo remarked in his interview, "is to achieve the equivalent of the Bayanihan" (the Cebuano interview transcription reads: *Dreams lang gyud namo maparehas lang mi sa Bayanihan*). Not only was the company's dancing not an unmediated manifestation of purely "native" Mindanao or Samal Island cultural practice, it was in fact a representation at least three times removed from any indigenous precolonial dance traditions. As presented on Pearl Farm's utopian stages, this "native" dancing had been filtered through the interpretations of the Bayanihan, their first- or second- or third-hand replicators, and eventually, the Toledos.

8. The Cebuano transcript reads: *Mrs. [Mayor]. "Naa baya nagasayaw diha sa Pearl Farm. Testing daw mo diha kay mga tribal man daw ilang ginapangita mga folk dance." Mao to among gi-try, nagpakapal mi didto.*

9. As it happened, the Pearl Farm management later became interested in the group's swing and disco dance repertory, which it used for social dance events on at least one occasion. Modern dance proved to be the only category in which the resort never expressed any interest. The resort's initial and primary interest, however, was in contracting presentations of "tribal" dancing.

10. The Cebuano transcript reads: *Diha [sa Pearl Farm] na ko nakakuan choreograph. . . . Diha lang mi naka-kuan tungod na lang nang Pearl Farm.*

11. Peñaplata's población or civic center was estimated to have a population of around 4,000 people, according to the Samal Island Profile document, a typescript in the files of the LAWIG Foundation office.

12. Although a minority, both gay men company members played prominent roles in the company. One was the president of the company, a pioneer member, and the individual responsible for persuading Dani and Heidi to audition the company at Pearl Farm. The other was the only dancer in the company to have performed with Davao City's most prestigious cultural dance ensemble, directed by a former Bayanihan dancer. The influence of the gay subculture on the dance company was significant, but beyond the scope of this study to address.

13. In Kaputian municipality in particular, only 4 percent of the population had any postsecondary or college education. Of those seven years old and older, the majority (67 percent) had completed an elementary school education.

14. The company made 4,000 pesos per performance, 1000 going to choreographers and 3,000 split among dancers (roughly 250–300 each, the equivalent of around two days salary for young office workers in Davao City, in local terms "good money").

15. Full-time Pearl Farm "frontliners" in contrast made upward of 6,000 pesos a month when service charges and salary were counted—roughly three times what Dani or Heidi made at their regular jobs.

16. The Cebuano transcript reads: *Na-divide na. Pero siguro kung focused gyud mi sa sayaw, sayaw gyud. Kanang siyempre kinahanglan tag income karon di ba? Lisod man ang kinabuhi. Karon kay di man gyud kaayo pirmi gyud ang show so kinahanglan gyud namo mangitag lain job.* It should be noted as well that, while the work with the Peña company was financially rewarding, it was something more than a business opportunity for Heidi. Part of her motivation for working overtime for the company came from a personal enjoyment of the practice. When it was suggested to her in her interview that she seemed to love her work with the dance company, she immediately responded in the affirmative.

17. The Cebuano transcript for the two quotations in this paragraph read: *Sus kay kun puwede lang atras mu-atras naman gyud mi unta. . . .Opportunity na unta-alangan first class gud na nga Pearl Farm.*

18. The Cebuano transcript reads: *Sa akong na-observe ha nga naka-experience kog mga choreographer, wa gyud koy na-experience nga choreographer na buotan. Istrikto gyud.*

19. The Cebuano transcript reads: *At least akong pagka-isog nakatabang sa ilaha. Kaya na nila mutudlog lain nga tao.*

20. The Cebuano transcript reads: *Naga-dagdag siya ba.*

21. The Cebuano transcript reads: *Mura gyud real gud mi nga mga Muslim.*

22. Heidi's husband Dani was asked directly about this in a joint interview, and when he confirmed that there had been no bad experiences ("Everything has been beautiful. We have had no bad experience there." *Guwapo tanan. Walay mga bad experience namo didto*), Heidi tacitly agreed.

23. The Cebuano transcript reads: *Pag dawat namo taas noo kaayo mi. "Uy nadawat mi no, mag-adto na mi," ingon ko uy taas-taas . . . "base makaadto pa mig abroad."*

24. The Cebuano transcript reads: *Sad experience sa mga Pilipino. . . . Dili halos namalakpak. . . . Grabe bitaw uy. Ang Pilipino tan-awon lang ang mali. Dapat silay mu-una unta nga palakpak gyud kay Pilipino gud. Sila may hinoon di mamalakpak, ginoo ko. Yawid-yawiran pa ka.*

25. The "crab mentality" was and remains a popular phrase in Filipino identity discourse to indicate dysfunctional group dynamics. Like a group of crabs trapped in a crate, pulling back down any individual that attempts to climb up and out of their common prison, the metaphor characterizes Filipino-identified group dynamics as having destructive consequences for individuals showing any initiative that might result in moving into a more advantageous position vis-à-vis their original group.

26. The Cebuano transcript reads: *Wala gyuy sila gihunahuna nga mga kaayohan sa barangay. Paminaw nako ana gyud.*

27. The Cebuano transcript reads: *Ana man siguro na mo-react man? ana gyud na sila. Number one gyud na ana ang ilang gibati is: dili sila mobalhin kay naanad na sila diri sa baybayon. Pero kung lantawon gyud nimo ang progreso sa barangay dapat balhin gyud sila kay kung once nga mo-develop ang barangay ma-develop ni nga area. Makatabang man pod sa ilaha. Dako nga makakuan sa ilahang pamuyo.*

28. The Cebuano transcript reads: *Always naa sila sa negative side ba.*

29. The Cebuano transcript reads: *Pero sa 200 ka residents siguro naa lay lima . . . lima lang . . . ang interesado.*

30. The Cebuano transcript reads: *Ay Oo, dako kaayog diperensiya kay sa income lang makatabang gyud kaayo. Maka-paeskuwela gyud ka kay ga-yuta lang siguro ang imong gikuanan lisod magpa-eskuwela.*

31. The Cebuano transcript reads: *Dako gani na silag kanang mga Taiwanese dako na silag tabang sa ekwelahan ba.*

32. The standard price for a young coconut, even at a tourist establishment, would have been closer to 25 pesos. The Cebuano transcript reads: *Usahay magpanon ang mga Taiwanese ana diha sa ilaha. Dugay kaayo mag-uli. Mangayo silag butong. . . . Pero dili man na siya magpabayad pero pagbalik nila usahay tagaan na siyag 200, 500 ana. Depende sa kadaghanon sa mga.*

33. Since the time of the research period, Pearl Farm Beach Resort has continued operation, although its management changed after the Estrada administration came to power in 1998. The name was changed to Barcelo Pearl Farm Resort sometime after 1997, indicating that Century is no longer involved with its operation. The ownership, however, as confirmed in a Philippine Daily Inquirer News Service report in May 2001, is still with the family of Antonio Floirendo. According to one of the individuals interviewed in Davao City in 1996, who was reinterviewed in 2001, the resort was taken over by individuals representing the Estrada administration shortly after it came into office, but was closed during part of the period as well, apparently for lack of business. In general, tourism in the Philippines entered a sharp decline in 1997 and has not yet shown clear signs of recovery. Pearl Farm, however, was again open for business in 2001 and currently remains open, though it is no longer listed on the Small Luxury Hotels web site (the Philippines is no longer listed as a country covered by that company). Pearl Farm's web pages currently use the same imagery and text that were used during the research period. Its rates, which had increased for several years, dropped sharply in 2001 and currently range from $70 per night for a hilltop room to $385 for one of the four-bedroom Malipano island villas, which are no longer reserved for the exclusive use of Floirendo family members.

Chapter 6. The Flagship Destination: The Samal Island Tourism Estate

1. Information on the early stages of the SITE development has come from unpublished government documents located in the files of the LAWIG office, Babak, Samal Island, and from personal communications with members of the 1993 commission representing the Samal Island residents during the project's early phases of negotiation with Ekran Berhad. Information has also been obtained from unpublished government documents furnished by the Davao City office of the Philippine Tourism Authority (a subdivision of the Department of Tourism).

2. Ekran Berhad is an investment holding company chaired by Ting Pek Khing. In addition to its investment holdings, however, the company has also been involved in construction and property development, which by 1998 accounted for 37 percent of its fiscal revenues. The company is also involved in trading and extracting timber and oil and in air transportation development and related aerial businesses. The company's activities have been primarily based in Malaysia, making the SITE joint venture something of an exceptional undertaking (the information here provided was available from the Wright Research Center in 1998).

3. For a concise account of the Ramos administration and its perception as generally successful, see Steinberg (2000: 193–208).

4. The statistical information given here, except for the infrastructure spending figure, appeared in a commencement address delivered by Carlos G. Dominguez to the Ateneo de Davao University, March 23, 1997 and published the same year in the journal *Tambara*. Dominguez quoted a 4 percent growth rate in the regional domestic product in 1993–97, contrasted with 0.5 percent in 1992. Telephone lines grew from 63,000 in 1992 to 148,000 in 1995. Energy consumption was reported as having risen 19 percent in the 1992–95 period and was characterized as having become "more reliable" (Dominguez 1997: 120–21). The infrastructure spending figure was announced by Paul Dominguez in an address to the Philippine Business for Social Progress membership on September 27, 1995, as is the rest of the information in this paragraph.

5. Copies of the tourism blueprint and Tourism Master Plan for Samal Island were obtained in 1995 at the Davao City PTA office in 1995 as well as at the LAWIG office. The quality of the reproductions was not adequate to permit reproduction.

6. Such reports were published at the national level as well in the *Philippine Daily Inquirer* (June 20, 1993: D-8) and the *Manila Chronicle* (May 29, 1993: 16).

7. This land area ratio for the estate in relation to the municipality of Kaputian is drawn from information in the Background Profile document in the LAWIG files, which was compiled from National Census and Statistics Office survey information around 1990. Kaputian's total land area was cited as 11,750 hectares. The land area ratio for the estate in relation to the island is approximated from figures in "A Brief Profile of Davao Province," dated circa 1990; a Samal Island Profile document, dated circa 1995; and the "Samal Island Profile" section of a Philippine Business for Social Progress document dated circa 1995, which cited as sources the Provincial Planning and Development Office of Davao del Norte, as well as the municipal planning and development offices of all three Samal Island municipalities. All these sources were unpublished typescripts found in LAWIG office files. Estimates of land area varied from 28,000 to 33,000 hectares. In subsequent statistical citations, I have deferred to the Background Profile and Philippine Business for Social Progress "Samal Island Profile" documents, regarding their information as being the most recent and probably the most reliable given the sources indicated.

8. There were a total of three municipalities located on Samal Island, all "fifth class" in provincial income rankings. Kaputian trailed the others in a number of

respects as far as its development was concerned, and it was a great deal more isolated. Babak municipality, at the island's northern end, was the most closely connected to Davao City, with hourly ferry boat transports to and from the city operating everyday. Samal municipality, located in the island's center, had been created in 1948 and originally contained the other two municipalities. Samal municipality included the port center of Peñaplata, which provided ferry service to Davao City several times a day. The island's only hospital and junior college were also located in Samal. Kaputian, on the southern end of the island, had ferries leaving the municipal center or población for Davao City only once a day. See note 12 below for further details on the municipality's underdeveloped condition.

9. Most sources checked described Kaputian municipality as being composed of fourteen barangays in addition to its población district. However, the Background Profile document lists fifteen, including the población district as one of them. I have adopted this latter strategy, hence the "eleven" barangay figure used in the text includes as one of the eleven the población district.

10. According to the Background Profile document for Kaputian municipality (which quoted the 1990 census statistics of the Philippines National Census and Statistics Office), the population and household numbers for the barangays were as follows: Pangubatan,1,255 population/236 households; San Remigio, 2,070/417; Libertad, 2,251/421; San Isidro, 1,207/231; Linosutan, 1,133/223; Santa Cruz, 3,777/735; Cogon, 1,944/343. The 1990 total for the Samal Island area was 6,783/1,305 and that for the Talikud Island area was 6,854/1,301. The 1990 resident population of all seven barangays came to 14,942, or 2,606 households. Given the estimated 2.78 percent population growth rate for the municipality in 1990, the 1995 resident population/number of household estimated totals came to 18,135/2,989.

11. The 1990 figure in the Background Profile and Philippine Business for Social Progress "Samal Island Profile" for the municipality was 23,923. The total number of households was listed in both sources as 4,069. The estimated 1990 growth rate of 2.78 would give a 1995 estimate of 27,438. The total population of the three Samal Island municipalities taken from the Philippine Business for Social Progress document was 68,577. However, it should be noted that this population figure differs significantly from the other "Samal Island Profile" document also located in the LAWIG office files (see note 7), which estimated closer to 50,000. With a 2.78 percent growth rate, the 25 percent estimate in the text is a rough approximation.

12. Although Samal Island was in most respects a satellite island of Davao City, it was not a part of Davao City Province, but rather belonged to Davao Province (still commonly referred to as Davao del Norte in 1996). This was generally considered to be an impediment to the island's progressive development, as the main stakeholders in Samal Island's development lived in Davao City and were not in control of the island's provincial political organization. According to the Background Profile document for Kaputian municipality, only around 300 of Kaputian's 4,069 households were supplied with electricity from the province's electric company, DANECO (Davao del Norte Electric Company) as of 1990. None of these households were located in the barangays affected by SITE. Only the municipal center had a water pipe system, leaving the households in the rest of the municipality without running water. The entire municipality had only a few hundred meters of cement roads. The municipal profile indicated that over 65 percent of the municipality's children under seven years of age suffered from some form of malnutrition, citing a Department of Health 1990 survey. Provincial surveys for 1990 ranked Kaputian fourth or fifth in the province of Davao in terms of problems with malnutrition.

13. The descriptions here are based on the documents located in the Davao PTA office in 1995–96.

14. See note 11 above for the derivation of this figure.

15. The projections are based on the documents located in the Davao PTA office in 1995–96. Estimates of total employment ranged from 17,000 to 18,650 jobs.

16. The Background Profile estimated that 52.47 percent of the municipality's population were between the ages of 15 and 64, which for the seven barangays would have generated a figure of 9,502. The municipality's labor force was estimated in 1990 to be 14,422; the exact percentage given for unemployment was 12.58 percent.

17. The Background Profile listed four types of economic activities for the municipality: (1) farming rice, coconut, corn, beans vegetables, root crops, coffee, and cacao; (2) animal production, of chicken or swine; (3) fishing yellow fin tuna, skip jack, anchovies, and big-eyed and round-eyed scad; and (4) small scale commercial activities, concentrated in the población district, such as sari-sari stores, *carenderias* (meal stands), merchandising stores, and baby cono rice and corn mills. The Philippine Business for Social Progress "Samal Island Profile" listed 64 percent of Kaputian's agricultural land as planted with coconuts, 25 percent with bananas, and 6 percent with corn. The other Samal Island Profile document in the LAWIG files also listed coconuts as the largest farming crop for Kaputian, with 4,890 hectares given over to its production, and listed "grains" and "fruit trees" as the next largest crops, their combined cultivation requiring approximately 1,500 hectares.

18. This figure (approximately U.S. $60,000,000) was given as the total in the undated document, Tourism Master Plan for the Philippines (sponsored by the World Tourism Organization, the Philippine Department of Tourism, and the United Nations Development Programme), probably written circa 1991. The same figures are reported in articles in the *Philippine Daily Inquirer* (June 20 1993: D-8) and the *Manila Chronicle* (May 29, 1993:16).

19. Accounts of the exact investment figure Ekran Berhad would contribute varied greatly, from 10 million pesos to U.S.$50 million. The 50-million-peso figure represents the amount most frequently estimated by the most reliable interview sources, although, given the budget estimates developed by DOT for the project as a whole, the figure seems extremely low. One DOT document, for example, estimated a total cost of $250 million for the first 1,720 rooms, built on seven different construction sites, and lists $50 million as the initial investment of Ekran Berhad. The Davao Home Page (updated February 13, 1998) reported Ekran Berhad spending $100 million to develop the estate, with an option to invest an additional $100 million in future estate development.

20. It should be noted, however, that Ekran Berhad was assisted in its initial investment by the Philippine government. The government granted several million pesos outright to Ekran Berhad during initial negotiations between Ekran Berhad and the Samal Island commission, when the commission insisted on a higher leasing amount than the Malaysian company was willing to pay (represented during the negotiations by Narzalina Lim of the Southern Pacific Resort Development Corporation, who was also the current head of the Department of Tourism). Given that the official roles the government had designed for itself as leaseholder and public works developer did not include this type of assistance, its willingness to grant funds to Ekran Berhad clearly indicated the importance the Ramos administration placed on seeing the project succeed. In addition, the budget estimates for the Philippine government's public works projects supporting the estate totaled over 400 million pesos, according to the DOT's Tourism Development Plan for Samal Island. These included building a circumferential road for Samal Island, upgrading the Davao City Santa Ana Wharf ferry terminal, and building a cruise ship terminal and a Samal Island port, as well as developing water and waste utilities, telecommunications, and a power system for the resort area.

21. Unfortunately, time constraints and the sensitivity of the topic prevented a

full investigation of the details of the Samal Island commission's operation during this critical early phase of the development process. I was not able in 1995 and 1996 to locate any documentation of the commission's activities, any record of the calculations used to determine the lease amounts ultimately settled on, or even a complete listing of the commission's membership and its official designation. Two members of the commission interviewed at some length, however, both characterized the meetings with Ekran Berhad as demoralizing, given what they perceived to be a lack of support from the DOT officials present at the meetings for the Philippine interests at stake. The negotiation of the lease price, in their recollection, involved the commission members bargaining alone against both Ekran Berhad and DOT representatives. The agreement achieved was brought about only when the commission members threatened to walk out of the meetings rather than settling for the Ekran Berhad offer, a tactic that would have caused a delay of several weeks at least in the negotiations. No evidence of dishonorable conduct in relation to the commission or its members ever came to light during the course of my research. All indications pointed to the conclusion that the commission served its appointed purpose effectively, if not heroically, and secured a degree and level of participation for community interests in the development process unprecedented in the history of Philippine tourism development.

As for the details of the payment agreement, accounts of the exact structure of the holding corporation (referred to in DOT documents as the Samal Island Resort Development Corporation) varied. However, somewhere between 20 and 27 million pesos of an original 47-million-peso lease amount was designated for investment in this corporation (the money coming from the Philippine government). The structure of the corporation determined that the organization representing community interests, a collective that was named the SLS cooperative, would never have more than a minority share of its stock, somewhere between 7 and 20 percent, and would never have more than one seat on its board of directors. The holding corporation was viewed by some as an evasive tactic to withhold much of the lease funds from the direct control of the community cooperative, but by others as a guarantee that the community members would permanently benefit from the estate's profits.

22. I have been unable to verify the exact nature of the connection of Don Carlos with the San Miguel Brewery. The relationship was mentioned by an interviewee whose her father had been a long-time employee of Fernández Hermános and who recalled living at Don Carlos's house in Manila. She described the family as "Spanish" and involved with San Miguel Brewery.

23. For a detailed discussion of the Aquino CARP legislation, its place in the history of land reform initiatives in the Philippine context, and its relative success and failure, see Putzel (1992), particularly 259–81. The plan is generally described as a compromised initiative that fell far short of its intended goals (see for example the summary in Steinberg 2000: 173–74).

24. According to one member of the Samal Island commission, the order to form a cooperative body that could represent the CARP beneficiaries in negotiations over the tourism estate came directly from "Malacañang" through DAR. The order, however, initially produced not one but three individual cooperatives, representing CARP beneficiaries from the three barangays separately. According to one interviewee, it took a second presidential order, which came down through the same channels, to combine the three cooperatives into a single one that then began to interact with the DOT. Bypassing the CARP legislation thus occurred at the direct order of President Ramos.

25. There was not complete agreement among sources on the figure of 27 million pesos as the initial amount of the cash payment, but the most reliable accounts

collected consistently did report this figure. The exact date of the payment is also uncertain, although sources commenting on the payment all placed it at about two years before the research period, which would have put it late in 1993 or early in 1994.

26. The relocation area was situated in an inland/upland region of the plantation. The new homes, built on lots ten or twenty by thirty meters in size, were chosen by raffle.

27. There were 29 cooperatives in existence on the island in 1995, according to the Philippine Business for Social Progress "Samal Island Profile," all but four based in Samal municipality. Twenty-five were consumer coops, two transport coops, and two credit coops. Only three, all consumer coops, were based in Kaputian. An NGO worker based on Samal Island familiar with these cooperatives estimated that their operating capital in every case fell far short of the 1-million-peso mark.

28. Since the time of the research period, the Samal Island Tourism Estate has remained incomplete and changes to the locality have been minimal. The entire EAGA initiative of which it formed a part was dropped by the Estrada administration and was only recently considered for revival by the Arroyo administration. Only one hotel was ever constructed on the estate territory, located near Tocanga. The hotel was completed during the Estrada administration and was designed as a casino. According to one Davao City resident interviewed in May 2001, the casino was a failure and closed shortly after completion for lack of business. However, it is advertised currently as an available destination for Samal Island on the Philippines Department of Tourism web site. While no current information on the SLS Cooperative or its members is obtainable, it is clear that the tourism estate never did result in the dramatic changes in employment or residence that the planning stages predicted.

Chapter 7. The Samal Island Tourism Estate: Tourate Perspectives

1. We used the following general interview format. After a series of background information questions, we asked interviewees to give their views on the positive and negative aspects of the SITE project. Some responses were of epic proportions, others no more than a few words. My NGO partner Ben asked the questions, initially, while I listened and made notes on the interview locations. After the main portion of the interview was completed, I asked a few follow-up questions.

2. Kadayawan translates roughly as "thanksgiving." The festival was designed around a harvest theme, which was intended to showcase Davao's agricultural and horticultural industries.

3. This is not to say, of course, that such linkages were severed entirely by this strategy. Ben's NGO was itself funded in part by a variety of regional, national, and international sources, although it was by no means an outpost or satellite of any of these in particular. However, the partnership, since it was not directly sponsored by any particular nonlocal agency, did not explicitly foreground or assert such linkages or associations.

4. A *sitio* is a subdistrict of a barangay with a concentration of the barangay's households. Roughly speaking, a sitio is to a barangay what a población is to a municipality. 28 of the 39 interview respondents were residing in the sitio of Tocanga.

5. The Cebuano transcript reads: *Ang akong trabaho man gud, komo kay nakatuon kog gamay, ako na ang maghimo sa ilang payroll. Ga ana ko trabaho na mga kapin sa mga 15 anos. Naa man lang ko sa opisina.*

6. The Cebuano transcript reads: *ang mga gagmay mga bata karon mahamugaway*

na gyud ang ilang pagpamuyo. . . . Mapa-eskwela na gyud ang mga anak nila kay naa na may mga trabaho muabot diri.

7. Margoles recalled that land sold for around forty pesos a hectare at that time, when laborers were making 2.50 pesos a day.

8. The Cebuano transcript reads: *Mao nga kining lugaraha nagtuo ko nga ma-develop gyud pag-ayo ang mga lugar ang mga tao sa mamuyo diri hayahay gyud sila kay nia namay trabaho. Mao ray akong ikuan ug mga kaubahon sa mga bata ug para namo nga may mga edad-edad na malipay santi nga musayo pag-abot diri ang mga investor para nakatan-aw kami ba sa pag-improve nila. Mutan-aw lang mga view kay guwapo man gyud ang lugar nga makuan na . . . guwapo man gyud.*

9. The Cebuano transcript reads: *Kini ang mga wild pigs kini adto diri manginhas pa . . . baybayon, mga wild monkeys, mga bitin. Sa kada 5 ektaryas, makakuha namig bitin ana. Kay usahay muabot tag 9 metros. Naay usahay tag imong bagtak, kana magluko na lang na sila kay busog naman sila kay mangaon man na sila. Pag busog na sila, magluko na lang na sila. . . . Kaniadto di pa mi mukaon ana kay naa pa may mga—has, mga isda.*

10. The Cebuano transcript reads: *Unya ang isda niadto diri daghan ang isda. Kinason daghan kaayo mga kuan pa gyud ni mga bag-o pa gyung isda. Mao na maski gamay ang suweldo, OK lang kay di man tung isda ug ang pagkaon naa man poy uma. Maabot sa imong uma so sobra pagkaon.*

11. Maria Mangahas (1998: 49) in an independent study has also noted in passing that land speculation motivated by the potential boom of Samal Island as a tourist destination was perceived on the local level as a significant trend at this time. Mangahas does not mention specific land value increases. The 1 million peso per hectare figure was mentioned by several Samal Island interviewees.

12. The Cebuano transcripts reads: *mahal man ron mga palaliton* and *nagkalisod-lisod mi dinhi mga tawo mi dinhi diri.* The concept *magka-lisod-lisod* is translated as "very bad shape."

13. The Cebuano transcript reads: *Kay ngano di magka-lisod-lisod nga wa na may tanom pagpanguma kay ang didto nahawa na sila sa 250 ektaryas? Mga hapit 200 ka-pamilya kana naa sa relocation. Nagpaabot na na sila sa mga investor kay aron makatrabaho. Way mga uma na, nangisda na lang sila, nagpasuhol na lang. Mao na nga maayo unta nga madali ang pag-abot ba sa mga investor kay aron ang mga tawo di na magkalisod-lisod.*

14. The Cebuano transcript reads: *Ang akong pangandoy karon nga kining akong mga bata makapanarbaho ta diha sa tourism.*

15. The Cebuano transcript reads: *Kay wa gyud ko magtuo nga maingon ining Samal.*

16. The Cebuano transcript reads: *Kay sa akong pagpuyo gani diri wa ko makapalit ug yuta nga dako-dakog yuta. . . . Wala gyud. Nakayuta ko karon kay ang. . . . Sa CARP na.*

17. The Cebuano phrase in the transcript reads: *Baybay ra.*

18. The Cebuano phrase used in the transcript to express abundance reads: *Sa una nag-uma kami, naa may daghang mga tanom, mga kahayopan.*

19. The Cebuano phrase in the transcript reads: *dili man sad istrikto ang tag-iya ani.*

20. The Cebuano transcript reads: *Maayo among kahimtang niadto gyud. Tinuod na. Naghayopan mi. Nagmanokan. Nagbaboyan. Hayahay kaayo. May baka pa. . . . Wala mi ingon naglisod-lisod mi.*

21. The Cebuano transcript reads: *Magmanokan pod ka diri, ang manok nimo dili gihapon magsilbi kay daghan silingan. Adto man sa uban ang mag-itlog. Kay naa bitaw among manok diring gamay . . . bisag asa na lang. Namiso man kuno hay pero mangamatay sad nga mahuman. Maing ana gyud ang amo diri . . . kahimtang namo diri. Lisod. Lisod gid na mi diri.*

22. The Cebuano transcript reads: *Wa may trabaho pa. Kay ang saad dunay trabaho makuha. Wala pa man. Ing ana gyud ang kahimtang diri. Bisag pangutana ka sa uban ing ana gyud gihapon.*

23. The Cebuano transcript reads: *Diri wala naman. Unsa may imo panginabuhi ani diri. Ing ana na gyud situation namo diri. Ing ana gyud. Hulat na mi kanus-a mi di tagaan. Himoog salmon ang mga tigulang. . . . Puwede pa—ginat-an. Ginat-an tingali puwede pa na. Mao bitaw ana intawon kinabuhi namo diri. Tinuod man na.*

24. The Cebuano transcript reads: *Ingon ni* [chairman's name], *"Kung kamo ma-relocate bisan tua namo sa inyo relocation pwede kamo makopras, puede kamo magkuha ug mga pagkaon pa, saging, bisag nabayran na kay wa pa man gi-develop." Karon, kay di naman.*

25. The Cebuano transcript reads: *Oo, maayo ang dinagan dagan namo uy. Daghan man mi didtog mga kahayupan kay ni akong mga anak silingan man gihapon na didto. . . . Among okupasyon? Dose ka hectares. . . . Di man [dako] kay gi-bahin man namo sa mga anak. Tag tulo tulo na lang. . . . Ing ana among kahimtang gyud, didto, mas hayahay kaysa diri.*

26. The Cebuano transcript reads: *Sa mo-interview ka sa lain mao lang gyud nang sitwasyon. Trabaho ang gikinahanglan nga. . . . Gi-ingon bitaw nako trabaho gyud ang importante.*

27. The Cebuano transcript reads: *Muingon pa ang chairman, "namalit man mo sa imong mga karowakwak dinha ug kanang mga TV—wa ninyo ayoha pagdumala inyong kwarta."*

28. The Cebuano transcript reads: *Kung ako pa giadto ingon man nako ay, "Wa ka nay pakialam kun unsay imong, among buhaton kay amo naman tong kwarta!"*

29. The Cebuano transcript reads: *Nahapit na lang mahuman ang tuig pero wa mi, wa mi hibalo sa among share kun pila, pilay tubo sa among kwarta—wa mi nahibalo niana kung asa niya gibutang.*

30. The phrase used for "our money" was *among kwarta.*

31. The Cebuano transcript reads: *O [mosugot man mi] kaysa usa lang ang mugamit.*

32. The Cebuano transcript reads: *Usa lang gatasan nila nang kwartaha na . . . gigatasan nila na kay ngano. Ang uban di man musugot ug bahinon labi na sa mga board of directors. Di bahinon kay gatasan man na nila.*

33. The Cebuano transcript reads: *Ang akon lang pagsabat sa tourism, kaayohan daw na, kaayohan alang sa mga tawo. Kay makabaton ug trabaho. Unya samtang karon wala pa man.*

34. The Cebuano transcript reads: *Wala lang ta kahibaw-an. Wala lang. . . . Wala, wala pa gyud. . . . Kaayohan lang maoy among . . . may nag-istorya.*

35. The Cebuano transcript reads: *Wala na. Wala na ikasulti sa project kay wa man ta kahibalo kun unsa na siya.*

36. The Cebuano transcript reads: *Wala lang gyud ta kahibalo ana kung unsa.*

37. The Cebuano transcript reads: *Tanang trabaho iyang gi-angkon. Mga tawo diri usahay mo-react niana. Ang iyang sakop iyang mga anak. . . . Chairman siya ang suweldo niya karon 7 thousand. 5 thousand diri sa coop, 2 thousand sa PTA. . . . Mao bitaw nga nagka-molomolo ang tawo. Siguro naka-safety na siya, bahinon na ang kwarta.*

38. The Cebuano transcript reads: *Baybay ra man iyaha. Nag-uling na man ug namalit ug kahoy.*

39. The Cebuano transcript reads: *Mao nay iyang project nga naistorbo ang mga tawo.*

40. The Cebuano transcript reads: *Busa ang gikinahanglan sa mga tawo trabaho gyud. Way lain gyud. Trabaho lang gyud gipaabot. Kun maabot na ang turismo kay made-velop. Maayo na lang makatrabaho sila. Di na magutman kaayo. Pero sama ani no adto pa sa sunod tuig, adto pa sunod tuig kaha ron. Wala. . . . Patay. Mao nang mulabas sila sa Davao manarbaho didto. Sa laing lugar para lang makakuan intawon sa mga pamilya. Ing ana gyud sistema namo diri.*

41. Individuals born during the Marcos regime are often referred to as "Marcos babies" in the Philippines. Those born during the Magsaysay presidency are here referred to in a similar manner.

42. Of the 39 individuals interviewed in the SITE study, 23 were chosen at random during unannounced visits to the research locations. The remaining 16 were identified in advance as particularly knowledgeable sources on the tourism development. The combination of random and selected interviewees resulted from a mixture of pragmatic concerns and research interests. Given the tensions the communities were experiencing during the research period, it was imperative for the safety and continuance of the project not to exclude certain key community members from the process and to be responsive to suggestions from individual community members encountered during the interviewing, which was often done in public places where onlookers and listeners could and did gather. Toward this end, leaders on different sides of some of the most important conflicts were identified and invited to participate in the interview process. These selected individuals included current and former barangay and municipal officers, SLS cooperative board members and employees, one prominent landowner, and a religious leader working in the barangays. In some cases, such as Paolo López's, the choice of interviewees was guided by the suggestions of community members encountered on research visits who felt it was important to include certain other individuals whose perspectives were considered to be particularly representative or well informed. To a considerable extent, who was and was not included in the interviewee pool was decided by members of the communities visited, albeit in an impromptu manner. However, as time and circumstances allowed, additional random sampling of the perspectives of community members who were not in leadership roles was also undertaken.

43. The Cebuano transcript reads: *Kasagaran na akon tan-aw gani mga 60 percent nga mga tawo diha nga di pa kaayo dugay diri. Swerte lang sila kay pag . . . during that time nga na-implementar ang CARP Law naa na sila.*

44. The Cebuano transcript reads: *Kay sa una, pipila lang katawo dinhi; unya ang eskwelahan up to Grade IV lang. Unya during that time mga year 1970s duna nay elementary diri natukod so buot ipasabot nagdaghan ang tawo.*

45. The Cebuano transcript reads: *Baligtad ang nahitabo. Ang eskwelahan . . . dool na ang eskwelahan pero di ta pa makapatunha tungod sa panginahanglan . . . way kwarta. Kaniadto layo ang eskwelahan adto sa siyudad sa Davao makapaeskwela man. Kung gusto gyud. Ang problema lang kay ang puy-an didto lisod pod kaayo.*

46. The Cebuano transcript reads: *For example kanang nahimo karon nga relocation site dinhi sa San Isidro gwapo kaayo kog plano diha kay dunay creek nga kuan guwapo developon. . . . It's the people nga mag-develop niana. Makapahatag na attraction sa mga visitors.*

47. The Cebuano transcript reads: *Looy ang coop.*

48. The Cebuano transcript reads: *Kay mao man gyud na sa agreement na ang mga tawo dinhi or ang SLS nga maoy mo-direct na mo-supply didto sa tourism. Unya ang nahitabo karon wala pa kaandar sila parte ana. Pag-abot dinhi sa project anha pa sila magsugod so late na. Dapat unta karon puwede na sugdan para pag-abot sa panahon kon anha na siya matukod na maong project maka-operate na puwede na siya. Anha ikahatag. Kay ngani ug makasugod sila karon mentras tanto nga wala pang project maka-deliver man tag Davao. In demand man kaayo na. Kinahanglan man na karon sa mga tawo. . . . Maplano bitaw ug maayo kun unsay angay buhaton ning mga tawhana.*

49. The Cebuano transcript reads: *Ang akong nakita karon hinoon medyo may gap gyud hinoon karon ang atong local government ngadto diha sa pagdumala. Kay sa akong nakita mura ug lahi ba ang nagdala karon dili kaayo mo-cooperate sa local government. . . . Dapat unta igkuan bitaw sila mag kuan diha sa lain-lain nga ahensiya. Di lang kay focus lang ilang panan-aw ngadto lang sa Department of Tourism. Mao ra man kana akong nakita didto lang sila nakatutok, wa sila manguan sa lain nga agency o lain nga grupo. Kalimot siguro. Sayang ba.*

50. The Cebuano transcript reads: *Unsay purpose nga gidako ang (lote) 20 x 30, that*

is 600 square meters. Kun kamao sila magmanage nianang loteha kaya nila na, backyard gardening. . . . That's tourism di ba?

51. The Cebuano transcript reads: *Mag-reserve ka ug kanang mini forest para bugnaw ang mga lugar. Unya kanang ilalom silag kahoyan ato nang developon. That's tourism. Sayang ba.*

52. The Cebuano transcript reads: *Ako na silang gisugdan ug plano parte sa liveli-hood, aw kining sa agriculture, mga technology sa agrikultura, katong kuan contour. Giplano nako ana. So kana maka-attract na sa kuan. . . . Duna nay gipreparar nga para sa mga goat-raising. Para kana pag-contour magsagbot so magsunod na magkuan na goat-raising. Unya guwapo na ang area. Pero katong tanan nawala. Wala may nakahunahuna ana gyud.*

53. The Cebuano transcript reads: *During the construction period gamay ra nang 1,000. Basta magdungan lang ang unit magtrabaho gamay ra 1,000. . . . More or less, basta diha dapita lang mga 1,000 m . . . kay dako gud na. Naa pod diha ang swimming pool. Pila ka units nang naa diha sa dagat ginbutang. May hotel. Daghan, naa pod diha ang ball-room. Kun mao na nay madungan daghan kaayong magamit. . . . Human sa trabaho sa construction, mo-open na sila so another employment na sad, chambermaid, kana roomboy bellboy. Naa na diha tanan kumpleto na maka-operate na. At the same time kun daghan ang tawo diha daghan manarbaho naa na poy mga negosyante. Ginagmay ra pod—. Mura ug duna nay kalingawan ang tawo panginabuhi. At the same time duna nay mga tourist musuroy dinhi katong wala manarbaho didto unya musuroy diri sa kabukiran. Siyempre naa may mga turista musuroy diri mamalit sila. Unsa poy ikabaligya nila dinhi naa poy sila makuha. Makakwarta lang gihapon sila diri. Dunay magtrabahog mga pang souvenir. (Usa sa akong giplan . . . . Nagpa-training na mi diri ug bamboo novelities. Sa DTI. Mga T-shirt printing.) Mao nang gi-ingon bitaw nako kun maandam unta ning mga tawo labi na gyud ang mga batan-on karon muandam na sila pag-abot ni maong project, diha na sila, maka-sideline na sila sa ilang panginabuhi. Ug siguro kanang panahona kun daghan na dinhi panahon na pod siguro nga ang Kaputian duna na poy college diri. Kay kun duna nay col-lege diri makaeskwela mga bata, the same time manarbaho diri, eskwela. So ang edukasyon magkataas.*

54. The Cebuano transcript reads: *Mao na ang akong nakita usa gyud na nga ilang na-focus sa employment.*

55. The Cebuano transcript reads: *dugay man nako ng mga tawhana nakauban. May limitasyon man gyud ang kuan sa ilang panghuna-huna ba. . . . Mao nay akong nakita sa ilaha nga usa lang ka step siguro, duha ka step lang, after that wala na. Mao na nga ako maproblema usahay maghunahuna pero—Mao lagi tungod sa akong commitment, duna man kitay commitment . . . so masakitan pod usahay . . . sa sitwasyon. . . . Maka-ingon ko unsa may akong mahimo? —Sa pagkakaron . . . unsaon ning mga tawhana makasabot unsay kaugmaon. Naa guy sila mga bata. Asa naman unya ang mga anak nila padulong kung ilang kunsinti mao na lang diha lang kutob. Magpabilin lang ta empleyado, mga tra-bahante. Maayo ta mangempleyo tag executive. Dili kay [pause] trabahante lang ta diha—looy kaayo. Unya kini sila mga laborer kun maminyo duna nay mga anak asa may ibutang? unsa may igasto sa ilang mga anak?*

56. The Cebuano transcript reads: *Karon latest na pod nako nahibaloan na gusto na pod nila bahinbahinon ilang kwarta sa tanang miyembro.*

57. The Cebuano transcript reads: *Naa lagi daw unya kahapon lang ko nakabati anang istoryaha nga mao nang plano. Mora kog nasubo ana maghunahuna. Kung bahinon ang kwarta after that kanang kwartaha kay sa akong estimate mga 23 million over 332. Kana more or less dunay mga 60 to 70 thousand each. Within how many months hurot na ang kwarta. After that, asa naman padulong? . . . Mao na nga giproblemahan nako hunahuna. Wa ko katulog kagabii. Akong pagkahibalo anang istoryaha ingon ko porbida sayanga tong pinangkamutan nga unta ang tawo makita ug dako unya karon ing-anaon na lang ang kwarta nila.*

58. The Cebuano transcript reads: *Duna koy plano kung ana man gali ang mahitabo. Ani lang ang akong ika-suggest kondisyon. Katong mokuha ug sa ilang share mas maayo na lang siguro nga mopirma na lang sila nga mohawa na sila sa cooperatiba. Ang katong dili mokuha sa bahin, ipabilin pod sa opisina magpabilin miyembro kay kato ra sigurong mga tawhana ang nakasabot nga bililhon kaayo ang kwarta para sa cooperatiba ug para sa ugma.*

59. The Cebuano transcript reads: *Sayang kaayo ang cooperatiba. Isip usa ka cooperators sa amoang cooperatiba mao na akong stand karon di ko gustong bungkagon ang coop. Gusto ko magpabilin ang cooperatiba. Kay ani ang sistema, o kana ang himuon nga hagdanan—stepping stone na alang sa mga tawo dinhi.*

60. This statistic was given in the Samal Island Profile document (typescript in the files of the LAWIG Foundation office) for Samalnon speakers in the municipality of Samal. According to the same source, Visayan ethnic groups comprised 85 percent of the island's population at this time. No "Muslim" Islamic-identified ethnic category was listed. Information for the other municipalities was not available. Given the comments of several interviewees residing in the barangay of San Remigio, however, it is likely that the percentage for Kaputian municipality was somewhat higher, perhaps as high as 30 percent.

61. The Cebuano transcript reads: *Murag ang akong mama murag wala mi ingon ginapakita sa ilang traditional gani nila. Dili kaayo istrikto akong mama* (My mother did not really show or teach us their traditions. My mother was not very strict).

62. With regard to Spanish influence, however, it should be noted that Ms. Duarte believed her grandfather on her mother's side may have been a Spaniard, who had married a "pure" Samaleña woman—Ms. Duarte's mother's mother.

63. The Cebuano transcript reads: *Unya akong bana usa ka laborer diri sa Fernandez Hermanos hangtod 1991 man siguro to sila na-relief* (Before, my husband was a laborer at the Fernández-Hermános estate until around 1991, when he was relieved).

64. The Cebuano transcript reads: *Tungod kay wa pa man ta kabalo ug maayo ba gyud ang ilahang pagpalakaw diri. Kay murag ingon nila Malaysia Ekran Berhad daw ang, ingon sila nga Ekran Berhad daw ang. . . . Mao na nga, murag nag, murag wala pa wa pa ko makontento, nang giingon nga wala makontento pa.*

65. The Cebuano transcript reads: *Ang akong kabalaka sa akoang, maayo ba ang ilang pagpalakaw kay naa man koy mga anak. . . . Ang ako la untang gipangayo nga maka-trabaho akong mga anak.*

66. The Cebuano transcript reads: *Naa mig gamay nga nakatuonan.*

67. The Cebuano transcript reads: *Ang akong gyud gusto ato housekeeping man gyud unta to pero murag direct direct man ang pagtudlo murag dili gyud ingon nga ma-catch up namo. . . . Running man gud ang kuan gani ang kanang pagtudlo na murag dili na man gyud puwede nga mubalik ka gyud kay direkta direkta man ang pagtudlo . . . pagka-ugma murag maglisod na pod na, mao na mohatag man silag test. Mohatag silag gamay nga test na makakuha kog usahay 1 to 10 makakuha kog mga 6 items lang. Murag kini siguro lahi naman gud ang pag-eskuwela nato sa una murag lahi na man gud ang sa karong bag-o. Murag nabag-ohan ko.*

68. The Cebuano transcript reads: *Murag akong mga kauban murag nakita pod nako kay sila mga elementary lang sila murag maglisod sila.*

69. Only six interviewees reported having any post-secondary education. The rest were mixed between a minority (five) who mentioned having had some high school education and the rest who for the most part probably had had an elementary school education only. Several interviewees did not bring up this topic, which, because it carried some sensitive status concerns, was not one that was raised directly in the interviews. In this regard, the information on educational attainment for the interview pool as a whole is not conclusive, but rather is the best estimate,

given all of the other information collected. No statistics reporting educational attainment for the municipality, or the island, were available. "A Brief Profile of Davao Province," reported that 57 percent of the province had completed elementary school only, and only 10 percent had attained post-secondary educational training or beyond.

70. Roughly 40 percent of the island's population was under fifteen, and only 4 percent were over sixty-five, according to the Philippine Business for Social Progress "Samal Island Profile" (typescript also in the files of the LAWIG Foundation office).

71. The Cebuano transcript reads: *Ang properties natin for tourism talaga. Its future is tourism. Agricultural is wala na. Ito na lang ang pag-asa natin.*

72. The English language concept "control" was typically used to express these concerns.

73. Both interviewees used the English language term.

74. In this respect the SITE barangays exhibited more strongly than Adecor the characteristics of a "fractal landscape" (Moore 1999: 674, Feierman 1990: 29). Such landscapes emerge when a layering of territorial identities occurs—in this case a plantation identity submerged by a tourism estate. When such layering occurs, competing cultural practices tend to produce alternative understandings of the locality, particularly with regard to power structures and historicity. The tensions in the SITE barangays can be understood to a large extent as the consequence of this kind of competition in the emergence of a fractal landscape.

75. As noted in the previous chapter (Chapter 6, note 28), SITE has remained largely incomplete. Only one hotel was ever constructed. No envelopment of the local landscape ever did occur, and the dramatic changes anticipated in 1996 have yet to come about.

Chapter 8. The Home Away from Home: Marjorie's Inn

1. The 1991 *Regional Tourism Situation Report* for Davao City, Region XI (DOT 1991) actually classifies one of these hotels as a "standard" not a "first" class hotel. However, in my own observation, taking into account price of accommodations, the type and class of facilities, the importance of events held on the premises, the economic class of the guests, and the decor and design of the hotel, the "standard" class was not an appropriate rank for either hotel. In all respects both were unambiguously first class hotels, on comparable terms with one another, and were generally described as such by everyone who discussed them with me. While the rooms of the "standard" hotel were not as expensive as those of the other, and while it was not under international ownership and management, it was nonetheless a top quality establishment, and the gap between it and the next highest ranking hotel (in terms of size, facilities, clientele, decor, and events) was significantly greater than that between it and the other first class hotel.

2. The 1991 *Regional Tourism Situation Report*, the most comprehensive source available for this period, lists thirty-one such "economy" establishments in addition to three "standard" and one "first class" hotels. The economy establishments are divided into the following categories: two hotels (averaging 300 pesos a night for double air-con), nine inns (averaging 350 pesos a night for double air-con), eight pension houses (averaging 300 pesos a night for double air-con), six lodging houses (averaging 235 pesos a night for double air-con), and six motels. As the motels generally rented rooms only by the hour and were not used for lodging purposes, they have not been included in the estimate above of "two dozen." In price contrast to these economy options, the first class hotel was charging 2,078 pesos a night and

the three "standard" hotels 1,271, 923, and 573 pesos a night respectively for a double air-con room.

3. If a "standard" or "middle class" average price between high and low end could be set as roughly 900 pesos a night for a double air-con room—the average of the high end and low end averages—only one hotel in the entire city advertised a room of this type near this price, one of the three "standard" hotels listed in the 1991 *Regional Tourism Situation Report.* All others were at least 300 pesos above or below this average, the vast majority 600 pesos or more. The other hotel in the 500–1,000 range aside from the one mentioned above was asking 573 pesos a night for a double air-con room. The economy class inns and pension houses were asking just under 500 pesos (488, 498).

4. See Morris (1993) for a more extensive theoretical discussion of the motel's general character.

5. See Smith (1997) for a discussion of the involvement of elites in tourism development.

6. Such hybrid forms of urban tourism are among the fast growing in the world. See Sieber (1997) for a more detailed account.

Chapter 9. Local Expressions of Leisure: Beach Parks

1. No statistics are available documenting the size or character of the beach park tourist population. Judging by the number of establishments of this type, which could not have been more than fifty in 1996, and their peak capacity, which on average could not have been more than 250, the maximum number this local beach park tourism industry could accommodate would be around 12,500 on any given day. In my own observation, such peak days occurred only on major holidays, however, perhaps ten days out of the year. The bulk of patronage was spread out over the year, on weekends and vacation days, perhaps at most one hundred relatively busy days, when the resorts were more likely to be operating at half capacity on average. The resorts sat virtually empty for half the year, during weekdays when schools were in session. This left around seventy-five slow days when roughly 10 percent of capacity might be patronizing the resorts. The total number of arrivals to the resorts could not have been more than 850,000 over the course of a year, given these estimates, and was probably considerably less. Since most people frequenting such resorts did so on average once a month, in my rough estimation, the number of actual tourists involved in the market was unlikely to have been higher than 70,000, although it could have been as high as 150,000. The ratio of nonlocal visitors to city residents on these excursions generally hovered at around one to eight (again, a rough estimate), so probably no more than 60,000 to 130,000 of the tourist population were local residents. This figure represented roughly 5–10 percent of Davao City's population in 1995. Another indicator of the size of the tourist population at these resorts was the patronage count of the largest and most popular resort, which estimated an annual arrival figure of 250,000 guests, 90 percent of them Filipino. In my observation, this beach park had captured at least half the tourist market, but even if it had only captured 30 percent, the estimate would still fall somewhere around the 5 percent mark in relation to the city's total population, assuming the same ratio of repeat usage. While there is a large margin for error in these estimates, it seems certain that only a minority of Davao City's residents patronized the beach parks, although the parks were undoubtedly the most widely used facilities for leisure activities outside of homes.

2. See Chapter 4, note 2 for elaboration on this point.

3. See Ness (1991) for an account of tourism development in the Philippines during the period of American rule. Domestic touristic practices of the type described in this chapter most likely emerged during this period throughout the provinces.

4. The Ati-atihan is the annual fiesta celebration of the town of Kalibo, Aklan, on the island of Panay. Regarded as the most popular provincial fiesta in the Philippines, the Ati-atihan draws hundreds of thousands of tourists to its Mardi Gras events every January.

Chapter 10. Conclusions

1. See Magdelena (1997: 9–10) for a brief discussion of Quezon's motivations for the "Land of Promise" slogan.

2. The summary here is oriented along lines suggested by Sara Cohen (1997: 86) in her study of urban tourism and musical practices in Liverpool, England.

3. As Hazel Tucker among others has recently noted (1997: 107), touristic play often includes more than visual practice or "gazing," and many forms of utopic landscaping anticipate and encourage a more complete participatory involvement of tourists in the various narrative-generating activities they animate and realize.

4. See Foucault (1982: 212). The concept of subjection is also cited and discussed from a cultural anthropological perspective in Rabinow (1986).

5. Wittgenstein's critique of a theory of "private language" ranks foremost among them. See, for example, the discussion of Wittgenstein in Geertz (2000: ix–xvi).

6. Mark P. Whitaker (1996: 7) has made a closely related point, noting the centrality of Wittgenstein's work, both to the writing of Geertz and, in what Whitaker describes as a "subterranean way," to the literature derived from Geertz's approach.

7. Whitaker (1996: 8) has characterized Wittgenstein's method in this regard as consisting of "trying" at learning, contrasting it with the formulation of meta-languages to (mis)apprehend" or "capture" epistemologies.

8. The phrase is taken from Cora Diamond, although her discussion of a realistic spirit in Wittgenstein's writings does not focus directly on the topic of method as it is summarized here.

9. Whitaker (1996: 8) has drawn this parallel even more broadly, arguing that standard ethnographic method used in all cultural anthropological fieldwork, is akin to the method of philosophical investigation that Wittgenstein developed in his later work, being composed of "pedagogic experiments." Whitaker argues further, however, that such method is "suppressed" in ethnographic writing, a point that is not argued here, and in particular not with regard to the literature of interpretive ethnography.

10. See Clifford (1997: 89) for a discussion of the practices of displacement and encounter as defining the role of the cultural anthropological fieldworker.

References

Abram, Simone, Jacqueline Waldren, and Donald V. L. Macleod, eds.
    1997   *Tourists and Tourism: Identifying with People and Places.* Oxford: Berg.
Abu-Lughod, Lila
    1991   "Writing Against Culture." In *Recapturing Anthropology: Working in the Present*, ed. Richard G. Fox. Santa Fe, N.M.: School of American Research. 137–62.
Adams, Kathleen M.
    1993   "Club Dead, Not Club Med: Staging Death in Contemporary Tana Toraja (Indonesia)." *Southeast Asian Journal of Social Science* 21 (2): 62–72.
    1995   "Making Up the Toraja? The Appropriation of Tourism, Anthropology, and Museums for Politics in Upland Sulawesi (Indonesia)." *Ethnology* 34 (2): 143–53.
    1997   "Touting Touristic 'Primmadonas': Tourism, Ethnicity, and National Integration in Sulawesi, Indonesia." In *Tourism, Ethnicity, and the State in Asian and Pacific Societies*, ed. Michel Picard and Robert Wood. Honolulu: University of Hawaii Press. 156–80.
Appadurai, Arjun
    1990   "Disjuncture and Difference in the Global Cultural Economy." *Public Culture* 2 (2): 1–24.
    1991   "Global Ethnoscapes: Notes and Queries for a Transnational Anthropology." In *Recapturing Anthropology: Working in the Present*, ed. Richard G. Fox. Santa Fe, N.M.: School of American Research. 191–210.
Bachelard, Gaston
    1958   *The Poetics of Space.* Trans. Maria Jolas. Boston: Beacon Press.
Baranera, P. Francisco X., S.J.
    1899   *Handbook of the Philippine Islands.* Trans. Alexander Laist from *Compendio de Geografía.* Manila: William Partier.
Basch, Linda G., Nina Glick Schiller, and Christina Szanton-Blanc, eds.
    1994   *Nations Unbound: Transnational Projects, Postcolonial Predicaments, and Deterritorialized Nation-States.* Langhorne, Pa.: Gordon & Breach.
Bateson, Gregory
    1972   *Steps to an Ecology of Mind: A Revolutionary Approach to Man's Understanding of Himself.* New York: Ballantine Books.
Beckett, Jeremy
    1982   "The Defiant and the Compliant: The Datus of Mindanao Under Colonial Rule." In *Philippine Social History: Global Trade and Local Transformations*, ed. Alfred W. McCoy and Ed C. de Jesus. Sydney and Quezon City: Allen and Unwin and Ateneo de Manila University Press. 391–414.

Behar, Ruth
　　1996　　*The Vulnerable Observer: Anthropology That Breaks Your Heart.* New York: Beacon Press.
Berger, John
　　1984　　*And Our Faces, My Heart, Brief as Photos.* London: Writers and Readers.
Berger, Peter L., Brigitte Berger, and Hansfried Kellner
　　1973　　*The Homeless Mind: Modernization and Consciousness.* New York: Random House.
Blair, Emma and James Robertson, eds. and trans.
　　1903–9　*The Philippine Islands, 1493–1898.* 55 vols. Cleveland: Arthur H. Clark.
Boissevain, Jeremy, ed.
　　1996　　*Coping with Tourists: European Reactions to Mass Tourism.* Oxford: Berghahn.
Bolles, A. Lynn
　　1997　　"Women as a Category of Analysis in Scholarship on Tourism: Jamaican Women and Tourism Employment." In *Tourism and Culture: An Applied Perspective,* ed. Erve Chambers. Albany, N.Y.: SUNY Press. 77–93.
Bonner, Raymond
　　1987　　*Waltzing with a Dictator: The Marcoses and the Making of American Policy.* New York: Vintage Books.
Boon, James A.
　　2000　　"Showbiz as a Cross-Cultural System: Circus and Song, Garland and Geertz, Rushdie, Mordden, . . . and More." *Cultural Anthropology* 15 (3): 424–56.
Boorstin, Daniel J.
　　1964　　*The Image: A Guide to Pseudo-Events in America.* New York: Harper.
Britton, Stephen
　　1991　　"Tourism, Capital, and Place: Towards a Critical Geography of Tourism." *Environment and Planning D: Society and Space* 9: 451–78.
Bruner, Edward M.
　　1989　　"Of Cannibals, Tourists, and Ethnographers." *Cultural Anthropology* 4 (4): 439–46.
　　1995　　"The Ethnographer/Tourist in Indonesia." In *International Tourism: Identity and Change,* ed. Marie Françoise Lanfant, John B. Allcock, and Edward M. Bruner. London: Sage. 224–41.
Bruner, Edward M. and Barbara Kirshenblatt-Gimblett
　　1994　　"Maasai on the Lawn: Tourist Realism in East Africa." *Cultural Anthropology* 9 (4): 435–70.
Burns, Peter M.
　　1999　　*An Introduction to Tourism and Anthropology.* London: Routledge.
Causey, Andrew
　　1997　　"Getting More Than They Bargain For: Toba Batak Wood Carvers and Western Travellers in a Utopic Marketplace." Ph.D. Dissertation, University of Texas, Austin.
Chambers, Erve
　　1994　　"Thailand's Tourism Paradox: Identity and Nationalism as Factors in Tourism Development." In *Conserving Culture; A New Discourse on Heritage,* ed. Mary Hufford. Urbana: University of Illinois Press. 97–110.
　　1997a　"Introduction: Tourism's Mediators." In *Tourism and Culture: An Applied Perspective,* ed. Erve Chambers. Albany: SUNY Press. 1–12.

1997b   "Tourism as a Subject of Higher Education: Educating Thailand's Workforce." In *Tourism and Culture: An Applied Perspective*, ed. Erve Chambers. Albany: SUNY Press. 183–99.

Chambers, Erve, ed.
1997c   *Tourism and Culture: An Applied Perspective*. Albany: SUNY Press.

Chant, Sylvia and Cathy McIlwaine
1995   *Women of a Lesser Cost; Female Labour, Foreign Exchange & Philippine Development*. Manila: Ateneo de Manila University Press.

Clifford, James
1986a   "Introduction: Partial Truths." In *Writing Culture: The Poetics and Politics of Ethnography*, ed. James Clifford and George E. Marcus. Berkeley: University of California Press. 1–26.

1986b   "On Ethnographic Allegory." In *Writing Culture: The Poetics and Politics of Ethnography*, ed. James Clifford and George E. Marcus. Berkeley: University of California Press. 98–121.

1988   *The Predicament of Culture: Twentieth-Century Ethnography, Literature, and Art*. Cambridge, Mass.: Harvard University Press.

1989   "Notes on Travel and Theory." *Inscriptions* 5.

1997   *Routes: Travel and Translation in the Late Twentieth Century*. Cambridge, Mass.: Harvard University Press.

Clifford, James and George E. Marcus, eds.
1986   *Writing Culture: The Poetics and Politics of Ethnography*. Berkeley: University of California Press.

Clift, Stephen
1994   *Romance and Sex on Holidays Abroad: A Study of Magazine Representations*. Travel, Lifestyles and Health Working Paper 4. Canterbury: Christ Church College.

Cohen, Erik
1974   "Who Is a Tourist? A Conceptual Clarification." *Sociological Review* 22 (4): 527– 55.

Cohen, Sara
1997   "More Than the Beatles: Popular Music, Tourism and Urban Regeneration." In *Tourists and Tourism: Identifying with People and Places*, ed. Simone Abram, Jacqueline Waldren and Donald V. L. Macleod. Oxford: Berg.

Corcino, Ernesto I.
1993   "Davao History: An Overview." In *Proceedings and Positions Papers of the Region XI Historical Convention*. Davao City: ARJ Printing Press. 28–30.

Craik, Jennifer
1997   "The Culture of Tourism." In *Touring Cultures: Transformations of Travel and Theory*, ed. Chris Rojek and John Urry. London: Routledge. 113–36.

Crick, Malcolm
1985   "'Tracing' the Anthropological Self: Quizzical Reflections on Field Work, Tourism and the Ludic." *Social Analysis* 17: 71–92.

1989   "Representations of International Tourism in the Social Sciences: Sun, Sex, Sights, Savings, and Servility." *Annual Review of Anthropology* 18: 307–44.

1995   "The Anthropologist as Tourist: An Identity in Question." In *International Tourism: Identity and Change*, ed. Marie Françoise Lanfant, John B. Allcock, and Edward M. Bruner. London: Sage. 205–23.

Crystal, Eric
    1989/   "Tourism in Toraja (Sulawesi, Indonesia)." In *Hosts and Guests: The*
    1977   *Anthropology of Tourism*, ed Valene L. Smith. 2nd ed. Philadelphia,
          University of Pennsylvania Press. 139–68.
Csordas, Thomas J., ed.
    1994a   *Embodiment and Experience: The Existential Ground of Culture and*
          Self. Cambridge: Cambridge University Press.
    1994b   *The Sacred Self: A Cultural Phenomenology of Charismatic Healing.* Berke-
          ley: University of California Press.
Dabbay, Gloria P.
    1992   *Davao City: Its History and Progress.* Rev. ed. Davao: G. P. Dabbay.
Daniel, E. Valentine
    1984   *Fluid Signs: Being a Person the Tamil Way.* Berkeley: University of Cal-
          ifornia Press.
de Certeau, Michel
    1984   *The Practice of Everyday Life.* Berkeley: University of California Press.
Deleuze, Gilles and Félix Guattari
    1987   *A Thousand Plateaus: Capitalism and Schizophrenia.* Trans. Brian Mas-
          sumi. Minneapolis: University of Minnesota Press.
Department of Tourism (DOT)
    1991   *Regional Tourism Situation Report, 1991.* Davao City: DOT, Region XI.
Derrida, Jacques
    1977   *Limited Inc.: abc.* Trans. Sam Weber. Published in *Glyph 2*, 162–254.
          Baltimore: Johns Hopkins University Press.
    1982   *Margins of Philosophy.* Trans. Alan Bass. Chicago: University of Chi-
          cago Press.
Desmond, Jane
    1997   "Invoking 'The Native': Body Politics in Contemporary Hawaiian
          Tourist Shows." *Drama Review* 41 (4): 83–109.
    1999   *Staging Tourism: Bodies on Display from Waikiki to Sea World.* Chicago:
          University of Chicago Press.
Dominguez, Carlos G.
    1997   "Mindanao and the New Millennium: Fulfillment in Progress." *Tam-*
          bara 14: 116–25.
Drummond, Lee
    1980   "The Cultural Continuum: A Theory of Intersystems." *Man* 15:
          352–74.
Dumont, Jean-Paul
    1984   "A Matter of Touristic Indifferance." *American Ethnologist* 11 (1):
          139–51.
Ebron, Paulla A.
    2000   "Tourists as Pilgrims: Commercial Fashioning of Transatlantic Pol-
          itics." *American Ethnologist* 26 (4): 910–32.
Eco, Umberto
    1986   *Travels in Hyperreality.* London: Picador.
Elder, Charles R.
    1994   *The Grammar of the Unconscious: The Conceptual Foundations of Psycho-*
          analysis. University Park: Pennsylvania State University Press.
Errington, Frederick Karl and Deborah B. Gewertz
    1989   "Tourism and Anthropology in a Postmodern World. *Oceania* 60
          (1): 37–54.

Farnell, Brenda
    1995   *Do You See What I Mean? Plains Indian Sign Talk and the Embodiment of Action.* Austin: University of Texas Press.

Feierman, Steven
    1990   *Peasant Intellectuals: Anthropology and History in Tanzania.* Madison: University of Wisconsin Press.

Fernández, Doreen
    1996   *Palabas: Essays on Philippine Theater History.* Quezon City: Ateneo de Manila University Press.

Fischer, Michael M. J.
    1986   "Ethnicity and the Post-Modern Arts of Memory." In *Writing Culture: The Poetics and Politics of Ethnography,* ed. James Clifford and George E. Marcus. Berkeley: University of California Press. 194–233.

Fowler, Don D. and Donald L. Hardesty
    1994   *Others Knowing Others: Perspectives on Ethnographic Careers.* Washington, D.C.: Smithsonian Institution Press.

Foucault, Michel
    1982   "The Subject and Power." In Hubert Dreyfus, Paul Rabinow, and Foucault, *Michel Foucault Beyond Structuralism and Hermeneutics.* Chicago: University of Chicago Press. 208–26.
    1984   "What Is Enlightenment?" In *The Foucault Reader,* ed. Paul Rabinow. New York: Pantheon.

Fox, Richard G., ed.
    1991   *Recapturing Anthropology: Working in the Present.* Santa Fe, N.M.: School of American Research Press.

Friedman, Thomas L.
    1999   *The Lexus and the Olive Tree: Understanding Globalization.* New York: Farrar Straus Giroux.

Garrison, Lloyd
    1989   "Tourism—Wave of the Future?" *World Development (UNDP)* 2: 4–6.

Geertz, Clifford
    1973   *The Interpretation of Cultures.* New York: Basic Books.
    1983   *Local Knowledge: Further Essays in Interpretive Anthropology.* New York: Basic Books.
    2000   *Available Light: Anthropological Reflections on Philosophical Topics.* Princeton, N.J.: Princeton University Press.

Ghosh, Amitav
    1992   *In an Antique Land.* London: Granta Books.

Goodman, Grant K.
    1967   *Davao: A Case Study in Japanese-Philippine Relations.* Lawrence: University of Kansas Center for East Asian Studies.

Gowing, Peter G.
    1979   *Muslim Filipinos—Heritage and Horizon.* Quezon City: New Day Publishers.

Graburn, Nelson H. H.
    1983   "The Anthropology of Tourism." *Annals of Tourism Research* 10 (1): 9–33.
    1989/   "Tourism: The Sacred Journey." In *Hosts and Guests: The Anthropology*
    1977   *of Tourism,* ed. Valene L. Smith. 2nd ed. Philadelphia: University of Pennsylvania Press. 21–36.

Greenwood, Davydd J.
>1972   "Tourism as an Agent of Change: A Spanish Basque Case." *Ethnology*
>11: 80–91.
>
>1989/ "Culture by the Pound: An Anthropological Perspective on Tourism
>1977   as Cultural Commoditization." In *Hosts and Guests: The Anthropology
>of Tourism*, ed. Valene L. Smith. 2nd ed. Philadelphia: University of
>Pennsylvania Press. 171–85.

Gupta, Akhil and James Ferguson
>1997a   "Discipline and Practice: 'The Field' as Site, Method, and Location
>in Anthropology." In *Anthropological Locations: Boundaries and Grounds
>of a Field Science*, ed. Gupta and Ferguson. Berkeley: University of
>California Press. 1–46.
>
>1997b   "Culture, Power, Place: Ethnography at the End of an Era." In *Culture, Power, Place: Explorations in Critical Anthropology*, ed. Gupta and
>Ferguson. Durham, N.C.: Duke University Press. Pp.1–29.
>
>1997c   Beyond "Culture": Space, Identity, and the Politics of Difference. In
>*Culture Power Place: Explorations in Critical Anthropology*, ed. Gupta
>and Ferguson. Durham, N.C.: Duke University Press. 33–51.

Gupta, Akhil and James Ferguson, eds.
>1997d   *Anthropological Locations: Boundaries and Grounds of a Field Science.*
>Berkeley: University of California Press.
>
>1997e   *Culture, Power, Place: Explorations in Critical Anthropology.* Durham,
>N.C.: Duke University Press.

Hall, Colin Michael
>1994   *Tourism in the Pacific Rim: Development, Impacts, and Markets.* Melbourne: Longman Cheshire/Halsted Press.

Hannerz, Ulf
>1992   "The Global Ecumene as a Network of Networks." In *Conceptualizing
>Society*, ed. Adam Kuper. London: Routledge.

Harvey, David
>1989   *The Condition of Postmodernity: An Enquiry into the Origins of Culture
>Change.* Cambridge: Blackwell.

Heidegger, Martin
>1977   *The Question Concerning Technology and Other Essays.* New York:
>Harper Torchbooks.

Helms, Mary
>1988   *Ulysses' Sail: An Ethnographic Odyssey of Power, Knowledge, and Geographical Distance.* Princeton, N.J.: Princeton University Press.

ICL Research Team
>1980   *The Human Cost of Bananas.* Manila: n.p.

Iyer, Pico
>1988   *Video Night in Kathmandu: And Other Reports from the Not-So-Far East.*
>New York: Vintage Departures.

Jackson, Michael
>1989   *Paths Toward a Clearing: Radical Empiricism and Ethnographic Inquiry.*
>Bloomington: Indiana University Press.
>
>1995   *At Home in the World.* Durham, N.C.: Duke University Press.
>
>1996   "Introduction: Phenomenology, Radical Empiricism, and Anthropological Critique." In Jackson, *Things as They Are: New Directions in
>Phenomenological Anthropology.* Bloomington: Indiana University
>Press. 1–50.

Jameson, Fredric
    1983   "Postmodernism and Consumer Society." In *The Anti-Aesthetic: Essays on Postmodern Culture*. Ed. Hal Foster. Port Townsend, Wash.: Bay Press.

    1984   "Postmodernism, or The Cultural Logic of Late Capitalism." *New Left Review* 146: 53–92.

Jokinen, Eeva and Soile Veijola
    1997   "The Disoriented Tourist: The Figuration of the Tourist in Contemporary Cultural Critique." In *Touring Cultures: Transformations of Travel and Theory*, ed. Chris Rojek and John Urry. London: Routledge. 23–51.

Kahn, Joel S.
    1997   "Culturalizing Malaysia: Globalism, Tourism, Heritage, and the City in Georgetown." In *Tourism, Ethnicity, and the State in Asian and Pacific Societies*, ed. Michel Picard and Robert Wood. Honolulu: University of Hawaii Press. 99–127.

Kaspin, Deborah
    1997   "On Ethnographic Authority and the Tourist Trade: Anthropology in the House of Mirrors." *Anthropological Quarterly* 70 (2): 53–57.

Kearney, Michael
    1986   "From the Invisible Hand to Visible Feet: Anthropological Studies of Migration and Development." *Annual Review of Anthropology* 15: 331–61.

    1995a   "The Local and the Global: The Anthropology of Globalization and Transnationalism." *Annual Review of Anthropology* 24: 547–65.

    1995b   *Reconceptualizing the Peasantry*. Boulder, Colo.: Westview Press.

    1998   "Transnationalism in California and Mexico at the End of Empire." In *Border Identities: Nation and State at International Frontiers*, ed. Thomas M. Wilson and Hastings Donnan. Cambridge: Cambridge University Press.

Kincaid, Jamaica
    1988   *A Small Place*. New York: Penguin.

Kirshenblatt-Gimblett, Barbara
    1987   "Authenticity and Authority in the Representation of Culture: The Poetics and Politics of Tourist Production." In *Kulturkontakt, Kulturkonflikt: Zur Erfahrung des Fremden. 26. Deutscher Volkskundekongress in Frankfort*, ed. Ina-Maria Greverus, Konrad Köstlin and Heinz Schilling. Frankfurt am Main: Institut für Kulturanthropologie und Europäische Ethnologie, Universität Frankfurt am Main. 59–69.

Krippendorf, Jost
    1984   *The Holiday Makers: Understanding the Impact of Leisure and Travel*. London: Heinemann.

Kruhse-MountBurton, Suzy
    1995   "Sex Tourism and Traditional Australian Male Identity." In *International Tourism: Identity and Change*, ed. Marie Françoise Lanfant, John B. Allcock, and Edward M. Bruner. London: Sage. 192–204.

Kuklick, Henrika
    1997   "After Ishmael: The Fieldwork Tradition and Its Future." In *Anthropological Locations: Boundaries and Grounds of a Field Science*. Berkeley: University of California Press. 47–65.

Laarhoven, Ruurdje
    1989   *Triumph of Moro Diplomacy: The Maguindanao State in the 17th Century*. Quezon City: New Day.

Lanfant, Marie Françoise
    1987   "L'impact social et culturel du tourisme international en question: réponses interdisciplinaires." *Problems of Tourism* 10 (2): 3–20.
    1995   "Introduction." In *International Tourism: Identity and Change*, ed. Lanfant, John B. Allcock, and Edward M. Bruner. London: Sage. 1–23.
Lanfant, Marie Françoise, John B. Allcock, and Edward M. Bruner, eds.
    1995   *International Tourism: Identity and Change.* London: Sage.
Lash, Scott and John Urry
    1994   *Economies of Signs and Space.* London: Sage.
Leach, Edmund R.
    1984   "Conclusion: Further Thoughts on the Realm of Folly." In *Text, Play, and Story: The Construction and Reconstruction of Self and Society*, ed.
Leed, Eric J.
    1992   *The Mind of the Traveler: From Gilgamesh to Global Tourism.* New York: Basic Books.
Lett, James
    1989/   "Epilogue." In *Hosts and Guests: The Anthropology of Tourism*, ed. Valene
    1977   L. Smith. 2nd ed. Philadelphia: University of Pennsylvania Press.
Lévi-Strauss, Claude
    1976   *Tristes tropiques.* Penguin: Harmondsworth.
Lewis, J. Lowell
    1995   "Genre and Embodiment: From Brazilian *Capoeira* to the Ethnology of Human Movement." *Cultural Anthropology* 10 (2): 221–43.
MacCannell, Dean
    1976   *The Tourist: A New Theory of the Leisure Class.* New York: Schocken Books.
    1989   *The Tourist: A New Theory of the Leisure Class.* 2nd ed. New York: Schocken Books.
MacIsaac, Heather Smith
    1995   "The Pearl Lagoon: Across Asia's New Horizon, the Philippines, with Native Daughter, Josie Natori." *Travel and Leisure* (April): 136–42, 146–50.
Magdalena, Federico V.
    1997   "Population Growth and Changing Ecosystems in Mindanao." *Philippine Quarterly of Culture and Society* 25 (1/2): 5–30.
Majul, Cesar
    1973   *Muslims in the Philippines.* Quezon City: University of the Philippines Press.
Manapat, Ricardo
    1991   *Some Are Smarter than Others: The History of Marcos' Crony Capitalism.* New York: Aletheia Publications.
Mangahas, Maria F.
    1998   "Modern 'Bongkog': "Temporary Weddings' and Dual Samal and Bisaya Identities in Samal Island, Davao Gulf, Philippines." *Pilipinas* 30: 45–62.
Manila Hotel: Tourist Guide to the Philippines
    1931   Manila: California Directory Association.
Mannheim, Karl
    1953/   *Ideology and Utopia.* New York: Harvest Books.
    1936
Marcus, George E.
    1998   *Ethnography Through Thick and Thin.* Princeton, N.J.: Princeton University Press.

Marcus, George E. and Michael M. J. Fischer
    1986   *Anthropology as Cultural Critique: An Experimental Moment in the Human Sciences.* Chicago: University of Chicago Press.

Marin, Louis
    1986   *Utopics: Spatial Play.* Trans. R. A. Vollrath. New York: Macmillan Humanities.

McKean, Philip Frick
    1976   "Tourism, Culture Change and Culture Conservation." In *Changing Identities in Modern Southeast Asia,* ed. David J. Banks. The Hague: Mouton.
    1989/   "Towards a Theoretical Analysis of Tourism: Economic Dualism
    1977   and Cultural Involution in Bali." In *Hosts and Guests: The Anthropology of Tourism,* ed Valene L. Smith. 2nd ed. Philadelphia: University of Pennsylvania Press. 119–38.

Minh-ha, Trinh T.
    1994   "Other Than Myself/My Other Self." In *Travellers' Tales: Narratives of Home and Displacement,* ed. George Robertson et al. London: Routledge.

Moore, Donald S.
    1999   "The Crucible of Cultural Politics: Reworking 'Development' in Zimbabwe's Eastern Highlands." *American Ethnologist* 26 (3): 654–89.

Moore, Henrietta L.
    1996   "The Changing Nature of Anthropological Knowledge: An Introduction." In *The Future of Anthropological Knowledge,* ed. Moore. New York: Routledge. 1–15.

Morris, Meaghan
    1993   "At Henry Parkes Motel." In *Australian Cultural Studies: A Reader,* ed. John Frow and Morris. Urbana: University of Illinois Press. 241–75.

Nash, Dennison and Valene L. Smith
    1991   "Anthropology and Tourism." *Annals of Tourism Research* 18: 12–25.

Nemenzo, Gemma
    1999   "Diary of a Balikbayan." *Filipinas* (August): 29.

Ness, Sally A.
    1991   "Sacred Progress, Secular Pilgrimage: Philippine Tourism Development in the Early 20th Century." *Pilipinas* 16: 45–62.
    1992   *Body, Movement, and Culture: Kinesthetic and Visual Symbolism in a Philippine Community.* Philadelphia: University of Pennsylvania Press.
    1995   "When Seeing Is Believing: The Changing Role of Visuality in a Philippine Dance." *Anthropological Quarterly* 68 (1): 1–13.
    1996   "Dancing in the Field: Notes from Memory." In *Corporealities,* ed. Susan L. Foster. London: Routledge. 129–54.
    1997   "Originality in the Postcolony: Chroeographing the Neo-ethnic Body in Philippine Concert Dance." *Cultural Anthropology* 12 (1): 64–108.

Nuñez, Theron
    1989/   "Touristic Studies in Anthropological Perspective." In *Hosts and*
    1977   *Guests: The Anthropology of Tourism,* ed. Valene L. Smith. 2nd ed. Philadelphia: University of Pennsylvania Press. 265–74.

Oakes, Timothy
    1997   "Ethnic Tourism in Guizhou Province, China." In *Tourism, Ethnicity, and the State in Asian and Pacific Societies,* ed. Michel Picard and Robert Everett Wood. Honolulu: University of Hawaii Press. 35–70.

Olwig, Karen Fog
    1998   "Epilogue: Contested Homes: Home-Making and the Making of Anthropology." In *Migrants of Identity: Perception of Home in a World of Movement*, ed. Nigel Rapport and Andrew Dawson. Oxford: Berg. 225–36.

Ong, Aihwa
    1995   "Women Out of China: Traveling Tales and Traveling Theories in Postcolonial Feminism." In *Women Writing Culture*, ed. Ruth Behar and Deborah A. Gordon. Berkeley: University of California Press. 350–72.
    1996   "Anthropology, China and Modernities: The Geopolitics of Cultural Knowledge." In *The Future of Anthropological Knowledge*, ed. Henrietta Moore. New York: Routledge. 60–92.

Paine, Robert
    1992   "The Marabar Caves, 1920–2020." In *Contemporary Futures: Perspectives from Social Anthropology*, ed Sandra Wallman. London: Routledge.

Pastells, Pablo, S.J.
    1998   *Mission to Mindanao, 1859–1900.* Ed. and trans. Peter Schreurs, MSC. Vols. 2–3. Quezon City: Claretian Publications.
    1994   *Mission to Mindanao, 1859–1900.* Ed. and trans. Peter Schreurs. MSC. Vol. 1. Cebu City, Philippines: San Carlos Publications.

Peters, Jens
    1991   *Philippines-Travel Survival Kit.* 4th ed. Berkeley, Calif.: Lonely Planet Publications.

Picard, Michel
    1995   "Cultural Heritage and Tourist Capital: Cultural Tourism in Bali." In *International Tourism: Identity and Change*, ed. Marie Françoise Lanfant, John B. Allcock, and Edward M. Bruner. London: Sage. 44–66.
    1996   *Bali: Cultural Tourism and Touristic Culture.* Singapore: Archipelago Press.
    1997   "Cultural Tourism, Nation-Building, and Regional Culture: The Making of a Balinese Identity." In *Tourism, Ethnicity, and the State in Asian and Pacific Societies*, ed. Picard and Robert E. Wood. Honolulu: University of Hawaii Press. 181–214.

Picard, Michel and Robert E. Wood, eds.
    1997   *Tourism, Ethnicity, and the State in Asian and Pacific Societies.* Honolulu: University of Hawaii Press.

Putzel, James
    1992   *A Captive Land: The Politics of Agrarian Reform in the Philippines.* London: Catholic Institute for International Relations.

Quiason, Serafin D.
    1993   "The Japanese Colony in Davao." In *Proceedings and Position Papers of the Region XI Historical Convention.* Davao City: ARJ Printing Press. 14–18.

Rabinow, Paul
    1977   *Reflections on Fieldwork in Morocco.* Berkeley: University of California Press.
    1986   "Representations are Social Facts: Modernity and Post-Modernity in Anthropology." in *Writing Culture: The Poetics and Politics of Ethnography*, ed. James Clifford and George E. Marcus. Berkeley: University of California Press. 234–61.

1989   *French Modern: Norms and Forms of the Social Environment.* Chicago: University of Chicago Press.

1991   "For Hire: Resolutely Late Modern." In *Recapturing Anthropology: Working in the Present,* ed. Richard G. Fox. Santa Fe, NM: School of American Research Press.

Rapport, Nigel and Andrew Dawson, eds.

1998   *Migrants of Identity: Perceptions of Home in a World of Movement.* Oxford: Berg.

Raz, Aviad E.

1999   *Riding the Black Ship: Japan and Tokyo Disneyland.* Cambridge, Mass.: Harvard University Asia Center.

Richter, Linda K.

1982   *Land Reform and Tourism Development: Policy-Making in the Philippines.* Cambridge, Mass.: Schenkman.

1989   *The Politics of Tourism in Asia.* Honolulu: University of Hawaii Press.

Ricoeur, Paul

1986   *Lectures on Ideology and Utopia.* Ed. George H. Taylor. New York: Columbia University Press.

Rojek, Chris and John Urry

1997a   "Touring Cultures; Transformations of Travel and Theory." In *Touring Cultures: Transformations of Travel and Theory,* ed. Rojek and Urry. London: Routledge. 1–19.

Rojek, Chris and John Urry, eds.

1997b   *Touring Cultures: Transformations of Travel and Theory.* London: Routledge.

Rosaldo, Renato

1986   "From the Door of His Tent: The Fieldworker and the Inquisitor. In *Writing Culture: The Poetics and Politics of Ethnography,* ed. James Clifford and George E. Marcus. Berkeley: University of California Press. 77–97.

1989   *Culture and Truth: The Remaking of Social Analysis.* New York: Beacon Press.

Said, Edward

1979   "Zionism from the Standpoint of Its Victims." *Social Text* 1: 7–58.

Savage-Landor, Arnold Henry

1904   *The Gems of the East: Sixteen Thousand Miles of Research Travel Among Wild and Tame Tribes of Enchanting Islands.* Vol. 2. London: Macmillan.

Schreurs, Peter, MSC

1987   *Angry Days in Mindanao: The Philippine Revolution and the War Against the U.S. in East and Northeast Mindanao, 1897–1901.* Cebu City: San Carlos Publications.

1989   *Caraga Antigua, 1521–1910: The Hispanization and Christianization of Agusan, Surigao, and East Davao.* Cebu City: San Carlos Publications.

Schutzman, Mady

1999   *The Real Thing: Performance, Hysteria, and Advertising.* Hanover, N.H.: Wesleyan University Press.

Scott, David

1989   "Locating the Anthropological Subject: Postcolonial Anthropologists in Other Places." *Inscriptions* 5: 75–85.

Seagrave, Sterling

1988   *The Marcos Dynasty.* New York: Harper and Row.

Selwyn, Tom, ed.

1996   *The Tourism Image: Myths and Myth Making in Tourism.* Chichester: Wiley.

Showalter, Elaine
    1997   *Hystories: Hysterical Epidemics and Modern Media.* New York: Columbia University Press.
Sieber, Timothy R.
    1997   "Urban Tourism in Revitalizing Downtowns: Conceptualizing Tourism in Boston, Massachusetts." In *Tourism and Culture: An Applied Perspective,* ed. Erve Chambers. Albany: SUNY Press. 59–76.
Smith, M. Estellie
    1997   "Hegemony and Elite Capital: The Tools of Tourism." In *Tourism and Culture: An Applied Perspective,* ed. Erve Chambers. Albany: SUNY Press. 199–214.
Smith, Valene L., ed.
    1989   "Introduction." *Hosts and Guests: The Anthropology of Tourism,* ed. Smith. 2nd ed. Philadelphia: University of Pennsylvania Press.
Spivak, Gayatry S.
    1999   *A Critique of Postcolonial Reason.* Cambridge, Mass.: Harvard University Press.
Stack, Carol
    1996   *Call to Home: African Americans Reclaim the Rural South.* New York: Basic Books.
Staten, Henry
    1986/   *Wittgenstein and Derrida.* Lincoln: Univeristy of Nebraska Press.
    1984
Steinberg, David Joel
    2000   *The Philippines: A Singular and a Plural Place.* 4th ed. Boulder, Colo.: Westview Press.
Stocking, George W., Jr.
    1987   *Victorian Anthropology.* New York.
    1992   *The Ethnographer's Magic and Other Essays in the History of Anthropology.* Madison: University of Wisconsin Press.
    1995   *After Tylor: British Social Anthropology, 1888–1951.* Madison: University of Wisconsin Press.
Stoller, Paul
    1989   *The Taste of Ethnographic Things: The Senses in Anthropology.* Philadelphia: University of Pennsylvania Press.
    1995   *Embodying Colonial Memories: Spirit Possession, Power, and the Hauka in West Africa.* New York: Routledge.
Truong, Thanh-dam
    1990   *Sex, Money, and Morality: Prostitution and Tourism in South-East Asia.* London: Zed.
Tucker, Hazel
    1997   "The Ideal Village: Interactions Through Tourism in Central Anatolia." *In Tourists and Tourism: Identifying with People and Places,* ed. Simone Abram, Jacqueline Waldren, and Donald V. L. Macleod. Oxford: Berg.
Tyler, Stephen
    1986   "Post-Modern Ethnography: From Document of the Occult to Occult Document." In *Writing Culture: The Poetics and Politics of Ethnography,* ed. James Clifford and George E. Marcus, Berkeley: University of California Press. 122–40.
United States Bureau of Insular Affairs
    1902   *A Pronouncing Gazetteer and Geographical Dictionary of the Philippine Islands.* Washington, D.C.: U.S. Government Printing Office.

Urry, John
    1990   *The Tourist Gaze: Leisure and Travel in Contemporary Societies.* London: Sage.

Van Den Abbeele, Georges
    1980   "Sightseers: The Tourist as Theorist." *Diacritics* 10.

Van Den Berghe, Pierre L.
    1994   *The Quest for the Other: Ethnic Tourism in San Cristobal, Mexico.* Seattle: University of Washington Press.

Volkman, Toby
    1984   "Great Performances: Torajan Cultural Identity in the 1970s." *American Ethnologist* 11 (1): 152–69.

    1985   *Feasts of Honor: Ritual and Change in the Toraja Highlands.* Urbana: University of Illinois Press.

    1990   "Visions and Revisions: Toraja Culture and the Tourist Gaze." *American Ethnologist* 17 (1): 91–110.

Whitaker, Mark P.
    1996   "Ethnography as Learning: A Wittgensteinian Approach to Writing Ethnographic Accounts." *Anthropological Quarterly* 69: 1–13.

Wittgenstein, Ludwig
    1938–46   *Lectures and Conversations on Aesthetics, Psychology, and Religion.* Ed. Cyrill Barrett. Oxford: Blackwell.

    1970   *Zettle.* Ed. G. E. M. Anscombe and G. H. von Wright; trans. G. E. M. Anscombe. Berkeley: University of California Press.

Wolff, Janet
    1995   *Feminine Sentences: Essays on Women and Culture.* Oxford: Blackwell.

Wood, Robert E.
    1997   "Tourism and the State: Ethnic Options and Constructions of Otherness." In *Tourism, Ethnicity, and the State in Asian and Pacific Societies,* ed. Michel Picard and Robert E. Wood. Hololulu: University of Hawaii Press. 1–34.

Yiannakis, Andrew and Heather Gibson
    1992   "Roles Tourists Play." *Annals of Tourism Research* 19 (2): 287–303.

Youngblood, Robert
    1990   *Marcos Against the Church: Economic Development and Political Repression in the Philippines.* Ithaca, N.Y.: Cornell University Press.

Zulaika, Joseba
    1988   *Basque Violence: Metaphor and Sacrament.* Reno: University of Nevada Press.

Index

abaca, 48

Adecor (Aguinaldo Development Corporation), 70, 72–73, 80–82, 83–89, 91–93, 99–106, 167–68, 235–36

America, 17, 105–6, 206, 225; American(s), 17, 48, 50–51, 55, 76, 98, 102, 161, 197, 205, 207, 224, 231; American rule, 35, 49, 54–55, 102, 144, 164, 205, 208, 230. *See also* United States

AnFLOCOR (Antonio Floreindo Corporation), 37

anthropology, xvi, 4–5, 7, 22, 223; cultural, 3, 5–6, 10, 238–40; "classical," 4, 6, 8, 10

Apo View Hotel, 39, 40, 41, 182

APTTI (Asian and Pacific Tourism Training Institute), 35, 162–64, 179, 182–84, 188, 209, 214

ASEAN, 3–4, 11, 28, 35, 41, 45–46, 49, 53, 56–61, 108–9, 111, 113–14, 149, 179–80, 189, 215, 229–31; "ASEAN-ization," 4, 45

Babak, 67, 91, 208, 218

Bachelard, Gaston, 19

Bagobo, 25, 49, 57, 75, 90

Bali, 27, 41, 58, 59

Balikbayan, 17–18, 228

barkada, 205, 215, 221–23, 226

Bateson, Gregory, 14

Bayanihan Dance Company, 90, 93, 94–96

BIMP-EAGA (Brunei, Indonesia, Malaysia, and the Philippines—East Asean Growth Area), 45, 110, 113, 118, 149, 182, 192

Bohol, 53, 101, 151, 164

Brunei, 40, 45, 110–11, 113, 192

California, 8, 48, 50, 180, 196, 224, 228

CARP (Comprehensive Agrarian Reform Program), 121–23, 130, 136, 140, 150, 154

Catholic. *See* Roman Catholic Church

Causey, Andrew, 12–13

Cebu, 17, 32, 51, 91, 164, 187, 226; Cebu City, 76, 212

Chambers, Erve, 10

Clifford, James, 8, 10, 18, 240

culture, 3–4, 6, 7–9, 11–12, 89–90, 96, 98–99, 108, 117 166, 169, 176, 180, 201, 205, 215, 231, 236, 238–39, 241; and naturalism, 10

Dakudao family, 34, 54, 175; Catalina "Kiling" Dakudao, 34, 42, 182, 183, 188, 189; Carmen Dakudao Locsin, 34

dance, 15, 38, 48, 57, 89, 90, 92–98, 106, 127, 215, 235; dancing, 56–57, 59, 90, 92, 94–98; Filipiniana, 90, "tribal," 90, 92. *See also* Bayanihan Dance Company; Peña dance company

DATA (Davao Tourism Association), 37–39, 41–47, 52, 58, 60, 75, 162, 182–83, 191

Davao, 6, 8, 23–28, 30, 32–38, 40–43, 46–54, 56–62, 74, 78, 92, 101, 109–11, 116, 119, 126–27, 129, 139, 151–52, 156, 163, 174, 176, 182, 187–93, 196–98, 202, 209–10, 214–15, 218, 221, 230–32, 234, 241–42; history, 48–50, 53–54, 62, 230–31; indigenous cultural groups, 25; "pioneer" families, 46–59, 74, 175, 198; violence in, 211

Davao City, xi, xiv, xvi, 3–6, 8, 13–17, 21–22, 31–32, 42, 45–49, 52, 54–55, 57, 59–61, 65, 67, 78, 80, 82, 91–93, 102, 109–11, 113, 117–18, 121, 123, 126–27, 147, 155, 162, 173, 175–76, 178–84, 191–93, 197–98, 200, 203–8, 210–16, 221, 229–37, 241–42

Davao Gulf, 28, 32, 49, 54, 67, 110, 117, 204

Davao Insular Inter-Continental Inn, 33, 40, 83, 208. *See also* Insular Century Hotel

Davao International Airport, 26

Acknowledgments

This research was made possible in part by an Advanced Research Grant for Southeast Asia from the Social Science Research Council (1996) and a Residence Fellowship Award from the University of California, Riverside Center for Ideas and Society (1998).

In the Philippines, grateful acknowledgment is due to the following organizations and institutions, whose assistance was instrumental in completing the research for this study: the University of San Carlos Cebuano Studies Center, Ateneo de Davao University, Philippine Women's University of Davao, the LAWIG Foundation, the Philippine Tourism Authority, the Ford Academy of the Arts, and the Davao Tourism Association. The businesses and families cooperating in the study are too numerous to mention individually, but all are most gratefully acknowledged for their participation and support. In particular, the following individuals have my most sincere thanks for their ongoing assistance and support: Mr. and Mrs. Danté Abaca, Imelda Bacon, Hur Camporedondo, Loreben P. Daday, Catalina Santos Dakudao, Mr. and Mrs. Peter Durano, Aida Rivera Ford, Heidi K. Gloria, the family of Mrs. Carmen Dakudao Locsin and Mr. José Locsin, Ann Pamintuan, and Victor Secuya.

To my colleagues in the United States who were kind enough to read parts or all of the manuscript—Audrey Bilger, Andrew Causey, Jean-Paul Dumont, Michael Kearney, Lynn Kwiatkowsky, Paul Rabinow, Christena Schlundt, and Eberle Umbach—I am deeply grateful. I would also like to thank Patrick Alcedo, who assisted in the final phases of manuscript preparation, and Fruto Corre, who painstakingly checked all of the transcriptions and translations of the quotations given in Cebuano throughout the text and who prepared the three maps provided.

On a personal note, sincere thanks also go to Senia Pizzo, without whose support during the early years of research and writing this work would not have reached completion. Finally, I wish to thank my companion and partner in life, Erich Reck, for his love and encouragement through the final years of writing up.

Earlier versions of portions of Chapters 4 and 5 appeared in "Tourism Transforming Dance: Experiences of Pearl Farm Beach Report," in *1998 Philippine International Dance Conference: Dance in Revolution, Revolution in Dance,* ed. Basilio Esteban S. Villaruz with Leonila J. Bondy (Mindanao: World Dance Alliance—Philippines, 1999).